MADONNAS AND MAVERICKS

POWER WOMEN IN SINGAPORE

LORETTA CHEN

Marshall Cavendish Editions

Published by Marshall Cavendish Editions
An imprint of Marshall Cavendish International

A member of the Times Publishing Group

Other Marshall Cavendish Offices:
Marshall Cavendish Corporation. 99 White Plains Road, Tarrytown NY 10591-9001, USA • Marshall Cavendish International (Thailand) Co Ltd. 253 Asoke, 12th Flr, Sukhumvit 21 Road, Klongtoey Nua, Wattana, Bangkok 10110, Thailand • Marshall Cavendish (Malaysia) Sdn Bhd, Times Subang, Lot 46, Subang Hi-Tech Industrial Park, Batu Tiga, 40000 Shah Alam, Selangor Darul Ehsan, Malaysia

National Library Board, Singapore Cataloguing-in-Publication Data

Name(s): Chen, Loretta, 1976-
Title: Madonnas and Mavericks : Power Women in Singapore / Loretta Chen.
Description: Singapore : Marshall Cavendish Editions, [2017]
Identifier(s): OCN 990165920 | ISBN 978-981-4751-22-3 (paperback)
Subject(s): LCSH: Women—Singapore. | Celebrities—Singapore.
Classification: DDC 920.72095957—dc23

Printed in Singapore.

To my readers.
For there is a Madonna and a Maverick in all of us.

Contents

Introduction

Writing the introduction always comes last for me. The journey and process of writing take you places, and you are never the same person as you were when you first started—neither is the book. The ideas and words morph with each person you meet and each story you hear.

I have had the privilege of meeting with and talking to 17 of Singapore's most illustrious and well-respected women, across diverse backgrounds and demographics. They have shared with me their childhood struggles, countless challenges, personal tragedies and little victories. In today's global climate, perhaps now more than ever, we need greater awareness of and united support for diversity against the rise of divisive rhetoric. And we can certainly do with more Singaporean female role models.

This book is a collection of honest, searing stories from many luminaries—leaders and specialists from various fields. In the sphere of politics and diplomacy, there are Ambassador Chan Heng Chee, Speaker of the House Halimah Yacob and Worker's Party Chairman Sylvia Lim. Three women have served as Nominated Members of Parliament on top of being professionals in their own fields: ophthalmologist and nature advocate Geh Min, stage actress Janice Koh and water treatment magnate Olivia Lum.

Many of them are entrepreneurs, expanding the job market in scores of industries. Nichol Ng and Janice Wong are both passionate about food, one as a grocer and the other as a chef, both leading teams of staff. Former CEOs Jennie Chua of Raffles Holdings and Fanny Lai of Wildlife Reserves Singapore are experts in their respective fields who have ventured to new, unchartered territories. Other remarkable head honchos include Odile Benjamin of F J Benjamin, Cynthia Chua of Spa Esprit Group and Tjin Lee of Mercury.

From the realm of sports, we are honoured to have Paralympian Theresa Goh; from the music circle, the celebrated violinist Siow Lee-Chin; and from the TV world, the evergreen darling Xiang Yun. And last but not least, the spunky and uncategorisable Gentle Warrior, Ivy Singh-Lim.

There is more than one way to list these luminaries as they are all so multi-faceted. As you read their stories, you will discover other lesser-known descriptors, because amongst these women, we have playful professors, artistic businesswomen, entrepreneurial musicians, sensitive souls, cancer survivors, poverty conquerors, nature champions, enthusiastic mothers, happy singletons, amiable divorcees, contented wives and so many more. All these women have courageously redefined what it means to be women of the 21st century, and have bravely forged ahead with their dreams—fearing nothing and no one.

At the initial stage of this project, I had wondered how best to organise their stories. I had wanted to write in prose and had not yet settled on a definitive title. But I knew that I wanted to explore the archetypes of women—Maiden, Maverick, Madonna and Matriarch. In fact, I even toyed with the idea of grouping the ladies under these headers.

But then, I conducted my first interview with Chan Heng Chee, and she quizzed me on my definitions. As I started elucidating on my thesis, I realised that few women could fit neatly into any one taxonomy or archetype. Besides, all had such distinct voices that my attempt at capturing their personalities in prose would prove ultimately futile. Eventually, I decided that my format would include an "op-ed" or a "first impression", followed by an edited transcript that captures their speech patterns and thought processes. I also figured that I would end the interview by asking them which archetype(s) they best relate to.

The title today stands as *Madonnas and Mavericks*. For the purposes of this book, I have defined Madonna as a steadfast and virtuous woman after the Judeo-Christian tradition. She is a disciplined professional with specialised mastery that has taken her many years to hone and cultivate. This contrasts with the Maverick, a character born out of today's fast-paced environment—a game-changer and a dynamic individual, who revels in taking the bull by its horns and seeking new adventures.

The process of putting the book together has been as intricate as these women's lives. Coordinating the time to meet was itself a noteworthy feat because I am based in Hawaii, whilst these women are either based in Singapore or always flying the friendly skies. Some of the interviews were scheduled in between a packed day of meetings. A couple opted to have their PR gurus and expert handlers on ground to assist. Some interviews were so intimate, we ended up trading personal stories that left me in tears. An interview was held in an industrial kitchen, another on a farm and one was conducted in a boutique hotel over Christmas (with *Jingle Bells* playing softly in the background, but unceremoniously overridden by the untimely arrival of a dump truck). One encounter blossomed into a firm friendship with subsequent meet-ups and frequent chats, whilst a handful of interviews allowed me to catch up and celebrate with friends from the past. Yet others allowed me the opportunities for close encounters with some of my personal heroines. Whatever the circumstances, all the interviews were unique, informative and ultimately inspiring.

One thing to note is that the Madonnas and Mavericks in this book hold distinct views on feminism and the role of women in society. Their perspectives on marriage, motherhood and career differ and many even challenge Sheryl Sandberg's notion of "having it all". Some argue that we still have a long way to go, whilst some maintain that we have it good in Singapore. A few share that motherhood is tough business, while some, like Earth Mothers, take it in gleefully and ask for more. Many agree that the workspace today can still be hard on women, and observe that women can sometimes be hardest on women.

Globally, Singapore is ranked 55th out of 144 countries in the Global Gender Gap Report 2016 published by the World Economic Forum. For a first world country whose per capita GDP is one of the highest in the world, we can certainly demand more progress and stage a concerted effort to increase the recognition of women in the work sphere. We should aim to offer better support and set up social structures to allow women to undertake and assert their multi-hyphenate roles.

To quote Brené Brown, "The real struggle for women… is that we are expected to be perfect and yet not look as if we are working for it. We want it to just materialise somehow. Everything should be effortless. The expectation is to be natural beauties, natural mothers, natural leaders and naturally good parents, and we want to belong to naturally fabulous families. … And when it comes to work, we love to hear, 'She makes it look so easy,' or 'She's a natural.'"

These women have unabashedly shared what they had to undergo to get to where they are today. The climb can be arduous and unglamorous and certainly not always "natural". But what does make it beautiful is their unyielding passion, strength in spirit and staunch belief that things will always get better. They have embraced challenges and pain; taken a stab in the back, a kick in the face and a slam of the door, and they all somehow find the courage to say in their own way, "Okay, this is how the world rolls. So this is how I will rock and roll." They have never allowed their circumstances to define them, and instead saw them as a challenges to overcome. None of them used the victim card, "Boo hoo, poor me. It's all my parents', ex-husband's, baby's and future lover's fault." None. Zilch. Nada. They instead had a similar rallying cry, "Whether I like it or not, this ball is in my court. So what can I do?"

Either consciously or unconsciously, these women have all marched on to the beat of their own drums. In so doing, they have crafted personal worldviews, distinct life philosophies and their own style of authentic leadership. Whether they are Madonnas, Mavericks or any other M's, they are true beacons of light, worthy of being exalted as Power Women in their own right.

The Renaissance Woman

ODILE BENJAMIN

Odile Benjamin is the Divisional CEO and Co-Creative Director in F J Benjamin Holdings Ltd which is an industry leader in brand building and management across Asia. It also handles luxury and lifestyle fashion, timepiece, retail and distribution.

Odile joined the company in 1993 as a brand manager before making the switch to the creative and licensing division. She is responsible for the design, development and strategic operational direction of the in-house brand Raoul, which was a favourite of the Duchess of Cambridge. Raoul is available in department stores in the U.S., Europe and the Middle East.

***

Elegant, petite, polished and soft-spoken, Odile Benjamin gives off the vibes of a forerunner of society's elite. After all, she is the Creative Director of Raoul, a Singapore-born, internationally recognised fashion label worn by the likes of Viola Davis and Zhang Ziyi. And she is also the wife of Douglas Benjamin, Group COO of F J Benjamin, a publicly-listed company which has offices in eight cities, manages over 20 iconic brands, operates 226 stores and hires over 3,000 employees. I had imagined she might be a pretty face with politically correct answers and "easy" responses. But I was to be blissfully disappointed.

Within the first moments of our introduction, I felt an affinity with her as if she was a distant cousin or a long-lost friend from elementary school. Ten minutes into our intimate chat in the Four Seasons, I found myself asking the maître d' for napkins as I was positively tearing from her searing story of war, death and the loss of her dearly beloved father, Raoul Mizrahi. In the glossy magazines, we are told that the label's name is inspired by her son, which is not untrue. But in our exclusive interview, we finally learn the dark reality and horrors of Odile's childhood in war-torn Lebanon, her days as a refugee leading up to the adoption of London as her second home, before her meeting and falling in love with Douglas and moving to Singapore.

Indeed, life is not always just about cocktails and society parties. Odile still battles lupus, an incurable disease, and went through a severe, malignant breast cancer episode in 2015 that left her with a mastectomy. She bares her petite soul as she gamely professes to not only share her story with us, but to show us that we need to make each moment of our lives count—we never really know what will happen next.

***

Share with us your eclectic background and how that has shaped you to become the person that you are.

I was born in Beirut in 1971 into a fairly privileged family. My father came from a background of diplomats and he started his own business in electrical engineering. He had a pretty substantial business in the Middle East doing electrical works for the government. We had been based in Lebanon for quite a while, and I consider myself Lebanese because that's where I was born and that is where my parents were from. But our background is actually much more varied than that. I have Italian and Persian blood, with grandparents on both sides of the family that came from Persia. Part of the paternal side of the family also came from Syria—my father was born there and he moved to Lebanon as his parents were diplomats there. On my maternal side, my great grandfather was an Ambassador and my grandfather was also an Ambassador to Persia, which later became known as Iran. My mother was born in Lebanon. You can see how varied our ancestry is.

I think of myself as Lebanese because of the traditions we uphold—the food that we eat, what I like and crave for is always Lebanese—I even look Lebanese. But I am also Jewish, so that has made me different right from the onset. We are one of the few Jewish families who are actually Lebanese that originated from Syria. My maiden name is Mizrahi which means "coming from the East". If you go to the Jewish temple, the Mizrah is the Ark where the Torah Scrolls are kept, and that always faces the East in the direction of Jerusalem.

I am one of those rare Middle Eastern Jews who lived through the war in Beirut until the late 1980s. The civil war in Beirut broke out in 1975 and I was three years old. Life was never the same after. My father moved us—my mother, my brother and I, and my grandparents—to Italy but he had to keep going back because of his business. In 1979, we moved back to Beirut when things settled, as my mother could not bear to be apart from my father. We lived there until 1984. I have seen some horrific things living through the civil war. There were days and weeks where we had no water. There were curfews, electricity and food shortages, and frequent bombs blasts around our home. I have friends who have lost their limbs because of shrapnel. I've seen it all.

I left when I was 12 years old, after my father's death. Prior to that, we lived through one of the most historic times in Lebanon, which was the

Israeli invasion of 1982. This was the pinnacle of the war. Airplanes were bombing the whole of Beirut and the country was a big ball of flame, and I am not exaggerating. We stayed in the shelter underground and had to be evacuated. We were taken through the borders into Israel to seek refuge. Crazy as it sounds, we chose to head back even after my dad's death as that was our home. I recall having a happy childhood surrounded by friends and all my loved ones. We made our own happiness there in spite of all that was going on.

Dad's death was a shock, and much more than a tragedy as he did not die of old age or illness but was kidnapped and murdered by the Hezbollah. It was the start of the Hezbollah movement and in hindsight, we now know that we had been under surveillance for weeks prior to his murder. Suffice to say, my whole world fell apart. The saddest fact was that it happened on my brother's birthday, which was on Monday, 2 July 1984. Strangely, I had a premonition before and insisted that we should celebrate my brother's birthday on Sunday. We did and even popped a bottle of champagne. The next morning, our lives fell apart. It took quite some time to find my father's body.

My father was the most amazing man and everyone who knew him would agree. My father's name is Raoul and he was fearless, strong and he kept our home and our whole world in order up till the day he died at age 50. He was multilingual, highly educated, highly regarded and everybody in Lebanon knew my dad. In fact, when I was younger, I would meet people and introduce myself as Odile and they will say, "Ah, Raoul Mizrahi's daughter." Lebanon is a small country, like Singapore, so once you make your mark, you will be respected and remembered. He fought his battles throughout the war, but he truly believed Lebanon was home and that he had a right to live there. We were not unlike *The Last of the Mohicans* as the only Jews living in there, but we paid a hefty price.

After we had found my dad, we had to find a way to bury him. It was not an easy thing to do as you need to get to a Jewish cemetery which way down in the south, and that was dangerous territory. Because I was young, I was not allowed to make the journey so I didn't get to say my last goodbye to my father. My brother who was two years older than me, and 15 at the time, undertook the journey with my uncle. My brother dug my father's grave himself and laid him to rest. So that was an abrupt end to one sad and significant chapter of my life.

We originally had planned to leave for the UK a week after my father's murder and arrangements for the paperwork had been done. However, with my father's untimely demise, all the documentation was nullified and we had to start from scratch. After that, my mum had us pack and leave for Cyprus and we had to figure things out as we went along. My mother eventually managed to get me and my brother student visas in the UK so we headed there in September while she had to wait for a while longer for her papers. It was a trying time as I did not speak a word of English and my brother spoke only a little, but we had to make it work, together with the help of my maternal aunt.

Share with me more about your mother. She had gone through something so utterly devastating and had to raise two children on her own.

My mum is one of the most incredible and selfless women I know. She is what you really would call a "woman of substance". She kept it all together for us even though she fell apart. Till today, she still lives her life for my father even though he has passed away close to 34 years ago. She lives in London and has dedicated her entire life to us, to our family and to my father's memory. I don't think it is possible for me to live up to her standards but that is what I aspire to do.

Honestly, given what my brother and I went through, we really had every excuse in the book to stray and not succeed in school, but my mum always knew how to get us back on track. In those days, we did not go to a therapist, especially coming from the Middle East, but our mother kept us grounded even though we had so much to deal with—change in country, new language, schools and culture. My mum resolutely kept us together and helped us overcome our trauma even though she never healed.

Her focus in those days was ensuring that we excelled in school and we did. Within a year, I moved from a French school to one of the top English all-girls' school and got 11 A's including English Language and Literature for my O Levels. Later, I graduated from my A Levels with straight A's. My brother excelled in school as well, and I think we worked hard as we wanted to make our mother proud, as well as to honour the memory of my late father.

We had gone from being Raoul Mizrahi's kids to virtual nobodies and we never got our old lives back. For that reason, I do not feel compelled to return to Lebanon nor do I feel any urge to return in the future. Lebanon took away something so fundamental to me so it is going to be too painful and futile to go back to the past. What would be the point? Nothing would look or be the same again so I would rather keep the past as memories and leave it as a chapter in a book or a movie, as if it was someone else's life.

Having said that, my father lives in me all the time and I still cry for him as most children do when they miss their parents. But my tears are tinged with the injustice of what had happened to him, even though I am proud of who he is and he will always be a hero to me. He was a hero because he never ran away and stuck to his home, his beliefs and his country. So this concluded the chapter of my life in Lebanon and the start of my life in London.

So how did Douglas come into your life?

I met Douglas when I was 17. He was studying his final year in the university in the UK and I was still in high school. We met at a friend's birthday party and he was as fascinated by my background as I was with his. We started talking and became friends. I had never met anyone from Asia before even though I have Asian and Indian friends from the UK. It fascinated me that Douglas is from and lives in Asia, looks Caucasian and is Jewish. I did not know there were Jews in Singapore and was ignorant about the little city-state. As we started talking, we found out that we had a lot in common. Doug's childhood had its fair share of trauma too, which was not dissimilar to mine.

Later, Douglas moved back to Singapore but we remained friends and kept in touch with letters. He would write me a letter once every few months and I would reciprocate. I knew he was attracted to me but probably felt that I was a little too young. Anyhow, during the First Gulf War, Doug was in Europe and was stuck there for some reason and he gave me a call. We connected again and started dating long distance. During this period, Doug would travel back and forth from London. I was 19 and he proposed when I was 20.

In December 1991, I went to Singapore for a holiday together with my entire family—brother, mother, uncle and my aunt and he decided to propose. I said "yes" as I knew he was the right guy for me. He checked all the right boxes, and I, having gone through what I did, had a clear perspective on life and knew what I was looking for that was quite different from your average 20-year-old. To be honest, it is not something I would recommend to even my own daughter. In fact, I had one more year to go at the LSE (London School of Economics) but I gave that up as I did not feel that I needed to prove anything to anyone. Again, this is not something I would recommend to anyone but at that time, I felt that what was most important was being with the man that I love who loves me and who would give me that stability I needed. Strangely enough, my mum was agreeable too and we got married six months later.

I moved to Singapore, and even though it sounds crazy, it felt right. Honestly, Singapore then was not like what it is today but I knew that I could make it anywhere having been through harsher times. While I found it hard to adapt at the start, I quickly made it my home. In fact, it was paradise compared to what I had been through. There were many *ang mohs* and expatriates even in those days, but I never saw myself as an expat as I was here with my husband who is so rooted to this country.

Doug is a third generation Singaporean so I knew this was going to be my home but for the longest time, I was looked upon as a foreigner. It was hard trying to find my groove in the early days. I looked distinctively different, there was a language barrier and I quickly figured that I had to adapt if I was going to make this work. And yes, now I am able to speak Singlish and even have a Singlish accent!

Share with us this new chapter of your life in Singapore.
So, we got married in 1992. I had plans to transfer my credits in London to a local university that had a partnership with LSE and the University of London but, unfortunately, I got ill with lupus. I was very ill for a few months and back then, Singapore did not have that level of medical expertise and experience that could effectively combat lupus. It took us many months to get to the source of my illness and it was indeed a very unpleasant way to start my life in Singapore. But I knew this chapter would be a milestone for Doug and me and it truly shaped our relationship. My being sick from the start of our marriage sealed us together and gave us a sense of "rootedness". It helped to mould our values as a couple and made us focus on what was important.

In fact, a few months before I was diagnosed, I had already acquired inflammation of the heart. It was unpleasant and the bedside manners of the doctors then were truly found wanting. There was no Internet and all I was given was a leaflet to read up on my condition. In fact, when I was in Tan Tock Seng Hospital, I recall the leaflet basically confirmed that death was imminent. As lupus is highly unpredictable and can attack any organ in the body, it was not uncommon for one to come down with kidney, lung or brain failure.

I recalled that I was devastated at the thought that we may not have children and I felt so guilty for having implicated Doug in this health crisis and he felt the same. But in hindsight, this has certainly glued us together to the point that many have said we are virtually inseparable and are truly bonded. Anyway, by December 1992, we received a clear diagnosis on my condition and it was a sheer miracle that I even got pregnant in March the following year.

I decided then that I was going to have the baby against all odds. My view was that I might be run over by a bus even before this disease takes over me, so I might as well have this baby. Doug, too, was not one to leave things to fate and went all around the world to search for the best medical care for me. Eventually, we found this incredible doctor in the U.S. who assured me that I would live a long, happy, healthy life and that I could have my children. All it took was having the right doctor to give me that sense of assurance and confidence.

I did have the baby and in less than nine months later, I was pregnant again! Today, we have four children, with ages ranging from five to 24, and my oldest got married this year in Jerusalem. I have been living with lupus for 26 years now and I can honestly say that it is not easy but I am determined to lead a full life and decided that I was not going to let lupus control my life, even though there is no cure for it.

Lupus affects everyone differently so how does it affect you?

Lupus is an autoimmune illness and, as you say, it has symptoms that vary from person to person. If I was diagnosed early enough, perhaps it could have been better controlled. Nonetheless, I am very disciplined about getting my regular check-ups and always ensure that I am on the right level of medications. I do not fool around with my health and live in full understanding of the limitations of my body.

In my case, lupus attacks my joints and muscles even though it started by attacking my heart. I have been on medication for the last 26 years and I continue to lead a full life, with four kids, full-time work and an active social life. I am careful to not expose myself to the sun too much, watch my diet and am mindful of stress and getting adequate rest. I am an insomniac and a busy individual so getting rest is a challenge for me but I try to keep things in perspective. I have learnt to listen to my body and will take a backseat for a few days if need be.

Honestly, lupus is now a part of my life and I did not even share this with my kids until quite recently. I live with pain everyday and learn to not focus on the pain which actually magnifies it. Yes, there are days when I wake up swollen and am unable to move in the morning but somehow, I manage to get through the day. I am my own cheerleader and have a "can do" attitude. I do not cancel anything on my schedule and continue to plough through the day. People sometimes look at me and ask if I am well. Honestly, I want to say I really am not well, but I keep a smile on my face and keep going on. This mental strength has kept me going and I don't stop until I am really ill.

So this is perhaps a great segue to your fight with cancer.

You know, I had a premonition that I was going to have breast cancer as my mum had it almost 20 years ago. I watched her go through the motions and was mentally prepared that this was going to happen to me someday.

I also had another strong hunch about my cancer in 2014. I knew something was not right as I started getting intermittent sharp, shooting pains on the side of my chest. I asked by GP and my Ob-Gyn and both said I had nothing to worry about. I then approached my lupus specialist who also agreed with the diagnosis of both doctors. However, he suggested that I should see a breast surgeon if I was worried. So in July 2014, I went to see one, underwent all the tests and was told I was all clear. However, I continued to be bothered and returned six months later in January 2015 and was instructed to have a mammogram and ultrasound. Again, I was given the all clear and told to return in a year. I was adamant that there was something not right but was told by the doctor that it was probably my hormones acting up.

Six weeks later, Douglas and our youngest daughter were getting ready to go on a trip. I suddenly felt this huge lump on the side of my chest. I instinctively knew things were not right but I chose to ignore it for an entire day. That evening, as we finished packing our suitcases, I asked Doug to feel the lump and while he initially tried to dismiss it, he did feel the lump right away. We were in disbelief as we knew that cancer does not happen overnight and Doug put it off to a bump I may have suffered in the course of the day. Anyway, we were scheduled to be at the airport at 11 a.m. the next morning so I shared with Doug that I would head to the GP in the morning.

The next morning, I was up at 7 a.m. and busied myself with all the last minute errands. At 9 a.m., Doug asks if I had visited the doctor and

I said "no" as I had clean forgotten about the lump. I decided then that I would see the doctor when we returned in three weeks. However, Doug was adamant that I saw the doctor as he did not want us to have this hanging over our heads throughout our holiday. For the first time, I did not argue with him and headed straight to the doctor. I told him that I would be home by 10:30 a.m. and that we would head to the airport thereafter. Famous last words.

When I got to the doctor, he quickly got me into an ultrasound and suffice to say, I never made it to the airport. It was a huge blow but at that time, all I could think about was my daughter, who was then in her final year at UCL and expecting me in London. My mother was also anxious to see me and my youngest daughter was so excited about getting on this flight. She had been ready with her little backpack, ready to board that flight. Doug was calling me while I was undergoing the scan and all I could think about was "What am I going to tell him?" By that time, my GP had confirmed my worst suspicious and shared that they saw a 3.8cm growth.

That was Tuesday. That afternoon, we went to see a breast surgeon who confirmed we needed surgery and we had to break the news to the family that very day. It was a huge blow for everyone but I knew I needed to keep the family together by staying strong and focused. I also asked Doug to stay strong together with me and help process all matters as I was not capable of doing so.

By Thursday I was in surgery, and the doctors removed a 7cm growth that had spread to the lymph nodes! All this happened in little more than 24 hours! Anyhow, with the lump removed, I knew that I had to focus on getting better and becoming emotionally stable for the family. Through it all, Douglas was my rock. He was just incredible. My mum, too, took the next flight out that same night and stayed by my side for the next six months in Singapore. Between Doug and my mum, they saw me through some of my darkest days.

I had a daunting surgery and needed to undergo chemotherapy. I must say it was an unpleasant thing and I was scared and felt as if my life was out of my own control. At that point, I felt so helpless and needed everyone to do everything for me. It was a huge emotional and mental adjustment. I underwent two more surgeries as the pathology after the first operation showed that the cancer cells had spread. I was so miserable then even though I knew I had to grin and bear it.

I remember waiting in the pre-operating ward at 7 a.m. No one was around and the nurses were trickling in to turn on the lights and conduct their daily chores. I recall being so nervous that I was crying and shaking uncontrollably. I felt then the full meaning of mortality—that there was nothing money could buy.

And yet at that moment, I also had my epiphany. Suddenly, I felt that there was indeed nothing I can do but trust the doctors and let my fate take its course. I knew then that my life was not in my hands and decided that I would surrender myself to the journey. I remembered looking up to the ceiling and imagined the heavens opening up to me. I said to God, "This is your child. I am in your hands and you do what you need to do". With that, I found my inner calm and headed into surgery. I even found myself joking with the anaesthetist as he was trying to find my veins.

I have to say the team at SGH (Singapore General Hospital) was amazing. I have nothing but the best to say about them as they were so supportive. I still go there for my follow-ups and also have my lupus treated there now as well. I tell Doug who accompanies me on all my visits that they are just really, really incredible and have a way of making a terrible situation better. You know, in fact, as a trivia, I was actually in the hospital at the same time Lee Kuan Yew was warded in the last days of his life. We were on the same floor. It was quite a time that I shall never forget.

Anyway, to date, I am still on the mend, recovering emotionally and physically. I am still trying to adapt and adjust to the effects of chemo and grapple with the notion of "cancer". It seems so unreal but I have come to realise that I am a cancer survivor. But have I really survived it? That we will need to wait and see. We commemorate our milestones from the time you complete chemo—one year, five years, 10 years and we will see how we go from there. But you know, I have come to the understanding that it is not in my hands, so I am going to live my life to the fullest as who knows what tomorrow will bring?

I have experienced that too many times in my life and know that one's life can change in a second. It takes only one second for your life to turnaround for the better or for the worse. It was in that one second that I lost my father; one second that I met Douglas; and both of them have changed my life—the former for the worst and the latter for the better. You just don't know what the next moment will bring and it may shape the next chapter of your life.

So you had to undergo a mastectomy.

Yes, and the only reason I am sharing this is not to deter anyone from receiving treatment but on the contrary, I wish to inspire anyone who has to undergo a similar surgery. Most procedures are simpler than what I had to go through. To be honest, mastectomy is not a pleasant procedure under any circumstances, and I opted to do a reconstruction at the same time. It was quite intricate for me as I have lupus, and was therefore not able to receive an implant. Suffice to say that it was a painful process and it took me months to recover from the surgery both mentally and physically. But today, I have come to accept my new body, and am grateful for the medical advancements that have allowed me to turn a new leaf in my life.

How did this experience change the way you view yourself as a woman? Many women grapple with their femininity and sense of identity as a woman after they undergo a mastectomy.

It's a good question because I went through all of these emotions. I felt like my body and I were mutilated. There is no other word for it as I was slashed, cut, and it was brutal. As my oncologist said, the experience is an assault on a woman's body. Having gone through this is probably one of the most humbling experiences of my life.

My husband disagrees with me, and honestly, it was him who made it all the better for me. Like I said, he never left my side for a day, or even a minute. He was with me throughout the entire process and he saw me through all this. I could not even bear to look at myself for weeks after the surgery but his love, care and the support from my family and friends, truly helped me through that difficult time. Sure, I can sit and cry about this all day, but it is not going to change the way my body looks. So I figured that since there is really nothing I can do about it, there is not point in brooding.

Has this affected the intimacy between my husband and I? No. In fact, I give my husband full credit for making me feel whole again as he has never looked at me any differently. In fact, I do not think that anyone views me differently.

On days that I feel that things are not right, I try to take myself out of my body and look at it from the outside. I would pretend as if I was talking to my best friends and I know that this would not affect that way I feel about them. Would I see them as less of a person or would I think of them as courageous? This is how I talk to myself and beef up my own self-esteem.

This is crucial as I have three girls and self-esteem is one of the key things on a list of things that I want to impart to them. If you don't have self-esteem, no one will have it for you. You need to work on it—self-esteem isn't something you are born with—you have to work on it. Everyone has their own practice and my way is to look at myself as an outsider.

I have always been super short and while that does not help with self-esteem, I have spun it around and worked my petite frame to my advantage. I have never had to lift a heavy bag in my life—people will always help me as I look so small and frail. Because of my tiny frame, I have always been looked after, always been cuddled and am not seen as a threat to anyone—and that in itself has helped me build my self-esteem—all five foot one of me.

I am sure our readers will find the honest, searing account of your battle with cancer inspiring. Kudos to you for not glossing over the pain, trauma and mutilation you endured. It is reassuring for our readers undergoing similar situations to know that it is okay to admit that there are days when they feel completely down and embattled, and not feel that they have to always glorify their fight with cancer or any other difficult moment in their life.

Yes, I do want to share, and yes, it takes time to heal. I can't speak for every cancer patient, but for me it was important. I did not want to hear that everything was fine because it isn't, even till today. I don't want anyone to pull the wool over my eyes and tell me that I will never have to think about it ever again. The reality is that you do and it changes your life. As my oncologist said, it is an existential experience. One is so close to death that it reshapes everything you think about. It does take a lot of time to get over.

As I shared, my mum had cancer 17 years ago and it was similar to mine. It is painful for any parent to go through this with their child and vice versa. She's a cancer survivor and she still worries. She is 69 and it is still a real threat. Cancer stays with you for the rest of your life but somehow you manage to gain moderation and perspective over time.

Share with us now on your career. Not many would know that you cut your teeth at a now defunct brand called Rachel B.

I always look at Rachel B as my learning platform and it was what I would have paid if I went to five years of fashion school. We had multiple brand stores at F J Benjamin and I was working on the sourcing, buying and curating of various brands. I started sharing with Doug that I wished we had this from this brand and that from that brand, and lamented that customers wanted pieces that we don't carry. So one day, he said, "Why don't we just make the stuff we don't have. We are in Asia, how difficult can this be?"

With that, we got an American consultant to come in to help us.

She was a designer and a product development person. At the start, we were a very small set up and had a tiny studio. The consultant started working on sourcing factories, and we soon hired our own pattern maker and started acquiring our own software, computers and a cutter. We also hired a seamstress and an in-house fit model.

The consultant then started designing and I found myself disagreeing with her on her choice of fabrics and started getting involved with the creative aspects. She, however, continued to do just about everything else. But I learned very quickly as I was with her all the time. Coming from a Mathematics background, everything makes sense—from how a pattern needs to be drafted, to how it is cut and shaped. I had hands-on, on-the-ground experience and I soaked it up like a sponge.

Soon after, there was a financial crisis and things changed. I had to leave the creative aspect behind and go back to my roots, to the scientific and mathematical side of things. The change began around the late 1990s and we were faced with anxiety and the crisis of the Y2K bug. Like all companies, we had to change all our software to one that was Y2K compatible. Back then, we were already developing our own software and had this great team of Indian programmers. Even though we had a manager, I was still hands-on and worked as a number cruncher for Douglas' uncle, Nash.

As I was working on the reports, I realised that I was lacking key information each time we churned out a report. We still relied heavily on manual data and could not seem to be able to process some information from our existing systems. I took it upon myself to look into matters. I saw that things were not where they needed to be.

I had a team of programmers who were very good at what they were doing and I had retailers who knew what they wanted, but somehow the two parties didn't know how to "talk" to each other. They had totally different lingo. The buyer, for example, wanted to know what the sales-to-stocks ratio is and the other has no idea what that meant. Or if I wanted details on my gross and net margin, the computer programmers would be at a loss. I realised there was a communications breakdown so

I made myself a systems analyst and stepped up to work for the next two years with the IT department.

I worked on everything from warehousing, accounts to retail—from front-end to back-end—and I literally drafted every report and provided them with every single formula and template that they needed to get the work done. I am not able to do any programming to save my life and IT has developed so phenomenally since my days in LSE, but I knew I was well-versed enough to understand the logic behind what needed to be done. This allowed me to sit with the professional programmers to literally map out all the reports and guide them towards understanding what was needed for our retail business. It was like being a creative director of the programming team. We also mapped out product trees which was actually a lot of fun and I enjoyed it.

During that time, we were also running Guess Kids. We had great business with Guess and we had about 30 Guess Kids stores when the Guess Kids licensee in the U.S. had to fold. We were at a loss as we had stores with no product. We quickly approached Guess and suggested that we would develop products for Guess Kids until they got their house in order, otherwise we would have to shut our stores or convert the stores into something else. I already had two children by then and was called into a meeting where I was told that I had to oversee the design for Guess Kids.

I went to the designers and the factories and was not happy with what I saw. As I had children, I knew what they needed and I started sketching for them. So those sketches went to Guess and they loved it, so we produced it and I had nothing to do with it after as I was soon pregnant with our third child in 1999. But in 2001, the person running Guess Kids left suddenly so I had to step up and flew to the U.S. to present the new collection. That ended up working very well for us. So in a way, these encounters became my learning ground in manufacturing.

As for the creative and design aspect, I picked that up when I was at Rachel B as I had to understand the structure of the garment, how to get the right cut, the finer details. For example, a 1cm margin could make a difference to a men's garment looking on-trend or off. In contrast, Guess Kids was less about design and being trendy than about comfort so we had a lot of room for play. In fact, most times, we took our ideas from what was "happening" in adult lines and translated that to the kids lines. What was key was that the clothes were "cute" so you can add a bow here and some sparkle there to make a cute little T-shirt.

There was certainly room for creativity and it was not as scientific. Guess Kids taught me what it takes to manufacture and I gained an understanding about how to order the right amount of raw materials and fabrics. I also learnt how to do the costing, tagging, shipping, labelling and testing. All this I learnt from Guess Kids in the 10 years that I was there. By then, Baby Guess and Guess Kids were in Asia Pacific and we started distributing to the Middle East as well. It was a very interesting business but I always felt that it was not my own as it still belonged to the Guess label.

One day, Douglas had the idea that he wanted to do a men's shirt line. He was tired of buying his own shirts and felt that it was silly to be spending so much money on his wardrobe. With that, Raoul was started. I initially thought he was crazy as I had my hands full with three kids, Guess Kids, Baby Guess and we were also doing Manchester United as well. I was by then involved in product development and the design for the mass sports line. We were creating all sorts of merchandise from coasters to T-shirts. By the way, Manchester United taught me how to do sourcing which was really interesting. So, in hindsight, I took all of this knowledge—sourcing, manufacturing, logistics, financials and the creative and put them all to good use in Raoul.

So yes, Raoul started as a men's line but we noticed that wives and girlfriends were coming into the stores to purchase the shirts for their men and were also buying the shirts for themselves! We then set aside a small corner in the stores and started to create a small range of shirts for the women and they picked them up like candy! As demand grew, we introduced more styles and expanded the range to skirts and shirtdresses. So Raoul grew organically from consumer demand. The whole DNA of the brand is reflective of my aesthetic that is feminine and elegant. I am inspired by the late 1960s and 1970s for its haute feminine flair for cocktail wear and I certainly have fun pairing white shirts with big ball skirts. As of 2016, we shut all our retail shores in Singapore, but we are still available in department stores in the U.S., Europe, the Middle East and online.

You are a self-professed mathematician at heart. Do you think you would have stumbled upon fashion if you had not married into the F J Benjamin family?

I have always been fascinated with fashion and am privileged that I am equally comfortable working with my right and left brain. Some days, I am more comfortable with one than the other, but I am both artistic and analytical and use it to my advantage. When I was doing my A Levels, I did Art in addition to Maths and Higher Maths. Maths was always my passion so I even did Extended Maths, but I also did what they called S Level Art.

But I was always interested in fashion but it just didn't occur to me that I would eke out a career there. One of my relatives is a designer. His name is David Sassoon and he used to design for the late Princess Diana and was a London couturier. When I was 16, he was over at our house for dinner and I expressed that I really wanted to work in fashion. He dissuaded me and told me that art school is really tough and that I needed to build a good portfolio. He also shared that I had to go to an art school before I could attend a fashion school.

I was, in fact, good at art but it was not my main focus as maths was my great passion. Soon, I gave up on that art school idea and chose to study Management Sciences, which was a very scientific and mathematical course. I enjoyed it and did really well. When I decided to leave, the Dean actually called Douglas in and told him that it was a travesty that he was marrying me and taking me out of school. Till today, I do not have a degree to my name but I have no regrets.

Did you have any expectations about Singapore before your move?
I didn't know what was going to happen in Singapore. I knew I wanted to work though I am not a highly career-oriented and ambitious woman. I am very passionate about what I do and very determined.

That is something I learned from my dad. Before my dad passed away I was never really interested in school—I was not very academic. My dad was obviously a scientist and I used to say I hate science and maths and that I could not do it. My dad would ask me, "If the person next to you can do it, why can't you? Are you saying they are smarter than you? If a question is being asked, then there must be an answer. You just need to work hard to find it."

So, my dad's words have stuck with me and it has become my mentality towards life and I impart that to my kids. I don't want them to give up too easily. Kids tend to participate in many different activities but I tell them that they must keep at it and achieve something out of what they undertake. My oldest daughter eventually graduated from UCL with first class honours in Information Technology for Business Management—something she did not want to do nor did she think she could do. I told her to persevere, succeed through that and do whatever she wants to after. She did and went on to read her master's in Psychology Applied in Fashion.

How is like working with your husband? Share with us tips on how you make your partnership work.
I think boundaries are really important. There is no hard and fast rule. For us, it is about respecting each other's abilities and work. It is also about defining the roles very clearly. As colleagues, we discuss, talk, put our ideas forward and try to come to an agreement but it is very clear to me that he is the boss, and that his final word *is* the final word. Doug makes the final decisions at work and whether I agree with them or not, those are the decisions that stay. After all, he is the one who reports to the Board, not me. He has to account for everything that happens.

As his wife, however, I argue and debate with him. Doug and I have so much that binds us together. Sure, we have our moments like any other married couple but we agreed from day one that we would never go to bed arguing. So whatever happens, we resolve our issues before we go to bed, fully at peace with each other.

If you had your life philosophy on a car bumper sticker, what would it say?
Don't sweat it if you can't control it.

Favourite fashion item?
I will have to say it's not a fashion item, but it's my hair. I lost my hair and I didn't have any hair for a while so that was really tough. Hair and nails really make a difference to how a woman feels about herself and not many women pay enough attention to that. Like a handshake, the way your hand feels and looks says a lot about your personality.

What pisses you off?
Dishonesty.

How do you want to be remembered?
As a kind, loving person.

Given what you know now, what would you say to a younger version of you?
Don't underestimate yourself.

What would you say to God when you meet him?
Thank you.

What role do you identify with? A Madonna, Maverick or any other M word?
I'll say I'm a Mere Mortal, Multi-tasking Mother and most recently, Mother of the Bride!

The Controversial Diplomat

CHAN HENG CHEE

Ambassador Chan Heng Chee is Ambassador-at-Large with the Singapore Ministry of Foreign Affairs and Singapore's Representative to the ASEAN Intergovernmental Commission on Human Rights. She is the Chairman of the National Arts Council and a member of the Presidential Council for Minority Rights. She is a board member and chairperson in various universities in Singapore such as National University of Singapore, Nanyang Technological University, Yale-NUS College and Singapore University of Technology and Design.

Previously, she was Singapore's Permanent Representative to the United Nations from 1989 to 1991 with concurrent accreditation as High Commissioner to Canada and Ambassador to Mexico. She was also Singapore's Ambassador to the United States from July 1996 to July 2012. When Ambassador Chan left Washington at the end of her appointment, she received the Inaugural Asia Society Outstanding Diplomatic Achievement Award, the Inaugural Foreign Policy Outstanding Diplomatic Achievement Award and the United States Navy Distinguished Public Service Award.

Ambassador Chan has received numerous awards in Singapore including the first Woman of the Year in 1991, The Meritorious Service Medal in 2005 and The Distinguished Service Order in 2011. She was also twice awarded the National Book Awards for "The Dynamics of One Party Dominance: The PAP at the Grassroots" in 1978 and for "A Sensation of Independence: A Political Biography of David Marshall" in 1986.

She has also been the recipient of Honorary Degrees of Doctor of Letters from the University of Newcastle (Australia) and the University of Buckingham (United Kingdom), as well as Honorary Degree of Doctor of Laws from University of Warwick (United Kingdom).

***

"So what is the title of the book?"

"Matriarchs, Madonnas and Mavericks. But I haven't really settled on a title yet..."

"So who do you consider a Matriarch, a Madonna and a Maverick?"

"I see Olivia as a Maverick, she became a serial entrepreneur with no formal education. And Cynthia Chua as a Maverick as she seizes opportunities, utilises market forces and manipulates social media and savvy branding to grow her business empire..." I was about to continue but she interjects, not impolitely, but more out of interest.

"How are you defining Madonna?"

"Hmmm. That's a great question. I started defining Madonna as the pop star Madonna, the queen of reinvention, as people identify with that better. But I later decided that I should define her in the traditional sense, as a role or archetype to contrast with Maverick, the game-changer. So Madonna is immaculate, pristine and virtuous—someone who has perfected a single craft and has longevity."

"So what am I?"

"You are a Matriarch but I am not defining merely in terms of age." I checked to see if she took offence. None was taken as she knew I meant it sincerely. "You broke the glass ceiling and were a first in many ways and domains..."

"But I can also be a Maverick," she said. "I hold many hats and have changed roles so many times, going with the flow."

"Indeed, I can see that... your resume is endless," I laughed with all due respect.

Suffice to say, Prof Chan is a poised picture of diplomacy. Her answers were measured and guarded, and there was a sense that there is always more unsaid. I interviewed her in her office in the Lee Kuan Yew Centre for Innovative Cities in SUTD (Singapore University of Technology and Design) where she is Chair, so I found it more appropriate to refer to her as Professor Chan instead of Ambassador Chan. Somehow one cannot help but use these terms of deference with her, which must say something about her bearing and countenance.

Unlike Ivy Singh-Lim who is all text and no subtext, Prof Chan is a study in measured accuracy and one gets the distinct sense that there are many filters at play (or at work) when she speaks. This is not to say she does not speak her mind, she does. She has distinct points of view that raises eyebrows and gets her embroiled in controversies, yet her demeanor is one that is practiced and calculated, like a stealthy jaguar on the hunt—cool, calm, collected. Though make no mistake, one false move and you are prey.

So we begin. And oh, it is perhaps no surprise that I also dropped the word "Matriarch" from my title.

***

You know, I didn't start out wanting to be a diplomat. I was never very ambitious, few believe that, but it is true. I actually wanted to be a librarian as that was the only career available to women educated overseas. That and a writer.

So you have always wanted to be a writer?

Well, I enjoy writing, I enjoy imagining. One of these days I will write another book and it will be my story. But I cannot decide if I should write it as fiction or non-fiction. I spend a lot of time reading novels in my down time. On board an aeroplane, I would prefer to read a novel if I am not writing a speech. I have a fond wish that when I become less busy in everything I am doing, and most of it is in the foreign policy, diplomacy and academic field, I would be writing a novel. Well, let's see!

Aside from all the numerous firsts you have garnered, what did you think you would be doing when you got your degree in Political Science?

If I tell people, frankly, I never thought I would be what I am today, nobody will believe me. I was just meandering through. The only thing that was constant, as I look back in my life was this: I always wanted to do my best. I am not always the top girl but I am competitive. If I am not top, I want to be near the top.

Now, I knew, when I finished school at O Levels that I wanted to go to the university. That was a very clear goal. When I finished getting my BA, I asked myself, "What are you going to do now?" I knew then that I wanted to work in the public sector. I didn't use the word "public sector" in those days because that was not the word. I didn't want to work in the commercial world—I wanted to work in something for the good of people—a general good. So, I decided I could be a teacher, work in the civil service, or be a librarian.

I wanted to be a librarian very much because I knew that the then University of Singapore gave scholarships to people to study library science. Most of the top women, when I was an undergraduate, went into librarianship because the other areas were not opened to them. So, I said, "Ya, that's where I want to be. I want to go overseas. So I'll be a librarian." Besides, I did love books.

But because I had a first class in Political Science, the head of my department said, "Look, why don't you take on a research scholarship? We'll try and get you one to do a PhD elsewhere." So the head of my department wrote to Cornell University and asked if they would accept me. I got the scholarship and I was not bonded.

I went over there but, you see, this is where the odd thing comes in. I was one of the first few Singaporeans to go to the United States for a PhD, most went to Britain and Australia. We had this idea that when you finish the PhD in say, three years, you would come home. When I arrived in Cornell, I had a shock because I was told, "Oh, a PhD in Cornell takes at least five years, typically five to seven years." You know,

Ben Anderson who just died? He was a cultural and political scientist. He wrote the book *Imagined Communities*, which is on nationalism and it is considered a great book. Well, Ben was in his ninth year in Cornell when I arrived. And I thought, "Oh God! I'm not going to stay here that long for a PhD."

I met all sorts of smart women, including Nancy McHenry who became my dear friend in graduate school. She later married an academic and is probably a good housewife and mother till this day. Anyway, back then, Nancy was from Stanford and she went to Thailand to serve as a Peace Corps teacher. She and I were the only two women in that batch. Then, she was trying to decide between marriage and her PhD as she was engaged to someone reading his postdoc. She kept talking to me about marriage that I started to think, "Oh God, if I stayed for five or seven years, I'll never get married. I do want to go home to get married."

The result was that she and I teamed up and decided we would not continue to read our PhD. We went to our professor and said that we wanted to drop out to do an MA instead. There, we found another two or three men also trying to drop out of the program. Now, Cornell was really crossed because it took in ten students for its PhD, and five of us dropped out to sign on to the MA. You can do it within the first two weeks and I did that. So, I did my MA, wrote my thesis and went back to Singapore as I was offered a job in the Department of Political Science at NUS. Back then, I was the first Singaporean to join the department. There was a Malaysian and the rest are British, Australians and Indians.

Anyway, Cornell is an institution that makes you question and think. I studied with the best in the United States for Southeast Asian studies and the education was very good for me. It helped that they liked my thesis too. In fact, my book *The Politics of Survival* published in 1971 was my MA thesis. It became part of the Oxford in Asia monograph series and that launched me into the arena.

Even after I came back, Cornell remained very helpful. Whenever there were Americans or friends of Cornell going to Singapore, they said to go and see Chan Heng Chee. Conversely, if they were organising a conference they would invite me to be the Southeast Asian representative. So even though I didn't have a PhD, I was getting into the circle and was thrown into the orbit of international conferences very young, at around age 25.

There were very few women in academia and I was the only woman in my department. The men in my department were very good to me so I didn't feel discriminated against and it helped that I wasn't a bad looker, was lively, interested, and in a way, rather western. My interests included literature, theatre and and the arts, and I was very much in touch with the architectural scene.

Back in Cornell, I had a host father and he was a professor of Architecture and I used to go to his house all the time. I looked after his kids when he and his wife went to New York for a spot of theater and I would stay overnight for the weekend. I would browse through all his books and sieve through his records, music, literary and artistic collections that fed my interest, curiosity, cultural education and really helped to deepen and broaden my horizons.

When I came back, I guess people found me interesting, and I had a sense of humor. So, I got on with my colleagues very well and never felt anyone was against me. In fact, I thought they treated me rather preciously. Fortunately or unfortunately, my life has been like that, which is why there isn't much anger in me.

During that period, I started writing to express my views which were not always in sync with the government. In fact, my monograph was seen by Alex Josey[1] to be critical of the government. I received a terrible review from him, which ironically led to my books getting sold out!

Yes, there is no press like bad press.

I suggested in my writings that the PAP (People's Action Party) had pushed too hard in the years leading up to the Separation, which led to the rise in racial tensions. I was also of the opinion that Tunku Abdul Rahman, then President of UMNO (United Malays National Organisation), took umbrage at the fact that the PAP stood for the elections. He thought Singapore would not and PAP said there was no such understanding.

1 Alex Josey was a British journalist and political commentator, best known for his biographies on Lee Kuan Yew.

Even though I ended the chapter on an upbeat note saying that Singapore will prevail because of the strong leadership, that was not good enough for Alex Josey. He pounced on me and cast me as this maverick who was criticising the PAP. Looking back, I now know that even if we didn't separate in 1965, we would have separated sooner or later as it was a matter of time.

Typically, I would write things when I disagreed and I disagreed on two things. One, that there was too narrow a space for intellectuals and academic freedom, and two, I felt that the government was too intolerant of and tough towards the opposition. These were the two issues I voiced my opinions on and I was never personal in my criticisms. My commentaries were always based on principle and I never spewed venom.

Honestly, I think that was why I was tolerated and nothing happened to me. In fact, when my book came out, Dr Goh Keng Swee gave a call and I was asked to go to his office to see him. He was then the Minister for Defence. He was curious to see who Chan Heng Chee was as I was the first Singaporean to write on Singapore politics.

So, when I showed up to see him, we chatted and he wanted to find out about my family background, my influences and defining moments to know what shaped me. He must have decided that I am not a dissident nor revolutionary, but was just being a Western-educated academic and university liberal who wanted to share a piece of my mind and my opinions. I think after meeting me he must have felt that I was okay. It is also for this reason that I always kept out of joining a political party. I felt that as an academic, I should not be seen as being partisan. So, I've always maintained that I am independent.

That is why you opposed the NMP (Nominated Member of Parliament) scheme?

Well, at that time, I thought that the NMP scheme is a retrogression. You have democracy and everybody is elected. Why are you doing this? I knew that this really was a strategy, or a ruse to deter people from voting for the opposition. I would say things like that, which was against the tide.

I remember an incident around in 1986. Francis Seow[2] was elected the President of the Law Society. I don't particularly admire or not admire Francis Seow. In fact, I don't know him so I am neutral. But when he took over the Law Society, one of the ministers said it was a political statement and issued an official memo that said interest groups should not participate in politics.

During the time that this matter raged on in the media, I wrote a letter to the press saying I believed that in constitutional democracies, interest groups should have a legitimate role in politics. I didn't write it in a rude fashion but as an even-tempered academic letter. This caused quite the furore and many people thought I was very brave to speak up as the PAP was quite tough in the 1980s. But, nothing happened to me.

I remember walking into an elevator one day and there was Mr Dhanabalan who was then the Foreign Minister. He asked me, "You took the position of Francis Seow?" I said, "Look, it's not about Francis Seow. It's about the principle." He said, "You did it on principle?" I said, "Yes." He nodded. The government didn't take action against me and I noticed, over the weekend, Wong Kan Seng, then Minister for Community Development, gave an interview to refine his position on the matter.

By 1987, I was asked if I would think about taking on the appointment as the Permanent Representative to the United Nations. My own sense is that I may have been on their minds as a potential. The interpretation by many was that the government was trying to get rid of me, but I disagree. I did not think it was fair to make that assumption of Tommy Koh's posting as well. The government could easily have handled me if they wanted to.

Anyhow, I shared with Mr Dhanabalan that I would like to consult with my then husband, Tay Kheng Soon as I was married by then. After discussing with him, I decided to accept the position. My co-workers

2 Francis Seow was a lawyer who served as Singapore's Solicitor-General from 1969 to 1971. He stood for the 1988 general election as a member of the Workers' Party and lost marginally against PAP. Just before the election, Seow was detained without trial under the Internal Security Act for 72 days. According to his account, he was subjected to torture, including sleep deprivation and intensely cold air conditioning. Amnesty International issued a public statement in 2007 mentioning Seow as one of two prominent Singaporean lawyers who were penalised for exercising their right to express their opinions and called him a "prisoner of conscience".

told me that as a political scientist, I should take on the role, otherwise I should have my head examined.

Up till 1989, I have never been a diplomat and nor has any other woman been appointed. The ministry and in particular, Dhanabalan was so very understanding. He said, "Look, Heng Chee, you know New York is a rough town, why don't you just go join the delegation of the UN General Assembly, and decide if you can see yourself living in New York." So, I went. In fact, before that, I attended a Non-Aligned Movement (NAM) conference just to get a taste of what the work would be like. You see, the Ministry wanted to make sure I was all right, and I appreciated it.

At that time, many had no idea that I am a night owl and don't sleep very much at night. One of the things that stood in my favour was my ability to stay up throughout the course, which I learnt was much needed in NAM. I was there for Cambodia and had to sit through the whole night in what is euphemistically called a demonstration of "S Power" (which stands for "Sitting Power" or "Staying Awake Power").

I was brand new, a trained academic, who is no stranger to late night reading and writing and so I sat there until 5 a.m. in the morning. It's a real test of manhood for many of the diplomats and they often fall asleep and opt to have a junior officer sit in their place. My tenacity rose eyebrows and people were asking, "Who is this young woman?" I was in my 40s and wasn't that young then, but I certainly won their respect. The international community was saying, "Gosh! She is awake, alert *and* she intervenes!" I am made for the UN because of my "S Power"—that and the fact that the Foreign Ministry was very generous with the first woman diplomat they were going to call "Ambassador".

The person I was meant to succeed was Kishore Mahbubani. He was gracious, generous and took the time to explain the workings of the UN to me. He introduced me to people and gave me encouragement and advice. He told me that I should be seen as a "serious ambassador" and not be regarded as the woman ambassador dressed in beautiful clothes like a supermodel. There were not many women ambassadors at that time, maybe four or five globally. I believe he also wrote to the Foreign Ministry to request for my use of the car and driver. You see, the Foreign Ministry is usually very strict about the use of the car for official duties, but Kishore wanted the driver to help keep an eye on me, not unlike a personal bodyguard. That's why I say, from the university to the Foreign Ministry, I have always felt well looked after. I felt that my colleagues were very kind and they all treated me very well.

I have to say though, that when I was in the university, my promotion to a full professor came a bit slow in the beginning, and people would ask me, "How was it? Were you promoted?" The answer was "no" and I would ask, "Did you think gender was an issue?" Honestly, I always felt that it was my politics rather than gender that affected me. Looking back, I would say it was probably both. In the 1990s, I was up against a male colleague for promotion. He was the head of my department but I cleared the hurdles before he did. The university tried to keep me back so as to wait for him to clear his hurdles, but he could not. In the end, they did end up making me a full professor but it was undeniable that I was held back for quite a bit.

So in many ways, fortunately or unfortunately, you were aided by your gender?

Yes. I think, for women to do well, they should not be angry. I was a feminine female and I was not angry, which is very important. I had too many other fights in politics so I did not think to fight my gender. I remained authentic to myself. If you bang the table, it doesn't come across so well. Although, now that I am older, I can make "angry women's comments" and people don't mind it so much. They think it comes with age.

What do you think is your greatest take away from having been in the U.S. for as long as you have?

My greatest take away is that the United States is a really creative place and I found everybody to be so helpful. The one thing I can say is this: women in the U.S. and Singapore seem to enjoy motherhood rather differently. I would observe the women in Washington, New York or even a small town in America. They look so happy being mothers. Whether they are well heeled professional women or middle income workers, they seem to view motherhood as part of their life cycle and have no qualms going back to work even with baby in tow.

I wish we could have that in Singapore and allow the women to go back to work and yet be integrated into the community. I've always said that we should find a way for women to get back at work easily even after they have their babies. For women who don't want to get married and have babies, it's okay too. The point is, I hope there is less stigma and judgment against working moms and childless career women. All should be acceptable positions and society should not judge.

The other take away I have is that the women in the U.S. are ambitious. Just take a look at Hilary Clinton. I don't think many Singaporean women harbour the thought of being a prime minister. That's the difference. The level of ambition is different but so is the level of understanding of what a woman's life can be like. I do think we need a mindset change. We have to have more crèches to free up the women's daytime hours and we must also "catch" and be aware of our own prejudices.

I have often noticed that people shun the mother in a party, choosing instead to talk to whom they see as a more powerful individual in the room. If you tell them you are a "homemaker looking after my baby", the person may turn around and talk to somebody else. So we need to change our attitudes to mothers and motherhood. Also, to mothers, here's a note: I know the hours are hard and tiring but do not give up. Keep up with your other interests even as you are looking after baby.

Do you think you would have come this far if you were a mother?
No, quite frankly. Though I think I would have been just as happy because I would not know what it is to come this far or to have this life. And by "this far", I mean, I am thankful in my life, I've always done what I want and love what I do. I probably have an instinct that if I

don't like something, I don't want to touch it. I also have quite a bit of energy, am interested and can get excited with a lot of things. These days, I Google and YouTube a lot. First TED talks, then movies, music, and now, I Google and YouTube all kinds of stuff.

So in other words, because you never had children, you have more time to pursue your diverse interests? And what do you say to your critics that say that you have "sold out" over the years?

Let me put it this way. I was divorced but I harbour no bitterness and I kept up with my stepsons. I don't as much now, but I know if I want to see them, we will meet even though we are all very busy. I wish my ex well and I am glad, I have no anger.

But here is something that connects with your idea of the Maverick. Many have come up to me to tell me that I sold out because the government made me an ambassador. To that I say, "Nonsense!" They made me an ambassador because they read what I was writing and probably found that I was calming down or mellowing. And why did I do that? I did it of my own volition.

Actually, I was married to someone who was quite rebellious too. He is an architect and a thinker in his own right but I don't always agree with him. Suffice to say we had very good discussions. And you know, I teach courses on development in other societies and you soon begin to realise that it is not that easy to build a nation.

Governance is not easy—just take a look at the different countries and you see different kinds of problems. Whether you agree with their politics—depending on what end of the spectrum you are on, if you are socialist-leaning or more democratic. At least I've always thought the PAP government was honest. I am a democratic socialist. I like the PAP of today where their policies are more inclusive. Their turning a little left is right for the times, and I do think you do have to look after people who are left behind. A pure free market doesn't work for me, in fact, it doesn't work anywhere else.

I have said that actually, with what is happening in globalisation, where you create structural unemployment, there will always be a group "in the know" and others who are "know nots". So governments do have to see what they can do for the people. I know the West is cutting back entitlements and they have to rethink if they can keep cutting back so many entitlements.

Singapore has gone counter-intuitive and headed the other way. We've started giving, which now leads to the question, "Can you keep giving forever?" and "Don't we have to raise taxes at some point?" These are issues Singaporeans will have to contend with and if we are pragmatic and sensible, we will know that there is some balance that must be struck. We cannot always be giving but we also cannot purely rely on a free market.

As I began to study other societies, I realised that this government is not so bad and is, in fact, doing a lot of good things. Yes, I agree they can be more democratic and allow more room for the opposition—that was always my big bug bear. The opposition is getting to the root but the PAP is extremely inventive and creative. They stepped to the left and incorporated more liberal policies. It's a bit like the new Labour and old Labour in the UK. New Labour incorporated the Conservative policies and the Conservative pulls in the Labour policies. You borrow a little here and there. I think the PAP of today has gotten a lot of good policies.

Anyway, as I began to have a more nuanced understanding of democracy and good governance, I started to not be as critical. It was a self-chosen position. I'd arrived at it myself and it was irrespective of position and appointments.

Speaking of a self-chosen position, you came under heat over...
Censorship. Well, look, if I had my druthers, in a perfect situation, there should be no censorship, which is great. But Singapore is a multiracial, multilingual, multiethnic and multireligious society. Like it or not, when there are differences, someone has to be the arbiter, so in this case, the government is the arbiter. I will say that no one does censorship with glee or joy. It's done with some pain and is seriously considered. I think all

parties should try to compromise, and where we can, government should see what it can do to accommodate societal demands.

But, extremism seems to be emerging and taking hold. Frankly, the Singapore government is generous and gives a lot of money to support the arts. But, there are some things we cannot allow and I guess if society wants it, then there should be funding and sponsorship from the private sector. In fact, I want to grow the audience and the patronage, so that the arts and artists don't have to just rely on government that has to then take on the responsibility to see where the money should be spent. It is not an easy task.

So, as the Chairman of the NAC (National Arts Council), I had to say something.[3] The artists were already angry when NAC issued the statement from Kathy Lai. I can't be the ostrich in the sand and not say anything so I said it very mildly. In fact, if you read the piece on what I said, it was quite balanced. I'm not trying to say you must crunch down on artists but many were upset because I said it at the opening of a film festival.

Have you had occasions where you felt that you faced a dilemma between your own values and the positions espoused by the organisations that you work with?

I feel I can be a bridge. In my role, whether as Singapore's representative to the ASEAN Intergovernmental Commission on Human Rights; as NAC Chair or in the other roles I have taken on, I have always been a bridge. While it is my role to try to change parameters, I also take it upon myself to explain to the diverse groups what the constraints are. Sometimes, I don't think this is sufficiently understood. Where I feel that there is the possibility for change, I would try to speak out for everybody but I am not going to stand up on a soapbox because that is not the way.

3 In November 2015, Chan spoke at the Singapore International Film Festival (SGIFF) to defend NAC's censorship policies, prompting calls to boycott the NAC. Chan did not warn the organisers, the strictly no-censorship SGIFF, of her talk's contents. This caused much anger and controversy within the arts and media community. Notably, NAC does not even oversee or supervise Singapore's film industry.

My role can be effective even away from the public eye—and what I take up, I don't have to tell the world.

Do you have any regrets in your life? I have read elsewhere that you have declined to talk about your divorce or motherhood.
I don't regret in a sense that I don't sit and mope about it. I did used to wonder what it would be like to have children of my own but I have two stepsons and they were with me for a while. That took a lot of motherly instincts out of me and also assuaged the desire to have my own biological children. Many of my friends tell me that I should have a closer relationship with them or else they will leave, but I honestly think that as long as you have strong, committed relationships and have somebody to love, that is all that matters.

So, I don't really regret anything, though I wish I could play the piano as I have always wanted to as a girl but my grandmother said "no". I begged to study it as there was a piano teacher two houses down my row. I could see the young girls going to the house and I could hear sounds of the piano. But my grandmother told my mother not to educate me too much as I was a girl. As a result, my mother didn't dare give me lessons without my grandmother's approval. But up till today, I still love music and I Google all genres be it classical, opera, pop, folk or jazz.

So as long as there are strong, committed relationships in your life, it does not matter if it takes the form of a spouse, child or confidante? I take it there is someone special in your life?
Let me put it this way: my life has not been man-less after my divorce.

(*Laughter*) **That is so good to know and an inspiration to many of our readers. Some Singaporean women still view sunset romances as taboo. Indeed, you keep a very active life. Speaking of youth, what would you say to your younger self?**
You know, I would not relive my life any other way. I think you go for what you are interested in. If you happen to have the IQ and brains,

then go for it. But, you don't have to set an ambition as you never know. Your ambition may be too low for what you can achieve. The other key is finding contentment in whatever you do. The word "contentment" is terrible as it makes you feel you are stagnant. It isn't. I guess the better word to use is "happiness"—as long as you are happy with what you do, then trust that you know better.

I used tell people that I never was ambitious, so I won't be disappointed. In fact, that way, you may feel a sense of surprise when you do achieve. So to my younger self, I'll say: don't be too fixed about what you want to do, just go for it. Whatever it is you choose, never look back and regret.

What would you say are your biggest victories in your lifetime?
I never think of it that way. People always ask me what I consider as the best thing I did or the most important accomplishment in Washington. I must say that's a tough question to answer. You see, as you move on in life, the last thing you've done is always the most important thing. So, I don't have a definitive answer although I do feel that certain things are more pertinent in the varying stages of growth. Mine can be delineated as childhood, marriage, divorce and life after divorce.

Speaking of a "life after", what will your epitaph say?
It's for others to write, isn't it? It's not for me to write. They will just put my name, when I was born, when I died. I am not one to keep scrapbooks of articles or stories published on me on myself. What I do have are some photographs in a photo gallery as a tribute started by my staff when I left Washington. I do however have stacks and stacks of photographs only because my ex-husband was a very keen photographer. At the time when we were together, we had many photos taken as a family.

So you will have problems writing your own biography?
Yes. I have not planned to write or start documenting myself, quite simply because I know if I were to write anything, it would be a piece of fiction.

Ah, so now you have your answer. When we prefaced the interview, you said you had no idea what to write just yet.
Yes, all I know is that I don't want it to be about me, and I want to explore themes that would allow me to utilise my knowledge of the history and politics of the times.

Do you believe in God's Will or Fate, or do you believe in choice and determination?
Oh, it is certainly choice and determination, but luck is very important. After a while, you make your own luck. How you think, behave and act all go towards building your luck as you do savings in a bank.

By the way, I have a sweet story about my mother and a fortune teller. My mother would take the birth date and time of all my siblings and me to have our horoscopes read by a fortune teller in Hong Kong when we are born. She told me he's blind—maybe just to make the story interesting. Apparently, the fortune teller told her that my life would be like a man's—that I would travel far and achieve a lot. So I grew up knowing that I would have a "man's life" so perhaps that inadvertently helped in my never ever feeling suppressed. My mother also said that the fortune teller told her I would take care of her when she is old… though I bet she added that in.

Are you religious?
No, but I am a lapsed Roman Catholic. I would say more accurately that I am not religious but spiritual, and I am not proud. If I am in a crisis or difficulty, I would mutter a prayer and draw strength from prayer and hope. There are moments when I've said prayers to myself and I know that I would go back to the church someday, although I do make it for Christmas Mass.

When you see God, what would you say?
My God! I made it!

I figured I might already know your response, but what would you identify yourself with: Madonna, Maverick or some other M word?

If we are defining Madonna as the queen of reinvention in your earlier definition, then I think I am both Madonna and Maverick. I have certainly reinvented myself many times. From anti-establishment to establishment and even in my ripe old age, I have taken on cities and novel technologies as my new academic focus. I am also very much a Maverick, especially in my younger days.

The Lifestyle Legend

CYNTHIA CHUA

Cynthia Chua is the founder and CEO of Spa Esprit Group, a company which owns multiple lifestyle, beauty and grooming concepts, as well as food and beverage brands. She is known as a lifestyle entrepreneur in Singapore and was awarded the Singapore Tourism Board's Tourism Entrepreneur of the Year in 2012. Her Spa Esprit Group was estimated to have an annual turnover of around $90 million in 2016.

She developed Singapore's first dedicated waxing salon named Strip in 2002, which has now grown to 48 outlets in 11 cities, including 15 in Singapore. The Group also runs more than 30 Browhaus outlets worldwide, among other brands. The Spa Esprit Group's F&B restaurants, cafés and bars include House at Dempsey, Tiong Bahru Bakery, Common Man Coffee Roaster, Open Door Policy, Skinny Pizza, The Tippling Club and others. Chua has made investments in local farming, taking a specific interest in consumption patterns and lifestyle choices. She recently started Open Farm Community, a community farming and dining concept.

Chua understands the limitations of Singapore's small market, and the Group is now focusing on developing new businesses in other parts of the world. Continually pushing the frontiers, she opened her first overseas F&B and multi-concept store in 2016 in Chelsea, London, called A Wanted Man. It is an espresso canteen with an attached brow bar and waxing salon. She has also increased the company's overseas presence with new Strip and Browhaus outlets in Beijing and a Common Man Coffee Roasters café in Kuala Lumpur.

***

Part flower-child, part hard-nosed entrepreneur, but 100% fun—that is how I would best sum up Cynthia Chua. Speaking to Cynthia is unlike speaking to any high-powered CEO of over 100 shops. She came in fashionably dressed and did not look the part of a head honcho, more that of an urbanite ready for an underground party after a long day at the bank. Indeed, Cynthia seems so comfortable threading these distinct worlds of corporate retail and the arts.

Trained in aromatherapy in London and hot stone massage in the Bronx, the self-professed essential oil fanatic may be mistaken as a hippie "Om"-chanting yogi—except that she has her head screwed on right for business. Her businesses are so novel that they remain the dreams of many millennials who seek to create unconventional businesses—and they now have a role model they can look up to. From being labeled the Pussy Ambassador to creating a men's grooming salon, to gentrifying Tiong Bahru and propelling the Melbournesque coffee culture in Singapore, Cynthia has done it all. In fact, she has even created a line of products called Farm to Beauty, which is made from plants harvested from a garden located on the rooftop of Raffles City!

Cynthia is warm, bubbly and speaks very fast. Actually, she thinks faster than she speaks, which is why it can be hard to keep track of her thoughts in a conversation. She flits from one point to the next, though she does always get back to answer your question. It is easy to see why she has become so successful—she processes information and makes connections very quickly. Her creative spark stems from her ability to dream and have the gumption to see it through. In fact, some of her ideas can sound so out of this world. She speaks of her love of chicken rice and hospitality, and wishes to create a Chicken Hotel quite simply because it has never been done. In the next conspiratorial breath, she shares that she is already eyeing a piece of real estate in Paris. This is Cynthia, so you never know if might just come to pass!

Despite her hectic schedule, Cynthia seems to spend quite a lot of time in introspection and credits her self-awareness as a core tenet and pillar of her success. While she is quick to share all her business ideas, quirks and failings, she remains rather tight-lipped on her private life. So it was a real privilege to have her share with me some of her views on marriage, motherhood, leadership and the role of women in today's complex world. You get the sense that she wants to provide PR-savvy answers but yet, her exuberance and passion for life comes through. She recently celebrated 15 years of Strip in 2017, but I know that when it comes to this Queen of Lifestyle, she is possibly just getting started.

***

Share with us what makes you tick?

It is true that some people are more positive and some people more negative. For me, I think my positivity comes from having a blessed family. I also have a weird streak. When I love something, I have to do it and I don't stop to think about failure at all. When I mentor young women, I remind them that their energy is finite. I find too many people worry too much about their failures, and drain themselves to the point that they decide to quit.

I always thank my dad for his positive genes. My mum and older brother are like that too but my youngest sibling is less positive. I think I lucked out in the gene pool and was perhaps born to have a positive thinking pattern and mindset. It doesn't mean you can't change but you need to be aware. I think positive and am never bothered by the 50 different concepts in my head. I incubate them and look out for the right factors and when it happens—boom! It explodes and it becomes something of its own.

Some people fall sick worrying about their potential losses or thinking about the stock market crashing. I've actually never ever thought about that. Let's say I want to do a bakery, then all I will focus on is how much fun it will be. Can you imagine the diverse baking goods that I get to taste? What about coffee pairing? My mind just works in that way and I attribute it to my childhood and my father.

My father has always been very encouraging. Even when he saw how my brother could not quite make it in the business that my father funded, he never grumbled or became disgruntled. He has always been supportive and told me to pursue whatever I want even if I fail. I never felt that he would judge me so his positivity really helps. I have learned a lot from him.

Do you think your success is attributed to your being born with a silver spoon?

I somehow have the tenacity to see things through. Yes, my father could help but it is not as if he has a lot of money to give me. He was responsible and he looked after us, but like everybody else, I went out to get a job in order to better understand myself.

I went for my first ever interview and got the job in a bank as a marketing executive for corporate credit cards. I had to travel all the way to Jurong to meet the CFOs of the big companies based there and had to present to them the value proposition of our bank's customised credit cards for the top executives. While I like meeting people, I was not an early riser and was always late. I also could not see myself waking up early to take a bus to work every day and soon realised that this was not what I wanted to do. It didn't help that I started to witness all the office politics as well. I figured I could not work in this environment, though I was very blessed as everyone was very nice to me. Perhaps it comes from my own self-awareness but if I don't like something, I am intuitive and my mind starts working to see how I can get out of the situation.

Soon after I quit the bank, I started to think what else I could do and turned to real estate. I knew that I was quite a good salesperson. In fact, by then, I knew that I wanted my own business but would need financing and I did not want to head to my father for money so I saw real estate as a good way to make money fast. I learnt quickly and had a great time choosing the properties that I loved.

I recall selling a property called The Summit in East Coast. I would imagine that the property was the best resort in town so when I sold it, I sold it from my heart—so much so that clients often tell me that I sounded as if I was selling my own house! I realised I could be very hard-working if I want something bad enough. I would find the way to build my connections, networks and contacts as that is what matters in real estate. I started from scratch to build up my own customer base. So for example, if the client says she wants Le Marc at Kheng Cheng Road, I would go and print out all the details of the entire building's listings and I would call each unit.

My work table would be set by 10 a.m. and I would start my day of calls. It was great as I did not have to wake up early and could be in my pyjamas calling you, "Hi Loretta, I'm Cynthia from the XYZ. Do you have an apartment that you would love to sell or rent?" And I would go on, checking off my list and building my contacts. I realised that I was tenacious, but I had to have fun in everything that I do. Soon after, I started to think about being my own boss and wanted to acquire a business, so I shortlisted a few businesses to purchase.

I used to do my massages at Belle Esprit in Lorong Mambong and thought that aromatherapy would be a good business. I loved my beauty treats. Besides, I got along with the owner Samantha very well. She was an ex-stewardess and was getting a little lonely in the business. We went into business together and had another partner. I was in charge of design, which was a lot of fun, but later I switched portfolios with my partner to run operations, I also had fun there. I learnt that being able to create fun and energy for yourself is very important. Even if I was on the floor, we would play music, so my staff was always happy and loved having me there. On days when we were quiet, I would envision the shop being filled with people and would think of strategies to achieve that. My staff would ask me how I intend to go about it?

Anyway, as part of operations, I would do a roll call at 4 p.m. daily and would set daily objectives and share with them the focus for the day. I will also ask questions such as "What is item no. 86?" just to see if all my staff knew our products. Yes, I can take charge but my staff know I like to have fun. They would sashay and have fun at work with a sense of pride. There was a sense of togetherness with the team and people who have worked with me will know that I like to work hard. I am not an easy boss as I am very demanding, but I also let them understand why and they always feel inspired. That is important. I am hands-on and don't just tell them what to do as they will definitely say, "Cannot lah." And if they do that, I will challenge them and ask them, "Why?"

I make them feel part of the team and have them head to meetings with me. I will ask them, "What have we learned?" to get them to reflect. I always share with them that nothing is impossible. That is my spirit and philosophy. I always remind my team that they have a choice, so do not be envious of others. I tell them, "Make your own journey but you must have a dream." Maybe not everyone is born with a vision and I do have staff members who feel that they don't have a personal vision. For me, I find that having a vision is key as it gives me direction and I work towards that.

Do you think leaders are born or nurtured?

I think it's inborn but you can make it better. People who are not born leaders can also learn, so it is a bit of both. But like I said, awareness is the key. In order to change, you need to be conscious before you can change your thinking patterns. I think that we are all flawed individuals and should always try to better ourselves and seek progress. I am always reflecting on myself and my interaction with others. I will ask myself, "Why did I react this way?", "How do I change?", "How can I be better?" These questions excite me as they signal progression and transformation.

What was the "Aha!" moment that made you realise the importance of awareness?

I think many people are protective of their own agendas as they think they are the best. But this lack of awareness means they have already shut others off and are in their own comfort zone. One should never stop looking in amazement and wonder—there's so much to learn. As Leo Tolstoy said, "Real life is lived when tiny changes occur." His wisdom slowed me down and these days, I feel I don't need to do so much, instead I focus on the little things and see to their improvement.

The other person that I find inspiring is writer Rainer Maria Rilke. Even after publishing many books, at the age of 45, he wisely said, "I have a long way to go before I am where one begins." Some people at 40 already go, "I am so old, I can't do this". To that, I say, "Don't give yourself excuses. How your mind works determines what your journey will be." If you are cocky, you shut out awareness and will not even know your own problems.

Learn to be humble. My father taught me that. Humility is very important. When people make a comment about me, I never go, "No, I am never wrong." I always listen to see what others have to say, and learn something from them if I agree that their methods are better. I am eager to learn and it is my curiosity that makes me different. People often see the surface that I have "made it" but there are times when I have failed. But I gain inspiration from my interactions with people and I would learn from them. It is a cycle and this is an important mindset to have.

Don't be afraid to make mistakes. Everybody makes mistakes but it is important how you progress from there. Even if you do fail in the end, you would have already learnt something in the process. To me, nothing is worse than stagnation. If I were to look back last year and reflect on what I did, I may see that I have developed in a particular way. You may not see it as development but I am happy with my own progress.

Self-awareness and mindset are key. But here's what I think. I think there is a third key: hope. Hope is bigger than anything and I am a subscriber of that belief. When there's hope and when you give people hope, they will shine. I saw that some of my own staff were broken and not educated. But when I believed in them, they started to shine and can now run the business better than some MBA or business graduate, simply because someone took the time to groom them. In turn, their hope gives me the energy to keep on wanting to do even better.

You speak of hope. Has there ever been a time when you felt hopeless or downtrodden?

There was a very difficult time. My business started with five girls and we are all really good friends, but of course it did not end that way. I was downtrodden and felt as if it was the end of the world. I am quite an emotional person so relationships mean a lot to me. I am very idealistic so people do call me Alice in Wonderland—the dreamer. I am 46 this year and I have made all my dreams come true and hopefully, I can continue to dream till I am 80. This is not just a fairy tale world; it is the world that I live in.

Anyway, we started as friends and I was the creative one and wanted to head to London to learn new trades. Once I set my mind on something, I am very focused and it is hard to move with four other partners and I don't like confrontations. It didn't help that three of them were lawyers and are much older than me. We had different vested interests and they did not understand my vision. So I decided that I would switch gears, give in and do something else. It was very emotional.

It was a difficult time and I cried my heart out. I prayed to God that if someone believed in me, I would make that someone a lot of money. I did not want to go to my dad and ask for money. Everyone else in the business wanted to get out. There was just no meaning in the relationship if everybody wants to leave. I was only 25 then but I told one partner to believe in me and that I wouldn't let her down, and she stayed even though she was on the fence for a while.

Ever since my three other partners left, my business grew by leaps and bounds. I did not have endless meetings and could work fast. I do think that I can work like a dictator but if you are a good dictator, it can be very efficient. Being in the UN where everybody has his fair share of talk does not work for me as we don't move and working by consensus can cause immobility—one would say no and we can't move. I can't work like that. When I have a vision, I am very passionate and need to act.

Share with us your early entrepreneurial endeavours. How did you get from beauty to vintage fashion to food?

I didn't go into beauty as I wasn't interested in beauty per se, I am interested in life, your lifestyle which is more than beauty. I love life, so I want to impart my love to all my customers—a great bakery, good coffee and wonderful clothes.

I have always loved fashion, so when I met Jerry, who has now been my best friend for 17 years, we decided to open a fashion boutique called Potion. Jerry used to sell vintage clothes at Queensway, and noticed "this crazy girl who always comes in" and we became friends. Jerry would put me in all these quirky clothes, which he would alter to fit me and they were great! We decided that that would be just what we would do. I was very entrepreneurial even back then.

So after real estate, I went into Belle Esprit. After the Belle Esprit partner got out, my new partners came in. We were five partners with a spa and started Strip at Holland Village before opening another at Wheelock. Potion at Chip Bee Gardens also provided manicures and pedicures and was great fun. We got very popular as we were featured in the media. Later, we were asked to leave Chip Bee and we moved to Paragon.

In sequence, I started with beauty, went into clothing, but I have always harboured dreams of setting up a café. The vision that I wanted was less about food than having a nexus or platform for people to connect. I started daydreaming again and soon House came about. Honestly, I had no idea how to manage a 35,000 square feet space with no experience, but I did it anyway.

What made you decide to take over the space then?

It was quite scary. Someone once said you need 10,000 hours to learn a trade or a skill and I agree. I literally spent almost three years running House full-time. My dad asks me why I would go into the oily kitchen since I am not a chef. But I feel that you may get burnt if you do not know the back-end of the business. I am thankful for my positivity and my ability to garner support from the people around me. When I say run, we all run. Jerry was a great help to my girls and I. We ran and had disco parties together. We would also get creative and create monster godzilla desserts and, in the early days, we would in fact be the ones dishing out the desserts. We would also act as House ambassadors and personally show the guests around. We were largely inspired by our childhood.

My staff always support me and believe in me as I have operational experience. I won't ask them to do the impossible but I think it is very important to push the boundaries. Our business grew because I have clear vision and we had fun. Our team constantly talks about our journey and the endless parties we've done. I figured since I had to stay till 3 a.m. in House, I might as well turn it into a party! We have had so many events—concerts, themed parties such as Halloween and Fashion Disaster Party, and we had so many guests. But it was tough. I will be doing my roll call at 4 p.m., tying balloons, dealing with complaints about the food, standing at the food counter, going to the kitchen to dish out desserts. Some guests don't know I am the boss. Once, someone approached and told me that my service was really good, "Why don't you come and work with me?" I joked and said, "You can't afford me." I took that as a compliment and we had a good laugh after he found out who I was.

I really had a wonderful time and am so blessed to have a team that believes in me. It's the little things. I think they love me and I love them. I feel that they are genuinely concerned about me, not just about work. And they are protective of me not just as a boss, but as a person.

I later decided to open the Tippling Club. I felt people were not taking me seriously as I had not ventured into food yet. I always like a good challenge, so I decided that I was going to try and become well-known in food by trying my hand at fine dining. Tippling Club was thus born over 12 years ago and is now well-recognised for our food and our amazing cocktails. The key was to have that gung-ho fighting spirit and tenacity.

You are great at trendspotting. What is the secret behind that?

I think you need the acumen to see what others don't, but it is also hard work. You need to be prepared to get help. I can tell you that I have tweaked my business countless times. It is not an easy process and there were times when we were not profitable so I had to keep tweaking, creating a ton of events to make the business profitable. If you love something, you want to see it happen and will not be afraid to work hard. You also need to find the rhythm to keep your business sustainable.

I am at work from 4 p.m. to 2 a.m. and have to ensure that our fries are delivered with no complaints, talk to the chef, deal with operational things and deal with staff stealing money—that's all in a day's work while people could be relaxing at yoga, having fun and a good massage, rest and spend time with their families in the weekends. Everybody wants to own a café but nobody wants to hear what goes on behind the scenes.

Give us some of the toughest situations you have had to combat, whether in terms of finances, HR or operations.

The business grew organically so we didn't need to have private equity. My father didn't have to inject too much money except for the first time when he bought my partners out. After that, I was left on my own. I put in my own money to buy the spa and my father helped me a little. The bigger portion of the investment came when he saw that I was really passionate about the business and my brother supported me too. He said I was crying every night praying for someone to believe in me. I have since repaid my father for the money he put in and he said that it was the best investment he has ever made.

I think people loved the spa as it was a homegrown brand—so if I can do it, you can too. I grew the brand from one shop to two, four, eight, 16 to over 100 today. It has been a 22-year journey and I learnt everything from being a massage therapist, to a receptionist and a customer service staff. In fact, back in the day, when my staff did not show up, I would do the massage for the clients myself. I don't have an easy life just because I am a CEO with 25 shops. In fact, one of my staff told me that he loves working with me because I am the only boss he has seen in the kitchen personally QC-ing the food.

When I opened Common Man, I was in the kitchen doing the plating and the staff were all very excited. I believe it is the little things that count. I saw to all the details and even checked the plates. I worked together with the potter and even measured the plates and cups. I have also gone to flea markets to buy little knick knacks like spoons. And I am the one who came up with the concoction for our aromatherapy in the bathroom, as well as the handwash. When they go to the bathroom and smell the essential oils I mixed, they know it is Spa Esprit and they know it is made from love.

There is no short cut. To be successful, you need to see and feel. You need to see how hard your staff are working and remunerate them well. You need to be interested in how or what they are thinking and finally, you have to make the judgment call on your staff hires. Understanding your staff's working conditions—knowing how hot and humid the kitchen is—and deciding how much bonus to give are different matters altogether. As a boss, have you walked the kitchen? If you do not have full information, you may not be able to make the right decisions. Your executives may not present you with a reality check or a fuller picture of what is really happening. That is why I like to be involved in operations as this gives me a holistic picture of the business.

You can't read all this from a book as there are emotions and connections involved. Like an onion, you need to peel off the surface and understand what is at the core in order to solve a problem. There's so much work to do before you make something work.

You have a distinct style with all your brands. How do you get inspired and come up with your quirky concepts?

First of all, I like to have fun in my life. I am dreamy and like to be happy and excited. I amuse myself with how I am going to do my hair today, with the clothes I wear, or the people I am going to meet. I also surround myself with positive energy to keep myself creative. I also read books, travel, and observe what others are doing. I think these are all important ways to keep myself going.

I like words, so I think my ideas start from there. I love touching, quirky poetry. I like humour and I like things that are not the norm. I don't like to conform. I like having creative interpretations to bring out that cheekiness. For example, who would take a *tau sar pau* and call it "Hot Buns Make Me Horny"? Well, I did it in Forty Hands.

I remember reading something on *The Economist* a while ago. The article said, "Go East, Young Man!" so I was inspired by the article and Asia and decided to create a *kong bak pau* for Forty Hands, as no one is ever going to serve that in any other coffee joint. I got my uncle who runs a Chinese restaurant to teach me the recipe, then I improved on it and called it "Go East, Young Man". I saw the Caucasians eating them and we started to call it Asian Sliders as they termed it so. Then, instead of french fries, I wanted taro fries.

Creative interpretations are fun especially when you have a vision. You can take something that has been neglected and harness it to propagate Singaporean culture. You dress up an Asian dish as Western and all the young people who have studied overseas would eat it off the plate the way they wouldn't in a typical Chinese restaurant which is too hot, humid or uncool. They may not even know where to begin to find a *kong bak pau*, but they know they can find it at House. Today, everybody's eating *kong bak pau* and the Caucasians know *tau sar pau* because of our inventions. These little anecdotes really excite me.

It sounds as if your inspirations come about very organically and are shaped by the business, and more importantly by this overarching idea of "fun".

Yes! A lot of it is based on what I like. One day, my father said he found the best *tau sar pau*. I remember saying, "Sure or not?" When I ate it, I agreed it was the best and decided to order from the supplier. But the challenge is how I could sell it for $2.50 if the coffee shops sell it for $0.80? I decided to make mine different by making it round, big and flat. It caught the eye of *8 Days* who hailed it the best and wrote a catchy headline, "Who sat on my *tau sar pau*?" Now everybody tells me my buns are the best! But at the start, it was tough to get it right.

At first, we didn't even know how to steam it. How many should we steam at one go? We even had to learn that in order to keep the buns piping hot at service, we need to take the buns from inside the steamer, because the ones on the display front are not warm enough. Simple things like that. I can't even begin to tell you how many steps you have to take to make one simple menu item successful. At least 25 steps! Later, we fretted on the plating. We wanted to use ceramic so the next question is, how do we style it? What do we call it? How should the poster look like? Or we may have issues like, "Oh dear, Uncle didn't deliver the buns today!" That's just one *tau sar pau* so you can imagine the headache!

Who comes out with all the concepts for your brands?

I don't think every tagline can be attributed to me but I think it has my influence. I have a very strong creative streak and when my soulmate Jerry travels with me to Prague or wherever, we may decide that for the next campaign, "Let's do Eastern European!" We share our dreams and are very connected so it is easy to work together. If I tell my designers to create an Eastern European creative concept, they will go, "Huh?" So we will show them references from *The Grand Budapest Hotel.* I love Wes Anderson's work, so our latest design was inspired by his film. I also love the train in *The Darjeeling Limited.*

Jerry got excited about an automotive-inspired theme. He was crazy about Singapore Airlines' Business Class flights on the A380, so we used that as our inspiration when we created our Paragon store. We also love barbeques and decided to create a caravan. And then we got inspired by vinyl. Despite the disparate inspirations, Jerry is able to synergise them all.

He came from a fashion background. No one thought he would be able to succeed in interior design, but he did. You can see that he does not think like a traditional interior designer. He is not formulaic, he's open to diverse styles, good with textiles and has a great sense of humour. It helps that he is not trained, so he thinks off-the-cuff and is quirky. That is what I like and most importantly, he knows what I like. I don't like things that look a dime a dozen and like having an edge. I am always looking for something different and yet it must make commercial sense and meet my P&L. It helps that I am also good with numbers.

So do you think you are more left or right brained?

I think I am a bit of both. My CFO is actually quite wary of me precisely because I am very good with numbers, so he knows he can't fool me! I understand what it takes to run a business, but am also clear when I do something for the sake of art which is not going to make money. The key is to have clear intentions, objectives and focus. But overall as a business, it has to deliver profits and you're only considered successful if you can make money out of it. Your business can fund your interests and your art projects.

But let's say when I support a music festival, I do that as I want to support the artists and young, creative people. Sure, I can also support cancer for our CSR but I would rather support artists as it is my passion and I like their spirit and am happy to mentor them. I like working with spunky, spirited girls who tell me that they do not have funding for their music and if I like their ideas, I would help them. For example, I have gotten involved with Super Zero. I love music, especially electro, which is why I throw parties. I love the underground scene.

Share with us how Strip started and developed.

I am very patriotic when I travel as I will look out for what Singapore lacks. Strip started this way. I was travelling a lot and was in New York to learn hot stone massage from an American guy. He shared that the Singaporean girls are very attractive, but Asian girls, in general, have poor grooming habits. In Australia, by contrast, most of the girls are waxed. I realised it was true as back then, I could not get a Brazilian wax in Singapore anywhere! It is very much a taboo in Asian culture—most mothers do not educate their daughters to be fuzz-free!

I felt that I had to defend the Asians so I decided to create a wax parlour and call it Strip as it is catchy and funny. I like quirky names, which is why I came up with We Need A Hero and Open Door Policy.

Anyway, I also wanted Strip to be the platform to educate the girls on grooming. You see, I always like to champion a cause, which will lead to a movement so I envisioned that 80% of the local Chinese girls would be my customers. At the start, my father said I was crazy. He said that I was a graduate in Economics and Statistics and should not get involved in people's private parts. Besides, most high-end spas may offer it as a complimentary service, so it was not a viable business at all. It was very difficult at the start as I was a pioneer. I started to think what the most economical method of marketing would be. By then, we had a second spa called Spa In The Village so I decided to convert the existing space into a boudoir. I spent $20,000 on the renovations as we already had existing rooms. I had to use very little money to prove my point and make the concept work.

I concocted a plan to first convince the media to play the role of an educator to create awareness. I shared with the journalist that Asian girls had to work on our grooming because we were being laughed at in the West. I also shared that once they start, it will be part of their grooming habit. I saw that waxing is like hair colouring—it was a taboo in the early days but it is a norm now so much so that you feel weird if you don't colour your hair. Waxing, I argued is part of a holistic grooming package and a necessity.

Meanwhile, I also hired a team of therapists and we had to undergo training. I went down for the training sessions at 8 a.m. in the morning and work with them on the floor. When Strip opened, I even went to Cold Storage to distribute flyers as I didn't think the public knew what a Brazilian is. For six months it was quiet. Nothing happened and I had to battle with people telling me that Strip has failed. I brainstormed how to interest the public and I decided to lure them in with $5 manicures and I trained my staff to upsell and rah-rah after their manicures to get them to try a $10 bikini or underarm wax.

Eventually, the magazines started writing and *Her World* gave me a really excellent write-up. I was there to see that the journalist had a painless waxing and even served her tea myself. Later, I did all the PR and customer service and was very hands-on with the posters and marketing. Once the first wave of PR went out, there was more excitement and motivation within the staff too. Energy is very contagious, so I always make it a habit to be positive and be very eager to share. I am a people pleaser and love the excitement I get from sharing.

Anyway, that was how Strip's business picked up and later, I started seeing the guys waiting in line too! It's funny but I saw the path of Strip and I had the vision of what it may become, though I never imagined that I would travel to Jakarta and Manila to talk about Brazilian wax. After that, I became known as the Pussy Ambassador!

After that, I decided to advocate for eyebrows and one thing leads to another. I saw all the guys waiting for their girlfriends outside the shop and decided to offer the service to men too. Years later, I collaborated with a London guy and we chatted about dating and girls. He said that he could tell if a girl at a bar has good grooming or not just by asking if she has heard or gone to Strip! It became a great pick up line and he would drop a girl if she doesn't know Strip because this means she is neither groomed nor in the loop. (*laughter*)

Things have changed. When I started, people will speak in hushed tones when they say "Brazilian wax" but today it is commonplace. Waxing has become mass and my clientele is 80% of the Chinese girls in Singapore, exactly how I had envisioned! I also recall that one of my clients from the outskirts of Kuala Lumpur would take a three-hour bus ride just to have a Brazilian wax! It was amazing how we managed to convert a population of non-waxers into waxers and we now have the highest concentration of wax saloons per square mile.

After I had achieved my dream in Singapore, I had my eye and my heart set on London and New York—all the fashion capitals. I once said that "We will wax a million bushes." In fact, by now we have de-fuzzed over three and a half million bushes! That was greatly helped by our funny, eye-catching memorable campaigns, such as "Strip Buddy" to encourage waxing with a friend. We also ran couples' promotion, the Boyzilian and an "Upsized Carrot" campaign. We had so much fun and started coming up with new wax formulas and even brought in the IPL machine. I saw a business where nobody saw any potential, but I had to combat everybody's negativity to finally have shops in nine different cities. After that, people say I am brilliant. In fact, when I first got on *The Peak* Power List in 2014, I was so happy as everyone else on the list were guys!

When I started with food, people said that I didn't know anything about food, that I was a beautician, "rolling in gold in beauty". And yet today, we are very well known for our food as well. If you are motivated by your interest and love what you do, you will go against all odds. But be prepared to put in 10,000 hours. You have to manage your own expectations.

Don't think owning a café means you get to wear nice clothes and tell your staff what to do. Owning a café means showing up when your staff and chef don't, handling a power failure, managing a food-poisoning complaint, carrying on when people quit or get poached, or when you run out of food and the delivery doesn't come. I usually channel all my energies to solve any problem as I like to see things come to fruition. But there are times when I have to let things go.

What are some of the other concepts that failed that we don't hear about?

There are many. For Potion, I think I was too involved in Strip and did not have time for it as resources are finite. Jerry is very creative but he is not a businessman. Potion became an unfeasible business. Each time I went on a buying trip, the travel and stock alone would cost me at least $50,000 and Singaporeans did not wish to pay $350 for a vintage dress that they imagine someone may have died in. We were ahead of the market. Singaporeans then preferred known labels and brands. I figured Potion was not going to work so we killed it and I got Jerry over as my creative director in Spa Esprit.

After that, we had a salad bar called 12 x 12 at Suntec City, which closed after six months of operation. We were ahead of the curve as I was very interested in studying raw beauty, organic products and farm sourcing. This was 17 years ago. I was very much influenced and wanted to promote a healthy lifestyle having been in the spa business for 10 years, listening to new age music and chirping birds.

I was thus keen to create a healthy menu that had food with low GI (glycemic index) and low sugar. We created fantastic healthy soups and served brown rice or what I called "fitballs". We catered to a niche group who loved our product but our rentals were too high. The food was forward-thinking but we were in a shopping mall in a business district away from the retail and food thoroughfare so we could not attract a big crowd so later, we killed that too.

My other big baby that I had to kill was Broadcast HQ. It was all about music. I wanted to create an underground place for people and local musicians to jam but I couldn't secure the license. STB wanted to help but it was an uphill task and it was too difficult for me to battle with the government as I kept getting called to the police station. My father was very angry and asked me why I had to keep going to the police station in the morning? It was such a heartache and I was drained having to deal with all the operational problems, staying till 4 a.m. in the morning, selling BBQ ribs with beer, dealing with the police when they arrive, only to head to the police station at 8 a.m.

I had chosen a place at a corner block near Desker Road. It is a red light district and I was denied a Category 1 license for public entertainment, which prevented us from playing live music even though we were next to a karaoke bar. I could only play recorded music as I was given a Category 2 license. Back then, the NMP Janice Koh tried to raise the issue in Parliament but even she could not understand the rationale and discrepancy. Apparently, the Minister said they had "run out of quota" for licenses. I figured there was some internal politics at play, but I did not have the spirit to keep fighting and this was draining my resources. I could not operate fully and the authorities kept coming to shut me down.

I did not want to be jailed for something like this. I am not a martyr, but I felt that I was contributing to the music scene and could really help to liven up the area that is typically associated with prostitution. I really wanted to support local music and talents and truly believed that the area has a lot of potential to be gentrified. STB agreed but I just could not understand the politics. Anyway, Broadcast HQ came to an end after nine months.

This was a learning curve for me too as I knew we had a great concept but I also realised not everything I wanted to do will work and I had to be careful as I have a big business with over 100 shops coupled with new projects coming up. As an entrepreneur, it can sometimes be very hard to let go. Even an ant in the shop bugs me but I have to really focus my energy. I realised I had to learn to let go, take care of myself, take stock of the situation and not think that I always have to be a Superwoman.

You can be credited for gentrifying Dempsey with House, Rowell Road with Broadcast HQ, albeit short-lived, and also Tiong Bahru with Forty Hands and Tiong Bahru Bakery. Share with us how do you have such an eye for old estates and its subsequent redevelopment?

I remember wanting to do coffee the way Melbourne does it with its hipster culture. It is so special there that even Starbucks could not survive. I saw a lot of potential in the hole-in-wall, alley-style type of indie café.

I first heard about Tiong Bahru from Charlie, who is the brother of my partner, Harry. Charlie was living in Tiong Bahru and he said there was a corner shop up for rent so I headed down. It used to be a fine dining restaurant. The rent was affordable at about $3,800 so we decided to give it a try. Tiong Bahru is at a very central location even though it is not the usual café hangout. It was a small and tiny outlet and we decided to call it Forty Hands.

The first six months were tough and the aunties in the neighbourhood were all very protective and told me that I have been cheated and said, "Aiyoh girl! Why you pay $3,800? The rental here is $1,800. You should not pay this much. Coffee shop sells coffee 70 cents but your coffee is

$4.50?" We had no footfall, only many roaming cats. But I tell you it was such a fantastic learning curve. We decided to print and distribute flyers to create awareness for the first six months. Our first campaign was called "The Great Leap Forward". Today, that poster is no longer apt as these types of coffee joints are now part of our landscape.

I also remember meeting Ted from Spring Singapore and I asked for his support in my coffee venture. Ted was uncertain as he felt there were already many coffee chains and brands. I pleaded with him, "If you believe in me and help me, I think I can propel the coffee culture." I had to meet a panel of 10 and eventually received an innovation grant. That kept me going at the start even though I had to keep the costs very low. I am very conscious about costs. We decided to have this raw, edgy look so it took us very little money to renovate.

In the beginning, we sold like 50 cups a day for six months which was barely enough to pay the rent but I believed in our product as it was interesting and unique. I started to think whom I could form an alliance with to launch Forty Hands. I was not merely thinking about my business but about curating a group of creative minds in the community to create that social spirit.

I love books and I was always going to BooksActually at Club Street for my poetry books and would go crazy and get very excited in the store. So one day, I went to BooksActually to meet with Kenny, the owner, and learnt that he was looking for a new venue. I suggested Yong Siak Street across from Forty Hands. He was unwilling as he said there is no crowd. I told him that I have already done the hard work and could sell 500 cups on weekends. I told him to come visit my café with his then-girlfriend and I would treat him to *tau sar pau*. So he came and we chatted on a Saturday and he saw the potential. I told him to call the property agent and he ended up renting the shop. That's how BooksActually came to Tiong Bahru.

At that time, I also started to wonder if I could create a low-price point, neighbourhood bistro the likes of Melbourne or London and a shop became available so I took it over and that ended up becoming

Open Door Policy. I was working with Ryan Clift and wanted him to head my kitchen but he was unconvinced. He said he was a gastronomic chef and had no intentions of doing a bistro with meals costing an average of $30—he saw that as a regression.

But I felt he would be great so I convinced him. I got him to see it as a challenge to deconstruct a burger and try creative recipes. Honestly, he said he didn't quite get the concept but he would take it up because I wanted him to and he trusted me. I remember my staff saying, "We don't understand what ODP is about, but we believe in it." And people believing in what we do was great PR. The support I received gave me that push to make it work.

Anyway, ODP was really fun and was part of my "curation" of the Tiong Bahru area, which was steadily getting gentrified. Later, the same aunty who spoke to me before came to tell me that rentals keep going up from $3,800 to $6,500 to $9,000. She was very happy because she owns the units in Tiong Bahru, while ironically, I don't! My unit at Forty Hands was bought by the landlord for $500,000, went up to $700,000, then $1.3M and is now valued at $1.9M. The Tiong Bahru climate was indeed changing with pop-up stores and new happenings so that was when I went "Wow!"

I won't say I gentrified the area but we certainly kick-started the idea and people came. This has been an inspiring process for me as it has inspired a lot of other people to look at their neighbourhoods differently as well. The F&B scene became really buzzy and now Tiong Bahru is alive with a café and bakery culture that I had dreamt of when I started Tiong Bahru Bakery.

How did the Tiong Bahru Bakery idea come about?

I have always dreamt of owning a bakery. I saw how Singaporeans tended to only eat this white, fluffy bread that is so bad for us as it is all refined carbohydrates. I think there is a lack of choice so I really wanted to have a Singaporean concept bakery that was fun and had good, healthy bread. That was the idea but I didn't have a baker so I did not know how to proceed. In fact, even as we speak, there are so many ideas incubating in here. (*gestures to her head*)

So I learnt to be smart and I waited. By that time, I was no longer so *kiasu* to do everything. I believe that if I channel my energy well, the right people will come. I met Gontran Cherrier who really fit the profile I was looking for—he is a fourth generation baker, not too famous, emerging, has a soul and is quite good-looking. When I tasted his croissants, I almost dropped dead and knew I found my master baker.

As for the branding, I did not want it to be known as a French brand because I am from Singapore and am proud of it and have benefitted so much from being Singaporean. I am bilingual, have travelled the world and tasted carrot cake and *chwee kueh*, and I am also able to eat French and Japanese food. So I asked myself, "What do I want to do for Singapore and for this bakery?" I also wanted to respect the heritage of the area and did not want my bakery to look too French as it would be out of place.

Anyway, while we were working on branding, I remember what I was always inspired by the old school packaging we used to have in Singapore: the white cardboard boxes we have to *tabao tze char*, the *chwee kueh* packaging with its grease proof wrapper and the take away *kopi kong* tied with the rope. I also love the *tau sar piah* packaging which comes in a box with a red chop which is so nostalgic, as well as the napkin from Long Beach Seafood with the girl in bikini posing with the crab. It's so kitchy and funny and uniquely Singaporean. Besides, everyone goes for the clean, minimalist look so I told my team to use the *tze char* packaging as inspiration for our Tiong Bahru Bakery branding and that was how it came about!

Most people are surprised to find out that Tiong Bahru Bakery carries top-notch French croissants and specialty coffee all under one roof despite it sounding so local. We played with the creative direction and reversed expectations. Today, you can see all the Lamborghinis and Ferrraris parked outside—their owners are coming in to buy bread from us instead of going to East Coast all the time.

Share with us more on your venture into a men's grooming salon.

After Tiong Bahru Bakery, I got bored again and wondered what to do next and ventured into the barber shop business and called it We Need a Hero. I think what keeps me going is that I am Singaporean born and bred so I can see the signs of a changing society. Singaporeans are changing. They are well-travelled and are so westernised, and barely speak Mandarin anymore. It is like they are Westerners trapped in Asian bodies and the new generation wants the same things they see in London and New York. I know Singapore will be as cosmopolitan as those big cities one day, but in the meantime, I want to fill those gaps and create the right channel and platforms for that demographic, but I also understand Singaporean culture enough to dish out these innovations.

Of course I will tweak the concept, but I am confident that what I love is also shared by many of my generation and the next. We are all influenced by similar media growing up so we are all influenced and are influencers. You know how you feel when you travel overseas and see something you like but you know you can't find it in Singapore. I feel that way, and once I feel that, I have to do it. So We Need A Hero came about because I think there is a need for male salons so here it is.

What have you learnt through the process of expanding the business to other cities?

I think it is important to hire a business coach, and really good partners. You may not be able to make a lot of money in some cities so you will need to learn. Everything is a work-in-progress and you need to find like-minded strong partners in different cultures. You map out the business, think of the gaps and look for support in those gaps. Being strategic and playing a strategic role is very important for me now. I have to be very careful with my energy and how I use it, but I have learnt to delegate.

What are some of those gaps that you want to work on?

My teams need time to get things right and they may not get it 100% right. I have learnt not to be in a hurry to fix everything and take time to smooth things out. I used to stay up to look at the books and want to come up with solutions right away. Sustainability is also an important word for me, so these days, if I find myself having the same problem then I know I should spend more time doing recruitment. I learned that I have to see the overarching problem and solve that rather than micromanage and fix everything myself. This is very difficult as entrepreneurs tend do everything themselves. I have to remind myself not to fall into that habit.

Do you think your gender has aided or impeded you in your career and development?

I think it has worked for me and I get things done. In fact, it helps in F&B as my chef may not want me to handle certain heavy loads or menial tasks and would take care of them himself.

I am glad to have done well too. I think it is an inspiration to the women in my company. And I think the guys are happy having a woman kicking their asses too! (*laughter*)

Do you have policies to help women?

I have a soft spot for girls with spunk. I don't have a strict company policy to help women but I adopt female artists through the "Adopt that Artist" programme. I mentor them and set aside funds to help emerging artists. Even within the organisation, I give the girls who have worked for me the avenue to develop and grow.

We wanted to create a CSR arm called "More FUNd" as a foundation to develop youth creativity. I have not firmed up these plans, yet though I am sure what I do must eventually must be something motivational and helpful to people.

What do you think a woman executive can bring to the table?

I think girls have a softer side that enables us to get things done and have our way a tad easier. It doesn't mean that just because you are a woman boss, you have to have a very hard demeanour and be "like a guy". In fact, people often say I remind them of "a little girl"—naive and innocent.

Sure, if I need to command an army, I can go "You do this!" But when I talk about my dreams, I never want to lose my gentle, feminine side as that is authentic.

Where are you headed in the next three to five years?

To develop other countries besides Singapore because I've been here for too long already and my business is already in nine different cities. I have put a lot of attention in Singapore and have equipped and empowered the team here so now it is my chance to lay the groundwork in Europe, where I see more avenues that I can develop. I also want to work strategically—the key for me is to effect change and always impact lives in a positive way.

I also like to create new types of business or find ways of relooking at current business. So Browhaus is not just about eyebrow shaping but it is about brow architecture as I love architecture. Business is not all about the P&L for me, but also the ideas. I am all about cross-breeding, fusion, creating strong branding and the "next big thing". I am thankful I have the luxury to experiment these days, so I don't know where that will lead me!

Sheryl Sandberg wrote in *Lean In* that "women can have it all" and she suffered many brickbats for that. What do you say to that?

I don't have children and that can be considered a sacrifice. I know I do not have extra time on my hands. I know that I would want to be a hands-on parent if I had children. Besides, I am divorced, am so involved in my businesses and live such a fast-paced life that I do not see children or a relationship in the works.

Regardless of whether I am divorced or single, what is more important is my personal development and progress. It does not mean just because I am successful in business that I failed in my relationships. Conversely, even if I don't have a career, I may still have ended up in a divorce, like many others I know. So no, I wouldn't blame it on having a career but I will say, yes, there is a sacrifice.

In hindsight, perhaps I should have set a cap and grow my business to only 80 shops instead of 100 and spend more time on my relationship. But the fact was and is, I am very happy working, learning and I honestly loved all of what I did. Love has always been at the core of what I did and this extends to love for my staff, my brands and businesses, and my family. I am very idealistic and created my own world, so no matter where I am right now, I always see it as progress and understand that my life is all about growing into the person that I aspire to be.

What will you say to your staff who is torn between having a career and a family?

If someone does ask me that, I will say, "You need to understand what you truly want." I know that is tough, for many do not know what they want. Everyone has that inner voice but it must first be developed. We also all have our subconscious but if you keep shutting it off, you will never hear it. If you are open and listen to yourself, you will know the answer. When you shut that off and move far away from your intuition and subconscious, you will come up with a series of hollow justifications. You need to go with your heart as that is the most sustainable.

That is why I go back to advocating conscious living and practice meditation to sharpen my senses. I am not a Buddhist but I believe in energy, frequency, meditation, rhythm, the importance of breath and introspection. I also like thinking and writing as it allows you to clarify your thoughts and answer the questions that no one else can answer for you. If you have to ask, it already means you are unsure.

What pisses you off?

When things don't work. I also don't like people who bully, self-sabotage or give themselves excuses. I also don't like complainers—if you don't like something, just change it yourself.

What would your epitaph say?

"I don't know how she did it but she did it her way!"

Do you believe in destiny or hard work?

I believe in destiny but I also believe in working hard because an action will lead to a reaction. You can't just sit there and dream of your destiny. It doesn't quite work like that.

How do you best want to be remembered?

She led a peaceful life? (*laughter*) Peace is such a big word for me right now. I did not use to understand what that meant but now I know it is being comfortable in your own skin and being totally confident even in the midst of distractions such as social media and Facebook, which I don't have by the way!

(*Incredulous and amused*) **You are a marketing guru and you don't have Facebook? I just assumed that you would!**

I don't have Facebook—I know I must be the only one. (*laughter*) I don't even have time to reply my emails or Whatsapp!

So back to your earlier question, I want to be remembered for being a happy girl. That's it. Simple.

Have you found your peace then?

It took me a very long time but I think I'm almost there.

If you met God, what would you say?

Thank you for my life and the hard knocks. I got what you wanted me to do and learn.

Which archetype do you identify with? The Madonna, Maverick or any other M word?

Medicine Woman.

The Grande Dame

JENNIE CHUA

Jennie Chua is a well-known icon of the hospitality industry, having helmed prestigious brands such as The Ascott Group, Raffles Holdings and Swissôtel. She broke the glass ceiling by being Raffles Hotel's first Singaporean and female General Manager in 1990.

She also became the first woman in 2009 to chair the Singapore International Chamber of Commerce in its 172-year history, and served for many years as the chairman of the Community Chest before becoming its adviser. She is also chairman in numerous organisations including The Old Parliament House, Sentosa Cove, Alexandra Health/Khoo Teck Puat Hospital, International Advisory Council of Tourism, among others. She was Singapore's Non-Resident Ambassador to Slovakia and is presently a Non-Resident Ambassador to Mexico. She is named one of Forbes Asia's "50 Women in the Mix" in 2013, and has also been affectionately called "Singapore's Grande Dame".

***

Talking to Jennie Chua is like chatting with a live Wikipedia. She seems to know everyone and has a clear and distinct opinion on everything. And I mean, everything. Unlike some of the other #Madonnas&Mavericks who urged me to stimulate them with thoughtful questions, Jennie needed no provocation. In fact, she led the interviews with her eagerness to share, frankness and candor that, in turn, led me to unexpected places. She was fully capable of highly engaging monologues that were savoury to the very last sound bite.

If I had to distill our conversation to three key takeaways, I would be very hard-pressed. Everything she shares with me feels like a life lesson I would like to cling on to. But if I had to, it would be that "poverty is always very glamorous when you look back" and in fact, one may even resort to inventing a "rags-to-riches story" in a bid to create one's narrative and raison d'être. Indeed, it is not uncommon for one to often look back with some sense of nostalgia, wistfulness and romance—for us to "glamorise the past", as Jennie says. None of the women here look back in anger, lament their present circumstance or think that their future looks bleak. Myth-making is not just fiction—it is fact. It is not just us homo sapiens who individually resort to that, but nations do so too to exact pride, patriotism and a sense of belonging.

The second key takeaway is on presentation, decorum and dressing. Jennie takes pride in her appearance, good manners and fashion sense, as these function as a mode of communication to another. Even in her youth, she always knew the importance of a few statement pieces—a good belt and nice buttons often maketh the woman. Even before the rise of social media and today's image-driven world, she has always intuitively grasped the power of personal image and its effect on people.

The last lesson that is etched in my head is her humility, modesty and deep embrace of her own mortality. Sogyal Rinpoche, the author of the bestselling *The Tibetan Book of Living and Dying*, reminds us that, "When we finally know we are dying, and all other sentient beings are dying with us, we start to have a burning, almost heartbreaking sense of the fragility and preciousness of each moment and each being, and from this can grow a deep, clear, limitless compassion for all beings." Somehow, I get the impression that Jennie embraces this Buddhist philosophy. Her ability to exercise compassion at all times underscores her sensitivity and espousal of our interconnectedness, which in turn must stem from a fundamental belief that we are all equal, despite all our physical trappings of wealth, looks, educational qualifications and status in life. And what can be more human than the fact that we all need air to breathe and that we shall all breathe our last, one day?

To say Jennie is like the big sister I never had—full of wise nuggets and zany anecdotes—is an understatement. She possesses more experience and gravitas than the average "sister". Yet, to call her a mother figure or mentor seems ill-fitting too, as she seems too cerebral, too hip and so "with it" that it is disarmingly charming. It is an uncanny combination and one feels as if one has to tread cautiously given her stature, yet her warmth and exuberance lures you in surreptitiously. Before long, you find yourself opening up to her and speaking candidly on all issues, no holds barred.

***

Today, I think, what I want to do is to say "Hello" to you and put a face to the email and the phone conversation. We may have to do our interview over a few sessions as this is not a journalistic article. A journalistic article is in the papers today, and tomorrow you use it to wrap fish.

Yes, newspapers are time-sensitive, but we have more time with this. Each of you will have your own chapter. I've sent the questions to your secretary ahead of time.

She only works at most three times a week as she is in her 50s and wishes to spend more time at home. I am okay with that as I don't need as much support as I did 25 years ago. She was with me at Raffles Hotel from say, 1989 to 2006 so it has been more than 17 years. She is not ambitious nor is she using this as a platform for something else.

Speaking of ambition, let's start our interview proper. Would you call yourself ambitious or did you go with the flow?

I think ambition is just not in my vocabulary. I guess women in my generation were educated because we had the opportunity to be educated in Singapore. I never felt that my boy friends or my brothers had better opportunities just because they were men. They may be physically stronger and are able to jump higher or run faster but as far as opportunities, I did not feel any different from them. In fact, I only became conscious of gender disparity and was introduced to this concept of work-life balance when I started to read Western publications.

I think for the educated women in my generation, we would complete high school and say, "Okay, what next?" In my case, tertiary education was very important while some of my friends opted to get married. I could have gone with the flow, but I wanted a tertiary education so that I could get a better job. I was thinking more for "tomorrow" rather than for the next 10 years. But I went into teaching for two years as I lacked the money for university. And prior to that, I worked part-time as a typist and a tutor before I got married, and then left for Cornell where I also worked as a bartender. It was fun but it was also hard work. When I look back, I always say you can wear that as a badge of honour. Poverty is always very glamorous when you look back. In fact, I might even venture to say that even if one was not poor in the beginning, one may still be tempted to invent a rags-to-riches story.

In my case, my story has a double badge of honour as I was born rich and then became poor. I had to transit from a life of nannies, cars, gardeners and a big house, to a tiny flat with three generations living under one roof from hand to mouth. I even recall having our electricity cut and receiving pink slips[1]. How far you had to walk to your school, how you had to interrupt your education... All these things, at that time, I tried to hide because poverty is not something you want to flaunt to your peers when you were a mere child.

1 A reminder to pay outstanding bills

As a teenager, you would pretend as if you didn't want something rather than because you couldn't afford it. At recess, you had to make the ultimate decision, would you rather buy a bowl of noodles or take the bus home? So in order to decide, you studied the weather—if it looked like it was going to rain, you would choose not to eat and take the bus home. And you wouldn't tell people you couldn't afford to eat, so you would just say "I am not hungry." When you do take the bus home, you would walk farther away from school simply because if you didn't, you could not afford the fare for the entire distance home.

So you didn't have the vocabulary for the concept of "face", but yet, you would intuitively embody and practice it.

Yes, you do, you do. When you are poor, you don't want to recognise it and you don't want to admit it either. Years later, when you have come out of poverty, you would boast about it.

I remember the school shoes I wore were very grubby. I had two sets of uniforms and one of them was torn but you hide it and patch it up, or you try to mask it strategically by placing your hand on the gaping hole in the hope that no one would notice because you did not want to be seen as being someone *without*.

Interestingly, my children were the opposite. They did not want to be driven to school as they did not want to be seen as someone *with*. Whenever my driver or I drove my two boys to school, they would say, "Please stop me far away." My two sons, especially the younger one—he attended a polytechnic before going to university—would always insist that I drop them off farther away, citing reasons like "Mummy would be late for work" etc. I could not fathom the reason then, and I finally figured out that my sons did not want to be seen as privileged as they were growing up, whereas I always felt I was underprivileged. It's a complete reversal of fortunes and psyche in one generation.

I only have two sons but I was one of 12 in the family. My father, because he was rich, had two wives in the days before the Women's Charter. Each of his wives had six children and we grew up in two separate HDB flats. My own mother was brought up as a *xiao jie*[2] but she was not a prima donna as she was raised a Buddhist, believed in karma and was very accepting of her lot in life. She believed that all in life, her marriage, children, were all pre-destined or 命中注定. So there was no need to celebrate nor complain, but neither was she a doormat. So when my father lost his fortune and became a teacher, she knew she needed to make ends meet and had no qualms going to friends and family to borrow money.

My second mother was also a tough woman who was not averse to hard work. In the 1960s when Singapore was going through its independence and industrialization, a lot of women went out to work in light and labour-intensive industries. But my second mother could not go to the factory as she had to take care of her children. So she would instead take the bus to Jurong and lug home a huge bag of pre-cut denim jeans, and she would sew them at home for 20 to 30 cents per pair. After she was done sewing the garments, she would lug them back to Jurong. Little by little, stitch by stitch, she managed to raise her children and all of us became professionals—there is a doctor, an accountant, an IT specialist, an engineer and an entrepreneur.

So to answer your question, women in that generation, even myself, we did not think of ambition. We just did what it took to survive. My mother could not sew, so I had to go out to work as I was the oldest. I could not complete my studies, even though I had a bursary. I gave tuition, worked as a typist and did odd jobs in a nutmeg factory, making about $100-200 a month in total, which was a huge help if your household was always getting its electricity cut.

When I went to the Teachers' Training College in Paterson Road, I was taught how to be a teacher in the morning and by the afternoon, I was practicing what I learnt by teaching at a secondary school. I gave half of my pay cheque ($90 for the first year, $190 for the second year) to my mother, and the rest I would use to buy pretty material to make pretty clothes. I wanted pretty clothes so I learnt to sew. One of my first lessons

2 A girl born into wealth and accorded social privilege

in life was that the material could be cheap, but a great design, expensive looking buttons and accessories would make a huge difference. I would take the bus to this shop at TANGS that sold nothing but buttons and bows and would spend $2 buying four good-looking buttons to make my dress quite wonderful. Or I may save the money to buy a nice belt, which would be the highlight of the outfit.

You are indeed known for your style and your dress-for-success mantra. You once said that you suited up in cheongsams all those years when you were in Raffles Hotel.

I try, or at least I try to evolve. I dressed a certain way when I was a teacher and my old students will still recall my earrings, which were at that time, nice, round buttons of varying colours. I would buy five different colours for each day of the workweek and match it with my different outfits. Bags were a luxury so I invested in one or two expensive accessories instead.

When I started making a little more money, I went to my tailor, Lani, across from today's Boon Tong Kee chicken rice at River Valley and paid her $5 for a slim-cut sleeveless mini-dress. And I would buy slightly more expensive fabric as I only needed exactly one and half metres!

Being petite has its benefits!

And at the time the minis were all the rage. In a month, I could afford to make say, two to three dresses as that would cost around $50.

Do you think that this need for survival in the early years and self-esteem in your early adulthood propelled you in your career? Do you think that you would have been as successful as you are now, in today's competitive climate?

I think, the answer would be "yes". As we didn't have much, I became quite good at seizing opportunities and was determined to do my best . I saw any offer that came my way as an opportunity for me to excel. You do not take something and be half-hearted about it. Instead, you say, "I will do a good job because there is nowhere to go back to"—simply because there was no fall back, no plan B. So poverty was a driver for me, as it was for a lot of people in my generation.

Indeed, your peers like Chan Heng Chee and Catherine Lim said quite similar things. It was not ambition that drove them but necessity.

Right, right. Yes, absolutely! When I finished my Cornell exams, I didn't even stay for the convocation. I completed the four-year course in two and a half years and people tell me that I am smart, but I did it out of necessity as I probably could not afford another semester. Studying for two and a half years was already a luxury. Today, people take their time and have gap years. I don't begrudge them as it is the environment and I say bravo to them. In our generation, we did not see ourselves as victims of circumstances. We don't say, "God, society is not fair to me!" but instead we say, "Hey, this is my lot so I make the best of it." I didn't even think I would end up being a hotelier.

So what would you have been? Have you ever considered that?

I guess, if you had asked me as a 17, 18-year-old, I would said I would like to be married to a very rich man, live in a white picket-fenced house, have four kids. He would take great care of me, gives me a car, jewellery and all that. That would have been my princess dream. It is equivalent to what my granddaughter would answer when I ask her, "What do you want to be?" and she would always reply, "I want to be a princess."

But I became a hotelier not by choice. I was in Cornell with my former husband and he was reading his master's in Political Science. He knew that the one unfinished ambition I had was to get a degree. So, we looked around in Cornell. It had a great agricultural school but that would have no application in Singapore. Engineering, Maths and Sciences were not my forte. They had great Law and Medical Schools but these were postgraduate programs. But they also had a great Hoteling School, so I decided, okay, Hoteling it is. We are talking 1968 to 1971.

Civil rights movement.

Yes. Anyway, during that time, Singapore was building hotels—Hilton, Shangri-La, Mandarin. You don't have to be too smart to figure out that you would get a job with a Hoteling degree. I am not an extrovert and if I were rude, I would go as far as to say I don't even like people. If I had my druthers, I would much rather sit at home, read a book and watch the sunset, which is what I do a lot now because I have a choice.

So, you are a born introvert but became a trained extrovert.

Yes, that must be the answer. Because I had to have a job and am in the service profession that says "people either make or break you", I had to become a trained extrovert. In the beginning, I disliked being in cocktail parties as I didn't know what to do. I would make myself smile, walk up to someone to strike a conversation by saying, "Hi, I'm Jennie." So, communication was for me a practiced art, so to speak, rather than something that came naturally to me.

I remember when I was the General Manager of the Raffles Hotel, I had to welcome VIPs. They would ask me how I was, and I would dread it as I did not want to tell them I really was an introvert and found it awkward to make polite conversation. As a woman General Manager, I had another challenge.

To illustrate, there was an incident when I had to greet one of our distinguished guests, an Australian politician at the North Bridge entrance. The situation became awkward as we both approached the escalator. If I were a gentleman, I would have ushered him up the escalator first as he was the VIP. However, because I was a lady, convention and etiquette required a role reversal and he gestured me up the escalator first.

At that moment I thought to myself, that is a wonderful reason to appoint someone to take on the role as the official greeter, curator or historian of the hotel. Later on, we appointed Leslie Danker for the role of Resident Historian and we also had my male colleagues take over the welcoming of VIPs.

Yes! That was ingenious. If you were a man, you would not be accorded this "reason".

Yes and I loved it that I had the advantage of being a woman and an introvert. That is where I think being a woman has its advantages. Which takes us to what I mentioned earlier, evolution. We need to evolve and move with the times although there are certain basic things that never change, such as integrity, honesty, trustworthiness and accountability. These values don't change but perhaps the way we exhibit them might.

As a person, you need to evolve with the times too and this means, at a superficial level, dressing the part. I wore a cheongsam—for the 10 years or so that I was General Manager—simply because it was functional and took me from day to night with a simple change of accessories and footwear. I wore my pearls in the morning, but donned a pair of dangling earrings and a cocktail ring for the evening. These are easy things to do to ensure that I do not have to live in the hotel and still have simple pleasures of real life.

And you keep your sanity.

Yes, you do. Amongst hoteliers, the divorce rate is very high which is understandable. You see, if you were a young twenty-something, you would probably be married to a gentleman of a similar age and would live in a modest home. And the disparity of what you see in a luxury hotel and your own home can be rather glaring and stark, which can give rise to discontentment. There is a huge transition.

What an excellent observation. That is good point which probably accounts for why there are many failed marriages amongst actors as well.

Exactly, because they do not work and live in the real world. In a luxury hotel, the men you see are decked to the nines, your husband is probably unshaven and at home in a pair of shorts. So you have to be very down to earth to see that real life is really this man in a pair of shorts who has not shaven for two days, not this guy who is perfumed in a suit without a crinkle, eating off silver and porcelain. This hoteling world is a different, almost artificial world.

If you are in sales, the lifestyle may be even more exaggerated. Calling for a bottle of expensive wine to impress may be very ordinary, as you are entertaining not out of your own pockets but at the hotel's expense. So when young women, in particular, ask me if hoteling is a good career, I always try to caution them…

Not to be seduced.

Absolutely. You need to realise you may be dragged unconsciously into this world of artifice which may not apply when you go home. Most people, after listening to me, just say, "It's okay. I can handle."

They don't recognise the depths of the repercussions. So would you attribute that to your divorce as well?

I don't think so. My divorce is a very simple matter of two very good friends getting married and then, going back to being very good friends. Our heads ruled the relationship more than the heart.

There was no more passion.

But one may say, isn't a marriage based on good friendship enough? Do you always need to have all this passion? Don't all good marriages end up as friendships? And isn't that more important than the original passion?

Honestly, I don't know the answer but the important thing is: we gave each other a chance to do something else. He got happily remarried again and we kept in touch with each other for years after the divorce. In fact, recently when I was doing some paperwork for my diplomatic visa, I wrote that I was "divorced", but could not remember the year, because we have stayed in close touch.

And there is the $1 alimony.

Yes, the $1 alimony. He owes me a lot of $1's because I never collected them as he took good care of me even after the divorce. In fact, he has one son from his second marriage and I went to Vietnam to officiate his wedding as Justice of the Peace. But, if you think back logically, is a friendship good enough for a marriage? Like I said, I don't know the answer but certain paths you take, not the well-trodden ones, will take you to interesting places.

Absolutely, which is really what this book is about too. How all the ladies made significant life choices given different circumstances and contexts. And to me, the context is important as we get to understand the circumstances, social mores, prevailing culture and your thought processes, which is interesting for the readers. Which takes me to, how did you deal with the stigma of divorce?

I don't think divorces were rare by the time I got mine, but it certainly was in the previous generation.

But do you think it is because of economic stability? Your friends and you had financial freedom the way a lot of women in your generation may not have.

Yes I think so, possibly. If you ask me now whether people should stay or go in a marriage or what the red lines are, I will say, it's quite clear. A friendship is a good place to stay even if you don't have the passion. You should also stay for the children. I'm very pro-children as they never asked to be born. So, you do have the responsibility to stay together for them.

But what the red line is to me is as follows, which is something I learnt from my mother. My mother's friends used to ask her for advice on how she could tolerate her husband having two wives. They would also share that they wanted to leave their husbands because at that time the word is not "divorce" but "I want to leave." My mother will always ask two basic questions, "有没有打你?" or "Did he hit you?" And secondly, she would ask "有没有回来睡?" or "Does he come home to sleep?" To my mother, those were her limits. A man should never raise his hands to hit a woman as there is no going back. The second question was premised on respect. She believed that a man can go out and "do business" as long as he comes home at night. That is a basic respect he has to accord to his wife.

But for me, how I interpret this is: If it is a mere lack of passion, it is all right to me. But, the red line that can never be transgressed is a fundamental sense of respect which means no physical, emotional and mental abuse. And this extends to the children too.

You are very forward-thinking and also vocal in your dating a younger man.

I didn't set out to date younger men as a choice. In fact, I did not date after the divorce as I saw myself as first and foremost a mother, and I have two boys who can be very sensitive and jealous if their mother started dating. There was a good 15 years where I did not date, but I would of course go out with good friends to concerts and the likes.

With Joseph, I would put it down to a karma thing. It was not like I went out searching or got online. We met the traditional way, through a friend, and we were mutually attracted to each other. He was in real estate before the Asian financial crisis in 1997, and turned to dancing, which was what he enjoyed doing, after his business went bad. I met him during that period and we have been together since 1999. So if you were to ask me 18 years ago if I would be in a partnership with a younger person, I will say no. But what I take comfort in, is precisely that, the comfort of being around him.

The mundane pleasures of life.

Yes. It is more like this. The joy comes from the companionship and not the ability to change the person. At my age, you do not need to mould your partner as you are already fully formed individuals, unlike how you are when you are younger and may need to compromise and adjust. We take us as we are.

I must say, now that I have met you face-to-face, you are genuinely very likable, although I have read stories about your Dragon Lady persona back then.

Maybe I gave that impression back then as I didn't like my job very much. But as you said, it is a learnt thing, and what I do is to make everything I do a success. Otherwise, how do I justify getting paid and promoted, and how do I account for the people who put their trust in me. But, did I enjoy it wholeheartedly? The answer is probably "no" and maybe that is why I took on so many other portfolios aside from being a hotelier as I was trying to find things that I enjoy.

Most people take on chairmanship of committees after they retire, but I was unusual in that I held a full-time job and took on all sorts of roles to find enjoyment in life. One such example would be my taking on the chairmanship of the Singapore Film Commission for the past 20 years. Joseph enjoys going to the movies so this role allows us both to keep up to date with the arts and cultural scene.

Perhaps you enjoy the challenges, stimulations, diversity and giving back to the community? You have over 20 directorships.

I do enjoy going into areas that I know not very much about. I also think that at the back of my head, I do wish to give back as I do think that life has been good to me and I have progressed along with the growth of Singapore. In addition, I am also motivated to do more while I can. Most people start to do charity when they retire but my sentiment is, I had better do it now while I am working and leverage on the network and connections that I have. When I knock on the door, it opens. One day, it may be less effective and the response may not be so enthusiastic.

How did you juggle your career and motherhood?

Maybe because we in live in Asia and in Singapore, in particular, the three-generation family is rather commonplace. Today, I live close to my sons. But when my sons were young, I was working and I had my mother to help care for my children. She lived with me till she passed away. My younger son was then only 10 and the older was 15. I didn't have full-time help, though I had *ah soh*[3] who came in on Mondays, Wednesdays, Fridays. She is still with me. She did all the heavy lifting, washing, cleaning and ironing. On the days she came to the house, she cooked. I did not have a full-time helper until five years ago, when my former mother-in-law passed away and I inherited her Filipino helper, Ruby, who had been with the family for over a decade.

Anyway, I think I acquitted myself fairly as a mother and spent what I considered was quality time with my children after work. But this all depends on how you define quality time.

So, let's say a member of your staff comes to you for advice as she is torn between career, marriage and motherhood. What will you tell her?

Staff *do* come to me about these issues. Diana Ee-Tan is an example. Diana started working with me when she was 24 after graduating in English and Economics. By the time she was 30, she had three children and her second daughter would cry whenever she went to work. Diana was at a crossroads and asked me for my advice.

I asked her three questions. The first is, "If you stopped working, will you be unhappy?" The second is, "Have you discussed this with your husband?" And the third question is "Can you afford it?" To which she answered: yes, she will probably be unhappy but she won't be any happier seeing her children unhappy; yes, her husband is fine with her taking off from work; and yes, she can afford it as her husband is an architect. So, she did indeed leave work for a couple of years, then came back part-time, and then went back to full-time work when the children were older. So if you use Diana as a case study, she would be an example of one who placed motherhood first, then came back for her career, and she still ended up as a Managing Director of Raffles Holdings.

---

3 A maternal lady who comes in to do odd-chores, a part-time domestic helper. Jennie speaks respectfully of these women who often manage two or more households. These unsung heroes take on the burden of Singapore's economy by assuming the household duties.

Let's talk about your recent role as an entrepreneur and a diplomat. How did that happen?

I've always been a manager my entire life. People mistakenly think I'm an entrepreneur but I am not. I am very much a creature of my "educated" generation who is very risk-averse and I think that was what made me successful. In my youth, I would not dare risk what I have built to go and sell hamburgers, which is why I am doing Jollibee now in my old age. I gathered a few friends together to sell chicken. It's like crossing the Yellow River.

Actually, that is true. Nobody has written about Jollibee as your first attempt at enterprise as you have always been so successful, but those successes were of you scaling the corporate ladder.

Right. And most people would assume that you should take chances in your youth. But I was quite the opposite and never dared to. I've had job offers from Hong Kong and the U.S. but I never ventured as I had my children and my mother was here in Singapore. So I guess I had to fulfill what I never got to be as a young person.

I never saw myself as an "international" person. I've travelled extensively but I have never worked internationally. Of course, when I was CEO of Raffles Holdings, we owned properties worldwide, but that was different from working for an extended period of time overseas. So I wanted to fulfill two things: I wanted to be an entrepreneur—so let's sell chicken—and I wanted to work overseas.

The diplomat route came in part also when the Permanent Secretary of the Ministry of Foreign Affairs called me to ask if I was willing to do more service for the nation, and immediately I said, "Of course, sure." I see no need to be shy and coy but just accepted the invitation to be a diplomat.

How would you describe your management style?

There is no style. I just make it a point to surround myself with people better than me. Diana at thirty was more capable than me at thirty.

You're being humble.
No, it's the truth.

Were you ever intimidated in a boardroom full of men?
No, I actually enjoyed that! I thought, wonderful! So many men! I remember when I very young, I was sent to Japan as part of my work with STB (Singapore Tourism Board). I was invited by the President of JTB, one of the largest travel operators in the world. He had invited me to an exquisite dinner. When I got to the venue, we realised all the guests were men. The President then looked at me and said, "Jennie-san, it's okay. Tonight, I make you honorary man."

Hilarious!
Some women may take this as a politically incorrect insult, but I thought it was wonderful! When I retold the story to quite a few "liberal" women, they said it was "condescending", while I thought it was rather sweet!

I think the key is, I never saw feminism as an agenda nor have I ever seen the proverbial "glass ceiling". I have been called insensitive but the truth is, I have never felt discriminated against as a woman. If you didn't get promoted because you didn't put in the effort, or you don't get the job because you don't have the right qualifications, and you start to blame it on your gender, then I think you are really falling into your own preconceived trap. This is not to say I have not been disappointed in my lifetime, I have, but I believe that that particular job probably went to a better, more qualified person than me at any point in time. Whether man or woman, it really does not matter.

So you would not implement policies especially for women?
I find that offensive, I find quotas and even the talk of quotas offensive. In fact, I think affirmative action is condescending as you're back pedaling the cause and inadvertently causing more harm than good. If you really want to help, just do it. Look out for good men and women and promote them. If you truly believe that we are all equal, why are you afraid? Why would you need a quota?

This is because you are progressive, Jennie. So you walk the talk and live it, not merely talk about it.

People have also looked at me and asked if I have regrets in life? I don't. I may sometimes regret being too harsh on this person or that, or taking out my bad mood on someone—but anecdotal things. I do not harbour regrets. I have made bad decisions but I learn from them and move on.

I recall an episode in Raffles City where I have a reserved parking lot. A young security person did not know that lot was mine and told me I could not park. I was in a bad mood and really chewed him up. That night, I went home and reflected. I thought to myself that he was someone's son and I would not have liked it if someone had spoken to my son in that manner. Years later, I still remember this story. It was not my finest moment.

Have you mellowed over the years?

Leslie Danker reminded me that on the day before we opened Raffles Hotel, I had said to the staff, "Forget your family tonight and only focus on Raffles Hotel." Would I have said the same thing today? The answer is probably "yes" as there is a job to be done. But certainly, yes, I could have mellowed. It comes with reflection and confidence. The more insecure you are, the nastier you are.

But it was also the same insecurity that led you to success as well.

It's a double-edged sword.

So what were the lowest points in your life?

Probably when I was in my late 20s, when I did not have a sense of purpose and was probably depressed and lost. That and my mother's passing. She died in 1988, close to 29 years ago and I still weep when I think of her. My younger son still carries her photo and lights incense in front of her photo in our house. Of course, there are disappointments in my career too, but I don't think it has led me to depression or tears the way personal matters do.

Speaking of personal matters, what has happened to your cheongsam collection?
I have between 200–300 pieces, which is not that many considering I was at Raffles Hotel for over a decade. They are all kept in a warehouse as I rarely wear them now.

You are often travelling. Do you think you have wanderlust in your soul?
On the contrary, no. I am averse to adventure and travelled largely for work as a hotelier or as part of my duties in STB to promote Singapore, or as an extension of being a parent when I took my children on vacations. It was not until I hit my 60s that I started to travel for pleasure. Even so, I tend to go on cruises to the European rivers, Alaska and around Asia. These are relaxing escapades where everything is taken care of. I am not one to strap on a backpack to go on an unknown adventure, even in my youth.

Which are your favourite destinations?
Back in the days, I would say the ryokans in Japan. Nowadays, I will say I love visiting my friends and staying with them or in their holiday homes. I enjoy my creature comforts and like having familial surroundings—the ease of waking up to fresh brewed coffee or having a family meal in the living room. I also love serviced apartments as they give one a sense of being home away from home.

What are your travel essentials?
Good old-fashioned common sense. Most vacationers or tourists tend to throw caution to the wind, have a false sense of invincibility and let their guard down. I think being in an unfamiliar or new surroundings should demand more awareness to the new cultures, contexts and customs not less.

Complete this sentence. Good manners….

Is culturally defined and has to be perceived by another. One cannot assume one has good manners as it is dependent upon what the counterpart perceives.

You have exquisite tastes. How do you define style for a gentleman and a lady?

It would be that innate ability to pull off something simple and make it seem timeless. It is what the French refer to as *je ne sais quoi*, an intangible quality that makes someone distinctive or attractive.

What do you think are your most memorable personal achievements?

On your death bed, you never think about your last promotion. It is known that the first sense you lose is sight, and the last sense that you lose is hearing. Because of that fact, your last thought cannot possibly be, "Oh, I was so happy about that promotion", but rather it would be what you hear around you. I can understand why in the old days, relatives were urged to call out to the dying person to go peacefully as it lets him or her know that their loved ones are with them.

People ask me, "What is your legacy?" And I think "What legacy?!" I am not Lee Kuan Yew, Nelson Mandela, Winston Churchill or Mother Theresa. People may remember me with the Raffles Hotel, or Community Chest, or not. So I don't think about personal achievements but I think about my children, loved ones, grandchildren and friends. I think that's important and certainly more memorable. I would rather be remembered as a fun mother and grandmother.

Would you have given a different response say 20 years ago?

Not in substance, but in nuance. A few things will still remain constant even when you go back 20 years. The only difference is all my interviews then were about my career. So my responses were first, surround yourself with good people. Second, I have never believed in the glass ceiling.

Third, on your way up, never step on anyone and do not use other people as your stepping stone. It's only been in recent years that there is any interest in me as a person.

What will your epitaph say? She was a fun grandmother?
I think so, and "She led a good life."

If you met God, what would you say?
If You didn't exist, mankind would have had to make You up, because that's what Man needs to survive. It's hard for humans to answer the questions, "Why are we here?" and "Where do we go after we die?" So by having a God, we can effectively answer both questions: one, "We are made by some superior being" and two, "There is no such thing as death because you go on to somewhere more beautiful so there is nothing to fear." So we would have made one up if there was no God, unless of course, if you are a Buddhist.

Finally, do you see yourself as a Madonna, Maverick or any other M role?
Since you are defining Madonna in the biblical sense, then probably not her as that would be too religious for me. I would say Mummy. But I am also a Maverick though I don't think I am very successful at that. So maybe Moderate Maverick or Mummy Maverick? What do you think?

The Quiet Renegade

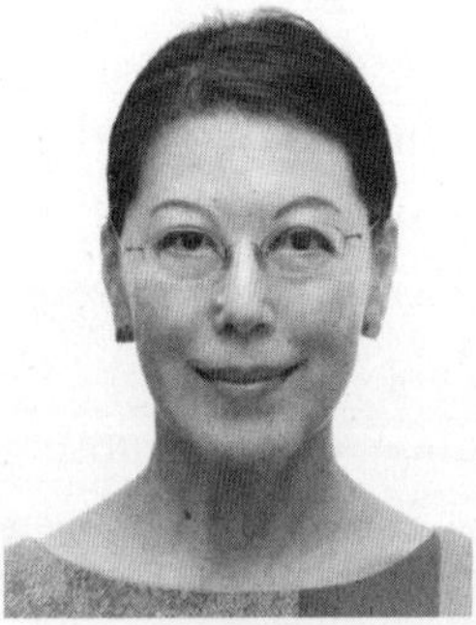

GEH MIN

Dr. Geh Min (MBBS, FRCS, FAMS) is a staunch supporter and spokesperson for the environment. She was President of the Nature Society (Singapore) from 2000 to 2008 and was sworn in as a Nominated Member of Parliament from January 2005 to April 2006.

She received the inaugural 2006 President's Award for the Environment along with Tommy Koh and the Waterways Watch Society (WWS). She is currently a board member of BirdLife International (Asia) and a member of The Nature Conservancy's Asia Pacific Council. Min also heads the Environment and Health Functional Committee of the South-West Community Development Council, the Water Network of the PUB and the Singapore Environment Council.

She is a medical graduate of the National University of Singapore and became a fellow of the Royal College of Surgeons (Edinburgh) in 1980. She works as a consultant ophthalmologist at Mount Elizabeth Medical Centre, and as a visiting consultant at the Singapore National Eye Centre and the National University Hospital.

***

Whenever I meet Geh Min, I am reminded of a quote from Susan Cain's book *Quiet: The Power of Introverts in a World That Can't Stop Talking*. She wrote, "The highly sensitive [introvert] tends to be philosophical or spiritual in their orientation, rather than materialistic or hedonistic. They dislike small talk. They often describe themselves as creative or intuitive. They dream vividly, and can often recall their dreams the next day. They love music, nature, art, physical beauty. They feel exceptionally strong emotions—sometimes acute bouts of joy, but also sorrow, melancholy, and fear. Highly sensitive people also process information about their environments—both physical and emotional—unusually deeply. They tend to notice subtleties that others miss—another person's shift in mood, say, or a lightbulb burning a touch too brightly."

In fact, being an extrovert, there is nothing more pleasurable to me than winning the trust of introverts and keeping them engaged in a conversation. After all, Min, a granddaughter of the late philanthropist Lee Kong Chian, is known to be highly private and prefers to be amidst the vastness and solitude of nature than amongst fashion conscious socialites in bling parties. Min would rather spend her time catching frogs, tadpoles and spiders than shopping for the latest, brightest object.

She speaks in soft, dulcet tones, but that does not prevent her from standing up for what she believes in. As a former NMP and past President of the Nature Society, she is known for not mincing her words, even under the bright lights of the Parliamentary Chamber. But she is equally adept behind closed doors, fostering an appreciation of nature and the importance of its conservation, whilst enabling a platform of understanding between government agencies and environmental groups.

Speaking with Min also brings to mind French philosopher, Jacques Derrida. He likened the concept of deconstruction to "pulling a rug from under one's own feet" and basically highlights the instability between text and meaning. Min's self-deprecating sense of humour and her constant self-reflection as she speaks is indeed, deconstruction in action.

Min breaks the mould of the medical surgeon and shared that she does not believe in living just the "one life". She chooses instead to indulge in a perennial sense of wonder that infuses her with a curiosity about life and everything under its big, vast umbrella. Rejecting the notion of the Unitary Self, she defies conventional wisdom and declares that she is elusive even to herself. Her lack of narcissistic ego is a departure from most born into privilege. She is able to laugh in spite of herself, even when she was being made a "laughing stock" when she stood for environmental rights in Parliament.

I also listened, intrigued, when she shared with me the patriarchal tyranny of her days in medical college and confessed that what kept her going was, at times, the sheer motivation of not wanting to let her "side" (the women) down. The common perception in those days was that women were just constitutionally weaker than men and thus not as capable as surgeons.

In her own quiet way, Min has come to embrace her inner renegade that speaks up when it feels compelled to, almost independent of her own volition. Like all superheroes who typically have a mousier alter ego, I am glad that her inner self speaks loud and clear when it has to be heard, for Singapore and the island of Chek Jawa is all the better because of women like Min.

***

Share with us your background as I know you are very private.

My whole family is very private and, in fact, I think I am almost the only member of the extended family who has ever consented to giving interviews. I am already looked on by some relatives as having betrayed the family by giving interviews although I try to specify that these be limited only to issues and not personal matters. As my grandfather, Lee Kong Chian is very well-known, I suspect a lot of the times when people want to interview me, it is because they want to hear more about the family.

I didn't know very much about my great-grandfather, Tan Kah Kee, because he left for China the year I was born in 1950—he was a great

Chinese patriot and he chose to go back. I read about him in history books because my family didn't talk very much about him. However, I do know my grandfather very well, or at least I should—we lived in the same house as I was growing up till he died when I was 17. I wouldn't say he's a private person. In fact, he was quite gregarious. My grandmother was the one who was very, very private.

My maternal grandfather had a lot of friends and he loved talking to people. But he never talked about himself—none of them ever talked about themselves. Frankly, the cult of the individual is just not present in my family. I think it's partly a generational thing to just not talk about yourself, or be seen as being too preoccupied with one's self. I don't know whether that is the family culture, a generational practice, or my own nature, but I am very uncomfortable about talking or reading about myself.

Andy Warhol once predicted that, "In the future, everyone will be world-famous for 15 minutes." This current social media climate must make you very uncomfortable.

It certainly makes me very uncomfortable. I guess everyone does have an ego, I definitely do and I think it's good to have self-awareness. But I must say, that is why I was having cold feet, prior to this interview. I was thinking about what you might ask as I don't know what sort of self I am. I don't feel I have a "self".

I can understand that people who are in the limelight—performers, actors, politicians, have to project themselves to the public. Very fortunately, I chose a career where you are not really required to be in the public eye. In fact, you shouldn't be projecting yourself but instead, you should actually be listening to other people and reflecting on what they say. So I suppose my upbringing and personality compels me to blend in, rather than stick out.

In fact, there's a sort of a joke amongst my close friends—you know grey is one of my favourite colours and I think grey is not a dull colour. If you compare me with a lot of other people, I come out quite colourless and I don't mind. I seem to have developed the art, without even realising it, of wearing something that blends into the environment I am in, even if I have never been in that particular setting before. I seem to have some sort of premonition of the colour scheme, and I will find myself blending in with the tablecloth, the carpet, the wallpaper or whatever.

You are like a chameleon and this is perhaps also a defence mechanism, which takes us to your love of nature. But I do think that it is interesting that you almost overcompensate for your family's successes and wealth by being so humble.

Yes, perhaps that is why I find nature fascinating because a lot of things "blend in" and you have to look hard and work hard to see them. I would rather be that than be a bright thing in a shop window that catches attention. Of course, there are also bright colours and hybrids in nature just as there are people who are larger-than-life. Perhaps, because of my family background, I have become very protective of my privacy and have my "protective colouring".

For a long time—and I am quite candid about this—I was seen as my grandfather's granddaughter and people were always comparing me to others and, of course, not in a complimentary way. You have to behave yourself because otherwise you feel as if you are a disgrace to your family. Even in medical college, I was pretty mediocre. It was not uncommon to hear comments like, "Oh, who would dare to fail her? Do you know who she is?" so you're not given any credit on your own merit. Frankly, we all felt the "banyan tree effect" because of my grandfather's success.

So I really only lost that sense of inhibition when I went abroad. If I may say so, I passed my exams there, where no one knew me or cared who I was, so I felt a certain satisfaction. And the thing is, actually, this is how people outside see me. In the family, we never talk about all this. It's not that we are trying to hide anything, we are just not even aware of it. My grandfather was a really simple, humble person and he always said he didn't want or like any fanfare because people tended to put him on a pedestal. It is also difficult for me to put myself in his place, but I think he felt that all this status and obsession with "who he was" hampered his relationships. People were self-conscious around him while what he really liked was one-to-one interactions.

My grandfather was a businessman. He was in rubber and banking, but as one of my uncles subsequently told me, he wasn't a businessman in the sense that he loved making money—he was a businessman by virtue of the fact that he was pulled into business. He was quite a scholarly person and was a teacher, and he came over to Singapore because he was fairly bilingual. He joined my great-grandfather, Tan Kah Kee, in the rubber business but as my uncle said, he never cared about money, which is true. He never really enjoyed the trappings of money, or flashy things like cars or status symbols. He wasn't interested in any of that. In fact, he was always wearing the oldest clothes until they had holes in them and my grandmother had to insist he buy new ones. He was a frugal man and hated any form of waste. He always insisted we ate every grain of rice on our plates and turned off every single light when we left a room.

Although he was a great Chinese patriot and supported a lot of educational institutions in China, he realised at some point in time, that Singapore would be his home where he would live and die. So he transferred a lot of his legacy to Singapore—unlike my great-grandfather, who was still of that generation who wanted to go back to China, and he did. I really think my grandfather, Lee Kong Chian, derived his main satisfaction from doing good for a large group of people. He, like his father-in-law, Tan Kah Kee, never believed in leaving a large inheritance to his family. They both believed that the best legacy they could give their children was a good education and the right values. He had six children with my grandmother and I am the daughter of the second daughter. I only had one brother but he died young in a car accident.

What were some of your challenges growing up and how did you cope?

My difficult time was in my teens and my early 20s, because that's when I had to cope with my parent's divorce and my brother's death. I was in the final year of university when that happened. Obviously, it's my mother who suffered the most from it. I don't want to make a big issue of it as lots of people have these problems too. In those days, you didn't talk about it, you just internalised it. We didn't even talk about it in the family but I remember thinking that I would have to live for both of us. My brother had very different interests from me but I tried to read some of his favourite books and take on some of his pet passions.

In hindsight, I am glad I found nature as a source of inner strength. I believe it is very important for every child to have something they derive meaning from whether it is the natural world or a talent or some other passion. I was exposed to nature when I was very young and I think that was where I drew comfort and companionship from without my realising it consciously. That is why I am a strong supporter of nature. Music and reading were also very helpful to me.

My mother was a literature teacher so she exposed us to books at a very young age. She's very strict about us not wasting our money on other stuff. In fact, we had to give all our birthday and Christmas presents away, except one. We could pick the one thing we liked best from amongst all the presents and she would give away the rest. She didn't believe in extravagance and in owning too much material stuff, and that was good.

How would you define yourself?

I think if you want to know a person, even if it is yourself, the worst thing is to talk about it as I don't think that defines what a person is at all. I don't feel that I can pin down a distinct personality. In fact, I don't believe much in personality and even individuality. Part of this is, of course, based on the science of consciousness which is still in its infancy. I don't want to go into psychology or neuroscience, but more and more, science is showing that we are just a composite, complex and constantly changing structure.

If I look at people, including myself, 10 years ago and compare them with what they are now, it's very different. That is why I believe there's no such thing as a "personality" as you are constantly reflecting your environment, your upbringing, your culture and experiences and these are almost always in a state of flux. There's of course the person whom you aspire to be and there's the person whom other people see you as but I don't think there is such a thing as the person you really are. I find that actually more interesting.

I remember as a child, I always used to think it's so boring to just live one life. You read about people who become this or that—a doctor or a lawyer—one of those stereotypes and you say, "I don't think I can last just living one life." I guess the only thing you had to stick to is your gender but even that can be fixed these days. (*laughter*)

As I said, books meant a lot to me. Books and literature do help you escape the "one life" problem and allow you to lead different lives. I think that, in many ways, helped me cope with my parents' splitting up. I was very concerned with conforming when I was a child—children can be terribly conservative and I didn't want to be different. I was also very conscious that I didn't live in a standard, happy family, though I didn't become aware of it until my schoolmates started talking about it.

I studied in Singapore all along and lived together with my mother and brother in my maternal grandparents' house because my parents had divorced. My brother later went to boarding school and to a university abroad. I stayed in Singapore, though I read many books on English boarding schools and I had friends who attended. I was offered a place but I was very, very happy in my Singapore school and had great friends there. I did apply and was accepted in a few universities overseas, but when it came to the crunch, I also decided to stay in Singapore—though I did go abroad to do my postgraduate training and examinations.

Getting back to living different lives, I remember consoling myself when my parents split up as I had to visit my father during the school holidays. He went to Malaysia and later took on Malaysian citizenship. I was thinking that while it was not a life I would have chosen, I was getting what I had wanted, which is living different lives. I got one life with my mother and another one with my father—and they were very different. It was my father who inculcated a love of nature in me because he used to take us on jungle walks and deep sea fishing trips, which I really enjoyed.

Aside from your love of nature, which we will explore later, what else inspired you?

My mother, as I said, is a great reader so she developed in us a love for books. She used to read to us regularly when we were young. In fact, that's how I learnt how to read. She just read to us all the time and one fine day when she didn't have time to read to us, I suddenly found that I could read all by myself!

She also had a sense of aesthetics, but it tended towards man-made culture rather than nature. She had a very good eye for clothes, design and interior decoration. In fact, because of her, I wanted to do architecture for a long time. Somehow, I think I was very fortunate because these two merged together. I don't just love the great outdoors, I also love man-made, modern architecture, design and fashion. In short, I just like anything visual. So these are the things that strengthened me and I was fortunate to have a lot of exposure to them when I was young. Maybe I should mention here that I wasn't aware of all these things until I looked back and reflected, of course. That is one of the advantages of being older.

I was reading this book by Rachel Carson, who is acknowledged as the mother of the green movement. She wrote one book that really put things into perspective. It's called *The Sense of Wonder*. It is about the impact of nature on children. She argues that for a child, it isn't as important to tell them exactly how things work or try to be too scientific with names and explanations. What is key, however, is to arouse their curiosity. Take them for a walk on the seashore, in the jungle or even a park and show them new things. That is one of my favourite things to do.

Children naturally have a sense of wonder and they will ask questions which you don't have to answer in detail. It's the questions that really make them think, and in fact, not being given the answer straightaway may be better as it makes them, with some encouragement, try to work out the answer themselves. This is something I believe I have and it doesn't matter whether you chose to go into the Sciences or the Arts. What you need to have is a sense of wonder about being alive. Why are things the way they are? You can have your special interests on people, animals, or plants or even machines but all this adds poetry and meaning to life.

I remember I had this eureka moment on the beach in Port Dickson where we used to have our vacations. In those days you don't fly anywhere, but went on long car rides. I loved being in Port Dickson as I loved seashells, so I enjoyed scavenging on the beach. It is probably the same hunter-gatherer instinct that makes people enjoy shopping in cities. City people don't have such nice beaches so they have to go and lose themselves in the shops. But give me a beach anytime, a real, natural, unpolluted beach.

So I was looking at these apparently identical seashells on the beach and they all looked alike initially. You see, I had the idea to stick them on a box and make a birthday present for my mother. But the more I looked, the more I found that there were rarely any that matched at all! Every single one was different and so I had this eureka moment that every single shell is different, so people, too, must all be different.

I asked my dad about it and he said, "Yes, they are all different. It's like snowflakes—every single one is different." He showed me some pictures from the encyclopaedia and that was an exciting moment for me as I was only five. Obviously I haven't really made that much of that experience or I might have become a famous scientist! (*laughter*) But I feel that sense of wonder at the natural world is something everyone should be awakened to and developed. How can you enjoy life if you don't have that appreciation for the world around you?

How did you go from loving nature to pursuing ophthalmology instead?

On my becoming an eye surgeon, I must say I was a bit of a reluctant doctor. I still think if I had shared with them all that I'm going to share with you in my medical candidate interview, they would definitely have kicked me out or not admitted me.

I became a doctor because my grandmother and mother wanted me to do Medicine. My mother's father wanted her to do Medicine but she read English Literature instead, which is why she was doubly insistent that I read Medicine even though I wanted to do Architecture. She felt guilty that she had disappointed her father and wanted me to make it up to him! I did not hate the idea of being a doctor and was attracted to the idea of interacting with people from all walks of life and being of help to them. But Architecture was my first love. I will say that the academic side was not a big problem for me and getting into medical school was not difficult so I decided to take the easy way out and please everyone. In retrospect, I am really very grateful to them as I really did enjoy being a doctor.

Anyway, when I was looking for a specialty, I did so partly by elimination. I knew I could not survive as a GP as it's just very demanding. I admire Generalists. Frankly, it is easier to pass a few exams and specialise in a niche area. Of course, everyone is different, but if you practised as a Generalist, you have to know a lot more across the board. I came upon the eye when we were doing our short postings where you get to explore various specialties, such as eye, ENT, anaesthesia but not the major things like surgery and gynaecology yet. Anyway, when I looked at the magnified iris of the eye, I found it really quite amazing!

It's like this shell moment again. I could see details that were so intricate. When you look into someone's eyes be it brown, blue or green, you actually see that it is composed of multiple threads and it is a wonderful intricate tapestry with so many secret compartments. So I really fell in love with eyes and decided to make this my specialty because I felt I could keep on looking and always find it fascinating. It is like a nature walk—each experience is different even if you are taking the same route.

Anyway, that was my epiphany all over again. It was a revelation that the eyes were not just a window to the soul, but it is also the window to the brain when you look through the pupil, because the retina is actually derived from brain material. So you are able to diagnose certain conditions such as hypertension that may affect the blood vessels in the brain. You are not able to look at the blood vessels in the brain so if you wanted to know what they may look like, you would look at the blood vessels at the back of the eye.

Share with us what it was like being in medical school back then.
It was rare for girls to specialise. There were plenty of girls going to Medicine, I would say in my year women made up about one-fifth to a quarter of the cohort. Women in Singapore have been doing Medicine for at least a generation or more so it was no big deal, but there was still a lot of inherent prejudice. In those days, they still allowed ragging and, of course, all the ragging was done by senior, male medical students. I received repeated warnings from male seniors that all the girls who do Medicine go in as "blooming young flowers" but end up as "withered old sticks" when they graduate. That used to annoy me. Frankly, flowers don't bloom forever either and I don't see anything wrong with sticks! (*laughter*)

Anyway, that actually didn't turn me off Medicine though it did turn me off a lot of those guys—but that was the norm then and I think they meant well… That was their attitude towards women and it may have been a result of a sense of insecurity rather than superiority. Of course, when it came to dating, most of them preferred to romance the nurses. But I was brought up to think that anything challenging was better, so their comments didn't really bother me much. In fact, they spurred me on. I also really like using my hands and I wanted to do surgery although women were not encouraged to then. It was thought that we don't possess the stamina or commitment as all the surgeons were male at that time.

There were also a few women surgeons already and I remember one of them, Alice Cheah. She was very encouraging when she found out I was interested in surgery. She gave me a lot of pep talks, always accompanied by a glass of sherry in her room. She was well respected by her male colleagues and I'm really grateful to her for taking the trouble. In fact, all the women were encouraging. Anyway, I liked using my hands so that was why I chose a surgical specialty, not because of any gesture against gender discrimination.

I became a specialist in 1980. In those days, there wasn't an exam here so I had to go to Edinburgh to do it. I remember the first letter I got after I passed was an acceptance letter was addressed to "Dear Mr Geh". Surgeons were referred to as "Mister" as it was the norm and women were a minority. I also recall there were no changing rooms for female surgeons so I had to share with the nurses, which is fine, but the male surgeons got a separate room from the other male staff. One of the female surgeons used to frequent the male surgeons' changing room and embarrass all her male colleagues, but I was not up to that sort of behaviour. The changing room gossip with the nurses was also very interesting and I learnt a lot.

Was it harder for you being a female surgeon in the early days?
I never had any problems with patients. I had problems really with how young I was, rather than what gender I was. The patients were okay and they don't judge. I was 30 when I had the paper qualifications but my training still had a long way to go. There were role models for me such as Kanwaljit Soin and Alice Cheah. The accepted wisdom then was that surgery was such a demanding profession that women had to choose between a career or marriage. But what about the men?

And do you know when I got into Medicine, I was harangued even by Dr Toh Chin Chye who was then the Chancellor of the University. He told me at a welcome tea for freshies that I should be going into teaching or something that is more compatible with marriage! I was quite shocked as he was a man of integrity, but he obviously felt strongly about the issue. It shows how difficult it is to separate your personal feeling from your official position. Yes, those were interesting times!

This was in the 1970s and so I was lucky that it was the time of the women's liberation movement in the States and I used to read all the literature. It was a really interesting time to be a female medical student. I got to meet a lot of people from different walks of life who gave me interesting insights. There was this young American girl who was travelling and somehow she ended up in hospital. You never have time once you are doctor but as a medical student you had a little more time and could talk to the patients. They would also let their guard down when they know you are a medical student.

Anyway, this American girl really stiffened my backbone. She was an ardent Women's Libber and she asked me certain questions such as,

"Did I consider myself equal to the men?" and "If not, why not?" She questioned conventional wisdom about why women do not specialise because they fear not having enough time to spend with their families, spouses and being labelled a "bad mother". She was assertive and of course, she said, "If a man can do it, why can't a woman?" Before that, I had a vague awareness of women's rights but I did not have the vocabulary to actually articulate my thoughts. The American girl articulated many ideas for me, so by the time I graduated, I was actually grateful to her.

"If a man can do it, why can't a woman?" That stuck with me. At that time, in order to specialise, you did have to go out of your way to prove yourself because the men were all watching you to see if you will drop out, fail, not do your share of the work, or be too temperamental. There was such a lot of pressure on and prejudice against women. And if you did fail, then of course you would be letting other women down. But in a way, that helped us cope collectively because it made us all pull our socks up as a team and get on with it because we couldn't afford to fail given this intense scrutiny.

Besides, I have always felt I had to try to prove to myself what I can do. It was also exhilarating riding on the tide of the women's movement because it opened up so many possibilities for us. I remember feeling quite sorry for the guys because we women had a larger menu of choices: we could be full-time mothers and housewives, or a full-time career women, or a combination of both. The men's choices were far more restricted and, of course, pressure on them to succeed was also greater. Whereas the pressure on women was partly self-generated, for men, it was the social expectations to be the main breadwinner.

When I completed my specialist training, I came back and worked at the Singapore General Hospital. The University in Singapore had just introduced a quota for the intake of female medical students. They always had an unwritten quota, but now they had a declared quota. I was quite outraged at that time as were all my female medical colleagues. We thought we worked just as hard as the men and felt a deep sense of injustice at this apparent relegation to being second-class doctors.

The justification for not having so many women go into medicine was that it was expensive training doctors and that most women would give up anyway because they would marry well, so it was a waste of taxpayers' money! It might be true in some countries where it was harder to get home help but I don't know of any women doctors who have given up practising medicine in Singapore despite having children, so I asked for the statistics from the Ministry of Health. This required some persistence on my part but finally, I managed to get them from a senior Ministry of Health officer who was female and sympathised with my desire to get a clearer picture of the career paths of women doctors. None of the men would give the statistics to me.

In my analysis, I found that the dropout rate after graduating from medicine is about 5% both for men and women. Those who do leave often move into some related profession or business, but frankly, who is going to work so hard for six years, training to be a doctor, just to give up? The implication was that women do it so that they could marry male doctors. Honestly, if all a woman wanted to do was that, then she could have chosen some other easier options, but, unfortunately, that was what some of our policy makers seemed to be saying.

I also found that some women did go into part-time medical work during their childbearing years because they had young children. Honestly, the support system was non-existent in those days. There was nowhere you could send your child to while you worked. There was no crèche and no childcare centres within your place of work so you and your family would just have to cope. That was why I was trying to advocate for a better support system, not just for doctors but nurses and other women within the hospital as well. Anyway, as part of my analysis, I also found that none of the women gave up practising, and in fact, once the women were done with the childbearing and child-caring years, they all returned full-time! In fact, because we now have a longer life expectancy, a lot of women doctors these days work well into their 70s.

So, I wrote the piece—in order to set the record straight and paint an authentic picture of what the reality was. The article was published in

Commentary, the University of Singapore's magazine, which largely ran scholarly and analytical articles of interest to the academic community including graduates and students. However, some journalists from our main newspaper got hold of the article and my analysis was made public. Of course they sensationalised it and quoted selectively to make it sound like a deliberate challenge to the University and the Ministry of Health.

So that was my first brush with political exposure and the media. My family, especially my mother, was furious with me because she worked at the University. I didn't know how to handle it as a junior doctor then. I hadn't expected to be put in the media spotlight and be shown by the media as contradicting the then Minister of Health who was my employer. You could say I was very naive in those early days and that a lot of my subsequent political career was accidental.

I had no political agenda, hidden or otherwise and I simply saw myself as sharing my own views on the matter. There were other women who were much more vocal on this topic but regardless, my article showed that the premise of putting up a quota on female students was not really a valid one. Kanwaljit Soin went to Parliament and she took up the issue. As for me, I was shell-shocked after all that unwanted publicity and I was told by my family to keep well away. It wasn't an issue that resonated with me too deeply though. All I wanted to do was to establish the facts. I left it to other people whom I felt were much more able to campaign and handle this politically, though I still felt strongly enough to speak about it later.

I was invited by Kanwaljit Soin to speak at AWARE (Association of Women for Action and Research) on the issue of abolishing the quota on female medical students. I approached this not as merely a gender issue but on a broader base of good national health policies and gave three reasons for abolishing the quota.

One of the reasons cited for reducing the number of women doctors was the fact that we tended to prefer to work in primary health care rather than in the specialties such as surgery that involved longer training and long work hours. There was a lot of emphasis in those days to promote ourselves as a major regional healthcare hub, so the more glamourous specialties, such as heart and neurosurgery, got a lot of attention. However, I pointed out that we were already seeing too much competition for surgical specialty training, and not enough people in primary health care. In fact, the Ministry had already begun to realise this and was trying to encourage more people to do family healthcare anyway.

The other area that women tend to do a lot of is the supporting specialties, like radiology, bacteriology, pathology. We were short of specialists in those fields because they were not seen as being glamorous or high-income generating, but they had more regular working hours, which appealed to working mothers. I thought it was a complementary fit in that it suited women and, in fact, was a good reason to have more women doctors as they were prepared to work in these less high-profile but equally essential areas.

The third point was that there was a discrepancy between the genders in how one defines "full-time" or "part-time" work. Back then, the Medical Association or Medical Council would ask you to fill in a form to state if we were working full-time or part-time. In the government departments, you are clearly one or the other as they didn't have that many part-time jobs anyway. However, in the private sector, the definition was fluid and self-defined. A male doctor in private practice would consider himself "full-time" even if he was just reading the papers or gossiping with his colleagues in the clinic. The women functioned differently. We multitask more and when we do not have a patient, we are usually running off to do marketing or perform childcare duties, and as such, we tend to define ourselves as "part-time".

Was this what unwittingly propelled you into politics?

I was never keen on politics. Kanwaljit Soin, who was in the first batch of Nominated Members of Parliament (NMP) and a leading spokesperson for Women's Rights had hoped I would play a more active role and urged me to go into Parliament but I declined. I really didn't feel it was my calling and felt that most women could fight their own battles. Besides, there were other women who were much more effective than I, even though I felt strongly enough about these issues. I must say that I was very fortunate and that's why I believe in serendipity. I did eventually end up in politics but that was because of nature conservation, and this again, was pure chance.

I always enjoyed nature but I never thought I would have to fight to protect nature—it's not my style of course. It seemed crazy to go into Parliament to further protect nature when you can do it from outside. Up till then, no one had done it from the inside and I heard that I was a bit of a laughing stock. Some of the other parliamentarians would tease me "Still fighting for gorillas?" and I would reply, "We don't have gorillas here but we have orangutans." But all that was just fairly good-hearted teasing though it was clear they didn't take me seriously at all.

So I learnt that if you believe in something, you shouldn't be afraid of laughter. But, you should question yourself as you shouldn't think that you know a lot more than other people or that your assumptions and beliefs are more valid than theirs. Anyhow, what really made me decide to get into Parliament was a conviction that I wasn't fighting for a cause that only I and a few people believed in. It was because I had realised that many more people believed in it than was evident to the policymakers.

For example, when I became President of Nature Society, we were fighting to protect certain nature areas even before Chek Jawa. One of the issues was that of golf courses as it was so obvious we had more golf courses than nature reserves, and they were legally protected in a way that many of the nature areas were not. The golf courses had clear boundaries and you can't just walk in freely. I am not against golf courses but we had 23 then when only a minority play the sport, while we as a country only had two gazetted nature reserves that were not always protected from encroachment by roads, highways and other developments.

The reasoning then was that everyone aspires to play golf, like owning landed property. So even if it was indeed a minority, we should have landed property and golf courses, even in land-scarce Singapore. But does everyone really aspire to be a golfer or is this another assumption made by males of a certain background and demographic? It is like the medical doctors' issue all over again except Nature Society couldn't do a survey because we didn't have the means.

I managed to get SEC (Singapore Environment Council), which is a government-initiated NGO, to help. They conducted an independent island-wide survey on attitudes of the public towards land-use for nature and other green areas and even I was stunned by the findings. I had assumed that I had a biased view on nature conservation because the people I hang out with are nature lovers, but the survey showed otherwise.

We asked them about their preference between golf courses and nature conservation areas. Over 50% surveyed said they wanted to keep the nature areas and over 40% said they wanted more nature areas—which means some 92-93% wanted to retain or increase nature areas! Only about 3% said they wanted more golf courses. About 5% were sitting on the fence. That was significant finding which was contrary to the impression that everyone aspired to play golf.

So this was a definite conflict to reality as at that time, the country clubs were expanding their golf courses into nature areas. They were cutting down trees—so we had a few fights on that. This survey was a revelation to the people in URA (Urban Redevelopment Authority) as they really thought everyone wanted more golf courses. To be fair, they did slowly change their policies after they realised the majority of Singaporeans don't really want to play golf. Even my husband, a heart surgeon in SGH and head of the department at the time, was told by one of his bosses that he should learn to play golf, that he would never get further up in his career if he didn't because the people responsible for his promotion played golf. My husband said he didn't have time to play golf. Today, golf is certainly not as popular as it was in those days, though I certainly won't say it's a sunset game.

Anyway, I am not against having golf courses but they should not come at the expense of nature areas. The survey findings reassured me that I am not out on a limb, because whenever you try to negotiate with the government, they will say they see the big picture and I was only seeing a facet and representing a narrow interest group. I said that might be true but if you really want to see the big picture, you should be prepared to take the views of all the people on the ground and not helicopter yourself up to see things from afar and miss out on the perspectives of the majority. Further, the government should also respect every perspective and every minutiae. To be fair to the government, it's not that they wouldn't listen—I think if you put the case reasonably, they will listen but they may have a rather distorted view as the people who speak up often tend to be the people who agree with them. That was of course in the days before social media!

Share with us more on Chek Jawa.

Chek Jawa was indeed a landmark event for Singapore and was, of course, totally unexpected. The government didn't know of the existence of this rich, marine ecosystem in the eastern corner of Pulau Ubin and for a long time, the nature lovers didn't know either. The marine specialists tend to go diving and while they knew where the corals were, they were not aware of Chek Jawa's existence. The terrestrial people didn't know either as it looks like another mangrove forest when it is submerged. So the spectacular part of Chek Jawa is the littoral zone and only a part of it gets exposed when you have a neap tide and that's so seldom, just a few days each month. That is why I love these liminal encounters as they are "neither nor"—neither here nor there, neither green nor blue.

Anyway, it was a totally serendipitous discovery when some of our members were taking a group of RGS students on a nature walk. They happened to be in the right place at the right time. The abundance of marine life there is truly stunning and anyone who sees it for the first time cannot believe their eyes! You wouldn't think that Singapore has that sort of rich, marine life.

It was such a spectacle and it's richer than any artificial construct such as, say, Sentosa, because it's real and changing all the time. It is even more amazing that it's ours—it's natural and an interesting counterpoint to Sentosa's multi-million dollar makeovers because those exhibits do become boring and repetitive over time. But nature never does—it is constantly self-renewing.

The problem was, of course, in preserving it—the land had been designated in the master plan for land reclamation in less than a year although there was no stated use for the land yet. So we were really frantic and we didn't have a hope but we went through all the motions of writing to the MP, URA and the Minister.

I was then already the President of Nature Society but I hadn't become an NMP. Besides, my practice is not to clash in public with the government as it didn't seem very constructive for me to do so. I always felt that unless you could give good reasons that would cap their rationale, you really couldn't win, so my policy was that it's always better to collaborate where possible and reserve an open clash as the last resort. At least, I was of the mindset that we had to show that we were working for the same goal, which was for the betterment of Singapore, balancing both progress and well-being. We could agree to disagree that we may want different things as what people want is indeed so diverse.

But Chek Jawa was very different as we just hadn't seen anything like that in Singapore for a long, long time. Everyone went mad. There were those of us who remember what it was like 30, 40 years ago in Singapore when we had a lot more natural beaches but even then it was still spectacular because the biodiversity was so concentrated. Nature had had the time to recover after the last kampong was relocated for the intended reclamation.

Suddenly, everyone started flocking there and we didn't engineer anything. Everyone just wanted to see it. One of the beauties of Chek Jawa, which I have spoken about, is that it's so photogenic. Nature photography usually requires a lot of special equipment and skill. It is very difficult for anyone to just take a good nature photo and share it with everyone. But Chek Jawa is so easy to photograph because it isn't in deep water or at the top of a tree, it is just there—if you happen to be there at the right time. And of course this was when we saw the rise of social media at the turn of the 21st century, and everyone started taking photos on their cellphones and getting on social media. So, we didn't have to do a big media event. Instead, the media themselves were rushing down to take photos. The ordinary men on the street were also heading down to take photos and the place had such tremendous appeal to children.

I'm reminded of Rachel Carson's "sense of wonder" because you had all these kids and they were just gazing at one spot, fascinated, looking at nature as it changed right before their very eyes. The crabs would come out, then the starfish, then the sea anemone would open up as the tide came in. The kids had never seen anything like that and it was so rewarding to see them so enthralled.

Then the-powers-that-be also went down, the various Ministers, the Prime Minister, the President. However, we were on a general consensus that we couldn't turn back the clock as the land had to be reclaimed. We were by then working very closely with NParks and I promised not to make a big public fuss because we had worked well collaboratively and I knew that they were pushing for the same agenda. It also would not have helped the cause for me to go public and criticise the government as a public fight would make them look bad. It would have been unconstructive in this instance, so I decided to approach the matter by playing a low-key, cooperative role.

This, of course, did not earn me brownie points with the rest of the nature people because they wanted me to be more vociferous and I couldn't say, "No, I am not speaking up publicly because I've got this agreement working behind the scenes." I was having closed-door meetings with URA and the Ministry of National Development. This resulted in a lot of other initiatives from individuals and nature lovers who had previously depended on the Nature Society to be the public champion to speak on their behalf.

Anyhow, because they thought we were not proactive, they turned their frustration into action and many independent nature NGOs stood up to voice their opinions. These were largely led by young people and that's how a civic society should act, by a broad-based spontaneous consensus. I think that this is one of the critical factors that made the government change their mind as it was not just one nature NGO standing up, but it was multiple voices, multiple nature NGOs and members of the public who had never shown any interest in nature before. How can you not believe in serendipity?

Anyway, in the meantime, Mr Mah Bow Tan did call all the nature groups and other stakeholder groups together and asked us to put in proposals on how we thought the biodiversity could be saved. But, he made it quite clear that he didn't think it was possible that the reclamation could be reversed. We had to look into translocating the species or provide some other solutions.

There were so many groups and we had initially thought we would put in a joint proposal, but it petered out and everyone decided to do their own thing. However, the diversity of proposals all ended up with one common conclusion which was that it would not be possible to save the biodiversity by any other means except by conserving Chek Jawa.

While we were all working on the proposals to explore ways to save all these rare species of flora and fauna, Mr Mah Bow Tan called us up again. Apparently, the Cabinet had made their decision and the government has decided to reverse the decision to reclaim Chek Jawa. You know, no one was expecting it. We were all in this air-conditioned meeting room in URA, and there was a deafening silence as all of us were so emotionally stunned. Mah Bow Tan asked if anyone going to say anything and that broke the spell and of course everyone cheered! We were all euphoric! It was not just a momentary euphoria as we had all done our best and worked on this together. I can still remember more than 10 years later the transformation of our mood from despair to joy at his announcement of this reprieve.

When Mr Mah made the announcement, he made it quite clear that he was not making any promises to convert this into a nature area but just to reverse the decision to reclaim for the time being, as long as Singapore could afford to do so. I used to resent that phrase "for as long as possible" always being applied to nature areas, but now, as I reflect on this, I actually rather respect the decision because to say "forever" could be an over-promise. No one can promise “forever”, so promising “as long as we can” was as good as it gets.

This was a real instance of how the government and civil society came together spontaneously and worked together. This event was, of course, later cited in four National Day speeches and even the PM used this to illustrate how the government and civil society can work together for a national goal. Personally, I saw this as a defining moment as to what my national identity was all about. It was such an emotional time for me.

Some may say that marine biodiversity is hardly an ingredient for Singapore’s national identity. But it’s actually the combined effort to protect it, and the fact that the marine life has been around a lot longer than we have, that added a lot of depth to what it means to be a Singaporean.

In fact, when I was giving an interview to URA for the archives, one of the youngest persons interviewing me shared with me that she was a student when it happened over a decade ago and yet she told me that she felt this bond of a shared experience over Chek Jawa and that it was a very different experience from, say, the National Day Parade, which is staged. It gives me great satisfaction to feel part of a collective memory that has brought so much pleasure and meaning to so many people here.

Is that the catalyst that made you decide to take on the role of Nominated Member of Parliament?

Yes, that was partly what made me go to Parliament. Prior to that, I didn’t even know if I really believed I could make a difference because as an NMP, you don’t represent any constituency so who or what are you really speaking for? But after Chek Jawa, I really felt that people who want to conserve and protect nature in Singapore were under-represented or not represented at all, so I didn’t mind sticking my neck out in Parliament and counter the belief amongst those who think that all Singaporeans are interested in is the cost of living. Indeed, Chek Jawa was a great experience for me because it was one of the most important memories of my life. I put it as an experience equivalent to becoming a mother and my daughter totally agrees.

Speaking of your daughter, did you plan for motherhood and how did you juggle that with your career?

Of course, I planned to be a mother, and if I may so say, I think I am quite a good mother. Why shouldn't I plan to be a mother? While I had some problems juggling work and motherhood, I really enjoyed becoming a mother and I still enjoy it, because being a mother is forever.

My daughter was a great little girl. I don't believe in trying to cater too much to kids and we continued to do whatever we liked to do. I would take her to art exhibitions, museums, nature walks and trips even when she was still a baby. I carried her in a kangaroo pouch and she was very well-behaved and adaptable. Children have a tremendous capacity for stimulation and I never believed in talking down to them or underestimating them but instead exposing them to as many ideas and environments as possible.

My daughter is a great companion and especially in those early years, it allowed me to see everything with a fresh pair of eyes. I began to appreciate everything that was stale to me as I saw it from her point of view. Motherhood also gave me a more extended perspective. Instead of looking into my own lifespan, I started to look beyond and imagined what the world was going to be like in the more distant future. This is why I've brought up issues on climate change very early on in Parliament, even though most people did not really pay much attention to it at that time.

Motherhood is one of the most exciting and educational journeys I've ever been on. By the time my daughter was born, I was already 32, but I felt that it was going to be difficult to be a mother and study my postgraduate at the same time. I was on a Colombo Scholarship administered by the Ministry of Health.

In those days, there was a fine print that read: if you are pregnant you have to come straight back without completing your course. We were clearly not promoting motherhood then and I know people who actually had to quit their scholarships to return home when they got pregnant. So that was another example of short-sighted policies. That was why I had to time my pregnancy after I completed my fellowship.

By then, it was not easy to find out I was not as fertile and had to wait for over a year.

So yes, it was tough to juggle. Anyway, I did become a surgeon before I became a mother. I could have been a mother more than once but it didn't work out. But it's better to have one child than none at all.

My daughter has very definite preferences and passions from a young age and is a great animal and nature lover. She really pulled me out of my comfort zone and I ended up doing a lot of things I might not have done without her prompting. For instance, many people think it was I who got her interested in nature but in fact, although I do enjoy nature, it was she who is much more passionate about her interests and spurred me on to get more involved.

Knowing what you know now about yourself, what would you have done differently?
I would have lived with more awareness, appreciation and enjoyment.

If your life philosophy was a car bumper sticker, what would it say?
Be Inclusive, Not Exclusive.

What are your greatest strengths and weaknesses?
I think my strengths and weaknesses are two sides of the same coin. I have a wide diversity of interests that help me see things more holistically and make connections, but this also means I'm easily distracted and can find it difficult to focus. I also have a bad habit of talking too much rather than listening. I'm working on that and I find that listening is very rewarding!

What irks you?
That humans have persisted in thinking we are separate from the rest of the living world. This has resulted in a lot of damage done including to our own species, not to mention the loss of valuable knowledge resulting from this distorted perspective.

What would you like to tell climate change disbelievers?
Your children and their children will suffer, and they will know that you are responsible.

Pick one thing from nature that best represents you?
Too presumptuous perhaps, but I would love to be a tree or a bird or even running water.

How do you want to be remembered?
I don't mind being forgotten. Leave it to posterity.

What will your epitaph say?
She came from the earth and is happy to return to it.

When you meet God, what would you say?
I'll leave the talking to God.

What do you identify with: the Madonna archetype, the Maverick or any other M word?
Maverick, of course!

The Power Paralympian

THERESA GOH

Theresa Goh Rui Si is a Singaporean swimmer and Paralympic medalist. She won bronze in the 100m breaststroke at the 2016 Summer Paralympics and holds the world records for the 50m and 200m breaststroke events.

She received the 2001 Sportsgirl Merit Award from the Singapore Disability Sports Council (SDSC) and was named Sportsgirl of the Year in 2002 and 2003. From 2004 to 2006, she was the SDSC's Sportswoman of the Year. Theresa received a special award at the SDSC's Sports Superstar Awards 2007 for outstanding achievements in swimming, and in August that year she was conferred the Pingat Bakti Masyarakat (Public Service Medal) in the National Day Awards.

***

Listening to Theresa's recorded interview, she sounds just like your typical, well-adjusted Gen Y-er—that incredibly sophisticated, tech- and media-savvy generation who has been exposed to endless marketing since early childhood. Her Singlish accent makes her hugely approachable, much like your average girl next door, except that Theresa is no girl next door. She is a top athlete who has represented Singapore internationally and has even been awarded the Public Service Medal for her achievements in the pool. Above all, her cheerful and warm disposition does not betray any hint that she was born without the use of her limbs due to a birth defect known as spina bifida. Her exuberance and confidence wins you over and none's the wiser.

She arrived for our interview in her wheelchair and wheeled herself easily and comfortably into Ben & Jerry's on the third floor where we had agreed to meet. Theresa Goh is very much as able as you and me—she had not ask for any concessions to meet at a wheelchair accessible spot or anything. In fact, she is certainly more able than me who was in a full brace because of a surfing accident and needed a walking aid!

One of the key takeaways from Theresa is the notion that we should not lower the bar for people with disabilities even as we strive as a nation and society to level the playing field. It may sound like an oxymoron but it isn't. Simply put, she urges us all to see disability not as a lack of but as a difference. Theresa makes a crucial point that in order for society to move ahead, we must recognise and accept our diversity and differences. Rather than keep navel-gazing, we should reach out to see how we can level the playing field by focusing on the similarities or the objectives we are trying to achieve.

Theresa is also no Pollyanna. While she has for the most part been spared the cruelty of bullies, she is well aware that the world can be a mean place and has shared with me that given a choice, she would rather not birth a child with her condition. I found this thought sobering—here is a woman who has triumphed in spite of herself but is unwilling to have another follow in her footsteps, which tells me—Dear World, there is still so much we can work on.

In fact, Theresa opted to come out as a lesbian in June this year and became a Pink Dot Ambassador. It was not an easy decision as most athletes choose to remain in the closet, and this is Singapore, after all. However, Theresa felt the need to embrance and live her life authentically and decided to make public her sexual identity both as a personal statement as well as making a courageous show of her support for the LGBTQIA community, and for human rights and the freedom to love.

Indeed, Theresa is inspiring not because she is a person with disabilities. She inspires because she has the strength and tenacity to surmount the odds to become a top athlete. She has been able to achieve more than what most able-bodied persons can achieve. And she has done so with much good cheer, kindness of heart and generosity of spirit. That, in my books, is a champion any day, able-bodied or otherwise.

***

Aside from medals and swimming prowess, share with us more about you, your family and your childhood.

I am the oldest of three and have two younger siblings, a sister and a brother who are both able-bodied. When my parents were planning to have my sister, they wanted to have a closer age gap as they didn't want me to be alone. They wanted me to have a sibling I could relate to, talk to and play with. My brother came into the picture, four or five years later by accident, but of course, we love him all the same. We grew up really close and my whole family is very close-knit. Of course, we have our own fair share of issues growing up as teenagers and all families have their own problems but we are always able to overcome anything together and we are as close as we can possibly get.

When I was born, thorough screenings weren't accessible and there was a lack of technology at that time. Throughout my mother's prenatal checkups, my parents had no reason to suspect anything. They assumed they would have a normal birth and a completely normal child with no complications. But when I was born, the doctors took me away from my mum and didn't tell her why. Of course she was very worried. The doctors then found out that I had spina bifida, which in basic, simple terms, means that my spinal cord did not fuse up properly and that affected my lower limbs and parts of my body. The thing about spina bifida is that the higher the location of the infection in the spine, the more parts of the body will be affected. My spina bifida is present in the middle of my spine so it only affects my lower limbs. I know if it had been higher, it would have affected my brain as well. Some of the spina bifida kids I met have shunts in the back of their brains to drain out the fluids.

When I was born, my parents were really worried. They had to measure the circumference of my head everyday just to make sure it wasn't growing bigger. I feel really lucky that I don't have a shunt, as my life would have been so different otherwise. From the time I was born, my parents were amazing. Of course, I am sure they had their moments of shock and fear, but they didn't dwell. They started becoming very proactive in researching on all the different ways they can help make me become as independent as possible.

In the days before the Internet, my mum started reading through the Yellow Pages to find out more about spina bifida. It took a lot of work back then, but they finally found a specialist who has dealt with spina bifida and they went to look for him. I ended up undergoing surgery when I was three months old to close the hole in my spine. I later had a couple of other surgeries on my legs and my hips before I was six or seven years old. Spina bifida requires me to go for yearly checkups to track my progress as it affects the bladder and I am unable to feel from my knees down. The doctors have to check on a number of things to see if I am improving, deteriorating or remaining constant.

As a baby, it was really hard for me to crawl as I would fracture my knees or my hip and my parents would have to take me to the hospital. Looking back, I should have been a lot more careful. I also had a catheter to enable me to pee and my mum had to help me all the time back then. Today, I'm very independent but my mum was there when my dad had to work. I was prone to urine infections too as I was careless in my youth.

So I was always in and out of hospital a lot and all the nurses and doctors knew me. Every time I was discharged from hospital, I would receive a present from my parents so I would always look forward to the end of my hospital visits.

My parents made sure that I didn't get special treatment as much and as far as possible. If I fell down, they'll help me up but they would also discipline me as a means of teaching me so that it made me feel normal. They wanted me to be raised "normally" and receive equal treatment as my sister instead of spoiling me. If I did something wrong, I would get scolded or even caned so I grew up without thinking too much about my disability. In all honesty, I didn't even realise consciously that I had a disability.

It was only when was much older and started to go to school that other people really opened my eyes and made me see how different I was. It was not that they treated me differently or poorly, but that I realised I needed a wheelchair or a pair of crutches to go to toilet which the regular able-bodied child would not require. Throughout my entire school life, everyone was very helpful and my classmates would even carry me up four flights of stairs so I can get to the computer labs. How could you ask for anything more than classmates who would help so willingly without expecting anything back? As a result, I grew up never really focusing on my disability nor was I kept cooped up in the house.

My parents were always very insistent on my achieving independence and set about to make sure that I could do almost anything on my own. I started reading about mindsets as I knew that in time, I would have to rely on myself and had to achieve full independence, even though my siblings were always helpful whenever help was needed. I don't know how they saw me from their point of view, whether they felt I was different from them, but the truth is, I was really happy growing up as a child. Maybe I should ask them one day but the fact is, I always felt that I had a pretty normal childhood. As a family, we played, we would eat out, head to swimming pool and did "normal" things. The only exception was that I spent a lot of time in the hospital.

Do you recall any bullying or negative encounters growing up?

I do not recall any negative encounters. I knew of a few of my able-bodied friends who were bullied in school. They were called names and I just cannot fathom how people can do that. I wasn't bullied and was, in fact, treated extremely well. It could be that most people overcompensated and treated me exceptionally nicely. My teachers were always helpful. In fact, when I was in secondary school, they kept me in the same classroom for five whole years so I never had to change my classroom venue!

My primary school was wheelchair accessible so I could move around easily. If the lift broke down, the teachers would carry me. It's just no big deal—if I needed help, I'll receive help which contributed a lot to making me feel included and never feeling left out. The only thing I didn't do was PE (Physical Education). It was also in part because I had already started swimming by the time I was in secondary school and had my own form of physical activity that I did every week. I think my teacher saw that as a good reason for me to not partake in PE with the rest of the students and exempted me.

Why and how did you start swimming and how did that become a serious part of your life?

I started swimming at five years old for fun, as any child would. I would go to a public pool with my family and played around, splashed water and start swimming simply for sheer enjoyment. Many kids enjoy being in the water because it makes you feel weightless and it certainly feels very different than when you are on land.

When I was about twelve, one of the volunteers from Singapore Disability Sports Council (SDSC) spotted me in the pool with my dad and asked him to take me to the upcoming National Disability Swimming Champs just to try it out. My parents said "why not" since I was swimming anyway and enrolled me in the competition. I ended up doing pretty well and was later selected for their training programs. That was my introduction to SDSC and how I started to learn about swimming, wheelchair tennis and horseback riding. There were so many different sports that I could choose from and try out. I tried out whatever I could get my hands on but I really enjoyed swimming and wheelchair tennis. Horseback riding was also quite fun and I recall riding around the tent with candy cane posts during the Christmas seasons. Horseback riding really trains your core and it was great fun being on the horse.

It came to a point where I had to choose one activity to focus on as I was doing way too much which took up too much time. Needless to say, I chose swimming. I selected it above the other sports as I really enjoyed it and loved how I felt in the water, and of course, it was also because I was doing really well. So I joined the program though it was not as well-supported as it is today. The coaches were all volunteers. I remember at one point, I was training five times a week with a different coach every day. All of the coaches were pretty good considering the amount of time each coach puts in—they gave whatever they could. Without them, there would have been no swimming program, so I really appreciated them, plus it helped that it was really fun.

One of the things I really enjoyed was the group dynamics. We were swimmers of different age and abilities, but we would all have fun in the pool. We were training, of course, but we thoroughly enjoyed each other's company. There was always a lot of laughter and we went through everything together. That was one of the key things that kept me in swimming—it was definitely because of the people. As time went by, I got increasingly better. It definitely helped a lot that I got more professional, full-time coaches. My first professional coach was Uncle Siong, better known to all as Ang Peng Siong. Before him, I had Edmund Lee. He is still coaching now and I am always grateful to him for training me to reach my personal best before I was to learn and train under Uncle Siong.

When I first met Uncle Siong around 2002 in the Commonwealth Games, he was not our coach yet though he was coaching able-bodied swimmers. He got to know us and we started talking and he got personally interested in taking on the program. So after the Commonwealth Games, the SDSC got him on board and he started training a couple of other swimmers and I. He was my first, full-time, regularly-paid coach. It was something new to all of us. It felt as if we were breaking new grounds, and I soon saw a really huge improvement in my timings and started to feel really strong and fast.

Uncle Siong had been a coach for a very long time so his experience, programs and his intense focus on me really helped. He certainly knew what he was doing. This is not to say that the other coaches didn't know what they're doing but he was certainly better as he was very technical. When I first joined him, I had a full two weeks of drills that I found so boring, but it was what was needed to make me swim faster because I had to get very smooth in my technique in order to progress. The key, I learnt, was for me to be on my side as much as possible as, because when you are face down with your head towards the floor, you have the most amount of resistance. These technical things were all new to me then.

Techniques have changed a lot over the years so there are always new drills. We would spend at least two hours on drills, followed by our entry into the water. We had to keep repeating these technical details as it required a lot of muscle memory. Once you do it often, your muscle remembers and you start to perform the actions without even thinking about it. I had two-hour drills every day for two to three weeks and I must say, it was so tedious but I learned so much from that and that was really important.

I had to make sure I got my technique down pat because even if I was fast and powerful, I would be wasting all my power and strength without the proper techniques. That was one of the biggest difference learning from Uncle Siong. I realised that while I was already technically more efficient than others, I needed to really master my technique to excel. That really helped to push me forward to the next level. By the time I headed to the Athens Paralympics, I participated in seven events and I made it to all the seven finals. That was beyond anything I had ever expected. I was 17 when I went for my first Paralympics game and was 21 when I was at my second. I have participated in three so far.

Which was the most memorable?

My first Paralympics was the most memorable as I had no expectations and went in just to challenge myself as a total newbie. I just wanted to make my personal best so making it to all seven finals was beyond my wildest dreams. I didn't win a medal at that time. I then headed to the Beijing Paralympics where I was hoping that I would place top three but I ended up in either 4th or 5th. Because I missed out on the medal, I became bent on getting one.

The Beijing Games was also memorable as it was where I felt my first real failure. It was probably the first time I ever cried over anything aside from the death of someone I knew. It was my first crushing defeat and I suffered pain, disappointment and devastation. I felt that I had spent four years training full-time for one event and still failed to get a medal. That incident left me so sad I had to stop swimming for a while as I just couldn't bear to be in the environment anymore. I didn't hate swimming but I felt so negative about myself. I beat myself up for not achieving and tried powerlifting for nine months. I wanted to do everything else but swim. In hindsight, I realised that even though I gave my best, there were others who were better than me. They did their best too. That's just how life is and just because I expected to win didn't mean I will win.

How did you come to this realization and when did you finally go back to swimming?

I went back only much later. Even after nine months, the wound was still fresh. But around that time, I realised no one dared to talk to me. I started to feel that if I wanted to continue powerlifting, I could not continue swimming or it will make it extremely hard to go back because each sport focused on and used different muscle groups. So I needed to make a decision. I asked myself if I really wanted to quit swimming, and the answer was "no". I knew I still had more to give. It was not easy to head back as there were many changes that happened in the interim. Even though I was still under Uncle Siong's club, APSC (Aquatic Performance Swim Club), he was not coaching me, but rather, it was one of the other club coaches.

I think at that time I was half-hearted. I wanted a life aside from swimming but I also wanted to train really hard. I was indecisive but the London Paralympics came around. It was to be my third Paralympics. I thought to myself, I would not be as hard on myself and would take things a little easier. For Beijing, I trained for four straight years non-stop, and was in training camps and competitions. Compared to that, what I did for the London was easy-peasy and paled in comparison. I was training but I felt as if I wasn't at my peak, all I wanted was to do my best. So I went to London with lower expectations and was more at ease. I enjoyed my swims and the experience of being at the Paralympics again. The environment and climate felt very different from all the other competitions.

In 2013, one of our coaches left for the U.S. to teach swimming which coincided with Pin Xiu and me receiving our sports scholarships. We were basically given the opportunity to train full-time and were fully sponsored. It was that very moment that I felt I had to be 100% committed if I was to take this on. I wondered if my body could handle another bout of full-time training and I decided that I did have more to give. Somehow, a new fire has been reignited within me for the first time since my loss in Beijing.

Over the next few years, I rediscovered my love for swimming and was so glad I did not give up. I was thankful to be given the scholarship and decided to dedicate the next few years of my life to the sport. I was, however, determined to pursue my passion in a smarter way. I learnt that I had allowed my whole world to revolve around swimming so much so that there's no room for anything else. I was probably stressing and burning myself out without knowing it, which certainly didn't help my emotional well-being.

Today, I train and live more consciously. Yes, I am getting paid and am under a contractual agreement, but I am training because I know I want to and not because anyone is saying I have to. This is a totally different mindset from the past when I felt as if I had to do it as an obligation. I feel as if I have been given a second chance and know that I am in a better state of mind. Whether I win or lose, I will have completely no regrets about what happens.

Back in the day, I would force myself to train and be unhappy about it, but today, I consciously choose to go for training. I am at peace and am happy. I like this balanced mindset which allows me time for friends, family, myself and of course, for training. There's a lot more self-awareness and I do not live life simply by going through the motions and not thinking about the consequences.

Has the level of support for para-athletes changed over the years? Share with us the changes you have experienced and what do you think needs to be done to take us forward?

One thing for sure is that support has increased tremendously. Case in point: I used to have volunteer coaches and now have a dedicated full-time coach. Disability sports is taken more seriously now even though we may still receive less media coverage. This could be seen as more an effect of demand and supply. Fewer people are interested in disability sports so there is less coverage. So this recent Asian Paralympic Games was really amazing. It was a game changer as we had huge outpouring of public support. People came to watch the Games. Sure, it may have a smaller turnout than the SEA games, but still, the size of the crowds was something we have never seen before. The amount of support after the Games was so profuse it was overwhelming.

Back in the day, my news would be covered in the Home section of *The Straits Times* which really felt like a slap in the face as you were not seen as a real sportsperson despite your efforts. Today, our news is featured in the Sports section, which is a significant change as this means we are now recognised as sports personalities. Granted, I'm not the kind to push for more as I'm always grateful for whatever I get, but I am thankful for this change in Singaporean mindsets. I was never bitter or upset as I knew the reporters were doing their jobs so I am thankful the powers that be have had a change in perspective. We certainly have more support these days. I wish it could have come sooner but I am just glad I'm around to see it happen and experience the whole paradigm shift. This really is a blessing as I came very close to quitting—I am very glad I persisted.

Based on your international experience and exposure, what observations can you make of how other cultures view athletes and para-athletes? What can we learn from them?

I will answer this based on what I have heard and my own observations. In order to achieve equality between para-athletes and athletes in certain very progressive nations, many people have had to put in a lot of hard work. I understand this as I myself have experienced differences in treatment. I am aware Singapore is still learning, and I know deep down, many Singaporeans still do not see us in the same light as able-bodied athletes, which is why they are not able to treat us the same.

For most, they feel that everything a person with disability does is amazing but that's not true. I would like to challenge them to have the ability to see our achievements alongside an able-bodied person and then be inspired thereafter. Don't set the bar lower for us. I would like to be inspiring for setting a world record—that's great! But don't be inspired simply just because I can swim, many can do that too. I hope for the day where most people could see us on an equal platform, minus our disability. If you keep emphasizing our disability then it will be hard to achieve equality.

There's a difference being able to see all abilities as equal and being focused on the differences. For example, there is a wall in front of you and you have a tall person and a person who is half that height side by side. If you place them both the same block, the tall person gets a boost to see over the wall but the shorter person still can't. When you talk about equality, it's not about both having the same thing per se. It's very different. What is key is to place them on a platform of varying heights so that both can see beyond the wall, and they will both have an equal ability to start from the same point of view. That is the part many have a harder time grasping. Many think that because I gave you the same platform, you must be able to achieve the same heights, but it is not the same. It depends on whether the platform is the right shape or the right height to help people overcome the initial barrier.

Here's another example. When I was growing up, if I had seen more athletes with disabilities or people who live like me in the news, I would have felt more "normal". But I didn't, so I always knew I was different from everyone else. The lack of diversity, difference and representation is why my disability became so pointed. I also don't agree that we should focus on abilities as this is not about making me feel better than an able-bodied person but it is more about starting us on a platform that allows us to see the same thing, even if it has to be different—that is when we can all see eye to eye.

There is equality when I feel that I no longer have to worry about unequal treatment. Able-bodied athletes are already seen as athletes simply because they are able-bodied. But para-athletes are only seen as amazing when they show how they manage to overcome their disabilities. They are not really commended for their athletic prowess. I want to be seen as good because I'm a good swimmer on my own merit, and not because I cannot walk but am able to swim. But I know that's a hard one to shake.

By that same token, there must also be a camp that plays up their disability?

Yes, indeed there is. And while it irks me, I cannot blame them as they grew up with these mindsets. I never grew up with a disability mindset though. I also worked hard to learn, read and be open to new experiences, and to challenge and form my own. Perhaps my perspective will change but right now, it is what it is and I cannot really expect everyone to be on the same platform as me. Similarly, there are also some athletes with disabilities who feel that they should receive special treatment and have everything given to them.

You have won all these awards but which moment in your career was the most significant and why?

I don't think all the past achievements are important as most people only remember what is current. Yes, I may have won a medal in the APG (ASEAN Para Games) but they may not know of all my other successes. People forget so it is not the achievements that matter but the kind of person I have become, or the stories I leave behind that is of more consequence.

I have taken part in so many games and won so many different medals and trophies but they don't mean as much as the experiences I've gone through. Of all the games I participated in, probably the most important was the very first one—the one that started it all. It was also in Singapore. I still have my very first national medal together with the very first medal I won internationally on my wall. They always say the first step is the hardest so if I hadn't taken part in my first competition, I wouldn't know where I'll be or if I'll even be here today.

In Singapore, we place a premium on education so even athletes have to do well in school. What are your sentiments about the Sports School?

In the Sports School, the school curriculum is more suited to an athlete's lifestyle, which is good, but on the whole, there is still a lot of societal pressure. I feel that the average Singaporean looks at athletes as supernaturals or robots, and thinks that they should be able to do everything, both school and sport. They seem to be held to a higher moral code as well.

Do you think that we have different definitions of success for different people? And if so, what can we as a society do to change these mindsets?

Yes, we do have different definitions of success for different people. In order for society to change, we, for one, have to be able to deal with failure better and expect that people will fail. You cannot always expect to see someone do well consecutively for three Games and then slam them when they don't do very well on their fourth. Thereafter, most people will focus only on the glaring failure instead of his or her past successes. I think the average person still possesses the mindset that is unable to view the athlete as a human being too. I think that's really harmful.

We should learn to fail. We should start them young and let them know that it is okay if your kids fail their tests sometimes. I think kids these days are really afraid of showing their parents that they have failed as they fear the repercussions. It is understandable to want your kids to be successful but parents also have to give them tools to guide them if they don't do well and instill confidence. They must also reassure them that failure is temporary and that there are other means of measuring success—such as being a nice person. Being a kind person is more important than being a smart person.

Have you ever been angry with your disability?

Honestly, no. I've never been angry about my disability perhaps because I grew up with it and my family has always been really supportive. I had a really peaceful, blessed, positive life and I'm thankful for that. I can understand how some may not be as fortunate as me and may feel angry at their circumstances and question why this is happening to them. I would imagine that those who were dealt with a disability later in life may be more negative, cynical or bitter about the situation. For me personally, I've never felt anger.

How do you deal with naysayers?

The first time I applied for the sports scholarship I was turned down and that was a slap in the face as I felt as if they did not believe in me. Of course I understood there were different criteria but at first, I was really disappointed and saw it as a setback as it meant that I would not be able to train full-time.

But on hindsight, maybe the time wasn't right and I figured that they probably wanted to see more achievements from me. On the year of the APG, I performed well and that helped me secure the scholarship. It was really good timing as we got our new coach and my old coach went off to the U.S. to teach swimming so I think everything happened for a reason and it was a blessing in disguise that I received my scholarship later.

Do you think your middle-class standing aided you to overcome your challenges?

I think that probably played a part. If I were born into a lower-income family, it may be a lot harder to get to where I am now so I'm blessed that we were able to do what we did and receive the medical support that I did. The medical bills are crazily expensive and I don't know how my parents did it. If I was born in a different situation, with different parents in a different income bracket, everything could have been different. In my case, everything worked out so that I could be here today.

If you met a genie and it gave you a choice to be able-bodied or be who you are now, what would you do?

Someone asked me this question recently. In the world we live in right now, it's definitely much easier being an able-bodied person. If it were so simple to choose, I would choose to be able-bodied for sure—not because I am not proud of who I am but because it's so much easier and I don't have to worry. But there's also a part of me that knows that I am the person I am because of my disability—the things I know, the way I think. I have been able to shape my mind and I wouldn't want to change anything too as I may end up an able-bodied person and an asshole! It is a complicated question to answer as I have definitely wished things could be easier for me, my parents and my family, but I'm really proud of who I am.

Have you ever been in a relationship and is it hard to find love as a person with disabilities?

I've never been in one. I have looked around but I've never been in an exclusive relationship. I don't think it is too hard for a person with disability to date in Singapore as I do know many of my friends who are dating, in a relationship or married. Perhaps it is me, as I did feel that I am not good enough to be with someone when I was younger. That may have contributed to my not being in a relationship.

Today, I'm much more confident and am in a better place. I don't think it's a priority in that I am not looking for anyone to date or be with. If it happens, great, but of course, I cannot just do nothing. I do think it is much easier now to consider dating as there is much more awareness on living with people with disabilities. There is more visibility on TV and online so I hope that one day, an able-bodied person may see that dating a person with disability is a viable option as well.

I read Nick Vujicic's book, *Life Without Limbs*, and in it, he wrote that he was once afraid no able-bodied person would marry him. Do you have the same reservations?
It is more our own mindsets than someone else's. There are many things to work through in a relationship anyway, able-bodied person or not. That is why communication is so important and one must be able to have discussions and be able to talk about anything with your partner. Right now, I'm at a place where I'm happy with who I am, my own body and the type of person I am. I am more willing to be open to someone else as well.

This is a hypothetical question. You shared that your parents had no idea about your condition when your mother was expecting. If you or your spouse is expecting a child diagnosed with a disability, would you choose to birth it into this world?
If I could have a child and knew that it has a disability, it would depend on what sort of disability and how severe it is. I would have to consider my financial situation, my partner's conditions and we would have to discuss. I really cannot say for sure, but if I have to decide right now, I would say I would not go on with it as I know how the world is. If I am unable to handle it then it may not be fair to bring this child to the world. After all, it's my choice and no matter how much potential the world has to become more and more progressive and accepting, I still think it can be a hard life. In the end, I want the best for my child. So I will say, if you ask me at this very moment, I wouldn't go ahead with it. It's just not fair.

Do you see any difference in the treatment of athletes based on their gender?

I do feel there's a difference though it is hard for me to articulate. Some of the more successful para-athletes in Singapore are female and those doing well are always in the headlines as the media likes these stories.

But I think, the difference in treatment is less male or female, but more abled or disabled. The standard view of an "able-bodied person" is to have two arms and two legs, standing. So I guess it may be hard to find the ideal, disabled body as there are various disabilities and the majority may have a shallow view on what an athletic, disabled body looks like as they are too accustomed to seeing the "normal" body.

However, this is not to say there is no outright discrimination of gender. For me, I'm more butch-looking and they are used to seeing more feminine looking athletes, whether able-bodied or not. I think there is more emphasis and expectation on how a gender should look like. So female athletes and para-athletes are expected to look feminine, just as the men are expected to look masculine.

So yes, I feel more discriminated in this regard especially in the past. It is better now and they are more respectful of how I look and want to look. In the past, I would be styled awkwardly feminine in the photo shoots and it always made me so uncomfortable but they didn't seem to care and would remark, "Oh, you look so pretty" while I am telling them I don't care to look pretty or feminine. Have you seen those photos? I was so uncomfortable and that was one of the more glaring type of discrimination that I have felt.

What do you do on your time off?

Read, watch TV and surf the Internet.

If you had your life philosophy on a car bumper sticker, what would it say?

Be kind, be brave and be yourself.

What's left on your bucket list?

I don't like to have a bucket list as I could die tomorrow, touch wood! But I don't want to regret not doing anything so if I want to do something, I'll do it now. Last year, I went skydiving for the first time with Pin Xiu, her boyfriend and my sister. I wanted to skydive to relax so we did it even though it was not on my bucket list. In fact, I didn't even think about it until I did it. I also wanted to go travelling solo so I went to book a trip. I thought about how I would get around but I wanted to do it, so I did.

Knowing what you know now, what would you say to your younger self?

Be patient and be open to new experiences.

How do you want to be remembered?

As a kind person.

What would you say if you met God?

Oh you exist?

Will you say you are more Madonna, Maverick or any other M word?

(*laughter*) So many M words to choose from! I would call myself more of a Maverick than a Madonna.

The People's Advocate

HALIMAH YACOB

Legally-trained Halimah spent over three decades as a unionist with the country's powerful National Trades Union Congress, and became a PAP Member of Parliament in 2001. She became a Minister of State in 2011 and was appointed Speaker of the House in 2013. The mother of five is a Member of Parliament for Marsiling-Yew Tee GRC (Group Representation Constituency), Marsiling Division.

***

Publisher's Note: At the time of press, Halimah has indicated that she may run for President in the coming election in response to reporters' queries.

Speaking to Halimah was strangely easy and fuss-free. I had anticipated more red tape, bureaucracy and surveillance but her personal assistant was swift and prompt. Like clockwork, I was ushered into the austere grounds of Parliament House with little more than a mandatory security check typical of a post-September 11 world we have all become accustomed to.

For the uninitiated, Halimah Yacob is the ninth Speaker of the House, the first woman ever elected to that post. She presides over the sittings of the House and enforces the rules prescribed in the Standing Orders of Parliament for the orderly conduct of parliamentary business. This is no child's play and Halimah runs a tight ship. I had thought that I would be gaining little real insights into her life. As a prominent politician, all that has to be said and can be published for public consumption is already out there. Yet, I must admit that our interview remains one of my most memorable, because she is genuinely, in my humble opinion, a people magnet, a servant leader and a kindred spirit. On top of that, she is also a mother, a wife and a daughter.

Whilst a large part of our interview features her career as well as the challenges she faced along the way, a sizeable portion is dedicated to the memory of her late mother who passed away on Election Day in 2015 and whom she adores and misses dearly. Halimah's honest and heartfelt tribute to her remains one of the key takeaways of our interview. One walks away feeling that she is very much a woman shaped by her poverty-stricken years, having witnessed her mother's struggles to single-handedly raise five children after her father's untimely demise.

At work, her love, fierce affection and loyalty for the people is driven by her ability to sympathise; her compassion stemming from having been in the shoes of the downtrodden. The self-professed *ponteng* queen once questioned her worth and decided to challenge herself to be better, to do more and scale the economic ladder. The aim then was to provide her mother and siblings with a better life. But today, she is able to extend her hope for more equitable welfare to a much larger group of society.

***

So, you say you are a very private person.

Yes, but once you enter the public office, it's not so private anymore. I try my very best to keep some private space as I think that's necessary to keep my sanity. Anyway, the nature of my job probably did not require that in the early days.

I started out in the Labour Movement in 1978 after I graduated with an LLB (Honours) degree from the then University of Singapore (now National University of Singapore) and that became a very significant chapter of my life. I spent 33 solid years in the Labour Movement until I became the Minister of State in 2011. Those were very good years as the experience really shaped my perceptions and sharpened my skills.

What would have prompted a young girl to join the male-dominated Labour Movement three decades ago?

You're quite right. In those days, it was even more difficult to find active women leaders in the Labour Movement. The first meeting I attended after I joined NTUC was in a room with 20 cigarette-smoking men. I was very happy when they decided to ban smoking in the meeting rooms and offices later. Back then, I would feel so unhappy coming out of a meeting as all my clothes would smell of smoke. But that was the kind of atmosphere and environment that one worked with in the seventies.

But the people were very passionate and they knew what they were talking about. They may not have degrees and high levels of education, but never underestimate them. They knew their ground and their issues very well. They knew how to deal with management and they can teach you many things. So, I cut my teeth in the Labour Movement and learnt so much from my time there.

Although I was a Law graduate, I knew that when the unionists came to seek help, it was not because of my degree. It is because they felt that I was approachable and was able to help them resolve their problems. Once you win their trust, it's a lot easier for them to accept your advice. You see, the Labour Movement is a place that teaches you the importance of trust. You have to build trust—trust with the union leaders and the workers, because along the way, and I can attest to that in my 33 years, you sometimes have to make very difficult decisions.

Such as?
The CPF cuts that we had to agree to, for example. We were faced with a very difficult economic climate and we had to help employers cut costs quickly and save jobs. If there is trust, the union leaders know that you are acting in the workers' best interest and they are prepared to support you. And by "best", I mean, the CPF cuts helped to cut job losses and ensured a faster recovery in the economy. So, trust is crucial.

The same applies in politics too. You need to secure the confidence of the people you serve. If they trust you, then half the battle is won as they know you are not there for personal, selfish reasons; instead, you are there because you want to serve them and this can be seen through your actions.

So, this career to serve the people was very much a calling. What do you think impacted you as a child or as a young person growing up that made you want to serve the masses?
I suppose it was because of my family background. My father died when I was eight years old. My mother was a single mum raising five children. She struggled very hard. We cannot underestimate how serious an impact poverty can have on people. It can be very debilitating as you struggle daily to survive, put food on the table and also grapple with the uncertainty of the future. It can limit your choices.

After my father had died, my mother went to help in a food stall to earn a living. She was a very good cook and I helped her there. In the mornings, I would help her with the marketing. In the evenings, when I was done with school, I would join her again. If I was in the school's afternoon session, I would follow her to the stall, help her to set it up by arranging the chairs and the tables and prepare the ingredients for cooking. After that, I would head home around 10 a.m. to get ready for school. That was my daily routine and I never had a chance to enjoy my school holidays which were all spent helping my mum in the stall.

At one Edusave Bursary Awards ceremony, I shared with the children that when I was their age, 10 years old, I knew how to make coffee. Not the 3-in-1 version, in those days, where got 3-in-1? I made coffee from scratch. I shared that I had to boil the water, know exactly how much coffee powder to add and I even knew how much coffee would come out of the filter. I knew how to make it *gau* or strong, how much condensed milk to add for the perfect cup. On weekends, I would help my mother to wash the dishes, wipe the tables and serve the customers. I reminded the children that I knew all that at 10 years old! Those were survival skills.

At their age, I also knew how to select and buy good fish—my mother taught me to look at the gills, to press the flesh to check for firmness and freshness. I didn't read all that from books. I learnt through real-life experience. In those days, we don't go to the supermarket to pick up nicely packed chicken or ready to cook fish.

Yes, we had live chickens in the coop back in those days.

Yes! Live chickens in those coops! My mother taught me to place my hands into the coop where there is a small opening and learn how to feel for the chicken. I was to feel the chicken's breast. If it was too thin with not much flesh, then that's a skinny chicken and I was not to buy it. She taught me to look out for plump chickens as they would have more meat. And I was to also look at the chicken's crown to check for its age. If it was fat but old, then the meat would be too tough and not palatable. So many things to learn! It was very interesting, these life skills.

So, coming back to the point, being poor is a real struggle. You struggle on a daily basis. You worry when you are not able to pay your fees, buy your books. I used to buy my books from the second-hand bookshops at Bras Basah Road. Sometimes, they don't have the books or perhaps someone else had beat me to it and I would have to go to school in the new year without the books, angering the teachers and inconveniencing my friends with whom I had to share the books.

You suffer indignities if you are poor. That is what led me to join the Labour Movement because I felt that there is something that I could do to contribute to the welfare of the workers. Whilst you work to earn a living, you are also serving the workers. So, I think, that was the reason why I joined NTUC and stayed for so long.

Education was key to you. Did you see it as a route to upward social mobility, as a way to get out of poverty?

Yes, I realised that helping my mum was no joke. Getting up at 4 a.m. even on the weekends. I saw her working every day and I was too. I felt that this was not the life that I want to lead. So, I asked myself what's the option? The only option I saw was to get a good education and a job to not just support myself but to alleviate my mother's hardship as well. She worked all the time from 4 a.m. to 11 p.m. and there were only three days in a year when she would rest—Hari Raya Puasa (two days) and Hari Raya Haji. It was a really hard life.

In those days, our country was also poor. Resources were scarce and whatever resources the government had would be invested in infrastructure—building roads, schools, hospitals, housing. Today, we have different schemes to help the poor but back then, everybody was relatively poorer so everyone struggled. We didn't look to the government for help as people were very resilient.

You were probably one of the few Malay girls to have studied Law.

Yes. I went to Singapore Chinese Girls' School (SCGS) in the mid-1960s and completed my studies in 1974. I was one of the few Malay girls there. In fact, in the years before I joined, the school was semi-private and was not open to minority children. Later, there were changes in policy. They received government funding and opened their doors. But yes, throughout my primary and secondary school years, I don't recall seeing many Malay students. It was the same when I was admitted to the University, where the minority numbers were very much smaller compared to today. Obviously, I was aware there were so few of us and there was this sense that the community was looking at you, so I did feel quite a bit of responsibility. I was active in the Muslim Students' Union in the university.

So, after you graduated, you joined the Labour Movement. What were some of your biggest takeaways?

I was elected as the Deputy Secretary General of the NTUC. My substantive work included appointments as Director of the NTUC's Legal Department, Director of the Women's Development Secretariat, and Director of the Ong Teng Cheong Institute of Labour Studies. I was also actively involved in industrial relations when I was appointed the Executive Secretary of the United Workers of the Electronic and Electrical Industries and Secretary of the Public Sector Unions. But I tell you, it was a really fulfilling period. The best part of the job is when you are able to help the workers, through policy formulation and relevant programmes that we ran.

For instance, when I was in charge of the Women's Secretariat, we started a programme called "Back to Work" in 2007, if my memory serves me right. It was a great project because we knew that many women who had left work to take care of their children found it hard to return to the workforce. Together with the Ministry of Manpower and WDA (Workforce Development Agency), we worked with the employers to help get these women employed again.

I remember, once, I was buying something from Mr Bean (the soya bean-based food and drinks retailer) and I noticed that they had many outlets located in housing estates. This meant greater accessibility for our homemakers living in HDB flats looking for work that could help them earn an income and still take care of their family. Flexibility was key, whether in terms of the hours of work or the time they report for work. I asked my staff to quickly approach Mr Bean and enrol them in our programme. We did that all the time—consciously keeping a look-out for partners to work with.

In the Labour Movement, you don't just come up with policies but you also have to see through the implementation. This way, we know the effect of the policy—how the programme affects people on the ground and whether we need to make any changes or refinements. We were very hands on. So, there was no disconnect.

Also, as the Director of the Legal Department, I represented workers in the Industrial Arbitration Court, fighting for better wages or retrenchment benefits or for the right to represent. My work also included representing them at the Ministry of Manpower and in direct negotiations with employers. My utmost concern was to make sure that workers were given their fair dues and were treated fairly at work, not as mere digits. They deserve to be treated with dignity. We also raised issues with the Ministry of Manpower when there were gaps in the law which affected the workers' welfare.

I also represented Singapore and the workers' group for 12 years at the International Labour Organisation (ILO), which is a tripartite agency of the United Nations, based in Geneva, Switzerland. I was the first Singaporean to be elected to the ILO governing body. It was a very enriching and challenging experience for me. As a worker representative on the ILO board, you have to represent the interests of workers all over the world, a very diverse group, and not just Singapore.

My last piece of work in the ILO was to represent the ILO Workers' Group in negotiating for a Convention and Recommendation on Decent Work for Domestic Workers. The Workers' Group had tried for almost 40 years to secure these two standards but had been unsuccessful. Finally, we managed to put it on the agenda and the Workers' Group asked me to represent them in the negotiations.

It was a huge responsibility but, if you look at the issue in perspective, we are talking about protection for domestic workers, the most vulnerable and globally-exploited group of workers. It was not just about Singapore, but it was a global issue as 95% of the domestic workers were women, including very young girls who worked in homes without much protection. International labour standards were needed to ensure that such workers were treated decently.

We held negotiations for over two years. In 2010, the Tripartite Committee managed to reach a consensus on the core issues and in 2011, we had to negotiate the actual wording of the text that goes into the Convention and Recommendation. It was a really daunting task as the employers, through their Global Employers' Federation, attempted to scuttle the Tripartite Committee's efforts and prevent the development of any standards. I worked with the International Trade Union Confederation and the domestic workers' organisations from all over the world, who came to Geneva to support the effort. We had people from North America, Latin America, Africa and Asia, and it was such an amazing, unifying moment.

In June 2011, I was already appointed as the Minister of State for the Ministry of Community Development, Youth and Sports and was no longer with the NTUC. But the Workers' Group wanted me to continue representing them and so I had to seek the Prime Minister's permission to do so and was grateful that he allowed me to proceed.

We were successful in securing the Convention and Recommendation and it was a great achievement. Both these instruments were later adopted by the ILO General Assembly. Singapore abstained in the voting to adopt the two standards and did not ratify it. However, some countries have placed these standards into their laws.

The work in the ILO was really quite memorable. The best part was that you get to see different perspectives from different parts of the world as each context differs. With such diversity, building a consensus among the unions was really tough but necessary to enable me to negotiate credibly as the workers' spokesperson at the Tripartite Committee with governments and employers.

I know there are many, but can you give me an example or an illustration of the diversity of those cultures, and how you had to suture them together?

Before I headed to the Tripartite Committee, I organised my own Workers' Group meetings first, to listen to the union representatives from all over the world. The Europeans would stand up and say "no" to certain clauses as the situation in Europe was different and they had to contend with the EU directives. Other regions would say, "Whatever you are proposing is not fair enough. We want to raise the standards even higher." Yet others would say, "I would support this provided you include that." Some of the things you could try to accommodate, but others you could not because the standards were meant for all countries and not just one country only. So, you have to be firm and tell them that your focus would be in getting the core and most important provisions reflected in the standards that would provide the core protection to the majority of the domestic workers.

You really need to do a lot of groundwork behind the scenes and talk to everyone. It was also useful to identify employers who were receptive to you so that they could help to moderate the more radical ones, particularly when they have their own internal meetings. We expected that the employers and the governments would have their own positions, but you need to be quite nimble to build alliances either with the employers or with the governments, depending on who was more receptive to your position. The worst is if the employers and governments were to form an alliance, then you would never win when a vote was called to adopt the standards.

It was not easy to get everyone onboard. You really need to exercise all your negotiation skills and practise international diplomacy. These were times when you just had to remind your own Workers' Group that we needed to compromise because that's what the employers and governments had to do as well to reach a consensus. So, we agreed on what was core to us and the rest were used as bargaining chips.

You went in with the clarity that you were representing the workers?

Yes, I was in no doubt at all. I went in not to represent the Singapore government, or any government. I only represented the workers.

What would you say to naysayers who believe that the labour unions in Singapore are rigged by the government?

They are absolutely wrong. The difference in our Labour Movement is people argue a lot behind the scenes. I know because I have my fair share with the employers.

We do not go publicly to disagree on record as that leads to more partisan positions. There is "face" at stake. If you fight publicly and say, "This is what I want and you must give this to me", then, invariably, the counterpart will say, "Why should I give it to you? I also have my own position". And that becomes fossilised and is not helpful. At the end of the day, the workers suffer. We are always mindful of that, which is why we keep the disagreements behind closed doors so that we can come to some sort of compromise and agreement much easier without appearing to be succumbing to pressure. What people see are the agreements, they don't see the disagreements, but there are a lot.

I remember going to the Arbitration Court as I had a case with a big manufacturing employer. We had asked for more bonuses for the workers as the company was doing well. The company was giving the management staff a lot of bonuses but wanted to pay the workers much less, purportedly on the ground that the workers contributed less to the company's profitability than the management staff. We objected very strongly and decided to refer the case to the Court. I told the company that they would have to convince the Court as to why the workers deserved less, and if the issue was reported, they would have the public to contend with too. The company finally succumbed and agreed to pay higher bonuses to the workers.

What was your experience of the 2008/2009 financial crisis?

It was really tough. Many electronic companies retrenched workers. We worked very hard in those days as we had to be on the factory floor when the workers were issued with retrenchment notices. I went down personally on many occasions, too. The industrial relations officers at United Workers Of Electronic & Electrical Industries (UWEEI) had to report to the factories at 7 a.m. when the graveyard shift ended, the usual time for workers to be told being retrenched.

Our presence was important to inspire confidence in the workers that they would be assisted. We told them that although they would lose their jobs, we would get them into training programmes, assist with job placements and help with financial assistance for those who needed help. We also assured them that they would receive fair retrenchment benefits. It was a lot of work that people didn't see. So, I do not agree that the Labour Movement in Singapore is toothless, or is not doing any work. We just do things differently as we have a different model and style.

Your discussion on "face" is key; we forget that a lot of the negotiation happens behind the scenes. It is contrary to what we see in the West, where everything is meant to be open and transparent. So, how was your transit from being the spokesperson for the worker to being a representative of the government, and what precipitated that change?

It was not an easy transition as I never felt that politics was for me. I had said "no" to entering politics before but the then Prime Minister, Mr Goh Chok Tong, called me up prior to the 2001 General Election. He asked me to meet him at the Istana and, when I arrived, he asked me if I knew the reason for the meeting. I answered, "I have a vague suspicion but I don't know." So, he said, "Look, the General Election is coming. I would like you to stand as a candidate" and I told him that I felt that I was already contributing to public service in my work in the NTUC. But he told me that he felt that there was a bigger role that I could play if I was elected as a Member of Parliament.

What he said to me later rang a bell and I also realised then that there were not many women MPs, in particular, there was not a single Malay female MP. I am glad that, today, women constitute 24% of our parliamentarians and are making significant contributions to policy making. It is significant to me that all the political parties continue to field female candidates, an important starting point before more women could get elected.

How did the Labour Movement take to that?

I think, in my case, people were already expecting the move. I don't think they were extremely surprised. Even my friends in the ILO knew that it was a matter of time. What is more important is how you continue to conduct yourself after you are elected. I don't think I've changed anything fundamental about me and I continue to work as hard as I did before.

I feel strongly that politics should not change a person. You are what you are, and you should live by your values and your principles. Whether you take on another responsibility or designation should not change your values and principles, unless, of course, you have been living by false values and principles.

There will always be those who will question whether I have become a "part of the Party" now. There will always be people who will question my priorities. But I think that the important question to ask is whether the Party takes care of Singaporeans. I am clear that if the Party is not taking care of our people, I have no business being associated with it. I would certainly not have stood as a candidate. We need people who work extensively on the ground in order to anchor the Party and ensure that the Party continues to reflect the voices of the people, which is important.

I read elsewhere that many have observed you in your Meet-the-People Sessions. Can you share any memorable stories?

If you come to my Meet-the-People Sessions (MPS), you will find many memorable cases. There are many people and it is the best place to ground you to reality as you hear the stories of the people every week. The greatest satisfaction I get is when I see a young person transformed by our work at MPS.

I have seen young people with limited means. I remember this girl who was raised by a single mum, and I helped her to access some financial schemes and she went from ITE to Poly. She subsequently graduated, got married and now has a child. I also started a free tuition programme in Marsiling for primary school children and the results have been encouraging as some of the children did well in their PSLE.

These examples give me a great sense of satisfaction and motivate me. What people remember the most is how you have directly impacted their lives. We have to give people hope so that they, too, can aspire to a better future.

At the start of your political career, were there assumptions made about you? Were there things that you had to debunk? Did you feel you have to work harder?

Well, I really don't consciously seek to change anything, but I always feel that I should try my best in whatever I do. It's not that people tell you to, but it is subconscious. I think, too, that, being a woman, somehow, I feel that I need to work hard to prove that I can do just as well as anybody else. I think that is the push factor for me more than being a minority.

I was a bit concerned that I would be the first Malay woman to stand for election. I felt a great sense of responsibility to ensure that not only was I able to do the job, but also to pave the way for other women. That sense of responsibility and duty is a big part of me. I certainly feel it personally even though I may not have articulated it too much along the way.

What were your biggest challenges and learning points when you became Minister of State?

When I became Minister of State for Community Development, Youth and Sports, which was later renamed the Ministry of Social and Family Development, I was very happy because it was aligned with my own interests. Community development is about welfare and the people, and I enjoyed the work tremendously. I used to visit the VWOs (Voluntary Welfare Organisations) practically every week. I visited the children's and girls' homes and that felt wonderful to me.

I was also very proud of the SG Enable project that was officially opened by Prime Minister Lee Hsien Loong at Redhill Centre in 2015. It has now become a dedicated centre for people with disabilities. It provides training, job placements and also allows for the building of a cohesive community that is very disabled-friendly. I had seeded the idea when I took over the portfolio in 2012.

Another memorable event, when I was at the Ministry, was when I had to defend Singapore before the CEDAW (Convention on the Elimination of All Forms of Discrimination against Women) Committee in New York, barely two months after joining. As a member state, we had obligations and had to report periodically on what progress we had made to fully comply with CEDAW. The CEDAW Committee asked many questions. It wasn't too difficult because, to be fair, we were not really down in the doldrums when it comes to the status, working and living conditions for women. Our women have done well on so many fronts.

As an MP, I focus a lot on staying engaged with the residents. House and market visits are two of my key touchpoints. I do house visits at least once a week. When I was in Marsiling, during the GE in September 2015, I did an entire round of 140 blocks over nine days. Immediately after the GE, I started my second round of house visits, so much so that the residents said, "Ah! I saw you two months ago." And I'd jokingly say, "Why, you don't want to see me is it?" I think this is a great way to meet people as some may not attend the MPS which I hold every Tuesday.

I am all for enhancing touchpoints—Meet-the-People Sessions (MPS), house visits, community activities and group events. You must have different touchpoints to reach as many people as possible. There are residents who will not come to my MPS but who need help, especially the frail elderly living alone. Sometimes, it's not material things that they lack but, rather, the human touch as they are lonely, and providing a befriender service helps them to stay connected to society. I am grateful that our RCs (Residents' Committee) and volunteers play a significant role in supporting me in this outreach work. We may not be able to solve all their problems, but at least people know that we are sincerely doing our best to assist them through all our various touchpoints.

Let's talk about the role of the Speaker of the House. How do you feel about this immense responsibility and how do you think you have measured up thus far?

The Prime Minister called me and asked if I could take over as Speaker when the position became vacant. I said, "Prime Minister, I have just become Minister of State for Ministry of Social and Family Development and I am enjoying my work a lot. I am not sure if I should move out after just a short stint of slightly over a year." He said, "Yes, I know, but we need someone to take over as Speaker." So, I suppose when I was asked, I saw it as a duty. When you are called on to perform a duty, you just do it.

But I also told him, "I do not want to be completely cut off from what I have been doing in the past and prefer to stay engaged. On-the-ground work is a part of my nature." So he agreed. As such, the National Council of Social Services appointed me as their adviser, which gives me the chance to continue to attend the functions of the VWOs. I also continued to teach labour law to union leaders at the Ong Teng Cheong Institute. The job of the Speaker can be quite isolating, with a specific set of duties. But as long as I am able to stay in touch and be engaged, it is an ideal arrangement for me.

As the Speaker, I think, what we need to do is to make sure that we conduct the proceedings fairly, and uphold the decorum of Parliament as it is a key institution. People may not realise the significance of Parliament as we have a peaceful democracy. But people need to understand that it is an important institution. If we looked back in history, we would have a better appreciation of Parliament. I honestly cannot judge how I have performed, Loretta, but I do my job and I give it my best. That is all I can say.

But I also have my challenging moments as Speaker, such as chairing the five-day debate on the controversial Population White Paper just one month after I became Speaker in January 2013. Mr Lee Kuan Yew's funeral arrangements, the Lying-in-State and the Special Parliamentary Sitting as part of his memorial service were also quite unforgettable.

What would you say to detractors who point out that the government often calls for snap elections? Many have critiqued that the 2015 election was held sooner to ride the wave of the SG50 high and Mr Lee's passing.

Actually, it is almost always clear from looking into historical patterns when and how elections are held. Most have already expected elections to be in 2015. The only question was when in 2015. To be fair, if you look at all the past elections, we have never stayed right up to the five-year term. We often called it around the four-year mark. So, I think people were prepared for elections to be called.

What is your leadership style?

My leadership style is consultative. I consult with people, listen, discuss and take their ideas onboard. But then, at the end of the day, after all the opinions and voices have been heard, you have to make your decisions.

Let's talk about your Malay-Muslim identity. You are very active in and also a big contributor to the Malay community. Do you think that more can be done for the community or do you think we, as a nation, have done enough?

It is always a work-in-progress. Nothing is ever enough, and there is a tremendous amount we can do. We have already done a fair bit over the years—the educational performance of Malay children have gone up and we see Malay graduates with First Class Honours. A matter of great pride for me and our community was when, for the first time, two students from the madrasahs were admitted into the university to study Medicine. Our community needs more role models, especially for the young. They would be able to look at these two students from the madrasah and tell themselves that "if they can do it, so can we." I am happy that many Malay parents today prioritise education as they recognise its importance.

I am also aware that there are issues we need to deal with—skilling up our lower-wage Malay workers to allow them to take on better jobs and earn higher income. That is something we need to do continuously to enhance performance. We have done well, but we need to do a lot better by continuing to push ourselves. We must never lose the momentum.

How can we encourage more entrepreneurship in the Malay women community?

For a start, we should try to boost our Malay women's employment rate which is much lower compared to the other communities; especially now when dual-income families are more necessary than ever, because of the fragmented labour market and higher cost of living. The problem is that once women fall out of the workforce due to marriage or childbirth, it is a lot harder to get them back to work. There are many schemes now to assist them and we need to be more proactive in doing that. On entrepreneurship, many women are actually quite resourceful as they can cook well and many use this skill to earn some extra income.

You have been very vocal against religious fundamentalism. Given today's paranoid climate, do you feel more pressure to speak up for your community and to be the voice of moderation?

I am satisfied with how we, as a community, have taken ownership and handled issues of radicalism and fundamentalism. Community leaders and asatizahs have been speaking up, which is important as they have influence over the community. How they view the issue, choose to articulate the right position and seek to shape and influence the minds of the people who follow them is absolutely critical. I am glad that we have been very cohesive as a community.

For me, I am most concerned with the youth. I worry most about radicalism through the Internet. In the old days, if you wanted to learn about Islam or any religion, you have to seek the guidance of a teacher. But these days, anybody can go on the Internet and the information you receive may be extremely misleading and dangerous. So, we need to constantly engage the young and encourage them to raise their queries or concerns with reputable religious leaders.

My other concern is the rising global tide of Islamophobia which is also very scary. Women wearing the tudung are viewed negatively and have become the target of public attacks which shows a lack of understanding of Islam and the inability to make a distinction between the small number who are abusing and exploiting religion, and the majority who are peace-loving. We have to guard against this happening in Singapore and I am glad that we have the Inter-racial and Religious Confidence Circles, which provides an excellent platform for people of different faiths to build bridges and to forge a consensus on how to co-exist peacefully. It also helps that our religious leaders of other faiths constantly remind Singaporeans not to stigmatise the Muslims based on the conduct of a few.

I was in a taxi recently and the driver suggested that the Muslim population has, in his view, increased after the rise of religious fundamentalism and that many of the new faithfuls are foreign workers coming together to worship with the Singaporeans.

We should not view all foreign workers, especially those who are Muslims, negatively. The Bangladeshi workers, for example, are active in the community, helping to cook food in their free time during the month of Ramadan in some of the mosques. They have religious needs, too, and it is better for our mosques to provide some space for their activities. In this way, we also help them to understand our religious context and practices and to respect them.

What do you think we can do to encourage more women to step up in politics?

I honestly hope I won't be the last female Speaker and that we will see more women in politics, unlike in the 1980s when we did not have even one woman. Sometimes, as I sit there as Speaker, I would muse to myself, "Imagine, there was a time when we didn't have a single woman in Parliament. The men were talking to each other and deciding on things which affect 50% of the population." I am so glad we have seen progress.

Women now constitute 24% of Parliamentarians, which is higher than the global average. However, I also accept that it is not easy for women to be fully engaged in politics as we continue to shoulder housework disproportionately. A more balanced sharing of duties may encourage greater participation.

Another source of immense satisfaction for me was seeing Chia Yong Yong, a lawyer with a disability, being sworn in as an NMP. In fact, we had to remove a seat and modify another to accommodate her, but that's great! Our Parliament must represent the diverse voices of our society.

Let's talk about social media for a while since it is the 45th U.S. President's de facto mode of communication.

Social media has become an important tool for politicians, though I only maintain a Facebook account. I don't have Twitter or Instagram as I am basically a face-to-face person. I prefer physical touchpoints, rather than be overdependent on technology. I would much prefer to head to the coffee shop, drink coffee, have my lunch and chat with the people. They are all used to seeing me. Sometimes, they will ask, "What are you doing here?" and I will reply, "I am eating lah, just like you!"

That's your version of Facebook—a "face-to-face book!"

Yes, that's funny. I know I have to adjust to technology as we accept that this is the new climate and environment that we have to operate in. I do not think that new technology will replace face-to-face interaction as you cannot get a sense of what the real issues and concerns are without directly talking to people. Technology cannot pick up the non-verbal cues and emotions. Only physical contact can allow for better communication and also gives us insights to better gauge a situation.

How do you juggle your various roles and responsibilities?

My children are all grown up now, so that's a bit easier. But when I joined politics, the two youngest ones were still in primary school. I would not pretend it was easy as that would minimise not just the sacrifice of one person but the sacrifices of so many women out there. I had to juggle between work and family, and it was very challenging.

In 2001, when I first entered politics, people would ask me how old my kids were. I would tell them that they were just this high (*indicates with her hands*) and they would ask me who was caring for them while I was at work. I would reply that my husband and family would help me. But the question was so frequent that I came to a point where I did the asking instead and queried them if they had ever asked a man the same question. They would look at me, stunned. They seemed to assume that only female MPs have a duty to their children and the family, not male MPs.

Today, the situation is different. We have women MPs who are pregnant and give birth while in office. This is now accepted as a norm, and that shows that our society has matured and our stereotypes, expectations and perceptions of the role of women have changed. This is a positive sign.

I hope for a day when I no longer have to write a book on women leaders but just leaders, though we still live in a society where we need books on women leaders.

Yes, when they write about Margaret Thatcher, they always say, "She was like a man." I always feel very tickled.

What is really important is having strong family support. Before I entered politics, I asked my husband if he would support me in parenting or else there is no way I could do this on my own. Our work hours are extremely long and it is not uncommon to return home at midnight. My husband has been a strong pillar of support.

I also had my mother who was such an amazing help. She passed away on Election Day in 2015 and I never got to see her though I was with her all of Cooling-Off Day the day before. On the day itself, I was at the polling centre and told myself, that I would visit my mum in Marsiling after that. But before I could do that, my daughter called me and told me "Grandma looks a bit different." My daughter had been taking care of Mum for the last one and a half weeks when she was hospitalised. I told my daughter that I would go soon, but two minutes later, my daughter called me and said "Grandma is no more with us" and so I headed straight to the hospital. That is one Election Day that I will never forget.

It is bittersweet.

Yes, really. We buried her at 5 p.m. but I decided to be with my GRC team at the stadium when the results were announced later that evening as I knew that my mum would have wanted that.

When my father died, people were wondering what would happen to us young children, but my mother said, "As long as I have two hands and two legs, we will not starve" and she lived to fulfil that promise. She was very hardworking, disciplined and had a big heart. She was very good with her hands and was always making these little decorations that you receive as door gifts at Malay weddings. I would ask her, "Mum, why are you doing this to yourself? You are already working so hard, why do you help to make these door gifts for our relatives?" She would say, "People ask me and I don't want to let them down." I was very fortunate to have her as my pillar of support and she lived with me for 30 years. She helped raise my children till the last few years when she became frail. I am grateful that she chose to live with me and my children.

Let's say today a staff came to you and she is torn between her career, marriage and motherhood. What would you say to her?

It is very tough, but I have worked all my life and believe that women need to be independent. My mum was a good example. When my dad died, we had nothing and she had to start from scratch. That taught me a very important lesson—women must have their own source of income and they must save for their own retirement to be able to take care of themselves.

I would say, as much as possible, don't leave your job if you can, as there are many childcare facilities available nowadays. Place your child in a facility and, more importantly, get the support of your family. When my children were younger, I hired a babysitter to help Mum as well. When the babysitter was ill, I relied on my older sister. While I had that family support, I understand that not many women have that.

So, the ideal arrangement really varies from woman to woman. She has to decide for herself and take into account her own circumstances. What is important though is that they are given the option to decide, without having to suffer too much pain for themselves or their family. Try to look for a job, or speak to your boss and ask for flexibility.

Will this be against the traditional values expected of a Muslim woman?

It is not so much Islam, but rather, cultural values. Islam strongly encourages education and social contribution for both males and females.

Many prominent Muslim women are distinguished and celebrated for their contributions to society.

Why don't we educate the men as well?
We should and attitudes are gradually changing among the younger ones who are now better educated. Social and cultural values are changing in the community.

Thank you so much, Halimah. We have covered much ground, so let's do some trivia. What do you do in your free time?
Not much free time, but I spend most of it reading.

What are your best and worst traits?
I am very impatient and tend to want to get everything done quickly. You can't see that, but I always tell my children that they are too slow and I'll ask "Why do you do this and why don't you do that?" My children will tell me I am a robot and remind me that they have their own way of doing things, too. That's my biggest challenge—wanting to do things fast.

Yes, our best strengths are also our greatest weaknesses, so it can be a double-edged sword. What irks you most?
People who give up too easily. Perhaps I may be wrong and shouldn't think that way. Perhaps because I grew up in such a difficult situation.

I never gave up even when I almost got kicked out from school from SCGS because I was a *ponteng* queen! Back then, I was helping my mum and at some point, it became too much to juggle that and schoolwork, and I would often not do my homework and was constantly scolded by my teachers. It was very stressful and I almost gave up until my principal knocked sense into me. It was only then that I told myself that I had to pull myself up and not engage in self-pity. I saw that my mother never complained and never gave up even when she was saddled with five children. So I figured that the least I could do was not to disappoint her. I feel sad when people decide to give up and not try.

I just realised you consciously or unconsciously mirrored your mother, having the same work ethic and even having five children, too. One of the key differences is that you had a supportive husband on your journey. Would you say you have made sacrifices along the way or have any regrets?

If I had a small regret, it would be that I wished I had more time with my mum. She was frail with dementia in the last few years. I tried to spend as much time as I could but I still regret that I couldn't do more. I wished I had spent more time talking to her about her past and recorded them, especially her wonderful recipes. I wish I had on record her life when she was young and her stories of the Japanese Occupation as well as her views about how her life had developed. She was born in 1925.

What do you think your mother would say about you?

My mother would be very proud of me. I had hoped that she would live past the elections. I remember a poignant moment when I fell asleep at her bed. I didn't know this but my children photographed the moment when my semi-conscious mum placed her hand on my head. I don't know what that means but I took it as an indication that she blessed me. I asked myself if I should have seen her on the morning before I headed to the polling centre, but my children say I must never live a life with regrets.

It was very challenging when Mum had dementia as she would always ask about my whereabouts and the family would assure her that I was coming home. At the end of the day, what matters most is the family. You don't want to go back to an empty house devoid of love. When there is no love, there is no point. Love is what anchors you and helps you do your work, not accolades. It's the love of the people that you really care about that sustains you. I used to hug and kiss my mother every morning before I go to work, because I didn't know when would be the last time. She would give me a bright smile as she warmed to the touch.

My sister would tell me that whenever mum sees me on TV or in the newspapers, she would say, "That is Halimah! That is Halimah." I teased her on Cooling-Off Day whether she remembered me and she replied, "Of course, I remember. You are my daughter." I am grateful for that. I have many memories and I hope, when my time comes, my children will have that relationship with me. That will be the greatest gift. I hope I leave this world as my mum did—well taken care of and remembered with love.

What is still on your bucket list?

I've always wanted to write a book on industrial relations and labour law but never had the time.

What would you say to a younger version of yourself?

I will tell the younger me that I worked too hard and have to loosen up. But I suppose there was no time to loosen up when I was young. If I did, I wouldn't have survived. I was in survival mode. I got married two years after I graduated and had the first child within a year before the rest followed, so I never had the time to loosen up. I have lived a full and fulfilling life and have no regrets.

Tell us something about you that people don't know about.

I like to cook though I hardly have the time.

How do you best want to be remembered?

At the end of the day, I just want to be remembered as a good person.

If you met God, what would you tell him?

Thank you, God. You gave me a good, full life. While you gave me many challenges, you threw me many lifelines, guideposts and let me find my own solutions. You helped to mould me to live a life of no regrets.

Which role do you identify yourself with—a Madonna, Maverick or any other M word?

It is difficult to box myself into any specific category. I've come a long way, experienced so many things and performed so many different roles. I guess you could say that I am a Multi-hyphenate.

The Champion of the Arts

JANICE KOH

Janice Koh is a stage and television actress, and a former Nominated Member of Parliament in Singapore, who currently serves on various boards in the non-profit arts and education sector. She holds an honours degree in Theatre Studies from the National University of Singapore (NUS) and a master's degree in Theatre from Goldsmith's College, London.

On television, Janice is well known for her role as the ambitious lawyer Angela Ang in the Mediacorp Channel 5 legal drama "The Pupil". Her performance earned her a Best Actress nomination for Asian Television Awards 2010. Film credits include Ken Kwek's "Unlucky Plaza", Kelvin Tong's "The Faith of Anna Waters" and "Hitman: Agent 47". Television credits include Channel 5's "Zero Calling 2", "C.L.I.F. 2", "Diary of Amos Lee", "Fighting Spiders", and "The Art of Conversation" for Channel NewsAsia.

A familiar face in the theatre scene, Janice won the Life! Theatre Award for Best Actress in 2003 for her performance in David Auburn's "Proof" and received Best Actress nominations for her roles in "Optic Trilogy", "Rabbit Hole", "Hitting (On) Women" and "One Flea Spare". Internationally, Janice has performed at various festivals and performing venues including the Edinburgh International Festival, the Kunsten Festival des Art in Brussels, Bristol Mayfest, the Shizuoka Performing Arts Festival, the International Summer Festival Hamburg and the Damansara Performing Arts Centre in Kuala Lumpur. In 2016, she performed in "Sandaime Richard", an international collaboration directed by Ong Keng Sen, which toured in

Japan to Tokyo, Shizuoka, Fukuoka, Kumamoto, Kochi and Suita.

Recent theatre production credits include "With/Out" by Loo Zihan, Dick Lee's "Beauty World", "Another Country", "Optic Trilogy" and W!ld Rice's "Cooling Off Day", Pangdemonium's "Frozen", "Rabbit Hole" and "Swimming with Sharks", The Finger Player's "Poop" and "Rant & Rave", and Tan Tarn How's "Fear of Writing".

***

Meeting Janice in the al fresco café of the Four Seasons was very much like meeting your star yogi mate after a challenging, but utterly satisfying, Ashtanga yoga class. She shows up prompt, fresh and without a hint of make-up. Blessed with a petite, lithe physique, Janice does not look a day past 25 even though she turns 43 this year. We were schoolmates in NUS—she was my senior by two years and she belonged to the inaugural batch of Theatre Studies students.

Over the years, our paths had crossed many times. Once when I was interning in Theatreworks in the Flying Circus Project, where Janice was a core member of the cast, and later, as fellow actors in a hard-hitting play on domestic abuse titled *Hitting (On) Women*. Even then, I recalled wanting to have the sheer physical and mental discipline of Janice. She would roll out her yoga mat in between rehearsals to practice her asanas while the rest of the cast would chat, snack and fritter our time in what we liked to call "cast bonding". This is not to say that Janice is not part of the team, she is. But there is always the sense that she was the quiet, cool, calm, collected leader of the pack.

Janice is what you would call a "serious actor". She comes to rehearsals with no baggage and she is always on point with her lines and blocking. Unlike most young actors, Janice had no drama—she was poised, confident and always sensible. That's the word—sensible. She is perhaps the poster child for Jane Austen's *Sense and Sensibility*. From her days as an undergraduate, to a thespian, arts administrator, mother, Arts NMP and a public figure, Janice is one of those women who seemed to always have her ducks in a row and inhabit a perfectly planned, manicured and curated life.

She has a high-flyer civil servant husband, two smart boys and a tight athlete's body to boot. There is every reason for a girl to hate Janice, except that she always makes sense and is polite to a fault. Her career in theatre has been nothing short of phenomenal and her time as an NMP was well-documented by the press, simply because she was always raising sensible yet thought-provoking issues. It is almost as if she is personifying what Bertolt Brecht said theatre must do, which is to hold up a mirror to society. As one of the few "double agents" in the industry, she is equally adept on stage as well as in Parliament, putting forth critical ideas either in the form of a scripted word by a fleshed out character or a fleshing out words not uncharacteristic of a seasoned politician.

It seems nothing fazes Janice and she remains passionate about the role of the arts, education and civil liberties in Singapore. We chat candidly on her views on everything, ranging from her time as an arts administrator in the National Arts Council, her take on censorship, local theatre, the vanguards in the industry, education, the role of women, motherhood to some of the other glaring issues she took on during the time she was a Nominated Member of Parliament. And as always, her answers are spoken with great passion, are well substantiated and always oh-so-sensible.

This is perhaps best illustrated by her 2014 speech as the Ambassador for Pink Dot SG: "There are some things in life we don't have a lot of choice over. We can't choose the colour of our skin. We can't choose the family we are born into. We can't choose to be tall or short, right or left-handed, just as how we can't choose to be born male or female, gay or straight. But I believe there are many things in life that we can choose. We can choose to embrace and treat our fellow human beings, including our LGBTQ brothers and sisters, equally, and with kindness, dignity and respect. We can choose to raise our children to be secure and confident in who they are and to teach all our young ones to be compassionate and accepting of those who are different from them. We can choose to be big-hearted and open-minded as a society, one where all Singaporeans—

no matter our race, language, religion, sexual orientation or gender identity—can feel included and feel a part of this place we call home."

***

Share with us about your background.

I grew up in a fairly working-class family. Both my parents worked. I grew up in an HDB flat in Marine Terrace. My mum was an executive secretary at Cold Storage and my dad worked at the Port Authority of Singapore. I am the oldest of three kids and I went to Singapore Chinese Girls' School (SCGS) for my primary and secondary education. Contrary to what many might believe, I wasn't exposed to the arts at a young age. In fact, I hardly attended plays or exhibitions until I actually studied Theatre in Victoria Junior College (VJC) at 17.

How did you decide to study Theatre if you had never been exposed to it?

SCGS cultivated my love for Literature, so by the time I was in secondary school, it was a subject I loved and did well in. When I went to VJC, I wanted to study subjects I enjoyed and I figured if I enjoyed studying Literature then I might feel the same about Theatre Studies. That's how I made the connection. It was more a process of elimination of what I didn't like as opposed to an active choice of what I loved. I knew I didn't want to go into the Sciences. I always say theatre found me rather than I found it. By the end of my time at VJC, I knew that theatre was going to be a huge part of my life.

When did you start dabbling in theatre and what was it about your theatre education that fascinated you?

In my first year of Theatre Studies and Drama under Rey Buono at VJC, I couldn't believe that as part of our course, we get to do things like lie on the floor, relax, warm up and play theatre games. We got to study all kinds of dramatic and literary texts, learnt how to analyse and develop characters and got to perform and direct scenes and stories. It made the world I lived in come alive for me in a way that all the other subjects never did. I was also encountering theatre at the point in my life when I was ready to understand and embrace different worldviews, and through the theatre, I was exposed to new perspectives and ideas, with no judgment.

Through the study of ancient texts and postmodern plays, from ancient Greek theatre to Asian performing art forms, I felt a whole new world had opened up to me, and that I gained insight into everything from history and philosophy, to psychology and sociology, and it helped developed a capacity for independent and critical thinking. I become someone interested in life and it gave me a sense of purpose. Of course, I enjoyed performing and acting tremendously. I did not always know I had a talent or even an affinity for the theatre. But once I had encountered it, I just found it tremendously enjoyable, pleasurable and almost cathartic. That's how I came to the theatre at a pretty young age of 17.

You were the first batch of theatre students in NUS. How did you make the decision to undertake this road less travelled?

I always try to make sensible choices, even as a young person. I knew that theatre and acting was something I loved, and it was very clear to me that I wanted to pursue my degree in it. At that time, NUS did not yet have a Theatre program, so I knew I had to go abroad. I was very aware that it would be an expensive undertaking, and I did not know how I was going to fund it. There were very few arts scholarships available then, and there's no way my parents would be able to afford a S$100,000-a-year program. Even if we had borrowed money to finance it, I could not imagine being able to pay it back as a working actor. But I was in denial for a while and applied to all the best drama schools anyway. I was accepted in a couple of very good universities that I had to eventually turn down. It was extremely sobering.

Fortunately, by the time I completed my A Levels, NUS had launched their Theatre Studies program. My parents were still hoping I would study Law, so I applied and went for the Law School interview. I figured it was probably the next best thing to studying theatre. You would not believe the number of lawyers-turned-theatre-makers there are in Singapore! I remember being asked very pointedly at the interview why I wanted to study Law. And despite having prepared for this question, I said, "Actually I don't. What I really want to do is Theatre." Sometimes when confronted with the right question, you are compelled to articulate clearly what it is exactly that you want.

And that was how I decided to take up Theatre Studies as my major at NUS. When I got accepted into it, I was aware that it was going to be an academic program. So throughout my four years there, I trained and acted with Ong Keng Sen and TheatreWorks. It was very demanding on my time, and I still recall having to attend rehearsals while preparing for exams, but it was my way of getting the practical hands-on experience that I needed—both on and off the stage.

Share with us how you got started as an actor, the experience working with Ong Keng Sen and TheatreWorks which was then regarded as Singapore's premier theatre company.

I think if you asked any actor, no matter which acting school you go to, nothing prepares you for the job until you actually do it. The experience I had working with TheatreWorks between 1992 to 2002 was particularly invaluable. I was very fortunate to have had the chance to learn from some of the best in the industry—Lim Yu-Beng, Ong Keng Sen and the late Krishen Jit.

I still work with the company today, but those early years were extremely formative for me as a young artist, not just as an actor but as a theatre-maker. I say this because Keng Sen works in a very collaborative manner as a lot of the work is original and often devised. The actors are often very involved in the making of the shows, and the exposure to that kind of process was vital and critical in how it developed me as an individual and a performer. It helped shaped my opinions towards art and art-making, and made me more open towards things that were new, risky or experimental.

TheatreWorks also initiated the Flying Circus Project, which provided an important platform to learn from and collaborate with masters of Asian performance traditions. In the day, I might be studying critical theory or theatre history, and at night, I would head to TheatreWorks and study with the masters of Kudiyattam (ancient Sanskrit theatre), Bharatanatyam (Indian classical dance) and Wayang Kulit (Javanese shadow puppet). It was as if I had a mirror image of my theatre syllabus but from a practical point of view.

In a way, I had the best of both worlds. Sometimes, I would say I "crafted" my own Theatre degree program because whatever practical component was not available at the university was supplemented by my training and experience as a working actor.

In hindsight, how was it like working in the 1990s with these local theatre luminaries?

In the early to mid-1990s, the idea of having a sustainable career as a full-time working actor was uncommon. Unless, of course, you were a full-time Mediacorp employee working in television. Most theatre actors held day jobs. Unlike today, where you might come across young actors and artists who start their career almost immediately after graduating, there was a lot more uncertainty about making a living from your craft.

As a young theatre student, I was interested in the theatre and very hungry to learn. I didn't care if I was working on stage or off, I regularly volunteered to work pro bono or for very little money just to get some theatre experience. I would help out with costumes and wardrobe or be a backstage hand or assistant stage manager for small black box productions. I also worked with fellow schoolmates like Kaylene Tan and Kelvin Tong to put up our own original works at the Substation or Drama Centre. There were no government grants or subsidies for amateur productions back then, so we had to be inventive and raise funds by doing school shows and assembly skits. It was a steep learning curve for all of us, but a necessary one.

When I first started working with TheatreWorks, it was not Keng Sen but practitioners like Lim Yu-Beng who let me cut my teeth as a young actor on stage. At that time, Keng Sen was away studying in New York, and the likes of Yu-Beng and Loke Meng Chu were helming some of the smaller productions under the TheatreWorks umbrella. Those were the first professional shows I acted in. Those were the shows that gave me the platforms to try, to fail and to be seen.

I don't know if young people still work this way today. I'm guessing that most actors graduating from LASALLE or NAFA come out with the expectation of starting their performing career on stage right off the bat. But back then, the arts and media industry was a lot less developed, and it wasn't perceived as a sustainable career for many actors until the mid-2000s.

I may be pragmatic about some decisions, but I don't plan very far ahead. I often listen to my gut instinct, and even though I knew it would be financially challenging to work in this industry, I was never discouraged or set back by how much money I was or was not going to make. Was it because my parents could afford to sustain my life in art? No, not at all. In fact, they couldn't. As an undergraduate student, my studies were paid through a loan on my mum's CPF account, which I knew I had to repay someday. I knew I had to be financially independent. But I also knew how fortunate I was to have found a calling, a life purpose, that I felt deeply passionate about.

When I got to my Honours year of Theatre Studies, I started thinking about what my next move would be. In a perfect world, I would pursue my Master of Fine Arts (MFA) or start finding work as an actor. But I had begun to develop a very keen interest in arts policy in Singapore, and there was a part of me that really wanted to bring about some change in an industry that was young, growing but had its flaws.

What did you realise was flawed about our arts industry?

In my fourth year at NUS, we covered a lot of issues related to arts administration, from copyright and fundraising, to government funding and regulation. It sparked my interest in arts management and the politics of art and art-making in Singapore. The Esplanade Theatres on the Bay, then referred to as the Singapore Arts Centre, was slated to be built, there was a lot of dissatisfaction over censorship, especially with regard to homosexual content, and many small theatre groups were struggling to find a voice and to build an audience with very limited funding. I remember feeling quite adamant that more needed to be done if we wanted to develop a mature and thriving arts environment.

This led me to pursue arts administration and policy as my master's. I felt it would be useful to have my feet in both worlds—as a performer involved in the process of art making, but also with some knowledge and experience in managing the arts. I was fortunate to secure a Public Service Commission scholarship to do my master's in Theatre Administration in London. I was bonded to the National Arts Council (NAC), where I worked for four years before breaking my bond to start a family and pursue my acting career full-time.

What were your biggest takeaways from your year in London?

When I was there for a year, I finally experienced what was like to work in a thriving, vibrant performing and visual arts scene. It was invaluable for me to learn how the arts was managed in the UK. The London arts scene is very mature and provided many lessons, for instance, on ways to develop corporate philanthropy, on business planning for the arts or venue management and programming for different spaces. It was a real eye opener.

When I came back to Singapore to serve my bond at the NAC, I did what I could to apply all I had seen and learnt through my work in strategic planning and funding. But all this while, I didn't stop acting. I did exactly what I used to do at NUS. I would work at the Council from from 9 a.m. to 6 p.m. and then head to rehearsals, which started at 7 p.m. and ended at 12 midnight. This went on for the next three to four years.

How did you finally decide to cave in to your passion given that you are such a sensible and practical girl at heart? Or was that your alter-ego doing the talking?

There is a part of me that tried to make it work, but there's another part of me that found a lot of pleasure in being a performer, and I wanted to do both. Unlike actors today, I just couldn't fathom how I was going to make a living from acting alone. Don't forget, I started working in the theatre in 1992, which was a very different time. We did not have a mature television industry and most people in theatre were only doing it part-time. Most of the actors I knew then were holding onto day jobs while they were acting. So that's where I was coming from.

Interestingly, by the time I left the Arts Council, things had changed quite significantly. A number of theatre companies were receiving two-year major grants that enabled them to plan ahead and hire actors at better rates. SPH MediaWorks just started out and were in competition with Mediacorp, so there was a lot more work to go round for actors in television and media. Actors such as Tan Kheng Hua, Neo Swee Lin, Lim Kay Tong, Lim Kay Siu were beginning to make a viable career out of television and working in the theatre at the same time. This growth in the arts and entertainment industry made the idea of becoming a full-time artist a lot more viable.

How did your time in the UK shape you as an arts administrator?
My one year in the UK was seminal as it exposed me to a mature arts industry and its working system. By the time I came back to work NAC, I knew that there were a lot of changes that needed to be made to the way we supported and funded the arts. Of course, I knew all things take time and just because it works in another context doesn't mean it will work in Singapore. In the four years that I was at NAC, I was very busy. I pulled in long, long hours but it was work that I loved because I genuinely wanted to make our arts scene better.

My first job at NAC was in the Strategic Planning Department which looked at policy planning for the Arts Council. At that time, there was a huge question mark on the future of the Old Parliament House. My department was in charge of putting up a paper to see if we had a compelling argument to convert the space into a viable arts venue. I helped to draft the paper to envision what an independent arts venue with multiple spaces might look like, which was submitted to the then

Ministry of Information, Communication and the Arts (MICA) and to the Ministry of Finance (MOF). I was over the moon when the proposal was accepted. I always had this pipe dream to run my own arts venue one day! My only regret was that I didn't stay long enough in the department to see the whole project through to fruition.

What did you envision The Arts House to be and what other projects were you involved in while you were at the NAC?

I wanted it to be a multi-disciplinary arts centre, one that could house several small, emerging resident companies. It would have to have a budget for programming and not simply serve as a bricks and mortar receiving venue. I would want it to commission and produce shows and house a bar and a café as a source of revenue. I envisioned a small black box space, an exhibition space and a small screening room for independent art films and the parliamentary chamber could host small recitals and concerts. As a young person returning from the UK, I was thoroughly excited by the prospect of having a venue like this, which I saw so many of in London.

I remember emailing and calling everybody from Jeremy Monteiro to Geoffrey Malone of the Singapore International Film Festival and having meetings with them, asking them to please share with me their vision for such a space. And then I tried to gather all the best ideas to see if it could happen in this venue. I met with property consultants from Knight Frank and asked them to help me work out the financial business plan for such a venue. I wanted to know how a bar or restaurant could be a viable source of income to support the arts.

With all these ideas, we drafted a proposal with a business plan that could support such a space. Yes, it was all on paper and theoretical at that stage, but the fact that I had this opportunity as a young arts administrator was utterly mind-blowing. It made me feel like I could contribute towards something good, that my knowledge and experience could translate into something useful for the arts and for Singapore.

The other thing I got involved in while I was at NAC was helping to draft the first Renaissance City Report. At that time, George Yeo was the Cultural Minister and was one of the few in Cabinet whom I thought understood and appreciated the place of the arts in society. In a largely pragmatic society, concerned mostly with bread and butter type of issues, the arts is often seen as icing on the cake. We had a Minister who could see the big picture, who understood that culture and the arts are instrumental in providing people with quality of life and a life worth living, and that society should not be preoccupied with economics alone.

So, when he said, "Let's write a paper and get some money from the MOF that will make Singapore a global city for the arts," a bunch of young officers and myself were excited and thrilled. We poured our hearts into drafting this paper and were successful in getting $10 million from MOF to be spent over five years. It might seem like a small sum today, but it was a very big deal in 2000. Soon after that, I was transferred to the Grants Department, which was the main department in receipt of most of that money, and one of my immediate jobs was to work out how to distribute it!

As the Assistant Director of Grants, I spent a lot of time developing a range of funding schemes to fill in the gaps in the existing funding system, but also to jumpstart new initiatives. I was very lucky to have such open-minded bosses at the time. The Executive Director of the Council, Choo Thiam Siew, and my immediate superior, was always open to new ideas. We tried new schemes to provide stability to companies, so instead of annual grants, we gave out two-year grants. I remember having to argue that in the UK, National Theatre companies and the Royal Opera House did not have to apply annually for funding as they typically planned for their season two to three years in advance. Long-term funding enabled arts organisations to plan better, and that kind of stability was good for the industry as a whole.

I also recall thinking that our Singapore writing scene then was suffering from a lack of new blood, so I suggested a scheme called the Mentor Access Project, where we would pair up emerging writers with experienced ones to give them the opportunity to be mentored and to develop their craft. I believe the scheme still exists today. We also decided to pour more resources into sending writers on writing residencies, and to allow local publishing companies to access publishing grants, in order to generate more interest in putting Singapore writers in print.

We also started a completely new grant called the New Media Fund to support "live" artists and those working in new media, because their works are sometimes genre-defying and fall in between the funding cracks. Overall, it was such an amazing time. We had the resources and the leeway to dream. I had such a positive experience working in the government at that time. Having said that, there have also been really trying periods, when my department had to manage censorship and licensing conflicts as well.

Do you recall any challenging episodes that you had to encounter as an artist and an administrator?

I recall the play *Talaq* by Elangovan as being one of the more challenging episodes during my time at the Arts Council. *Talaq* is a monologue based on the real life story of a woman, and examines issues of rape and marital violence within the Indian Muslim community. I thought it was an important piece, and a well-written one. But it caused an uproar amongst certain groups, who were vehemently opposed to it being staged, the protest escalated to higher authorities.

At that time, NAC would usually provide the Public Entertainment and Licensing Unit (PELU) with our views and advice on licensing these plays, in consultation with the Drama Review Committee. However, due to the political nature of this case, the decision was completely taken out of our hands, and eventually, the play was denied a license by PELU on the grounds of it being offensive to religious sensibilities. I remember feeling quite helpless then. For an artist and an arts advocate, it was a challenging position to be in and it was made more complicated by the fact that Elangovan was also one of my staff at NAC then.

In some ways, my time at NAC was akin to doing social work. I say this because for those of us who feel deeply, emotionally and passionately about the arts, and who are constantly advocating from the inside—we face a high level of burnout. The relationship between the artists and the government has always been tense, and the arts managers and administrators are sometimes caught in between.

All this time, while I was at the Arts Council, I was still performing, and very much a part of the theatre scene. Choo Thiam Siew would say jokingly every time I headed into his office to discuss a policy, "Okay, put on your NAC hat and tell me what you think." Then he would say, "Okay, now put on your artist hat and tell me what you think." I appreciated his effort to see alternate points of view, even when they clashed, and it was something I did often during my term as a Nominated Member of Parliament—deliberately putting on different hats or different lenses so that I could see things from multiple perspectives. My time at NAC provided me with the foundation to do my work as an NMP later on—managing differing interests and artistic conflicts, being empathetic yet understanding the wider interest of what the government thinks is best. I don't think that kind of line is easy to tread.

After four and a half years though, I was beginning to feel burnt out. I was only 28, but I felt physically and emotionally exhausted. I was uncertain if arts administration was going to be my career or if I should pursue my passion as a full-time actor. I took a six-month sabbatical, during which I performed in at least six theatre productions and undertook television projects as well. I even spent two months in Bali completing my yoga teacher training. The time I spent there, away from Singapore and my daily routine led me to realise how much I desired to be an actor and an artist. It was not an easy decision, as I would still have a bond to repay, but it felt right at that time.

Now that this is your career, what do you like better? Theatre or television and why?

In the theatre, the actor is the one in control once the curtain opens. The director can't shout in the middle of the play or yell "Cut!" if something goes wrong. There's something wonderfully risky and magical about performing live in front of an audience—to not only bring them along on your character's journey but to hear their response, their laughter or tears. It is a communal experience and it's very powerful. It's the reason why I fell in love with acting and the stage. And I find the whole rehearsal process equally enjoyable. I sometimes joke that once a show opens, I want to move on to my next project because I love the sense of discovery on the rehearsal floor, the unravelling of the playwright's thoughts, the characters' mindsets—all these things are very exciting for me. But once you open, we have a different of set of problems, which is keeping what you have found alive and new, night after night. For an actor, the theatre is a very special medium.

Having said that, I like doing film and television too, even though camera acting is very different. If you are fortunate enough to be involved in a project that has a great script and which reaches out to many people at once, it is amazing to be part of that. I also like the intimacy of the camera. It took me a while to appreciate the difference between performing to a room of 300 people and performing to a small camera lens, but I have grown to love both.

Which is your favourite role to date?

I always considered one of my very early roles, *Descendants of the Eunuch Admiral* as one of my favourites. I did that role when I was 22. The reason I still enjoy it today is because it was my first Kuo Pao Kun script—he was still alive at that time and was consulting on that production—but also because the themes in the play resonated with me deeply. The condition of Zheng He was the Singapore condition. It was moving and poignant for me at the time. I have a few other roles I love—including playing the lawyer Angela Ang on two seasons of *The Pupil*.

Where and how do you envision the arts, film and theatre scene and industry in the near future?

Art movements come in waves—sometimes it depends on the movers and shakers of the time, how influential they are across disciplines, the state of the economy and patronage during that period and so on.

I think Singapore film is going through a wonderful burgeoning at the moment, and I feel that some important stories are being told through film right now, similar to how it was in theatre say, 15 or 20 years ago. I also am very optimistic about where our independent music and literary scene is heading. There's a lot of buzz and interest, and I think a new and younger audience is slowly building for these genres, which is great. I am very heartened by the growing support on local radio stations for Singapore music, and I hope that will continue in a big way, especially for non-mainstream music tastes.

I am less optimistic about our theatre scene. I feel it has gotten expensive to produce theatre in Singapore, which does not bode well for new writing, younger practitioners and emerging talent. The fact that cost of production has an impact on ticket prices also means it will be harder for lower-income Singaporeans to afford and access the performing arts. At the same time, I'm concerned that censorship and over regulation has had an adverse impact on risk-taking and innovation in the arts. I think this is something we need to be careful about. A vibrant arts scene is sustained on the back of a thriving underground or fringe movement. The arts provide a safe space for society to reflect upon and think about the issues of the day. If we put too many restrictions and OB markers on what can or cannot be said in the theatre, there will be less room for the groundbreaking and experimental, and eventually we would find our theatre less and less relevant.

In the mid to long term though, I think Singapore needs more producing houses rather than receiving venues. We need performing spaces who have the budget to commission and programme works by emerging and mid-career artists. A performing venue with an artistic direction can play a vital role in building new audiences through creating a brand name or a distinct reputation for certain kinds of work, like the Royal Court Theatre, Riverside Studios or Sadler's Wells. I think the contemporary dance scene, for instance, could really benefit from having a performing space dedicated to dance.

How do you think social media has changed our perception of entertainment?

I think it changes our idea of entertainment but I don't think it changes the need and desire for good stories and good storytelling. It doesn't matter whether you are doing theatre, film, blogging or video clips on YouTube, you will still need to be a good writer. You need a good story and we will always need good actors to bring the stories to life. It's still very much skilled-based, and my belief is that the core components of what makes good stories don't really change.

Let's talk about your bid for NMP. How did that start?

I would say that I was kind of pushed off a cliff, because when the idea was proposed to me, I said I would consider it. The next thing I knew, my name was quoted in the papers as a potential nominee. Once it was out in the press, I realised I had little choice but to throw my hat in. But maybe that was the best way—there are some things you can't think too much about. Just do it. This was at the end of 2011.

Why did you want to take on the role?

The idea of running for the position of Arts NMP had always been at the back of my mind. Perhaps it was something I didn't consider earlier because I wasn't confident that I could do it well. It's a little like parenthood—you will never feel prepared if you've never done it before. But when you finally do, you realise you just have to learn on the job!

While we were searching for other potential candidates for this post as my term was coming to an end, many suitable individuals whom I approached said to me, "Not this year. It's not a good time." But, honestly, there's no good time for anybody really. We all seem to agree it's an important role, but not many people are willing take up the mantle to do it.

For me, the NMP post is important because it's about having representation and a voice at the highest level of government. It is a vital and powerful platform to raise issues that need to be heard by the wider public, by Singaporeans and by the media. This was the primary reason why I felt it was important to step up. Having worked both in government as well as in the arts sector, I had the added benefit of seeing how policies are formed and executed from both points of view, and felt I could be useful by applying that experience.

One of my main objectives was to raise awareness about the state of the arts and to provide a cultural lens on issues that affect Singapore and Singaporeans—be it education, urban planning or manpower. Culture and the arts should not merely be the business of artists alone. I didn't see myself as simply representing artists. I was representing a segment of the population who cared about our heritage and our cultural development.

I think the NMP for the arts can play a significant role in being a community mobilizer. As much as it was important to advocate and raise awareness within Parliament, the NMP role also has the potential to activate the ground and serve as a bridge between the constituency you represent and the government. Many of the issues I raised were results of extensive discussions and consultations with diverse groups from within the creative sector. I think that made artists and art-makers realise that all of us have a role to play in the advocacy process, and in making an impact on public policy. You can't just depend on your NMP in Parliament.

In one of my Parliamentary speeches, I once said that Singapore needs loving critics and critical lovers. Sometimes, government can be overly sensitive to criticism from Singaporeans, and view pushback or resistance as ingratitude or being unpatriotic. A strong opposing point of view, one that disagrees with the status quo, can come from a deep sense of patriotism and belonging. This includes the sometimes dissenting voices of artists, who raise a mirror to society.

How do you think you fared as an NMP?

I'm not sure what the benchmark should be to measure success. I can only say that I'm glad I spoke up on all the issues that I wanted to cover during my term in Parliament. Some of these include advocating for more financial support for the arts, highlighting the role of literature, creativity and critical thinking in our education system, and pushing for greater support and visibility of our creative industries, including Singapore fashion, design, music and film, which I feel are our more "portable" arts products.

Headway was made on some issues. For instance, it is nice to hear songs by Singapore bands and musicians being played on our local radio stations these days. This was something I advocated for at every opportunity and every Budget debate because the radio stations were resistant to playing local music up until recently. As a result, our Singapore musicians were hardly getting support from the public. It was very heartening to work with the local music community and see some changes in this area during my term. Today, most young people would recognise The Sam Willows, Gentle Bones and Charlie Lim as part of our music scene.

In the same way, having raised the topic of funding for the arts countless times in Parliament, it was very encouraging when the Ministry of Culture, Community and Youth (MCCY) managed to secure substantial monies from the Ministry of Finance to start the Cultural Matching Fund. The Fund provided dollar-for-dollar matching grants for any donations raised by charitable arts organisations. This was hugely significant for the arts community, and we were extremely fortunate that I raised the subject at a time when the new Ministry was keen to announce some impactful initiatives for the Budget.

On the other hand, I would have liked to see some progress made in terms of loosening up guidelines on arts regulation and censorship. Unfortunately, the government is still very conservative on this front, so this kind of change needs to be supported by the Singapore public at large, and cannot be the battle of artists alone.

I think, ultimately, my objective was to raise issues that I felt were important to Singapore or Singaporeans, and which needed to be debated or discussed at a wider level. My audience was not just the politicians. It was paramount that the issues reached as many Singaporeans as possible, and as such, it was critical to find the right platforms to be heard. That meant knowing how to tap on both online media as well as traditional print and broadcast channels.

It's not useful or impactful to simply preach to the converted. For positive change to take place, Singaporeans need to first appreciate that a rich and vibrant cultural life and an openness to innovation, creativity and diverse points of view are vital to Singapore's future, and not just our economic success. I felt that I managed to achieve some level of this in some areas. These instances include the time where the role of Literature and the prevalence of tuition became hotly debated issues in the media after I had raised them in Parliament. Sometimes, my intervention as NMP may not necessarily bring about change, but I think it is still impactful when it can generate dialogue on a complex issue.

Overall, I felt that my two and half years in Parliament was extremely meaningful and rewarding. But it was also a lonely journey at times.

Given what you know now about the NMP role, what changes would you like to make to the position?

I think it would be helpful to increase the NMP allowance to provide them with sufficient funds to hire a legislative assistant or researcher during their term in Parliament. Few people know that NMPs receive about $1,600 a month, which works out to be about 10% of what an elected MP receives. For an NMP to make a significant contribution in Parliament, especially with the complicated processes and research involved in debating and drafting Bills and so on, they could really benefit from some legislative support. It is unrealistic to expect the NMPs to be able to represent well if, like everyone else, they have to manage day jobs on top of their Parliamentary duties, without any form of external help.

During my term, I had to cut down on my projects in order to focus on the NMP work, and whatever fee I was given went to my PA intern, or ad hoc assistants, who helped me organise community town halls meetings, write minutes and conduct ground research.

Is it harder for a woman and a mother to be in politics?

I think politics can be very challenging for women, especially those with children or tasked with caregiving. There were times when I would stand up in the middle of a Parliamentary sitting, and leave the Chamber thinking, "Am I the only one who has to go pick up my kid from class? Does everyone else not have this problem?" The kinds of responsibilities and duties expected of our elected MPs in Singapore are quite tremendous. I cannot imagine it being easy for women with families to take care of to be able to juggle all that. Until there is a change in mindset about the balance of gender roles at home, and until more men are willing to take on a greater share of caregiving in the home, I think it will be hard to see more gender equality in politics and in Parliament.

Do you think your gender has hindered you in any way? Or have you used it to your advantage?

I think that women have a certain way of achieving their goals and objectives that are different from men. We have a different approach to communicating and listening. I am not saying men can't do it; it's just a different touch.

I sometimes call my time in Parliament a "dance" because I had to tread on sensitive, controversial themes and issues during the course of my term—be it LGBT, censorship or funding. How do you raise topics which might be thorny or which government may not want to talk about and yet keep the discussion constructive, productive, diplomatic and civil? Sometimes you have to be critical or reflect on an opposing point of view, but at the same time, you need to express your views and find support from those in government to find the room for change. It's a dance.

Knowing how they work on the inside was very important and, in a sense, it is more complex than going into Parliament and banging on the table. It's a lot to do with timing. You learnt that there was a time to play hardball and there were times you needed to be soft or pull back, depending on the public mood and political climate. So, if you want to make something go along your way, you need to be quite sensitive to when is the right time to say your piece.

I was in Parliament during the debate over *And Tango Makes Three*, a book about two male penguins taking care of a baby penguin. There were energetic exchanges online and in the mainstream media, and people generally fell into two camps—those who felt the book should be removed from library shelves because of its LGBT overtones, and those who felt the book had value in welcoming diversity and difference. I acknowledge that there is a clash of values, and this is not an easy one to resolve. But the government tends to be take the conservative approach in such instances. They become ultra sensitive to those who take offense. It's like there is a fear of debate, a fear of having to negotiate differences. So, removing the book is the easier option, because if the book is not there, no one will argue about it.

In this case, I felt it was important to have a clear position to articulate and reflect the views of the many who are more liberal and open-minded—those who felt that they wanted the right to exercise their choice in reading this book to their children, and that it wasn't the place of National Library Board to make this decision for them. This was the time to be "hard", to ask questions regarding internal decision-making processes—not to stir up controversy, but to ensure that the procedures and the system are fair and transparent to all, and not just to a vocal minority. There will always be uncomfortable issues for our society, and yes, we do need to tread them sensitively and carefully, but it is also not healthy for us to close off discussions or sweep them under the rug.

What were the biggest challenges you faced while you were NMP?

I think the biggest challenge is not having enough empathetic voices in the Parliament and in the government, who understand or recognise the role of the arts in society. I think many people acknowledge the idea that culture is important, but lack a deeper understanding of what it does or can do. So there is a great appreciation of art as a thing of beauty, as a platform to represent our cultural diversity, as an activity that brings people together through shared experience. But there is less acceptance of art as the medium to seed new ideas; that it might challenge or question the status quo; that it also strains to test the boundaries of established practice and holds a mirror up to society to expose its strengths and flaws.

As a society, in order for us to progress, innovate and seek new ways of thinking about ourselves and the world, we need to give our storytellers and artists the license to not only reflect on our past actions and our history, but also to challenge and to test the norms. That is the beauty of art—it provides a safe platform to play pretend, to project, and to look at the world through another pair of lenses. I find the government quite resistant to this aspect of art-making, and as such, the arts, publications and broadcast media are often regulated and controlled with a heavy hand in Singapore. This can have a chilling effect, not just on art-makers, but also on Singaporeans at large.

One of the few people I really appreciated during my time in Parliament was Deputy Prime Minister Tharman. He was the only one in Cabinet who would come up to me to tell me how much he enjoyed my speeches even though it may have contained subtle criticisms of certain policies. He always appreciated where I was coming from, and I value that.

And speaking as a mother, I felt that the all-consuming nature of the work did not justify my spending so little time at home. I spent so little time with my children in the course of those two and a half years. The upside is that my kids have become very self-reliant and independent in their school work and travel arrangements.

Let's talk about you as a wife and a working mother. How does your husband respond to your multiple hats and undertakings?

My husband and I have very similar outlooks towards our roles as parents. As individuals, we feel it is important to be able to pursue what we do to our best ability. He has always been supportive of my work as an actor and of my short stint as an NMP, because he felt that that was an important part of my development and an important contribution to Singapore. The fact that I am also a mum shouldn't necessarily be the reason why I stop doing all those other things.

Sheryl Sandberg in *Lean In* said that a woman can "have it all". Do you think a woman can have it all?

I think Singaporeans are still largely conservative and patriarchal in our outlook, and we don't really question when a man is the main breadwinner, while the woman bears the burden of being the one who takes care of the household, even while pursuing her own career.

In this sense, I think it's a fallacy that a woman can have it all. Unless there is equal support at home from your spouse, even the most successful career woman would have to make sacrifices. They are either sacrificing time at home and leaving it to another caregiver to take care of the kids or they are sacrificing some kind of career move at work because they've chosen to scale back and spend more time at home.

We are nowhere close to the Scandinavian countries, where there is greater acceptance of an equitable balance of roles at home. Having said that, I think we are making progress, and I'm very encouraged that the government has increased the paternal leave allowance to signal that change. I think a lot more can be done to make childcare more accessible and affordable, so that Singapore households can become less dependent on live-in help and domestic workers.

Let's shift gears and talk about your personal coping mechanisms. Is it hard to read scathing reviews or negative criticisms? How do you handle that?

I think it's always hard to receive negative feedback. However, it's par for the course really, when you are an actor, so I've had to grow a thick skin! You do learn to take things in your stride and it is part of the journey. As a public figure, you just have to acknowledge that it comes with the territory. If you want to lessen the pain, don't read the reviews. Simply believe in what you are doing and continue to do your best anyway. I always try to see where there is room to do better, and I've always learnt something from criticism, even from my worst acting reviews. What is more important is not allowing any negative press hold you back and doing what you are capable of.

How did you deal with your naysayers while you were an NMP?

When I first stepped up to run for the NMP post, I think some people brushed me off as just another Mediacorp actress. I don't even work for Mediacorp! Perhaps few people knew of my experience in government and that I was trained in arts policy, but what can you do? There will always be naysayers. It did wake me up to the very public nature of this role and signaled that I had to be prepared for that. It woke me up to the idea that you can't please everybody and you can't represent everyone. And so you speak up on issues that are closest to your heart, that you believe in, and that reflect the views of the community you are meant to represent. For me, it was important to always be authentic and honest, but gracious.

How are you now that your term as NMP is over? You must have more time for the family and acting now.

My kids finally got their mum back! Being an NMP and acting at the same time was all-consuming. As an actor, I just go into rehearsal or go on set to do the work. I don't bring my characters home when the day is done. But as NMP, I had countless sleepless nights agonizing over speeches, policies, research—there was no day off.

I developed a newfound respect for all MPs. It's no easy task to take on this kind of public role—to find time for your constituency and still be able to juggle a family and a career. I couldn't imagine doing all that I did without the support of a helper at home, or the help of a strong support system. This is especially true for female MPs.

Knowing what you know now about yourself, what would you have told a younger version of yourself?

I would tell my idealistic student-self to be braver about chasing my dreams. I would have been less of a realist. Sometimes it's better to don't think, just do. I don't know what life would have brought if I had just decided to go away to do my degree in Drama anyway, and worked to pay it off on my own.

What is your favourite book?

One of my favourite novels is *The Great Gatsby* by F. Scott Fitzgerald.

Who is your favourite director?

In television, I really enjoy working with Lee Thean-Jeen, who wrote and directed *The Pupil.* He's one of the few writer-directors I trust to understand character development and the actor's craft, and we are always on the same page when it comes to the story and the approach. I recently had the privilege of working with film director Jon Chu on *Crazy Rich Asians,* and was totally blown away by how precise, calm and gracious he is, even under intense time pressure.

It's so much harder to pick one director in the theatre! I love working with Ong Keng Sen, the late Krishen Jit, Ivan Heng, Chong Tze Chien—all for very different reasons, but mainly because they have strong visions and a great love for their actors, and they have made great contributions to the artform.

How do you best want to be remembered?

I want to be remembered as a loving mother and wife, a steadfast friend, a passionate LGBT and arts advocate, and an inspiring actress. Oh gosh! So much more needs to be done for me to fulfill all that!

If you met God, what would you say?

I don't know really. If there was just one God, I would ask him why mankind can't be kinder and more loving towards each other. I would ask him why he made man to always fight each other over God—it is so ironic.

Maverick or Madonna?

I am not a Maverick nor a Madonna—I am neither a rebel or a saint. I see myself as a Mobilizer. I like moving people into action and bringing people together.

The Wild Child

FANNY LAI

Fanny Lai was the Group CEO of Wildlife Reserves Singapore, taking care of Singapore Zoo, Night Safari, Jurong Bird Park and the development of the River Safari. During her leadership, the parks were transformed into Singapore's leading tourist attractions.

She was also the Director of Communications for McDonald's for 12 years and is often credited as the brains behind the phenomenally popular Hello Kitty campaign. She also had extensive experience in advertising and was a Chinese journalist.

Today, the retired corporate executive has taken on a new role as a nature conservationist as well as a cartoonist, even though she has had no formal training in art or cartoon illustration. Her Nini and Polah books are inspired by comic books read in her youth, such as "Old Master Q", "Mad Magazine" and "Mr Kiasu".

She enjoys a good laugh and now spends her time travelling around the world exploring wild places and conducting field conservation work. She resides in Singapore and Denmark with her husband, Bjorn, an avid conservationist and photographer. She has two grown up children.

***

When I first met Fanny over a decade ago, she was the head honcho of the Wildlife Reserves Singapore (WRS). I was a rising theatre director, and we were in constant contact trying to create a series of educational and entertaining theatrical programs for the visitors. We discussed the conception of school tours for students and musicals inspired by the movie *Madagascar*. What struck me was Fanny's ability to listen, and her genuine interest and support for the arts, which was such a breath of fresh air for a young artist like me.

Unlike most CEOs who seem concerned only with the bottom line, she was always more keen on project ideas, which truly inspired creators to work harder to see the projects come to fruition. What also took me by surprise was her colourful dressing and big hair. Back in the day, Fanny would wear comfortable and brightly coloured jeans with animal prints, which struck me as being rather bold for a head honcho. Later, this creative streak became even more obvious after her retirement. Fanny has taken her love for comics seriously and has gone on to publish a series of cartoons and conservation books with her husband, Bjorn.

Our chat took place in Goodwood Park Hotel where nobody seemed to recognise her. Back in the day, she was easily recognisable and was often featured in the papers. She was undoubtedly a great PR asset for the Zoo given her stellar background in the area.

A decade on, I am thoroughly impressed with Fanny's ability and choice to pursue what she has always set out to do. Many executives I know get seduced by the comfortable lifestyle of being a CEO and never get back to pursuing their dreams. Fanny, however, seems immensely happy in her newfound freedom and is actively pursuing her childhood ambitions.

Effectively bilingual and articulate, I had been afraid that her answers would be press ready. Indeed, there are times when they were, but those moments were related to questions on her divorce, children and when other personalities are involved. However, with all other personal questions, Fanny was delightfully open, though thoughtful. Perhaps due to her Chinese proficiency, she answered the questions in a short, sharp and succinct manner without excessive hyperbole, verbosity and garrulity that most native speakers of English can sometimes unconsciously affect.

Her creativity, it seems, is tempered by a pragmatic head on her shoulders. She always knew she had a passion for art but chose a practical path in marketing, which she saw as a great combination of creative artistry and career feasibility. What I admire about her is her ability to live in the moment while planning ahead for her future. She always knew she wanted an early, comfortable retirement and consciously worked towards that.

Today, Fanny seems completely at ease doing what she loves most—drawing cartoons, working on conservation and travelling to far-flung parts of this world with her husband and soulmate. It seems, after years of corporate captivity, this innate wild child is finally able to roam free.

***

Share with us your background.

I grew up in Changi Village with my family of eight—mum and dad, and six children. That was in the 1950s and 1960s. We moved out of there when the government redeveloped the area for the construction of Changi Airport in 1974 and we relocated to town. You can say I'm very much a village girl. I studied in Anglican High School and then Ngee Ann Polytechnic and graduated with a diploma in Business Studies. I later went to King's College, London, for a Business degree and completed my MBA at the University of Chicago.

How was it like growing up?

It was comfortable. My dad was running a retail shop in Changi Village. When we moved to town, we had shops in Shaw Centre and Lucky Plaza. They were small souvenir stores selling anything that tourists would want to buy in the 1970s and 1980s—sporting goods, jewellery, knick knacks, collectibles, antiquities and the likes. There are just only a handful of these stores left in Singapore.

How long did your dad's business last?

All the way until my sister took over the business. But eventually, the concept went out of fashion. None of us are doing this anymore because we all have our own careers, so it closed in the 1990s when we got married and led our own lives.

Are you effectively bilingual?

My primary school and secondary school were all conducted in Chinese and I learnt to read and write in *fan ti zi*, Traditional Mandarin. At the time when I was in tertiary education, Singapore eradicated Chinese-dominant education and brought in a system that emphasised English. Schools started to teach Simplified Mandarin and introduced the use of *hanyu pinyin*. These days, when I start to write in Chinese, I find myself having to relearn the Chinese characters as today we use only *jian ti zi* and so I do feel a sense of loss with my Chinese heritage. That is why I decided to write Chinese versions of my books, I did not want to lose my Chinese background and heritage. Yes, I am effectively bilingual and am very influenced by Chinese culture and traditions.

But when I went to the UK, I had to learn all things British—the etiquette, history, humour and the afternoon tea culture. When I was working at McDonald's for 12 years, I was influenced by American culture—celebrities, consumerism, marketing, branding. It has a huge talking culture, so I also learned to come out of my shell, to be a little more talkative. Before that, I was introverted and did not like to open up myself to others and brag about my successes. But to succeed in America, you have to be larger than life, so I was persuaded to come out of my shell in order to market my company and my own capabilities. I will say I am a hodge-podge of Singaporean, Chinese, British and American culture.

How did your career begin?

Like everyone, I started work right after I graduated. I began with the now defunct Chinese newspaper, Sin Chew Jit Pao before it merged with Lian He Zao Bao. These days, no one speaks of Nanyang Siang Pao and

Sin Chew Jit Pao. I was a junior writer and we created commercial stories for clients. These writings functioned as advertorials. You see, back in the 1970s, newspapers had to write a positive spin on their clients' services or products, before their advertisements were published in order to boost credibility. I call myself a junior writer as opposed to a journalist as I was basically writing press releases for advertisers.

On the upside, I got to meet many entrepreneurs, advertisers and marketers, so much so I ended up working in an advertising agency. One day, a client who liked my work style recruited me, and I crossed over to the client's side for about seven or eight years. I worked on the KFC and McDonald's accounts for several years and eventually became the Marketing Manager for McDonald's. I was there for 12 years and worked my way up to Director of Marketing and Communications.

How did you get started in fast food?

When I was on a holiday, I read *McDonald's: Behind the Arches* by John F. Love. He wrote about McDonald's founder Ray Kroc and how he had started his business when he was 55 years old, quite late in life, and became very successful. It was an inspiring and interesting story. I like autobiographies of iconic personalities such as Walt Disney and others. Anyway, I also read *Grinding It Out* by Ray Kroc and other books on McDonald's. In the 1980s, the fast food industry was booming in Asia. They are strategic and systematic and are really in the business of real estate rather than restaurant operations. I decided then that I wanted to be in this game.

What did you take away from all these differences in cultures?

I have been privileged to work in different local and international organisations, and encountered diverse corporate and social cultures. It taught me to be humble, tolerant, self-aware, inquisitive and to learn to understand and embrace diversity, not only in the nature conservation sense of the word, but in terms of cultural diversity. One needs to be more open and accepting of national and social differences. I find that travelling to somewhere you haven't been before is an excellent exposure to experience cultural diversity.

Do you still think in Mandarin?

I don't think so, most of my knowledge sources are in English, but I do subscribe to Lian He Zao Bao to supplement my diet and I have been a member of the Promote Mandarin Council for many years. However, if I picked up a book on philosophy by Zhuang Zi and started to read again, I can relate to it immediately. I have made an effort to improve my Chinese consistently, for example I am now reading Lee Wei Ling's book about growing up in Singapore, and it is in Chinese.

Share with us your time and career in McDonald's, the backbone of your marketing prowess.

I was working for its ad agency for three years and McDonald's for 12 years. I did thousands of promotions and a few hundred TV commercials. They taught me international marketing, how to go global and think local. I received the latest marketing training and was involved in regional as well as global marketing.

I have loved marketing from my Ngee Ann Business Studies days. When I received my Philip Kotler Second Edition marketing textbook, I actually read it cover to cover and finished it two weeks before school started. I have never read a textbook with that kind of intensity and interest before, but I did for Philip Kotler. It remains the one and only textbook that I finished entirely.

It was a book about marketing principles. At that time, we had learned the four P's of marketing. Today there are seven P's. Before my education, I never knew that there was such a discipline as Marketing. A lot of people think you use common sense and a lot of bullshit, but there is a complex science behind it, supported by research and consumer psychology studies. I was very interested in the topics and even while I was in Ngee Ann, I knew I wanted to be a marketer.

I was later sidetracked into advertising, which is one of the key pillars of successful marketing, essentially the creation of a successful brand image. In the late 1970s when I started out in my career, public relations was not well respected in the Singapore market and very few clients would pay a retainer's fee to engage PR consultants to establish positive image.

What would be your key takeaway from your years in marketing?
Being able to manage a crisis is important to turnaround a brand—how you turn an adversity to your benefit. Often, companies get dragged down by a crisis but there are also opportunities that are available to engineer a turnaround depending on how you handle the situation. Consumers often can help to steer companies into the right direction.

On that note, what were some of your biggest crisis management takeaways in McDonald's?
One of the most important things is to know how and when to kill a story by not allowing it to come out in the press. I often spent more time killing stories than getting stories out.

You need a lot of preparation establishing a crisis management protocol, conducting training, engaging stakeholders, and finally testing the communications plan before the crisis happens. It is also very important to prepare solutions for different situations, as well as worst-case scenarios: food poisoning, accidents, fighting and the likes. That's the reason why the Hello Kitty crisis in 2000 turned it into such a positive story.

You are cited as the person behind the Hello Kitty phenomenon. How and why did you decide to create a campaign like that?
In the late 1980s and early 1990s, we created many local promotions that were new to our head office in the U.S. The cute factor or kawaii culture in Asia was very strong. By 2000, Japanese kawaii was on the downtrend and K-pop was rising, but even so, I knew that Hello Kitty was a gem that only needed a bit of polishing.

Anyway, we were already doing a lot of toy marketing to young adults, not simply to children who received a toy with every Happy Meal. The fact that we did a series of toys to cater to young adults was unseen and unheard of in American marketing. We brought in Snoopy, Winnie the Pooh and Disney characters that were extremely popular with the young. I remember when I first approached my boss with the Hello Kitty idea, he was unimpressed. He said, "Who is going to buy this cat without a mouth?" He could not relate to it, and he ignored it. Later he relented, and the rest is history.

We kick-started the release of the dolls a week before 1 January 2000 with six pairs of designs: Space, Romantic, Japanese, Korean, Malay and Chinese. We ordered a huge quantity—400,000 per doll, which is 800,000 pieces multiplied by six. That is a lot of Hello Kitties for an island with five million people, but the promotion just snowballed. It was the first time McDonald's went online, we had people bidding for the complete set of six pairs and the successful bid was over a thousand dollars! Today, Internet shopping may not seem groundbreaking anymore; we are already so consumed by it as we are by social media. But Internet shopping was certainly a novelty medium back then.

The first pair started to sell out within three days and by the time we had the fifth pair on sale, we had 300,000 people queuing at the 113 restaurants. There was just such outrageous queues in the restaurants that we had to get the customers to purchase coupons to place their orders. I even had people ambush me as I was getting into the office! We prepared ourselves very well in crisis management as we had anticipated the demand.

But when the glass broke in one of our restaurants and people started to fight over these little dolls, the police came to reprimand us and told us that we would need a police permit the next time we wanted to do a promotion. We all wanted to laugh when the police spoke to us because we were getting censured over the Hello Kitty plush dolls, but we had to be respectful and abide by them. Subsequently, I was interviewed by BBC and other international media, for this peculiar consumer phenomenon. It was a huge media circus over this Hello Kitty incident, and I had to enter my office through the back door for one full week.

Would you say this was the most successful campaign ever run by McDonald's?
In terms of profitability, it was. But in terms of marketing legacy, I am not sure if I would have wanted it this way. I would much prefer to have less drama. Now that it's been close to two decades, we can have a good laugh, but it would have been better without all the side stories.

You had mentioned that the kawaii culture was on the downtrend and the hallyu influence was rising. So why did you still decide to launch the Hello Kitty campaign?
It's a mixture of my own preference, experience plus research trends. At that time we were very systematic in fishing out what is popular, we conducted trend studies and constantly scanned the pop culture and music scene. We would also benchmark against the programs from overseas.

Which do you think is key—instinct or research?
I read widely on global, regional and local current events, environment, government, politics, arts, films, theatre music and lifestyle. I think it's a mixture of both. Research indicates the trends but you have to take the risk to innovate, create and experience. Remember it took Einstein more than 25 years to prove $E = mc^2$. We all live and learn.

Was it a calculated guess then to order such a big supply of Hello Kitty dolls?
We thought we would have enough just for the promotion with some leftovers which is typical of most promotions. We had 4.8 million Hello Kitty dolls for a population of five million. But even my best guess was completely off.

Looking back as a marketer, what do you think was the secret of the success of the Hello Kitty campaign? What was the draw?
Herd instinct to procure a scarce object, demand and supply imbalance, plus the right timing. When people started to grab the first few pairs,

collectors got frantic and it just got more and more frantic till it snowballed. This limited edition concept really works. Even after 10 years, people are still queuing for it.

What were some of your biggest gains from McDonald's that you took to your next appointment?

I learned a lot about global and local marketing. McDonald's taught us business discipline systematically. I learnt about hands-on operations and the importance of paying attention to detail. In the beginning, I learnt the business by working in the kitchens to flip hamburgers and scrub toilets, just so you really appreciate the day-to-day operations from the ground perspective. This training gave me an excellent insight to management before drafting a marketing plan in the comfort of an executive's office. It was the same at the Zoo. I started off as a docent working in different exhibits and learned about animal sciences for two years before I was employed by the Zoo.

Did you volunteer because you wanted to work at the Zoo or was it just a stroke of good fortune that you ended up working at a place that you love?

I volunteered because I was interested in wildlife. I grew up watching David Attenborough on black and white television. The people I met when I was a docent are still my friends today as we are wildlife and nature lovers.

I started off as a marketing director for the Zoo. Prior to that, I had left McDonald's and joined Singapore Management University (SMU) as their Director of Student Affairs to recruit students. When they inaugurated SMU, they wanted it to be distinct from the other universities, new pedagogy, new faculties, new facilities and they wanted a new breed of students. Meanwhile, I was planning for early retirement; even though I was in my 40s, I had had enough of corporate life and I wanted to experience something different.

Anyway, I was there for only a while and then joined Wildlife Reserves

Singapore as a Director of Marketing. They had consolidated the group as prior to that, the Zoo and Night Safari were one entity, and the Jurong Bird Park was another. The three parks merged into one Group. Soon after, I was promoted to Zoo Director and then became the Group CEO.

What do you think your bosses saw in you to have you promoted so quickly?

I really have no idea, maybe you have to ask them! (*laughter*) I think I am strong in branding, marketing and achieved good results fast. Temasek Holding was and still is the owner of WRS and they needed to make it profitable and financially independent.

At the time, the Zoo and the Bird Park were both losing a couple of million dollars a year, despite receiving government grants. It was pertinent for these institutions to become financially independent. Within a comparatively short time, I was able to focus the team on customer service and marketing, bringing business and commercial operations into a culture that was rather based on animal science. After a comparatively short period, we were able to show a profit with progress in science and education.

Was it, up till then, a very male-dominated environment?

Yes, it was. The Zoo was initially run by a zoologist with little or no commercial background. When I took over, I had to win the trust of my co-workers, as I do not have a zoologist background and was tasked to commercialise the park; this was not a welcome scenario for the scientists there. However, to me, conservation without money is talk only.

At first, I had various team building sessions for everybody to get know each other, create mutual understanding and to start a dual-channel communication. I looked into staff welfare and changed HR policies to benefit the staff so they could share our successes when we started to make a profit. It incentivised them and made it more rewarding for them to work for the company.

Around the time when I joined in 2003, there was an economic crisis, which was followed by a major retrenchment exercise in 2003 and 2004. Morale was low, so I knew we had to work on that as well. Before then, we didn't have a staff appraisal system and the salaries were way below market rates. Sure, they may have some perks as government servants, but it was certainly not on par with commercial organisations. I adjusted their salaries up to market rates, included profit-sharing as part of their bonus, created free staff meals, eliminated unnecessary paper work and finally implemented a five-day work week. I reached for all the low-hanging fruits.

Were people easily won over?

The first two years were spent mainly to build the team and win their trust and respect. We started to change things and created F&B outlets and retail shops, and the various departments for training, sales, communication, marketing and advertising. We changed the service attitude to focus on customers and the community besides animals and plants.

We upgraded the customer touch points and the infrastructure step by step: toilets, ticketing lobby, theatre, exhibits and education centers. We aspired to see the smiles on the faces of our visitors. We took over, renovated and developed a dozen new restaurants so that our customers could enjoy a break in a comfortable area with good food at reasonable prices. We redesigned all the exhibits to provide better conservation education and easy to understand interpretive signage, and created our own gift shop.

I remember the gift shop was previously operated by a third-party. When we took over the business, we made more than a hundred thousand dollars a month right away, which was way better than merely collecting rent. But it was a lot more work because I had to set up a merchandising team and create our own brand of toys, books, collectibles and memorabilia. However, the process was rewarding, fun and exciting.

You introduced many innovations and transformed the Zoo from a local park to a world-class tourist attraction. Share with us your thought process and strategy.

At that time, my vision was to make Singapore Zoo a learning Zoo. To do that we had to make sure that we were financially successful, so we developed the park's F&B and retail outlets, plus sales promotion and advertising to increase local and tourist visitors. We generated revenue and profit to fund improvements of infrastructure for our animals and staff, and to focus on conservation education. The entire process took about three years.

What is your management and leadership style?

I focus a lot on pacesetting and affiliative matters. People come first. Before me, the staff never had their bosses come round to do team building. I implemented many events so we had to go out and do outdoor activities and adventure camps to build trust. I feel it is critical that the team has a strong sense of belonging to the organisation and bond with each other. You bond a lot better when you are in a non-work environment. We had a lot of those sessions.

I learnt as much as I could about the day-to-day running of a Zoo by having a close network with great international zoo directors, and I put in extra hours to read all the zoo management publications I could get my hands on, so that I could set higher standards. I also worked a couple of months on the ground as a zookeeper, and I can say I've never seen so many different kinds of poop in my life!

What did you learn from being on the ground?

When I work on the ground, I appreciate the staff's contributions and efforts. Which is why once I am back in the office, I benchmarked and adjusted their salaries to bring them up to par with similar functions in other industries. I also included cross-training, as I noticed that ground staff lacked inter-departmental understanding, because their knowledge was compartmentalised. It was a great experience for me, especially when we restructured the education department, and implemented a new conservation supplementary syllabus. We could see its impact on the primary school students immediately.

What are some of your key milestones or personally memorable achievements?

I had memorable achievements both in McDonald's and the WRS. When I was in McDonald's, aside from the marketing, I worked on the Ronald McDonald Children's Charity, which helped kids in need of hospital care. Similarly, when I was in the Zoo, I raised funds to rebuild the Children's Zoo with a large water playground to make them happy.

I inaugurated the Wildlife Reserves Singapore Conservation Fund and we put in a couple of million dollars to support local researchers with grants to pursue projects in biodiversity, conservation of fauna and flora. A percentage of WRS profits goes into that fund on an annual basis.

I also added an educational emphasis. When I first started, I saw countless signboards all over the Zoo to commemorate so-and-so minister who had inaugurated the exhibits long ago. I quietly replaced all of them with educational, interpretive signs that would appeal to the visitors. Little things like that made a difference to public education.

From the generated profits, we invested in the things that matter—animals, customers and community. We created an animal hospital in the Zoo and a research cum discovery centre in the Bird Park, improved animal welfare, enlarged exhibits, improved staff welfare and promoted the conservation of native fauna and flora. These were things we could only do when we were profitable as we did not have to go and beg for money.

What would you have done differently at the Zoo?

I would have taken it a bit more slowly, and not bring about the financial turnaround so soon, in order to enjoy the journey in a less frantic fashion.

Do you think your gender aided or impeded your career?

Everyone knows that in the animal kingdom matriarchal societies are common and successful. For example the bees, bonobo apes, killer whales, lions and elephants just to name a few. Gender has definitely not been a negative factor in my career.

But I noticed that most people are instinctively territorial and they don't like new species coming into their territory and comfort zone—be it male or female. They are afraid that this strange animal may invade their territory and lower their status. Once they experience that this new addition can improve everyone's living conditions, they will start to embrace and support it. Using that analogy, I think it is fair to say I didn't have any problems being a woman helming the Zoo or managing Singapore's largest advertising budget in McDonald's.

Throughout my career, I did not need to do strenuous physical tasks such as restraining the crocodiles or moving heavy cartons of food. As a team, I feel men and women can complement each other in harmony, if we focus on our strengths instead of weaknesses.

Did you implement policies to aid women in their career while you were in the Zoo?

Not specifically for women, but I focused on the family; such as the implementation of Family Day, when families of staff get to preview new exhibits, gain free admission and the kids get to visit mum and dad's work stations to experience their job and understand why they may have to work long hours.

I encouraged staff to head home early to dine with their family. We also gave free meals to our staff. Not only did it cut down travel time, but there's also a certain magic in how people bond over meals. We did many things that benefitted both sexes, for the married and single employees. It's like having flexible hours because we all have different priorities at various stages of our life.

Was there any big crisis you had to battle while you were at the helm? One of the biggest stories, when you were there, was the White Tiger incident.

Animal escapes are inevitable in any zoo. It's like McDonald's where you serve more than a million customers daily, you might have food contamination cases someday. The key is to implement preventative and recovery measures. We spent a lot of time on exhibit design to ensure security, wildlife enrichment activities for the animals and safety protocols for keepers, especially for dangerous animals. I learnt through the years to always be honest and transparent. Don't cover up anything. Apologise when you have made a mistake. Be humble and compassionate. Learn from your mistakes and rectify them as soon as possible.

You broke the stereotype of a CEO and have always dressed flamboyantly with your loud jeans and big hair. Was it a deliberate attempt to break away from convention or pure self-expression?
It was impractical to wear high heels, long sleeves and suits in the Zoo. The distance from the car park to the office is one kilometer and it was without shelter. I dressed for comfort to suit the working environment. As I was running the three parks, sometimes one set of clothing has to stay fresh even after 12 hours of perspiration, especially when I worked in the Night Safari. Wildlife does not care about your makeup and hairstyle, so I didn't comb my hair at all. Most of us simply dressed in uniform or jeans and T-shirts. When I was in the Zoo, I wore the Zoo polo T-shirt most of the time as it was our standard uniform.

Do you think your management and leadership style evolved between your two careers?
When I was in McDonald's, I was Marketing and Communications Director. When I was running the WRS Group as a CEO, my job scope had expanded, so yes, I had to evolve.

Not surprisingly, as a high achiever in McDonald's, I was an opportunistic go-getter—persuasive, demanding, precise in time management and in achieving priorities. I was also task-oriented instead of people-oriented. An epitome of an up and coming lady boss. However, to lead the team in WRS, I had to mature into a leader that is able to inspire and delegate, to instill confidence and positive attitudes and most of all, to use creativity and commitment to transform the business. So yes, I have certainly evolved. There are different seasons of our life and as we grow older, we add value to life.

As the stakes became higher, how did you cope with the responsibility of caring for both humans and animals?

It's easier and sometimes more fun to deal with animals. They don't talk back and they behave in a completely natural and honest manner.

One of the biggest challenges that I faced in the Zoo was the anti-zoo groups. They don't believe in animals in captivity and demand animal rights. I felt that the bad zoos in the world have dragged the good zoos down.

The Bird Park, the Night Safari and the Singapore Zoo are probably among the top 10 best zoos around the world and there are a few hundred accredited good zoos in total. We are well-run, with excellent animal welfare, high standards of ethical practice, conservation and are education-oriented. Balanced with excellent customer service and an amazing animal collection, it is a group of world-class tourist attractions with a purpose.

Some of the keepers, who take care of the animals become so very attached to them. They also become passionate about nature preservation. When Ah Meng died, the keepers were crying so hard, as if it was one of their close family members. Anyway, when I thought I had done enough, it was time to move on.

After you left the corporate world, did you miss anything and is there anything you wished you could have done more of?

I wished I could have done more in conservation. It would have been beneficial to use the Zoo to generate funds and volunteers to conduct more conservation work in the field. Not necessarily in Singapore but in nearby regions such as Indonesia, Malaysia and Southeast Asia in general. There are countless conservation projects that need assistance.

My husband and I now spend our time traveling to wild places in the Amazon, Africa, Antarctica and the forests of Asia. Besides my graphic novels *Nini in Changi Village* and *Nini Eat First Talk Later*, Bjorn and I have published two conservation books *A Visual Celebration of Giant Pandas* to raise funds for World Wildlife Fund, and then we did another one titled *A Visual Celebration of the Wildlife of Borneo* to raise funds for Fauna & Flora International. The one we are now working on *Asia's Wildlife: A Journey to the Forests of Hope*, is to raise funds for BirdLife International.

Instead of cutting a cheque to make a donation to the conservation NGOs, we want to help them publicise their stories. Bjorn takes the photos and does the research while I write the text. Most conservation NGOs are strong in conducting fieldwork, but weak in broadcasting their efforts. Just like whispering and blinking to a pretty girl in the dark, only you know what you are doing, but nobody else does. As I said, conservation without money is talk only. You need to tell the story, ask for funding, create awareness, educate the public and shout out loud in our cluttered media space.

For the BirdLife International project, we have visited eight forests in Asia. All I could say is, there is an urgency for us to be connected to nature and give our helping hand.

What have you learnt from working at the Zoo?

They taught me a lot about conservation and how difficult it is to get conservation work done. Of course, the biggest thing that I learnt is that you need resources for conservation. Funding is essential for field conservation work. It is not just about seeking resources to save the animals. We have to take into consideration the communities, the policy makers and the government, plus the complex political issues surrounding them. The process is time-consuming and daunting.

As an outsider, we often think that prevention of animal trafficking is an easy task—simply enforce the rules. But there are many layers, and the bureaucracy is entrenched and complicated. It involves transborder policy, security, control, corporation and corruption. The communication with top level might not filter down to the ground. We also face differences in work culture, inefficiency, lack of technology, information and education. It's like peeling an onion—every layer may make you cry. You have to be patient and persistent to do it step by step. It is a long journey that might take many generations to complete, hopefully by then our biodiversity is still around.

So we need to rid systemic bureaucracy and give violators other means of income besides poaching and killing wildlife?

In 2015, I visited a village in Sri Lanka, outside of an elephant conservation area. Basically, the villagers place bells on some of the elephants and tin cans on their fence to alert the village when the elephants arrive. They don't have money to install hot wire or a strong fence to prevent the elephants from eating their crops. These crops are only harvested twice a year and are their only source of income for the entire year, but when the elephants come, they will eat or damage the crops.

In the comfort of our air-conditioned room on social media, we often ask, why do people kill these majestic elephants? When it comes to bread and butter issues, it is often interlaced and knotty. There are economic needs, lack of housing, jobs, education, water scarcity and a whole host of other issues you have to deal with before you can get to the root of saving wildlife. There are so many humanitarian problems that will break your heart. We need more intelligent and well-informed people to spend their time on these issues, but most of us are not willing to give up our careers to undertake this Mother Teresa task for animal conservation.

What gave you the push factor to live your dream?

I want to live my life the way I want it, and not the way that people expect me to do. People don't expect a CEO with a good income to just give that all up. They assume something must be wrong with you or that you were sacked. Why can't you choose your own path, have your own deadlines and live your life? Must we always dress like what people expect you to do and talk the way they expect you too? I don't care. I don't need lots of money to be wild, free and happy.

There is a Chinese saying that translates to "Your worldly possessions should not become the remnants of your will." We have more than enough for our lifetime, and our children will take care of themselves as they have a good education. For now, my husband and I just want to focus on living our own lives. He has a passion in photography, but he's been working for over 40 years, so now he's finally living his passion of photographing exotic wildlife and donates the work to NGOs. As for me, I want to live my dream as a cartoonist, I've always wanted to do that when I was young, so I decided to try it.

You are a CEO-turned-artist. What would you say to a young girl who comes to you today and tells you she wants to be an artist?
After I had graduated from Secondary 4, I wanted to pursue art in Nanyang Academy of Fine Arts. At that time, we don't have LASALLE and all these art schools. My mum killed that idea and advised that most people who do art will be poor and "starve to death". She insisted that I went to a business school. However, I carried that dream with me for more than four decades. My advice to the younger generation—you have to be pragmatic but don't study something that you could never practice. So when I chose a course of study, I found subjects that I was passionate about: business, marketing, communication, and advertising—I could apply them and make a livelihood from it.

Throughout my adulthood, I never gave up my passion for drawing and doodling. I would draw, paint and sketch during my free time, and when I was working, often I would doodle during seminars and long, boring meetings. I am also a cultural vulture for art museums and art books.

For young people, it is never too early to plan for a good retirement. A lot of people don't spend enough time to plan their life. To retire comfortably, you need financial independence, as you don't want to compromise your lifestyle too much after you retire. You also need to establish a new social circle before your retirement, to keep yourself active and current. People who know you through work may not fit into your new lifestyle. You also need to cultivate a sustainable hobby to provide a sense of purpose. It is not advisable to nurture it after retirement, as it might not be what you are truly passionate about. Cultivate your garden early in life, fertilise it often and enjoy the fruits during retirement.

You seem to subscribe to the belief that life, and all its riches, are transient. What contributed to that philosophy?

Yes. Since young, I had an understanding of the concept "This too shall pass." Be it glory or humiliation. I have little attachment to wealth and material things, and would much rather enjoy beautiful nature and good times with my loved ones. So much so that every time when I visit a new place, meet a new person or have a new experience, I always say to myself that this may be the last time, so I savour the moment like it is the last.

Life is short and I want to live every day like it is my last without regrets. At my age, I have had many friends who have passed away. I know that I do not want to work until I drop dead at my desk. I want to live the way I want it to be—free and wild.

Sheryl Sandberg gained much criticism when she said that a woman can "have it all". What are your thoughts on that?

It is not easy to be a man with growing feminism. It is ideal if women who are very successful in their careers can find a man to complement their strengths and work as a team. I think we should interview the men behind all the successful women, and find out the qualities of good men behind successful women. "Behind every successful woman is a great man." Finding the right companion on the onset is like striking the jackpot in life.

How do you think women fare now compared to how you were when you started?

We have a lot more opportunities in Singapore now compared to the 1960s and 1970s. We have access to the same careers, receive the same education and compensation. Many also venture into industries that were formerly "men's fields". The last I checked we were ranked #55 out of 150 odd countries in terms of gender equality, according to World Economic Forum. We are still lagging behind Scandinavia and some European countries, but we are way above all the Asian countries. We are quite fortunate to be women in Singapore.

I have travelled to places where women have no basic rights. The girls and women have to fetch drinking water from the rivers for their families, walk for miles under the scorching sun just to bring water back to their homes for cooking and drinking, while the boys are in school. We live in a privileged situation so I hope we will value our "entitlement" and help others to move forward and not backwards.

Is that anything we can do to move forward?

One of the key things is for women to be engaged in politics in Singapore. I think they are under-represented. We have 92 MP seats and only about 10 seats are occupied by women. That's only about 10-15 percent of women in politics. If you want to make a difference, you have to be among the decision and policy makers.

I, on the other hand, do not think that I am cut out for politics, as I have no passion for this. I can better contribute to getting people to appreciate and respect nature. That's the path I've taken so I want to focus on that. You need passion in whatever you pursue in order to be successful.

When was your lowest point and how did you overcome that?

You may find it silly, but it was when my mum passed away in 2008 at 83 years of age. I was very close to her. I knew she would go some day but when death hits, it is still hard to say goodbye. I remember lying on the bed and the tears just rolled down. Parting with your loved ones is really difficult. Eventually, I consoled myself that what lives in my heart will never die. I rest, reboot and distract myself with other things, and life goes on.

What do you do in your free time?

I paint, I read and I like to take long walks with my dog. With my husband, we exercise a lot, we do yoga and we run about 30km a week. We swim, we eat, we wine and dine, and we have sex!

What irks you?

When people make a lot of noise trekking in the jungle. They chit-chat, talk and laugh loudly, instead of being calm and try to appreciate and understand Mother Nature. I hope they can open their hearts and cultivate their senses to enjoy the sounds, scents and sights of nature.

How do you want to be remembered?

Funny Fanny!

What would you say to God?

"Hello, Madam!" Why do we presume it's a man?

Would you consider yourself a Madonna, Maverick or any other M word?

People around me say I am Mischievous and Mad!

The Media Meister

TJIN LEE

Tjin Lee is the founder of the Mercury Group, which grew from a three-person outfit in 2000 to a recognised agency that employs 60 people for its creative, events, public relations, marketing and communications arms. The company is also known for organizing Singapore Fashion Week (2015-2016) and Audi Fashion Festival (2009-2014), which showcased designers such as Diane von Furstenberg, Roberto Cavalli and Victoria Beckham.

She is a serial entrepreneur who has co-founded numerous other businesses including Trehaus, a family-friendly co-working space, Wolfgang Violin Studio and Baby Style Icon, an online baby clothing store. She started a non-profit social enterprise called CRIB, which aims to empower women to become successful entrepreneurs through networking, matchmaking and business incubation. For her role as an entrepreneur, and in the Singapore fashion and lifestyle industry, she won the inaugural Singapore Tatler Young Achiever Leadership Award 2010.

Tjin is born to parents who raised their four daughters to be strong and vocal. She studied in Singapore and left for Canada at 17 to pursue a degree in English Literature at the University of Western Ontario. She is married with two sons.

***

Tjin talks very fast—hers was one of the toughest interviews to transcribe because her thoughts, and subsequently, her words, rattle off at the speed of light. It probably explains why she currently has nine businesses under her belt and counting.

The media meister shows up for our interview at VivoCity dressed in a chic black and white outfit with a Peter Pan collar, and does not look a day older than 28. While seemingly aloof and Ice Queen-ish upon first meeting, she warms up quickly once she feels a genuine camaraderie. It is perfectly understandable for one who has established herself in the dog-eat-dog world of public relations, international fashion and high-end luxury.

Tjin presides over her own empire of businesses. The biggest among them is Mercury, which was started in 2000 because she was bored with the cyclical nature of fashion and yearned to do more creative endeavours. One might be tempted to dismiss her achievements as sheer luck, but she bared her soul during our chats and shared that she had been gutted so many times over.

It was especially devastating when, in 2009, Singapore Tourism Board (STB) decided to withdraw its funding support from the fashion festival she was organising. She had to work ceaselessly to garner enough support to still hold the festival, which became Singapore's first privately funded consumer fashion event. It subsequently led to her running of the marquee event till 2014.

The amount of politicking and negativity in the industry can be overwhelming but Tjin stands resolutely by her principles and relies on the support of her team to get through her darkest days. Today, Tjin is bona fide creator and producer. She is a regular face in the society circuit and organises the biggest parties in town.

Motherhood, however, took her by surprise. She found herself so in love with her children that she felt a need to change and restructure her life to afford time with her two bundles of joy. It led to her next phase of entrepreneurship, starting a string of baby-and-mother-related businesses. CRIB is a platform for mothers and women to network, and

Trehaus provides the space for working mothers to have a career and yet be there for the baby's first moments.

What I most appreciated about our conversation was her honest take on pregnancy and motherhood, which is not usually spoken in the local media. She shared that she felt discriminated against as a pregnant mother. Many companies did not award the commissions to her or her company because they consciously, or unconsciously, saw pregnancies and future maternity leave as a liability and an antithesis to efficiency and productivity. This perception, while arguably warranted, can severely curtail a woman's competitive edge in her career. On a macro level, this is also one of the key, unspoken reasons for low birth rates in Singapore and is an unaddressed stigma. It is a politically incorrect observation but I feel it is nonetheless something we should see to as a nation.

In this day and age, we know that image and perception is everything, and if there is anyone who knows that best, it would be the public relations meister herself. So it is certainly timely and necessary that we have this "mama-preneur" champion this cause and use this as her rallying cry—all while showing up immaculately styled and coiffed.

***

Share with us a little bit more on your family background and your famous sister. Was there ever sibling rivalry?

I am the second of four sisters, born to a doctor father and a remisier mother. Min is very much younger than I, hence there wasn't any sibling rivalry. Also, I never envied the many hours of violin practice she had, which was needed to make her what she is today. I admire her discipline and I wouldn't ever compete with that!

Is the middle child syndrome fact or fiction for you?

Fact. But you can make the most of it. I learned to be very independent and socially outgoing as a result of being a middle child.

Before we start formally. Just how many businesses do you own—I have lost count. Can you list them here for me?

I have co-founded more than nine businesses. The key ones are Mercury PR, Mercury Live (Events), Mercury M&C (which runs Singapore Fashion Week), Trehaus (a family-friendly co-working space), Wolfgang Violin Studio (with my mother and sisters) and CRIB (a not-for-profit social enterprise which empowers women through entrepreneurship).

How do you manage your time juggling your businesses and family?

When I was growing up, I was always a tomboy. I didn't really identify with babies and didn't find kids particularly endearing. I felt as if I was always a child—a dreamer, traveller, wanderer as I have wanderlust in my soul. I never thought I could just settle down and have children as it's the opposite to everything I am. I am an intrepid person always on the go.

I sleep very little, just six hours a day, and I believe the less you sleep, the more you do. A typical person sleeps eight hours a day, so I get two extra hours every day, which is 14 hours every week—an additional work day. I did the math and figured I get an additional 30 full days a year! My mind is always active. People have asked how I juggle motherhood and the running of multiple businesses. The truth is I really don't think about it—I just do it as a way of life.

Managing businesses really is about having a very good support network. Every single one of my businesses has a driver or a business manager, and it is not me. It is a matter of empowering yourself and building confidence. I no longer believe that I need to be the one doing everything on my own. I am now driving the business or networking which is what I do a lot better than running the day-to-day business.

You were quoted in *The New York Times* talking about "The ABC for Every New Business". Share with us more on that.

I have a theory about the ABC's of entrepreneurship. Fundamentally, the A, B and C are the three things you need for any business to succeed. Entrepreneurs are usually a combination of one or the other but rarely all three. A's are Angels who have resources to invest but don't necessarily have the skills or ideas for a business. B's are Business Managers, a majority of the population are that—they are good at accounting, are task-oriented or have strong organisational skills. C's are the Creatives—dreamers, movers and shakers. These are the ones who are full of ideas but will die running a business and dealing with numbers, spreadsheets, bottom-line and cash flow. If you are a combination of all three, then I call you a D, Divergent, and that's rare.

I'm a C. I like to create things that I wish existed. If there's a really good idea, and no one is doing it, I figure I'll do it. That's how my businesses start—with a really good idea and an opportunity.

Being a C, would you say creativity is born, bred or both?

I think a lot of it is nature. In the past, Singapore had this curriculum that evaluates students and places them into Science, Commerce or Arts stream where Science was reserved for the top performers, while the students who fared less well were streamed into the Arts. It meant that the arts and creativity were not a priority and less valued. I was channeled into the Arts because I didn't make the cut for Science.

I was naturally creative but faced challenges growing up. I was punished by my teachers when they assumed that I did not write my own essays or create my own art. My mummy had to constantly come to school to defend this renegade middle child. Basically, the school did not think that a 12-year-old was capable of writing a story the way I could. The teacher would embarrass me by reading the entire essay to a class of 40 and ended by saying that it was good, but that I didn't write it.

I am told it's much better in schools nowadays. But if you take a helicopter view, you can see why most companies are not deemed creative. They are run by people of my age, and in my generation, the schools then had systematically killed all creativity. Nowadays, everyone talks about "thinking outside the box" but this lack of local creative talent can possibly be attributed to the quelling of creativity back then, though I am not saying it is the only reason.

What are your thoughts about entrepreneurship, and how did you start your first business?

Success is really not just about dreaming, believing and having passion but it is more about sweat, blood and toil. Neither is it about just having few hundred thousand dollars to start. I know because I've been there and have struggled. You can die simply because you don't have enough cash flow. You may have the passion, drive and the readiness to work hard but if you have a $300,000 debt and can't pay that sum, you have to let your employees go, you can't deliver and the business fails. A lot of first-time entrepreneurs are not equipped and don't understand this. They just think, "If you can dream, you can do it."

People have asked if I always knew I was going to be an entrepreneur. The answer is no, I never had aspirations for it. I was happy to go where the wind blows. But what happened was that I worked for six years at Club 21 and got frustrated with doing fashion as it was very cyclical—I wanted to get out and be creative as I had so many ideas. During the economic downturn in 1997, one of our team members was retrenched so she set up her own PR agency. It seemed to do very well and it gave us the idea to set up our own agency.

Further, at the back of my mind, I knew that if I had children, I knew I didn't want to be working. My sister had a baby at that time and I once saw her two-year-old daughter clinging to her leg and crying for her to not go to work. It was heartbreaking to witness. So I knew I wanted that flexibility—to be able to work and also be there for my child when I did have one. It's not about working less hard. Instead, it is about working harder and yet having the flexibility to control your time.

I believed entrepreneurship was that solution especially when I discovered that many stay-home mums were not content because they are well-educated and resourceful, but are unable to continue with their full-time jobs because there is not enough support. Conversely, many full-time working mothers felt they were missing out on their children's growing up years. At the core of it, I believe entrepreneurship is the key to achieving work-life balance. In my idealistic mind then, I believed that if I worked very hard, I could grow the business to become independent and in five years, I would be the owner of self-sustaining, revenue-generating business. Of course, that is not to be.

I started Mercury with $10,000 and two partners. That failed within a year and a half when my partners couldn't agree. That was a grind as there was not enough money coming in and I was paying myself a minimum income. The business would have folded if I didn't take it over, take on its debts and powered on simply because I had to. The turning point was landing the contract for the Singapore Fashion Festival in 2004.

Share with us what happened with Singapore Fashion Festival.
Fundamentally, I think it was where I was forged. Some women are destroyed by fire and others are forged by fire. I was 29, bright-eyed and bushy-tailed when that happened to me and it was life-changing. Fashion Week made me who I am and I always believe what doesn't kill you makes you stronger—that experience certainly empowered me.

It is the source of strength I draw from as well. Sometimes, when the team says to me that we don't have the resources to operate, I tell them that I did it in 2004 with an intern, a receptionist and me. The three of us made a 16-day Fashion Festival happen!

We had a Chanel Opening Show, Christopher Bailey from Burberry coming to do a fashion talk, a gala show of the Red Carpet Designer of the Year from the UK, Julien Macdonald, and 18 other shows. I thought I brought in really good content for a 30-year old and her team of two. Today, Fashion Week is five days long.

What happened was that we had just landed the Singapore Fashion Festival contract, and my partners decided to leave. We were all quite sheltered in our previous work experiences. Anyway, a year and a half of start-up life meant salary cuts and you never know when you would get paid. We were a very small team of three. The first partner left to move to Kuala Lumpur. Later, the second partner disagreed on the direction. She decided that this start-up life is not for her and she needed more security and wanted to be part of a bigger entity, with a corporate dimension. I was passionate about lifestyle and fashion, but I feared being alone more than I did going the corporate route, so I went with her.

In that process, a few ugly things happened. We landed the Fashion Festival contract, and at that time, the agency that was going to acquire us thought it was going to be a very glamorous project and welcomed us. But after a few months, they realised that sponsorships were not easy to secure and they decided not to continue. They cut me adrift, or you could say I was kicked out of the office, as they took my staff and team and left me alone with a contract I still had to fulfill. Jasmine, the receptionist, and Karen, the intern, were the only ones who stayed with me but everybody else left. It was a tumultuous time but I knew I had to keep going.

My team and I worked every day for months from 8 a.m. to 3 a.m. I would drop Karen home and head back to nap only to pick her up in a couple of hours. I was very proud of the girls as we did the first festival all by ourselves. I remember when the Fashion Festival wrapped after 16 days, what I felt wasn't a feeling of accomplishment and joy, but sadness. I am a perfectionist and kept thinking of what I could have done better, which was what drove me to make it better in the Fashion Weeks to follow.

To my great disappointment, I didn't win the contract for the Singapore Fashion Festival the following year; it went to an international agency instead of my two-woman team. At that time, I was gutted and devastated but I believe things happen for a reason as that led me to work on building a stronger, better Mercury. I took the time to acquire my customers, team and experience so that when the tender came up again in 2008, we could bid against agencies much larger than Mercury. We did, and we won.

As luck would have it, STB changed the three-year contract into a one-year contract as they wanted to reevaluate the two fashion events: Singapore Fashion Week and Singapore Fashion Festival. They asked if I wanted to do it if I only had a one-year contract. I shared that they would lose money on a one-year contract as we could not amortise costs the way we could for a three-year contract but circumstances were what they were.

I was, however, very driven by this vision as I always believed that we could be the fashion capital of Asia and saw the opportunity like a jewel in the crown, especially back in the early noughties. In 2004, Singapore was the right place to be with Orchard Road and all its glamour. There were no IRs (Integrated Resorts) at that time, but I saw the potential in the Fashion Festival, so I decided to take on the contract.

I was truly passionate about developing the events scene and Singapore as a fashion capital. It was really hard at first because top international designers didn't want to come to Singapore—it is a very small market compared to Hong Kong, Japan and China. If an A-list designer like Carolina Herrera or Roberto Cavalli gets an invitation to go to an Asian country, he would certainly prefer to go to Japan or China where he has more stores and potential buyers.

So initially, many designers were not keen and would ask who came the year before. Today, it is less challenging, as we have built up our credibility and the heritage of the events, and we have had designers such as Victoria Beckham, Carolina Herrera and Roberto Cavalli grace our event since. But back in the day, it was hard to succeed without a single big name so I invested out of my own pocket in 2008 and delivered a successful program with six international designers in attendance including Matthew Williamson.

But at the end of the Fashion Festival 2008, STB informed me that there would be no more funding for the Fashion Festival as they were exploring other plans for 2009. I had already invested so much and I was devastated. Any ordinary person might have given up but I refused and decided to offer a strategic partnership to Audi who ended up becoming the title sponsor for the next six years. In 2008, I went out on a limb and my sponsors saw what I could do and believed in me. That was how the Audi Fashion Festival started in 2009. We were also grateful that in 2010, STB saw the potential in our new, private-sector driven Audi Fashion Festival, and came back on board with support for the event that would take us through the next five years.

That was how I came to own it and piloted my own destiny to ensure I would keep control of the event, unless I choose to not do it anymore. Contrary to what many thought, the Audi Fashion Festival was organised, funded, and hence owned by Mercury, with the support of Audi and STB. It took a tremendous amount of private sector fundraising and sponsorship activation to ensure the event was kept afloat at a world-class standard. It was a great partnership and I am grateful to Audi and STB for six years of successful collaboration.

We parted ways with Audi in 2016 because of a change in direction when they had a new management team on board. Yes, that was challenging and naysayers said negative things but I am sure we would make it happen again, for as long as we wish to. Adversity always leads to new opportunities and we will continue to innovate to stay ahead.

What is the new journey of Fashion Week in Singapore?
The Fashion Week continues to evolve year on year. We learn through successes and failures as we evolve. Our greatest challenge to both Singapore designers and the sustainability of any Fashion Week on our shores is that Singapore is a very small market with a population of only five million people. This also affects the size of our local partners and their corresponding marketing budgets.

With tech and digital disruptions, the traditional format of the Fashion Week grows archaic, and we have to evolve beyond being Singapore Fashion Week if we are to grow and thrive. I have had my sights set on the larger Asian stage for a few years, the future will depend on our ability to create a platform that is greater than Singapore and the sum of its designers and partners, beyond just fashion shows and retail pop-ups. We will soon be unveiling new plans—fly or fail. We can only make that leap of faith.

The fashion and luxury industries are known to be bitchy, so how do you stay on top of it and deal with all the negativity?
The industry is bitchy, but this doesn't mean I have to be. In fact, I admire Diane von Furstenberg, whom I invited for the Fashion Week in 2015. She decided early in the game when she entered the fashion industry that she wasn't going to do "that bitchy thing". She was going to

be "a nice person" and do it her way. When I heard her, I thought, "That's exactly it." It is not that I had to consciously tell myself that I am going to be nice, but that I was not to let any of the bitchiness and back-stabbing get to me. I should remain fundamentally who I am, but more armoured and less defenseless.

The fashion industry is filled with big enough egos as it is. I am happy to stay behind the scenes doing the work and never coveted the spotlight. For me and my team, integrity and loyalty are all the driving principles behind everything that I do. It gives me the strength to deal with all negativity.

What does it take to be an entrepreneur?

Perseverance. Entrepreneurship is not for everyone. You must be the kind of person that can get back up, because it is not about how many times you fall but how many times you get back up. I love this Eleanor Roosevelt quote, "The future belongs to those who believe in the beauty of their dreams." It was one of my favourites when I was young. Right now, it is "It doesn't matter how many times you fall, what matters is how many times you get up." I love inspirational quotes as I identify with them and they inspire me to keep on fighting the good fight, but I am not sure if they are realistic as entrepreneurs do have a really challenging time.

There are no safety nets, at least for me. If you jump out there but still want your safety net and day job, it may be hard to succeed in either. You have to be passionate about your product and dive in, or else, it may not succeed. You have to give your all. As an entrepreneur, I've done that many times. Each time I jump, there is no safety net and there never was.

Every business needs to have a USP. If you don't stand out, it's really hard to gain traction. Everyone is using social and digital media and anyone can be an entrepreneur these days but this also sets us up for more failure. Some people think that starting a business is simply buying some inventory, listing it on the website and purchasing a few Facebook ads and it will miraculously take off. That's naive as hell. If your product has USP, you have a better chance.

Do you think being a woman has aided or impeded your career?
Only three out of 10 businesses in Singapore are started by women. And seven out of 10 businesses fail in Singapore within the first three to five years so there are very few successful women entrepreneurs out there.

I don't think being a woman has hindered my progress but being a mother has. In fact, being pregnant was the biggest inconvenience; we realised we secured fewer jobs when I was pregnant. Clients did not want to work with us when they saw that I was in my third trimester. They would rather award the project to another company whose leader was not going to be on maternity leave. People don't want to see a pregnant woman on their account or project, even though I had a reputable company and a team of 60. Eventually, I stopped going to meetings during my pregnancy as I became a liability to my team.

How did that make you feel?
It is a perception. No law could fix that one. When you are looking at someone who is eight months pregnant, you are never going to know if that person is going to come back to work because many women quit. And many of my clients are women and they know their priorities change after a woman has her baby. Even if you assure them of a good team, clients still get nervous. Thankfully, I have bounced right back after my second son. That was a blip on the radar, albeit an eye-opening one.

What would you say to a woman who comes to you and says she would like to be a mother and an entrepreneur?
Come up with a plan because dreams are only dreams. If you can put it on paper, it becomes a reality. I mentor a few women who ask me for advice and I find time to chat with them as I think people should pursue their passions and dreams responsibly.

How has motherhood contributed to your life, personally and towards your businesses?
A lot of my businesses stem out of motherhood. I used to not like children

nor did I want to be a mother—but when I did, it caused a shift in the way I ran my life. When my son was born, he changed my life. I was so enamoured with my baby, I wanted to step back from the business to spend more time with him. I didn't want to miss a thing: his first word, first step, first crawl. I was so distracted and my partners shared that they needed me as I was only pulling in two days a week. I realised I had to prioritise and rearrange my schedule.

While I was taking time out, I met a lot of women, mothers like myself who just had babies. I saw that many of them were very distressed about leaving their children to go back to full-time work, so I have huge respect for women who can. You do get so attached to your child after four months of bonding.

I understand Singapore is an expensive place to live so most people will need two incomes and the baby is usually raised by grannies and nannies. It is also why we have such a low birth rate because if you work full-time, you don't have time for the babies and if you don't work, you can't afford to have more babies. This happens to so many Singaporeans. We don't have the luxury of not working.

Share with us how you started CRIB.

CRIB stands for Creative Responsible Innovative Businesses. It is a social enterprise to help women find a community of entrepreneurs and find work-life balance. We advocate responsible entrepreneurship and educate women on the ABC's. We create an environment where we help minimise the chance of failure by connecting you with potential business partners that complement your skill set.

That is essentially what CRIB is about. After 15 years of being an entrepreneur, I uncovered that that is one of the weaknesses that many entrepreneurs have. Most businesses are started by C's as they have the idea, but they do not have the right team, manpower or the skill sets to drive it and make it multiply and succeed. For this, you need B's. For the lucky ones like myself, I met some B's along the entrepreneurial journey and this is why Mercury was able to take off. Seven out of 10 businesses in Singapore fail. Many people don't realise how challenging entrepreneurship is without the right support and help.

So, I'm advocating responsible business ownership for start-ups because I think these are people's dreams and savings we are talking about. It would be very irresponsible for me to go out and say you can do it through passion and hard work alone—because it's not true. A lot of these businesses fail because they don't have the right people, the right team members and the right skill sets to drive the business. If you know your strengths and gaps early, you can make sure your ABC's are checked off before you start.

I would tell stay-at-home mums to start something and many have said to me that they would like to. It led me to start CRIB and "matchmake" these A's, B's and C's. These women will empower each other so they do not feel isolated or alone or under-utilised. CRIB is three years old now and we have over 200 members. That has been very satisfying.

Share with us your inspiration for your latest venture, Trehaus.

The concept of co-working spaces is from the U.S.—I saw that model and found co-working exciting as it also functions as real estate play where you have all these funky entrepreneurs with cool businesses and the property becomes valuable. While I thought co-working was interesting, it didn't speak much to me until someone raised a question to WeWork, a hugely successful co-working space in the U.S., "Why do you have a hundred outlets and not a single breast-feeding room?" and a light bulb went off. Then, I was at a co-working space in Singapore and I noticed that one of the women had brought her daughter along. She was getting restless and telling her mother that she was bored playing with her iPad. The other women were glaring and being hostile towards the woman and her child, and I thought, "Where can this poor mummy go?"

Trehaus is Asia's first family-friendly co-working space. Entrepreneurship is booming in Asia, especially in Singapore. In 2015, with all the incentives the government is giving to set up new businesses, 71,000 businesses were registered and 31,000 babies were born. The opportunity from the number of people who may want the option of working flexibly out of a corporate office is immense. Twenty co-working spaces opened in Singapore in 2015 and not a single one catered to the family, so I figured I should think about it because one or both parents may want to run their dream businesses. I envisioned Trehaus as a place where I could work and keep my little ones nearby.

I also realised that because we are based in Singapore, the concept has to be adjusted to Asian women. In Singapore, Malaysia and Hong Kong, we have access to good domestic help, so this concept will be different from in the West, where a child-care may be set up close to the office. They also don't have nannies the way we have live-in help.

Trehaus was conceptualised for the Asian entrepreneur who can have access to great help but requires the tools and environment for the child when he or she does not need the help and wants to have independent play. At first, I said to my partner that this idea wouldn't work as my son needs bouncy castles, slides and ball pits. My original idea had a playground next to a working space and I realised that was naive because if you really wanted to work and want your child to last all that time with you, he or she cannot be overstimulated and be drenched in sweat. What you want is an environment where they can play and explore quietly. It all came to life when I met my partners at Trehaus through CRIB.

Clearly, you feel very strongly about motherhood and creating opportunities for working mothers to work. Do you have policies that you implement in your businesses that empower women?

Yes, that is why I set up Trehaus as I realised that it is one thing to say to employers to give your staff a creative space and flexibility but it is another to provide it.

Trehaus is not just a co-working space with family-friendly facilities; my goal is to have it is to be rolled out in the heart of the CBD with Grade A office spaces where I could get corporations to come to us. The future would be to collaborate with some of the many amazing co-working spaces that are popping up downtown, exactly where we want to be. Perhaps we would work with them to offer Trehaus Family facilities so we can grow and scale with more partners on board.

I am a big believer in collaboration over competition. This way, the female employees can go have their meetings, take the conference calls, catch up with their clients and their colleagues, but have their children nearby. These companies may not even need extended maternity leave as the women can come back to work sooner with their children.

You had a business called Wonderland. Share with us about that.
I gave birth to nine businesses, but one has folded. I still say nine because I feel they are part of my history. I don't think of it as a failure, but as a lesson.

It failed was because we had two A's and a C. I found this artist who was immensely creative and talented and we decided to set up a photo studio for babies and kids. I found an investor and together we invested $100,000 and felt we could not fail. But it did because we lacked a B. The artist could not get her website up, was unable to take the appointments and was ill-suited to manage the team even though we gave her money to hire an assistant. Everything fell apart because she was not cut out to be a business person.

I pondered on our failure and that was what led to my ABC theory. Wonderland led me to the realisation that later inspired me to set up CRIB.

What is next for all your businesses?
Regional expansion for Mercury, and a new concept for the Fashion Week in Singapore. For Mercury, we have an Events team, a PR team, a Creative Marketing agency and the Singapore Fashion Week, which makes four entities. As I see opportunities in the social and digital space, I will be steering the Marketing and PR teams towards that direction. We have to constantly evolve to stay ahead.

Wolfgang Violin Studio is set up with my mum and I see that as a family business. She is an intrepid person and she is sometimes up writing music into the wee hours of the morning. The business is now independent and profitable, so we are looking for opportunities to scale the business beyond our shores.

CRIB is thriving in terms of membership growth and community impact, and we have organised our first CRIB Summit to overwhelmingly positive feedback and response. It is certainly gratifying to connect with women and their businesses and I hope to do more of that in time to come. We have also received expressions of interest to start up CRIB communities in other countries including Malaysia, Australia and Indonesia—so perhaps starting regional outposts for CRIB to spread our social cause could also be in the pipeline.

Having said that, we are facing a challenging economic climate in Singapore for many businesses. In good times, it's easy to do well. In hard times, only the strong, or innovative will survive. I am consolidating the businesses and shoring up the ones that will survive the downturn. Not all businesses will pull through, and that is okay too. Businesses are not babies, or people—they exist to make money, or to serve a function or purpose if they are a social enterprise. When they cease to be competitive or viable, I also advise entrepreneurs to know when to pivot, and when to pull the plug, to live to fight another day.

There is no shame in folding a business. Many successful entrepreneurs wear their battle scars with pride, and many had to go through several businesses before learning what they know, to start up the one that would succeed. It is okay to fail—the important thing is to learn. You can always try, and try again.

How do you manage to stay ahead of the pack?

I think competition makes you better than you are. I am never afraid of competition. When you have someone at your heels, you run faster.

What were some of the toughest decisions you had to make in your career?

Working with friends is very difficult. Sometimes, you need to do things that you wish you did not have to, but you do it for the sake of the business.

For me, integrity is my number one driver. It helps me sleep at night, knowing that I did the right thing. The partners that I work with have to have integrity, if not, it won't work. Sometimes, we face conflicts between what is the right thing for the person and what is better for the business. Sometimes, you forge friendships with people you work with and these people don't perform to the best of their capabilities. As an entrepreneur, the right thing is often the right thing for the business. Having said that, there are grey areas, but I believe that everything happens for a reason and there are no mistakes, only lessons.

What are some the biggest challenges women face?

Work-life balance. Why do you think the birth rate is so low? Lee Kuan Yew said it is a threat to our survival above scarcity of land or foreign workers. Sure, we give incentives for Singaporeans to have a baby but it doesn't help and makes things worse. What women want is work-life balance. If you empower them with that, they will have more children.

Trehaus gives women options, and once they see that, they could be persuaded to have more children. The government is trying to support fathers by giving more paternal leave; they are trying to get the daddies to be more active in care-giving and supporting the mother, but it is a knee-jerk reaction. The answer to me is more concepts like Trehaus. Many don't see the point of having another if they can't even see the first one grow up.

You married a younger man. Was there societal pressure or did you feel any stigma?

I don't think there is a stigma. But I do do things ahead of my time. I guess I've always done things my way and it doesn't bother me. We married when I was 35 and he was 28. As you progress, the age gap lessens and I don't even feel there's a gap now except we do have different sets of friends.

The only fear was the family's worry that I can't have children. But fortunately, I had two boys, at 40 and 42. My parents also thought that my husband and I wouldn't work out and they were concerned for me, but sometimes you just follow your heart.

What is your parenting style?
Is there one? I am quite chill. It takes a village to raise a child. I am very fortunate to have support from my mum, John's mum, family members and helpers. I love the boys and can't imagine life without them now.

Do you want them to inherit your businesses?
I would love it if they set up their own. Mummy will be there to mentor.

Who is your favourite designer?
Carolina Herrera.

What is your biggest splurge?
My biggest splurge is on travel and experiences. I rarely spend my money on things. I would generally prefer to invest my funds in a business.

What do you do to unwind?
Create new business ideas.

Knowing what you know now, what would you tell to your younger self?
It's going to be all right.

How do you best want to be remembered?
For making a difference in women's lives, being able to provide them with options and inspiring young women to pursue their dreams.

You are a multi-hyphenate so what would you say is your occupation?
Dreamer. Though my name card says Director as I am always directing my life and a hundred other things.

What will your epitaph say?
She finally rests.

If you met God, what would you say?
Can I do it again?

Would you consider yourself a Madonna or a Maverick or any other M word?
Maverick. I'm not a saint. Like most business people, you do what you need to do to succeed, and steer the team forward. The important thing is to maintain a moral compass, and not lose sight of your guiding principles and values.

The Brave Heart

SYLVIA LIM

Sylvia Lim is a Singaporean politician, lawyer and academic. She is currently the Chairman of the opposition Workers' Party (WP) and an elected Member of Parliament (MP) representing Aljunied Group Representation Constituency (GRC). She is in charge of the Serangoon Division.

She holds a Bachelor of Laws (Honours) from National University of Singapore, Master of Laws from University College London and Master of Science in Criminal Justice from Michigan State University.

In 1991, she joined the Singapore Police Force for three years as a police inspector. She did investigation work at the Central Police Division Headquarters, and then became a staff officer in the Criminal Investigation Department. Sylvia then joined the law firm Lim & Lim in 1994 where she handled litigation work for both civil and criminal cases in the High Court, Subordinate Courts and Juvenile Court. She started working in Temasek Polytechnic in 1998 as a law lecturer.

Sylvia ran as a candidate in the general election for the first time in March 2006. In the 2011 General Election, she contested as a candidate in Aljunied GRC and her team won. It was the first time that an opposition party won in a GRC since the system's introduction in 1988. One week after the election, she resigned from Temasek Polytechnic after 12 years of service to devote her time to her MP role as well as Parliamentary duties. Sylvia later re-entered the legal sector and is currently senior associate in Peter Low LLC.

***

It is uncanny how some of the biggest political figures can be so down-to-earth. You read about them in the papers and you imagine they are the stuff that dragons and myths are made of, and when you meet them, they are disarming in the most pleasant way. Likening Sylvia to meeting the Wizard of Oz would not be befitting as she is neither male, insecure nor is she a mere projection of smoke and mirrors, because this woman has brains, guts and (dare I say it) balls—perhaps even more than most men I know.

Sylvia Lim is arguably Singapore's most well-known critic of the establishment, having risen to the prominent role of the Chairman of Workers' Party (WP). She has taken on anything from ministerial pay, (she illustrated that a university graduate's median gross monthly income, about $4,450, is equal to what an average minister would earn in one day), to raising public concerns on the equitability of Singapore's legal system (she used plastic surgeon Woffles Wu as an example), to even the Population White Paper (she contends that the government's strategy of using immigration to "top up" the shortfall in Singapore's total fertility rate "will further dilute national identity" and cause Singapore to require "even more population injections in the future").

She was inspired by her father, Lim Choon Mong, who worked in the police force and who used to give briefings to the late Lee Kuan Yew whenever he visited the army barracks. What is most impressive about Sylvia is this innate drive to do what is right. Her drive to serve the masses is a call to duty of the highest order. It is clear that she is motivated by an altruistic impulse to serve the community even if it is a tough, lonely and rocky road.

Theatre director Ong Keng Sen once said that Sylvia is the most sensible person he knew in law school—a huge compliment given that they were in the same cohort with some the most brilliant and creative minds today, people such as Ivan Heng and Claire Wong. Indeed, Sylvia is that perfect mix of sense and guts. She works very much as a leader in service of her party and, more importantly, her constituents, her people, her country and her belief in democracy.

Articulate, eloquent and witty, Sylvia speaks with a huge dose of fervour. It is easy to see why the party and its supporters love her as I listened to her speak her mind and heart. She is careful with her words when it comes to matters of political sensitivity, but she is unexpectedly candid about her personal life and romance with footballer Quah Kim Song. I also found it refreshing that she is one of the few women who actually acknowledge that hormones play a role in our genetic make-up and that it can influence our lives and our sense of control. Too many women in power or visible positions tend to gloss over this, or mask it with an appearance of manicured control, almost as if in a bid to de-feminise themselves or to eradicate stark biological differences. Sylvia embraces her emotional side—however, she also states unequivocally that she would consciously put her feelings aside when she is at work and when she is wearing her political hat.

The avid reader hopes to be able to go back to teaching when she hangs up her political gloves, but she also aspires to be in a position where she could work with burgeoning democracies on their policies and legislation. She quotes from Brené Brown's book *Daring Greatly* and wistfully hopes that she will always find the strength to tread where angels fear. I assured her that in my view (and I am certain I speak for many Singaporeans here), she has already gone further, faster and deeper than most will ever deign to even try in their lifetime on this little red dot.

***

Share with us your background and reason for going into politics.
I decided that I wanted to go into public service in some form so that I could use my law degree and serve society at the same time. I remember I was driving along the highway one day, going home, and it was raining quite heavily. I saw this police officer dressed in a yellow raincoat, directing traffic in the rain. I felt so strongly that that's how we should serve our society, and I wanted to be part of an organisation which does that, so I did.

My father tried to dissuade and stall me by saying, "Okay, I'm going to send you to do your master's in London for a year. When you come back, think about this again." So I went to London, and when I came back, I was still certain about joining the police force. My father and I quarrelled and all that, but I went into the police force anyway. I left after three years, but I have never regretted my time there.

What were the key lessons that you took away from your years of being a police officer?

One of the things that I took away was the pragmatic and practical nature of police work. I also have an appreciation of the people in the police service and the fact that they have a "working personality".

Depending on what job you are in, certain people need to behave in a particular manner, say, teachers may need to be fussy about perfection and precision in language. For police officers, they are practical and need to look at what's critical so that they can just get things done. Sometimes, it doesn't matter how it's done so long as it gets done. Often, you may have to compromise as there's no perfect way to get to the end point. For example, if you are investigating a case and you are quite certain that this particular person has committed some offences, you need to weigh out how are you going to get the evidence and get a conviction. You have certain procedures to follow, but if you follow procedures too strictly, you might not get the evidence that you want. There are compromises along the way and I find that lesson very useful to bear in mind. In the end, you need to have a quick helicopter view of what's important, and you just work towards that. I found that to be an interesting lesson.

You literally are the embodiment of law and order—you have both the legal as well as the law enforcement background.

Yes, and as a lawyer, you have your dilemmas too. You have this thing called "due process", and no matter what, even if that person is guilty of the most heinous crime, he still deserves the protection of a fair trial and fair investigations. So you are constantly having this dilemma and questioning yourself if you should do this or that. You observe and you share with your colleagues, but if they were to follow what you prescribed as a "due process" person, the investigation might be affected and jeopardised. So as lawyers and police personnel, I don't think we are the best people to judge because we are always having these dilemmas and can see all these points of view.

Do you find your ability to see both sides of the coin helpful in politics?

Yes. Sometimes, even in Parliament, I find this to be something that's useful; and yet, at the same time, it can be a bit of baggage. Let's say, the government is proposing something for homeland security or internal security. I know the problem in terms of making legal compromises and, at the same time, I can understand the problem they are trying to solve. So it puts me, as an opposition MP, in a bit of dilemma, because I can't be too critical of certain things if I can understand the rationale. That's why I have also gone on record to say that we have to be moderate and honest with ourselves, and ask, if we were the ones making the decisions, would we have done the same as well?

So what was the push factor that started your political career?

I've always been observing politics. As children, we were sensitised to it because of my father. But what made me decide to make personal contact with a leading opposition figure was an incident in the late 1990s.

There was an election held in 1997. After that election, Mr J. B. Jeyaretnam, who was the leader of the Workers' Party at that time, faced multiple lawsuits because of something that happened at a rally at Yio Chu Kang Stadium. What happened was he held up a document and said to the crowd that in his hand was a police report that his comrade, Mr Tang Liang Hong, had made against Goh Chok Tong and his team. That statement alone led to lawsuits brought on by Goh Chok Tong, Lee Kuan Yew, Lee Hsien Loong and several other PAP ministers—they said that he had defamed them.

I felt really bad for him because I did not believe there was a legitimate legal case and it smacked of political bullying. So, I actually wrote to Mr

Jeyaretnam to give him a small donation as a gesture, because anyway, I knew that we could not really support these cases financially. It's like a bottomless pit when it comes to lawsuits. But we became friends, and I learned a lot during that period. I learnt what he had to personally go through as one of the PAP's biggest opponents, and he was eventually made a bankrupt in 2001.

When an election was called at the end of 2001 just after 9/11 in New York City, it was largely a walkover. I think two-thirds of the seats were uncontested because it was called at such short notice and the opposition parties didn't have time to prepare. I didn't want the elections to become a farce. I mean, how can you call it an election when two-thirds of people were not even voting? I decided it's time for me to do something about it as I've been thinking about this for such a long time anyway. So, I wrote to the new Secretary General, Mr Low Thia Khiang, who had been re-elected MP for Hougang constituency, to say that I wanted to join the party and that was what I did. To answer your question, it stemmed from a strong concern that our democracy was going down the tubes, and this was 16 years ago.

Do you know what has since happened to Tang Liang Hong?
From what I know, he's probably living in Australia. I am not sure whether he's wanted by the authorities here. But he gave me a call in 2006 when we contested in Aljunied—that was my first election and we lost. He asked me to challenge the result and ask for a recount. I remembered telling him, "Mr Tang, according to the rules or legislation, we're only entitled to a recount if the margin is within a 2% window and I don't think we are within that." And he said, "Okay." I was surprised because I never spoke to him prior to that, nor did I know him personally.

Was there fear when you first decided to put yourself on the line?
Fear was irrelevant when I made the decision. This tends to be the way I react to things. There are certain things which I want to do, which I know fundamentally have to be done, and I am very convinced that I

have to do them. So I'll just go ahead and worry about the fear later. Because if you were to think too long before you make a decision, you'd probably end up not doing anything.

What did your friends and family say?

You can probably still Google and find this article called "Stand Up For Singapore" which I wrote it for *The Hammer* in 2001 or 2002. I spoke about some of these initial reactions from my friends when I told them that I had joined the Workers' Party. Someone said, "You better start sorting out your assets." And another asked, "Do you have any skeletons in the closet that they can dig out?"

Besides, you do know there's always a risk, but then again what can you do about it? You can't change what you've done in the past, so you just have to move ahead. During the initial period, there were always these episodes of fear and paranoia. When I was going to the party's office, I would be wondering if anyone was following me, and silly things like that. After a while, you just get over it, and you realise a lot of it is actually self-imposed and irrational.

Share with us some anecdotes on your early political forays. You were the first woman to step forward in oppositional politics.

I joined at the end of 2001. In June 2003, one and half years later, I was elected as the Party Chairman. That made news because I was a fresh face on the scene and a woman. There was a lot of interest, and I found that daunting as there were endless media requests at that time.

At the same time, of course, there were some observers who predicted that this would actually be a strong encouragement to women to come forward to join party politics, but it didn't happen at all. It's very interesting to examine why. I think in Singapore, or maybe all over the world too, it seems that women don't really like this kind of work. Perhaps because it has a very public nature and the fact is that you are putting yourself up for heavy criticisms. In the Singapore context, of course, when you're in the opposition camp, you'll be facing a very strong and formidable incumbent party, which has been the government since before the Independence. So that is why I imagine it is not everyone's cup of tea, and I would say, especially so for women. I would imagine that taking such a step would probably involve consulting with their family members, whether it be a spouse or parents, and various people would probably voice their concerns. I think that's why it's hard for many women to feel an affinity to this role and type of work.

I was just saying recently at a women's seminar that even among single women or women without children, there's still a large pool of them who will not come forward because they probably feel that they do not want to get involved in all this public fighting. It may be a perception that being a frontline player in such a rough world is not a good image for a woman.

Share with us some of your most vocal political dissents and how these are taken by the government.

One key debate has been on ministerial salaries. It had reached astronomical levels by public reckoning, without the risks that usually accompany those in the private sector at similar pay levels. It had gone overboard in the years before the recent changes. I suppose it struck a raw nerve with me because I tend to think people come into politics because they want to contribute to society in some way and therefore if you say you can't get people to come forward unless you pay them top dollar, I think they must be getting the wrong people in. Because how much money do you need in order to function and have a decent standard of living in Singapore? At one time, I think the ministers' pay was well over S$100,000 a month! I think it's way beyond what even some well-paid professionals or civil servants get, and at the same time, it puts people out of touch with the common man when they live at that level of financial comfort. So that was one speech I made in 2007, which got much attention from the media and the masses.

In fact, I almost didn't get to make it to the debate because, during that time, we didn't have advance notice of when the Parliamentary sitting would be, so you only know when the next sitting is like a month before and I was actually already on my way to New Zealand to visit my sister when the dates were released. It was quite difficult for me to come back in time for it as I wasn't even sure how long the sitting would last. As things turned out, I managed to come back a day earlier and the sitting actually stretched out, so I was home and could attend the final day of the sitting. It was also helpful it was the final day so the ruling party didn't have time to prepare a comprehensive rebuttal during that final day. I think that was partly why some of the points that I made during the speech had a life of their own. The speech can still be found on YouTube and social media.

Can you shed more light on the issue of means-testing for hospitals?

It was something the party had been looking at for some time and it was not just my personal issue. Basically, the government's policy is that somebody who lives in a slightly more expensive home will get less subsidy when they go to a public hospital. That is something people feel very unhappy about because people who have the means would have probably contributed more in taxes anyway, so how far should we discriminate against them? Means-testing in hospitals is now in place, but many people were very critical of it as assessment of means can never be perfect, and secondly, people will always need healthcare—you never know how long your health will last. But anyway, this is more the Party's issue, and Mr Low Thia Khiang has been speaking more about this than I have.

What were some of your more memorable debates in Parliament?

Between 2006 and 2011, which was the period when I was a Non-Constituency Member of Parliament (NCMP), I had to take part in a not-so-simple debate about the NCMP scheme. There was this provision in the Constitution that states that if less than three opposition MPs are elected, then you can make up the difference with NCMPs. That means the highest "losers" will go into Parliament to make up a total of at least three opposition MPs. Then in 2008 or 2009, the government amended the Constitution to provide for more NCMPs, saying that we had to entrench at least nine NCMPs in Parliament because Singaporeans wanted more non-PAP voices.

We discussed this issue within the party. We have never embraced this NCMP scheme because we feel that people who are in Parliament should be voted in by the people whom they represent, as elected MPs. And of course, because of the inherent unfairness of the GRC system and how the boundaries are always changed at the last minute, in the end we still have to look at the NCMP seat to have your voice heard in Parliament. This is not an ideal situation—at best, it's a stop-gap measure. So I had to stand up to oppose this revision to provide for more NCMPs. People wondered why we were opposing this but we had our reasons for doing it. Basically, we just feel that if we revert back to single seats, then we won't need this NCMP seat at all. This also lulls voters into thinking they don't have to cast their vote for the opposition parties.

When I was an NCMP, I came to see the difference between having elected MPs versus NCMPs in terms of party development. If you are an NCMP, you don't have any territory under your charge and therefore your presence will always be itinerant. You can visit the Singaporeans but you can't hold any activities because you need space and you need permission from the powers that be that control the space. Whereas as an elected MP, the Town Council is under your charge, so you can organise activities in the common areas and you have space to build your grassroots. It makes a very, very big difference.

How did you cope with this limited scope as an NCMP?

We continued to do our house visits in the areas that we wanted to contest. For myself, I was doing a lot of work in Aljunied GRC. At the same time I wanted to be constructive and active in Parliament because it was also a chance for people to see what I can do and contribute. Hopefully by the next election, I'd be a known face and be familiar to them, and there will be some level of comfort to vote for us again.

During my NCMP stint, I spent quite a lot of time in Parliament and it was not easy when you were holding down a full-time job. I was teaching at Temasek Polytechnic, so it was quite tough at times. For instance, in February to March, Parliament would have budget debates and that will be a daily affair for two weeks. In the meantime, the Polytechnic would be having exams so I have invigilation duties, the marking of papers and the filing of reports under tight deadlines. There was one incident when I had to leave my students in the middle of a test and head to Parliament to do something. That's really not ideal.

So now that I'm an elected MP, it's better in the sense that I have left my full-time job and am better able to give it my all. I'm still licensed to practice law, but there's flexibility of time.

Did you not go on record to say that Temasek Polytechnic changed its HR policies to allow you to continue your work in politics?

I didn't say that but people linked the events to me because of what happened and my proximity to it. In 2005 or early 2006, the HR policy was still this—if you had less than 10 years in service and wanted to stand for election, you had to resign from your job. After the election, you could apply to come back but there's always the uncertainty, especially for those of us who stand for the opposition, on whether our employers will take us back.

Some other polytechnics did not have that restriction. You'll find, for example, PAP candidates who are lecturers in other polytechnics need not resign. They would stand for election and their job security continues. So I think the Polytechnic decided that it was best to have a consistent policy for everybody. They changed it just before the 2006 election so people tended to link that episode with me because I was the most visible person in the Polytechnic who was in the opposition. I wouldn't say they did it as a personal favour, no way.

But anyway as I said, now that I'm an elected MP, I've resigned from my full-time job, so with the flexibility of time, my law practice and my boss being so very understanding, I only need to do work when I can.

The 2011 General Election was a political watershed. What do you think were the factors that aided you?

I think there were many factors that came together at the same time. First of all, there was a lot of public unhappiness over many things like population overcrowding, concerns over the cost of living, immigration concerns, public transportation and the ministerial salaries. And I think, linked to the debates about the ministerial salaries were episodes like the escape of Mas Selamat. It appeared as if the ministers didn't pay any price, nor hold any real accountability over such a grave incident as the escape of a dangerous terrorist; the public was unhappy about that. So the general landscape and climate was one thing.

Then I think, politically, it happened that that was the election where the two elected opposition MPs, Mr Chiam and Mr Low, decided that they would come out of their comfort zones and strongholds and contest in the GRCs. I think the voters were very aware they could no longer rely on these two guys returning to their safe havens of Hougang SMC (Single Member Constituency) and Potong Pasir SMC, where they had been incumbents for decades.

That caused a heightened awareness for voters in Aljunied. If they did not vote for our team, there would be a real risk there might not any opposition elected in Parliament. At the same time also, we had been doing our work consistently on the ground in Aljunied for many years before 2011, and we probably also had better candidates with higher profiles and visibility joining the party. I think all these things came together which led to a swing away from PAP in that sense. For us, opposition victories are usually in the 50% range, so at 54.71%, we won by a bigger margin than we ever expected! It was a very clear victory at that time and many factors came together.

Share with us the challenges you faced after you won.

On the ground, there would always be challenges particularly when opposition MPs are first elected. We have to build our own grassroots because the People's Association would never work with us. In fact, they still consistently try to promote PAP candidates in a political way.

And one of the biggest indications of government agencies being involved in promoting the ruling party occurred shortly after we were elected in Aljunied GRC in early May 2011. The HDB decided to select 26 open spaces within Aljunied GRC, such as basketball courts and amphitheaters, and lease them to the People's Association for their exclusive use. This meant that even though we were incumbent, the Town Council would no longer have the management of these 26 sites. We were advised that we were not even allowed to step in there, and that residents who organised events there were not even supposed to invite us! In this case, the HDB got involved, so it just shows you that it's taken as perfectly legitimate for such things to happen.

One of the heartlanders' biggest gripes is the fact that they are denied upgrading in oppositional wards. What are your thoughts on this?

I think in a way that was used as a stick. During the years from 1991 onwards, when WP was running Hougang SMC and Mr Low was incumbent, that was used against Hougang residents, as well as residents in Potong Pasir (with Mr Chiam as MP). But this also made people angry because they were being threatened with their own money—they were withholding taxpayers' money for their political ends—so it ironically only served to harden the voters. In one sense, we have to respect the voters because they were defiant and refused to be cowered by the ruling party. Even though there was no upgrading, the residents continued to live in whatever circumstances they were faced with. "If you don't give us MRT, we'll take the bus. If you don't give us the bus, we'll walk." They have that kind of attitude and I really admire them for not giving in.

What were some of the challenges you faced between the 2011 and the 2015 elections?

We had to build up our own grassroots and it was not an easy thing. But one of the things we find gratifying is that we have been able to build up a significant base of volunteers who are also residents. There are people who care enough who want to volunteer their time to help us to succeed and serve the community.

Of course, we had a series of successes since 2011 and also in the Hougang by-election when Yaw Shin Leong was expelled from the party and left a vacancy. Despite that, we had managed to retain that seat. In 2013, we had the by-election in Punggol East where Lee Li Lian won. We were on a roll and I think the ruling party had increasing concerns about the WP and did not want WP to gain any more momentum. So they really put us under a microscope, and we had many challenges to overcome.

You would have read about the Town Council and some of the observations put up by our auditors, which became a big issue and we had to go through the Auditor General's audit. After that, we had to go through Parliamentary debates and a lawsuit. It has been very challenging and sometimes the circumstances truly push my limits as a leader.

What are your thoughts on the last 2015 election?

I think, first of all, it is well-timed and the Prime Minister, obviously, is very smart and well-advised on this. We had the SG50 celebrations, the passing of Mr Lee Kuan Yew and the constant replaying and retelling of the official narrative of Singapore's history—it drilled home the message that the PAP has not failed them all these years.

Looking at what has transpired, I think Singaporeans are not ungrateful people. No matter what, the respect for Mr Lee Kuan Yew is inherent, widespread and deep. Of course, the recognition of the Pioneer Generation via the launch of the Pioneer Generation Scheme captured not only the hearts of the Pioneer Generation itself but all of their family members who would correspondingly pay less for their elders' medical bills—which means this outreach touches probably everyone! I mean, if you have been able to secure help for your healthcare, your father or grandfather's healthcare, surely you would have found that beneficial to you.

At the same time also, I think the growth of the opposition may have stirred up some voters' fears. They were worried when they saw the size of the rally crowds for the WP. They started to fear that WP might win too many seats. On the one hand, there was a greater understanding of the opposition's capabilities and popularity that was helped by social media, but at the same time, it scared conservative voters.

Interestingly, during the election season, there were also these SMSes that were being spread like wildfire. They were purportedly the bookies' odds on the GE results, that WP would win Aljunied by a huge margin, win East Coast by a certain margin and Marine Parade would be 50/50 and all that kind of stuff. I think when the SMSes were sent, people were afraid that the PAP would weaken significantly and may have decided to vote against this happening, even though it may not have been the reality at all.

And at the same time, I think global economic uncertainties made people feel quite worried, especially those who ran businesses. They did not want the PAP to be weakened because they felt that they and their businesses might be personally affected. So we did see a shift in the middle class votes that swung to PAP to a significant degree. I think these are all the things that worked against us, even though, I feel that we probably fielded better candidates than we've ever done. It's truly a timing issue.

We were personally surprised by the results. We had, of course, hoped to do better but we have to accept the results as they are, try to understand them and look at the factors that we can change and recognise that there were probably some factors that were out of our hands anyway. I know that Singaporeans want some opposition and acknowledge its place in a democracy, but the real question is how many or how much?

What are your plans for the next elections?

I would say that we would probably need to work harder on the ground and smarter too. All the while, it's never been our style to trumpet what we do, but it seems we might have to do something like that. For example, if we were to visit residents, it's never been our habit to put up a banner or advertise what we do in this area. But after doing some introspection, we realised that we probably need to do this as people may not know that we're there.

For instance, if we were visiting people in the private estate in this street, people in the next street may not know or they may even think I'm not there at all! It may be necessary to do these things now. It is not in my nature to do so, but it looks like we have to up the ante and keep on telling people what we're doing and we may have to change the way we work.

Have there been other instances when your beliefs and your ways of working have been at odds?
One of the things I do struggle with is that I never like to get nasty with people. For example, we'd like to work with the People's Association. If they are doing things solely for the benefit of residents, we'll never oppose. But if these events turn political, then the question is how far should we accommodate them? That is something that I grapple with.

Has social media changed the way the Workers' Party works?
Definitely, in the past when we were stuck in mainstream media, the editors are king and the public may not know the reality if the editors do not want them to know. But of course, now the public does know with all these alternative media outlets. There is ground-up reporting from the citizens, and we can also put up our information inexpensively, and the reach is tremendous.

I'm amazed at how social media has expanded the reach of campaigning. For instance, for election rallies, it is no longer just about the numbers in the crowd, but also online viewers, as all our speeches are uploaded on our website. For example, nowadays, I have people coming up to me to tell me that they are watching a video their grandson sent them. The reach has benefited from a multiplier effect because of social media. We will also have to bear this in mind because we also have to think of the people watching the video, who may not necessarily be on the grounds. We need to ensure that there is substance they can hang on to in our speeches instead of merely feeling the atmosphere of the rallies, which can be quite intoxicating.

What are thoughts on the gerrymandering?

For Hougang and Aljunied, the boundaries did not change in GE 2015, so we cannot use gerrymandering as a reason to explain the election results; there are other reasons as mentioned earlier. Of course, the change of boundaries does affect voters in other areas and is clearly political.

There was an announcement from the Prime Minister to say they would move towards smaller GRCs because they, too, realised that a few constituencies have become too huge. But after the new boundaries were announced, the new boundaries did not square with PM's statement. For instance, Pasir Ris-Punggol GRC remained so huge. Ang Mo Kio, too, was still huge. In Singapore, re-districting is done just before elections. By contrast, it's quite an established principle internationally that electoral re-districting is usually done at regular intervals due to population movements, but this is clearly not the case.

I do think that makes people angry. That maybe also one reason why some people don't vote for the ruling party. It wrecks havoc into one's sense of place and identity, as you could be in Hougang but you can see in front of you a sign that says "Bedok Reservoir-Punggol" or you could be in Serangoon Central which bears a sign "Welcome to Marine Parade Town". It can be very hard for the residents to identify with that.

It is more important that if you want the Singapore identity to evolve, you can't keep being told your constituency is changed again and again without your moving anywhere. It is already hard enough as we are dealing with urban renewal. How many of us still have our old schools in place? Some people can't even go back to the places they used to be at as a child. We are already grappling with a loss of memory and physical markers.

What have you done to try to connect to the Mandarin-speaking population given that you are English-educated?

When I joined WP in 2001, I also had to plunge into cultures, sub-cultures and the different ways of life that I was unfamiliar with. For example, Chinese Taoism with its Seventh Month dinners and temple dinners. I've had little connection with it growing up, being raised in a

Catholic, English-speaking environment, but it's so much a part of life in the Chinese community and Singapore life.

And of course, my Mandarin has improved, conversationally at least. I have also started to read in Mandarin, which is good, but I still acutely feel my limitation when people start to joke or make a witty comment where you have to read between the lines. At those moments, I am always lost. Sometimes I just remain quiet and listen because I don't quite know what the implications or subtexts are and what people actually mean. But it has been good overall, and I think people are very generous and forgiving towards me as they know my background. They also do appreciate the fact that we turn up at their functions and try to support their activities as much as we can. It's has been a wonderful, cultural experience.

What were some of your lowest points?

One of the low points would be the Parliamentary debate over our Town Council's audit issues, which took place in February 2015. We were heavily attacked by the ruling party for the inadequacies pointed out by the Auditor-General as well as accused of other mismanagement. The news reportage overwhelmingly carried the ruling party narrative. After the debate, which was just before Chinese New Year, I was actually thinking to myself, "Have I failed the party as Chairman of Town Council? Could I have done a better job? Would others have done a better job?" It was a very difficult time. I knew it was an episode that the party needed to recover from, and I felt a big sense of responsibility about that.

Of course, how much I could have really changed things is a question mark, but it's the way you were being portrayed in the media that matters. Of course, there were some lapses, but the media was portraying us as people who acted in bad faith that was totally false. The weight of responsibility is tremendous, and I felt very bad in the immediate aftermath. After that, I decided that we needed to recover from this and I started to think about the areas of work that needed to be done. I also wrote to accountants to see how they could help us. I guess you need to give your emotions an outlet, to have a sense of catharsis, before you refocus on your work.

What is your style of leadership and how has it evolved?

I would generally like to be consultative, but I realise that after a while, it's not good to consult too many people as you may end up with analysis paralysis. I guess what I've learned is one thing—consult maybe two or three people whom you think are key stakeholders in that particular decision you are making, or have particular insights to give and then you just have to make your own decisions thereafter.

I often talk to Mr Low about things. He's such a veteran and I find that I'm able to draw great leadership lessons from him. People always wonder how we get along because we are from such different backgrounds. He's obviously Chinese-educated, a graduate of Nan Da, and his wife is also a Mandarin-speaking person. They are outwardly very different to what I am. But we actually get on very well, because I think, fundamentally, we have a common understanding of why opposition politics is in the national interest, why the party is important to us and to Singapore.

We feel that we are companions on this important journey and we bring complementary perspectives to this mission. I have great conversations with him to try and understand more on how heartlanders think as he has a great understanding of that aspect of things. At the same time, I may be able to give him a perspective on how the English-educated population may see things, and it can be quite different altogether.

In terms of leadership, as an inexperienced leader in the beginning, I used to find it very difficult to work with people who have priorities that are different from mine. One of the things Mr Low told me, and my father also tried to tell me, was that as long as people were generally moving in the same direction, it's okay to have different priorities. It is also acceptable for people who come into the party to have personal ambitions, as long as they also have the party's interest at heart. I have learned a lot of things from the both of them. When I encounter problems and am not sure how to solve it, I find that talking to Mr Low will clear my mind and he is able to map out the possibilities and repercussions of each choice to me. He has had the experience of seeing things unfold so that's very helpful to me. He's been a great sounding board and he leads with a steady hand, which I admire.

One of the biggest challenges is to keep a clear head when everybody around you is screaming. That's a challenge which requires a certain steeliness and strength that can only come about if you have discipline and know yourself well. You have to be able to make decisions, and also know when you probably should not make any decision. That is something that comes through with experience and a sense of self-awareness that only comes through time.

Who are your role models?

It's hard to really name specific people but I was actually very influenced by this TV series called *Band of Brothers*—it's a bit cheesy to say this. It is project by Tom Hanks and Steven Spielberg based on these real characters that lived through World War II. They were fighting in Europe and the story revolves around this American paratrooper company and the main character is based on a real person called Dick Winters who passed away in 2011. He was portrayed as a quiet leader who would not make a good first impression, but he ended up inspiring his men by being very disciplined in the way he assessed any given situation, leading from the front and trying to get people to excel in their different roles. I find leading with a steady hand, being able to think under fire and empowering those around you to be indispensable traits of a good leader.

One of the great motivational people I was introduced to is Dr Brené Brown from Texas. She wrote three books and the one that was very inspiring to me is *Daring Greatly*. She noted that people who put themselves out in the arena are going to fall short time and time again. Armchair critics will always be there. But what matters is to recognise that you dared to do something difficult, so give yourself enough credit for it and pick yourself up again.

Does it sometimes feel like you keep fighting a losing battle? What keeps you going?

The people who see the value of having an elected opposition and vote for us.

Election results send important messages that change lives. Many people point to the great introspection the government did after 2011 when they lost ground at Aljunied GRC. They openly said they were taking time to introspect, and Prime Minister Lee even talked about "going into meditation" to understand why they lost votes. So that's the true value of having oppositional politics.

Even for us, when we didn't do as well as we had hoped in the recent 2015 elections, it was a time for introspection for us too. That is the value of giving people the right to vote. There are many people who try to explain away the election results, but I don't think we should do that. I think we should really look at it squarely and assess what is within our control and what is not.

I think essentially you still have to go back to the fundamentals of why you went into the arena in the first place. I felt that there was something fundamentally inadequate about the Singapore political system, and we have played our part to bring some balance to it. It is something that is still important to do and we hope more people will join us on this journey. That way we can also take turns to support each other and also allow for others to take over. That's very important.

What would you consider as your biggest contribution to society?

It would certainly be my decision to join Workers' Party. I think that has also helped to give a new perspective to the party whether it be on a gender basis or otherwise. Each of us who joined brought along our own contributions to the party, whether it was Chen Show Mao or Pritam Singh. The good thing is that the party is growing and we are attracting good people. Mr Low is very happy about this but, of course, the recent election showed that it is not enough to win elections. Even if we work, there may be other factors out of our hands that may affect the overall outcome.

What cause do you feel you would champion personally?

There are not enough outlets for alternative voices. During SG50, I found that to be so true. There's only one narrative that counts and that narrative would be bombarded through every possible channel; everybody will be singing from the same songsheet. It can be very stifling. While we all had reasons to celebrate SG50, we could have done it on different levels and perspectives. We could be celebrating some of the weaknesses in our leaders and how they had to compromise when there were bigger issues at stake, or put an emphasis on other less heard names who have sacrificed themselves to bring Singapore to where she is today.

I don't how to describe it, but sometimes when I talk to people who are connected to the establishment, I find us just speaking about the same issues or sharing the usual anecdotes and I wonder if there's nothing else to talk about. I think we have a long way to go and we can allow for more diversity and plurality in voices. So by that token, you can say that I would champion for greater diversity and plurality of expression in our society.

What are some sacrifices that you had to make?

Definitely having peace of mind. In the past, before I had all these public responsibilities, I would travel for two weeks and not have to worry about anything. But I find that that's not possible these days. Privacy is another thing—it's part and parcel of the job, and while it's nice to get encouragement from people, but at the same time, our loved ones also have to pay a price. For example, Kim Song shared that he gets upset whenever we get attacked in the press, as he cares for us. My mother, being ever-practical, says that if it gets too hard, I should "just go get another job". That's a good bottom-line for me to remember—while we may do our best, in the end, it is the people who decide if they want to support us. And if they don't, then we just have to accept that and move on.

What would you do if you were not an opposition MP?

I will probably go more into teaching criminal justice and make a career out of that but right now it's not possible for me. Recently, I managed to get my Master of Science in Criminal Justice through my part-time study with Michigan State University. It took me some time to get there but I managed to and I really enjoyed studying policing and law enforcement. I was also teaching a lot of night classes in Temasek Polytechnic, and because I worked in law enforcement before, the police officers and security people would attend my classes. I used to enjoy that so much.

I enjoyed teaching working adults as they can relate well to case studies by drawing on their life experiences dealing with these issues. Full-time students, being young school leavers, had a more innocent view of the world. I remember one particular lesson when I was discussing a hypothetical case of a minister's son being charged with an offence. Typically, defence lawyers may write to you to try and get the charge reduced, and you may need to decide whether you want to put up certain papers to the public prosecutor for advice.

I asked both cohorts whether the fact that he was a minister's son was relevant or not. The young students said, "No, everybody is equal before the law." But the working law enforcers all said, "Yes, of course that is important!" It's not that their decisions would change, but they believed they needed to be much more careful in the way they managed the case. You see, these instances illustrate that we have may a certain concept of the world when you are young, but after working for a couple of years or more, you are wiser in the ways of the world.

What is your greatest strength and weakness?

Ong Keng Sen once told me when we were in law school that I was one of the most sensible people that he's ever met. I was really taken aback by that comment, because I never thought myself as such. But I think I try to be as rational as I can. Fundamentally, I think I'm quite an emotional person but when I make decisions about work, it's seldom emotional.

One of the weaknesses I have is sometimes I get too affected by things that have happened. Women tend to be more introspective. But I think one of the things which I still want to do better, is to compartmentalise and calibrate my reactions to things so that I am not down for too long. I have learnt to pick myself up faster.

You shared earlier that your dad was your role model so how do you cope with your dad having dementia?

I'm very blessed that my mum was a nurse, so she's not afraid of illness and she's able to talk to doctors on very intelligent levels about medication. She is also able to observe my father's condition with medically-trained eyes.

When I talk to my father now, I can sense that there's still that fundamental person that's still there—his determination and style—but it's being impeded by many medications, which dulls his mental ability. But you can see he is aware as he will sometimes give you a wink, or there's a glint in his eye and you know he's still there. It's just that he's not able to function at that level he was before. I used to have great talks with my father. We used to go to Holland Village, and the two of us will sit, enjoy wine and talk. He read widely and knew something about almost any country in the world. I miss those days so much.

Has your father's condition influenced how you think about policies?

It definitely has given me more opportunity to observe how the healthcare system works. Having to accompany my father to healthcare facilities allowed me to see what's happening to the other patients and what the staff is going through. You get first-hand observations and it is certainly helpful.

The cost of medication is definitely one issue, but it's very complicated because drugs can be expensive, especially those that are patented. The question for every government is how far it should subsidise the cost of drugs, and if so, which drugs and what is sustainable for government's budget. These are very difficult questions to answer, but you can see that if you have more money, you probably get better healthcare and that is just the reality.

Recently, I went to the A&E at Tan Tock Seng Hospital to accompany someone, and you could see that the waiting time for beds was about 20 hours! I was in the Observation Room looking at some of these older people and these days, our senior citizens are very articulate and there was this guy who basically asked the nurse how long he had to wait. He said that he came to the hospital to get better and not get worse! Some relatives of the patients also came to talk to me and shared some of their concerns. Some also asked if we should have spent so much on SG50 when there were more important things to spend money on. These are all relevant questions from the people.

Share with us your romance with Quah Kim Song.

It's really interesting because Kim Song said what had attracted him to me was actually a debate I had with Minister Shanmugam on television on the Woffles Wu case. Basically, I had a Parliamentary question about this famous surgeon who was found guilty of getting somebody else to take the rap for speeding, twice, and it was an elderly man who worked in his clinic.

He was fined $1,000 and many people wondered if that was a valid and justifiable punishment because that was merely a small sum to Woffles Wu. More importantly, what does it tell us about somebody who gives false information to the police? Anyway, my question was more about the public reaction to this verdict and what was going to happen next but I am not sure why the minister decided to turn this into an attack on me. The way he cross-examined me was unexpected and forced me to respond as I did on the spot with whatever I could marshall. Kim Song was so impressed with this, that he started asking one of my friends about me!

Later, in January 2013 the Worker's Party organised its first ever variety show at the Jubilee Hall at Raffles Hotel. We put together acts performed by many of us, as individuals and in groups. We also had some residents perform, and one of them knew him, so somehow they invited him to come and sing as well. That was how I got to know him and I could sense there was an attraction. And of course, I knew that he was a football pioneer who has contributed so much to Singapore and I found him quite an attractive man too! He was a widower and available to date. So after some time and quite a few false starts, we started going out together. We are still together and very happy.

Is marriage in the cards?

There is no plan. Anyway, I am already menopausal so I am not going to have any children. He also is a grandfather, and he's already been there and done that. Right now, we are happy with the way things are. We don't know if things will change later on, and we may have different thoughts about this, but right now, no.

Do you think your gender has aided or impeded you in your career?

I think it helps by virtue of the fact that there are fewer women so I tend to be remembered more easily. But at the same time, as a woman, you also have more things to manage, especially emotionally. That's just the way we're made, especially women going through hormonal changes, which can be a double whammy! We go through hormonal changes during our 40s and 50s, which is right smack where I am now. There are days when you feel very panicky and anxious, and on other days, you just take it in your stride. So you just have to try and manage it and also make sure you have a work-life balance that keeps you on an even keel.

What can we do to get more women to join politics?

I think mentoring is quite important. But at the same, I also feel there's nothing like somebody feeling the desire from within to come forward. That I think is much more powerful than somebody persuading you.

What makes you happy?

I take pride in our collective achievements, but also find joy in the people around me who stick with me through thick and thin. One of the things we tend to forget as we are fighting bigger battles is that we may take the people around us for granted and that's wrong. People don't have to stick by you, so it's important to spend time to appreciate the people who weather the journey with you, and enjoy those moments.

How do you best want to be remembered?

For me, it would be someone who has played a part to enhance democracy in Singapore. I think that would be a compliment. I hope that people will say that I dared greatly.

If you met God, what would you say?

I have tended to ask God, at times, whether certain challenges were just too much, so I may ask him about that when I meet him.

My colleague, Aljunied MP Faisal Manap and I do talk about these things when we are faced with particular difficulties. There's something in the Bible that says, "You'll not be given a burden that's too hard for you to bear" and the Quran has something similar, "One will not be tested beyond your capacity." Somehow, if you have faith, you will think that you can handle whatever comes your way. We just hang on to that!

Would you consider yourself a Madonna, Maverick or any other M word?

I like "Mover".

The Water Magnate

OLIVIA LUM

Olivia Lum is the Founder, Executive Chairman and Group CEO of Hyflux Ltd., a leading Singapore-based water treatment specialist with landmark desalination projects in Asia, the Middle East and North Africa. An orphan raised under adverse circumstances, Olivia now heads a multi-million dollar business. Her drive to succeed has earned her numerous accolades, including the Ernst & Young World Entrepreneur Award in 2011.

A chemistry graduate from the National University of Singapore, she started corporate life as a laboratory chemist in Glaxo Pharmaceuticals, where she learnt about environmental control and saw the potential in water treatment and recycling in water-scarce Singapore. In 1989, she founded Hydrochem, which later became Hyflux Ltd. The company traded in water treatment equipment but soon ventured into research and development. Olivia secured her first big break in 2001, when Hyflux was awarded the first municipal water treatment project in Singapore, to supply and install process equipment for the nation's first NEWater plant in Bedok. Two years later, the company won the tender to build Singspring Desalination Plant, Singapore's first desalination project. Since then, Hyflux has gone on to build landmark plants in Singapore and abroad, propelling it to the position of largest desalination provider in the world in 2016.

Hyflux has been expanding its expertise beyond water to include other utilities such as power generation and waste-to-energy. In 2015, Hyflux partnered Mitsubishi Heavy Industries to design and build Singapore's *sixth waste-to-energy plant. More recently in 2016, Hyflux was awarded a US$500-million project, commissioned by the General Authority for the Suez Canal Economic Zone, to construct the Ain Sokhna Integrated Water and Power Project in Egypt.*

Olivia was also a Nominated Member of Parliament and is currently a member of the Singapore-Tianjin Economic & Trade Council, Singapore-Jiangsu Cooperation Council, Singapore-Zhejiang Economic & Trade Council, Singapore-Oman Business Council and Singapore Business Federation Council. She also sits on the boards of International Enterprise Singapore, Singapore Technologies Engineering Ltd and the Singapore Mediation Centre.

***

It is not everyday one meets Olivia Lum, ranked by Forbes as one of the richest and most successful persons in Singapore. After all, she is very private and I am truly honoured to have been given this opportunity for an exclusive interview with her. Indeed, her schedule is packed, and our interview was interrupted by several gentle knocks on her door, which functioned to signal that she had to be whisked away from meeting to meeting. But Olivia betrayed no hints of slowing down even though she admited that she has learnt to delegate as well as take more time off for herself to travel and unwind.

And if someone ever tells you that you can judge someone from the tone of their voice—I suggest you think again, especially when it comes to Olivia. I am thankful that I have transcripts and recordings of all my interviewees; this way, I'd never forget how they sound like and the energy they project. Reading Olivia's interview transcript and listening to her voice presents a strangely jarring experience in a pleasant way. On its own, the transcript conjures the image of a fast-talking, go-getter who is driven by a fundamental need to elevate herself from poverty. Yet, most may assume from just listening to the recording that the voice belongs to a soft-spoken schoolteacher. But while she coos, Olivia has that steadiness in tone that emanates a cool, quiet confidence. In fact, she is actually amazingly adept at engineering, cutting deals in China and the Middle East as well as having a penchant for the arts and interior design. Is this even possible?

With Olivia it is. Hers is a classic story of self-mastery against all odds. She describes herself as an artist, who subjugated her passions to train herself to become a consummate scientist and businesswoman in a bid to give herself and her family a better life. She was only 28 when she saw an opportunity as a young chemist at Glaxo, and decided to strike out on her own to create a new water-recycling technology using membranes.

How she saw water as a viable business when no one else in Southeast Asia could is, in hindsight, shocking. After all, water is a necessity of life and a very scarce and precious resource. Clearly, pre-empting the needs of water supply is one of the key factors to Olivia's success. But life is constantly surprising, and by that same token, when I was her age, I was probably deciding which pair of shoes to buy for a dinner party and not "how can I create a master plan to solve the world's water crisis?" But I digress.

Her stories of tough childhood are probably well-known to all but her honest sharing sheds light on how poverty can work in two ways—it either motivates you or it utterly demoralises you. For Olivia, security and financial independence were her driving forces, and she never let that veer out of sight.

She built her business empire literally with her own hands—in the early days, she did have hands-on involvement in the construction of her plants! Today, Olivia is estimated to have a net worth of over US$460 million but her humility still prevails in all that she does and touches. In fact, her staff shared that she remembers little details, like where things are kept, demonstrating that while you can take the girl out of the village, you can't take the village out of the girl.

In the fast modernising Singapore, Olivia's story is held up by many as an inspiring example of entrepreneurship, perseverance and hard work. She reminds us that there are still pockets of poverty amidst us—that many still suffer from the injustices of life that come from a lack of basic necessities and decent opportunities. Olivia makes sure she always gives a little something to the children in developing countries, because once, in a not-too-distant past, there was a young girl in a kampong town selling freshly plucked papayas by the roadside. This is her story.

***

We have often heard of your rags-to-riches story but do share with us your experiences growing up.

A lot of people ask me about my background as it has shaped who I am today. I always say I was fortunate to make it big in life, but there were a lot of people like me where I grew up, who had no opportunity. I think if they were given the opportunity they might have made it too.

My early harsh environment toughened me, though I had a very happy childhood. I was carefree and did not yearn for anything that I did not know of. As a child, my house had no electricity and water, and we had a zinc roof and wooden walls. We had a river in front of our house. The river was usually dry, but when it rained, the water would fill up the entire riverbank and flood our home. We liked to sit on old tyres and paddle about the house, which would be full of water—it was fun. I always liked rainy days because I could also swim in the river as we had no swimming pool nearby in my town, and the next closest was an old mining quarry.

I was adopted by my grandmother when she was 63 years old. We are not related but I called her *por por*—the whole village calls her *por por*. It was a simple life in the kampong with a lot of freedom. I say freedom because if I felt like going down to the river to swim, nobody scolded me and my grandmother would only remind me to be careful, as opposed to parents these days who will say "No, no, no, better not try your luck because you will drown."

I had a lot of freedom when I was young and could do many things without fear of getting scolded. I did not have to eat when I was told, could wander about and head to the plantations to pluck papayas and sell by the roadside. I did anything I liked. It was a childhood without any boundaries but one thing really shaped me was when I opened my eyes to the fact that others had more than me.

This only happened when I went to school. I realised then that I did not have a lot of things that other children had—new shoes, brand new uniforms. My uniform was black and white in primary school—my grandmother bought me a white shirt and my black skirt was made from her black pants. I was still quite happy but when the school classmates started to make fun of my uniforms calling them "old", that was when I realised I didn't have a lot of things.

I began to ask my form teacher "How could I become like you?" I thought all teachers earned a lot of money compared to where I came from. And my teacher said, "Knowledge is power. You have to study hard." Somehow or rather, that got stuck in my mind. To me, and in my home and environment, nobody taught me anything. So when I went to school, and the teacher started telling us how to become a good person, that stuck with me. I said okay, "Okay, I want to study hard. I want to score. I want to be able to make it in life."

I also really began to notice that some people could afford things that I couldn't afford. Some could eat in the canteen while I had to sell papayas in order to get pocket money. It was common in those days—many of my neighbours used to sell small cakes and fruits along the roadside, so I simply followed them. Papayas were also easily available. I avoided rambutan trees as they always have big ants and I always got bitten. Anyway, those situations while I was growing up made me determined to want to make good and, at least, earn my own money.

To fast forward, I started getting involved in odd jobs since I was eight or nine years old. It was very common in my village, and I was working with a couple of factories that employ children. Back then, there were no such concept as "child labour" or "child abuse". Being a factory worker was the norm. So I worked in a factory making rattan bags that people would carry to school and work. The rattan had to be soaked in chemical sto soften so that it can be shaped. You would then pull at it hard so that when it dried up, it would take the shape you want. At eight or nine years old, my hands were very fragile and would swell because of the chemicals. When I went home, my grandmother would soak my hands in a pail of Chinese herbal wine to lessen the swelling so that I could work again the next day. It was difficult, manual labour. I was also a rubber tapper, and that was even harder because the mosquitoes will bite the life out of you. In my little mind, I thought, of all the odd jobs I did, the easiest was selling papayas along the streets because there was no stress, provided you had nice papayas for your customers! But that also made me realise that I wanted to become a businesswoman.

Anyway, at school, my teacher's husband was a jeans trader. My form teacher saw that I did so many odd jobs and had experience in selling so many things that she asked her husband to let me sell jeans and T-shirts to the students in school. So I did. Every pair of jeans that sold for about 10 ringgits meant that I received one ringgit, and for every T-shirt which was two ringgits, I got 20 cents. I was so happy selling jeans and T-shirts and became a super saleswoman in the school. Every day, I would lug a big bag of jeans and T-shirts and have the students try them on during the recess. I must have sold to all the students. It was fun and easy and confirmed in my mind that doing business is the way to go, even after I became a chemist.

Anyway, I went to Singapore and did well in school, and I did my A Levels in Hwa Chong before going to university. I actually applied for Engineering, but when I went to the orientation, I was the only girl in the entire cohort. I didn't want to be the odd one out, so I decided to do Chemistry because there was more diversity in gender representation.

Actually, I liked the arts too, but many people told me when I was young that I must not be an artist because there was no future and I would starve. During my time, doing the sciences meant you are a better student, and I was drawn to that fact and hence chose to read pure science all the way while I was in school. But I never forgot that I wanted to do business. In fact, during my university days, I would set up a mobile canteen in the construction sites and would do little trading businesses here and there, so it was always a part of my DNA.

When I graduated, I went to Glaxo to work as a chemist. I didn't know it was so boring being a chemist. Of course, I don't mean that all chemists are bored or boring, but it's not my cup of tea—I was so active and energetic in my childhood and was always thinking of new things. Eventually, after three and a half years, I felt I learnt as much as I could, and I chanced upon an opportunity.

I was looking after the water waste treatment in Glaxo and I thought to myself that Glaxo was such a big company, it can pump all this money into water treatment in order to satisfy the environmental regulations. I looked around and saw that no one in Asia was doing that, especially the developing countries who had to take care of their economic growth before looking into the environment. During that time when I was a chemist there, there was so much water pollution happening all over the rivers in Southeast Asia. I said to myself that one day, all these rivers would be totally polluted by industrialisation. I also knew that once the river is polluted, it will take years to clean it up and it was not going to be an easy matter. I thought if I started to clean up waste water and provide good, clean water to people, I would be starting a sunrise business.

So I told myself I had to do this. But my Glaxo boss told me that I had no experience, no knowledge of the industry and not a single customer in the business. I said, precisely because I don't have all these and have no money that I needed to resign from full-time work so that I could do my own research and understand the market. While I was at Glaxo, I worked all day in the factory and had no time to do anything else, so I boldly resigned. But it was very tough because I had no income, so I sold my little apartment and my little car and collected $20,000 to start the business.

It was very tough going, and I felt like giving up many times. As an early start-up, I had no product, so I went to all the big water treatment companies and asked to distribute their products. Two companies agreed to let me distribute their products and earn a commission, but without exclusivity. In Singapore, it was so difficult to sell these products as the big companies were already here, so they had no reason to purchase from an agent. I had no choice but to go across to Malaysia. With my name card which has a Singapore address, the Malaysian companies thought I was from a multinational company when it was really just me. I did not dare to call myself Managing Director or Founder, so I gave myself the title of Sales Manager. Eventually, I managed to sell this product but I had to work 14 to 16 hour days, so it was fortunate that I was a very energetic person.

After doing this for a while, I told myself that I needed to create my own product which was why I got interested in changing the dynamics of water treatment. I did not want to use conventional methods and wanted something that would save space, is energy efficient, environmentally friendly, uses fewer chemicals and was more focused on filtration—which was why I introduced membranes. But membranes were not known at all 20 years ago, so I had to source for them on my own.

How did you conceptualise the membrane idea?

I went to exhibitions. There was no Internet yet at that time and we were using 486 computers. But as I said, knowledge is power. I would go around the world looking at exhibitions, picking up great ideas for research and was always on the lookout for interesting ideas that were not commercialised yet. I felt that this was a step in the right direction, so I started going around looking for membranes, but nobody could give me the kind of membrane I was looking for.

Eventually, I went back to my university and sought the help of my Chemistry lecturer. My lecturer recruited a PhD candidate to help me and that was how I started: doing my own research and piloting. As I was the pioneer in recycling water in Singapore, I soon became a household name, and the rest is history.

How did Hyflux as we know it today started out?

I started on my own and the company was called Hydrochem. It was set up as a private limited. At that time, when I was exploring how to create my own product. I met many suppliers and chemical companies, but I was the only shareholder right up to the time when I listed the company. I had another trading company where I had tried to work with another person to trade chemicals, but I eventually sold the business to him because I didn't want to focus on chemicals, only water. Until today, this company is still our regular supplier to my factories and plants.

What were the milestones that shaped your career?

There are many milestones. The first is coming to Singapore—that was huge. Second would be securing the contract in the large water-recycling plant in Jurong Bird Park because that really launched my business. Prior to that, nobody had believed that we could recycle water on a large scale. I had recycled water for factories, but I had up till then not yet done larger scale projects. Things changed when the Jurong Bird Park gave me an opportunity.

I figured that if the birds didn't die, then humans won't die either, as birds are more fragile than humans. Of course, the Bird Park manager warned me not to kill the birds because they are special. So I had to demonstrate the purity of the water by drinking it first after it was recycled from sewage. I was the first one to have drunk the water before it even flowed into the Bird Park. This gave me confidence.

It was also around 1998 that the Singapore government started promoting water recycling. The companies remembered us from our earlier work doing pilot plants and demonstrations, which got us in through the doors. I went to PUB and told them about my recycling plants. I was certain that I was able to recycle water on a big scale. I reasoned that since the birds in the Park had been drinking my water for close to two years and were still alive, this meant that my water should be safe for human consumption. Of course, there was a lot of research done by the PUB team and I was very fortunate to win the contract for the first NEWater plant.

Later, in 2001, I raised S$6–7 million by listing Hyflux as a public company, even though it was in the middle of another financial crisis when the dot-com bubble burst. Nobody wanted to subscribe to my shares, and I had to sell it very cheaply to the market.

Anyway, we persevered. Four years later, in 2005, we built and opened Singapore's first major desalination plant. It is a 136,380 m^3/day

Singspring project. At the time, I can claim I built the largest desalination plant globally. Singspring was a real breakthrough for us even though it was a huge risk. We have been handling membrane systems since 1992 and had nearly nine years' experience. Membranes are a very scalable technology, so we accepted the challenge and built the first one.

Later, we also became the winning bidder for the Magtaa Desalination Plant in Algeria, and I was sure that we could use our membranes for the 500,000 m^3/day plant. The plan was to build the largest membrane-based desalination plant in Africa. We also signed a water purchase agreement for the 200,000 m^3/day Independent Water Project (IWP) in Qurayyat, Oman and the construction of the US$250 million plant just started in May 2017. The water will be supplied to the Oman Power and Water Procurement Company (OPWP) under the Design, Build, Own and Operate (DBOO) model.

How did you figure out how to build a plant and scale it up?

I had done so much research. Building a membrane plant is like building your own fridge—if you can build one, you can build a thousand because it is modular. Fortunately, I had the luxury of growing this business on my own, so I took the time to learn welding, piping and plumbing. I knew how to do this not because I studied engineering but because I had to learn plumbing on the job.

You see in the early days, I could not afford to hire a very experienced technician, and the technician who worked for me was not of a professional standard; but he was always telling me as a big brother that he is the "best in the industry" so I had to "just listen". I didn't want to be fooled and being a scientist, I always had to verify, so I enrolled myself in ITE (Institute of Technical Education) and did a night course in plumbing. I also enrolled in many other piping courses organised by my suppliers. So in the end, I was able to build my own small plant and even taught all my early technicians how to build good plants.

Some of my technicians are still around and I personally taught them how to do the welding, the piping, etc. The first few plants were really, literally built by my own hands. Nothing can stop me from doing things myself. If I do not know, I will learn, and I did. I am a little smaller in stature, so sometimes I need a technician to help me lift heavy things. But I would undertake the measurements myself. In fact, I would even teach the technicians how to take the proper measurements so that it would result in perfect plumbing. Without that kind of knowledge, I am sure I would not have succeeded.

That is why I always encourage my engineers to not be afraid of getting their hands dirty because they will have exponential learning by having hands-on experience. Sometimes, they may see a task as too small for them as they have a degree and are intelligent, but I always think that hands-on experience is the best. But yes, these days, the youngsters are a little bit spoilt and are different from how I was when I was growing up.

Anyway, we also saw the membrane trend overtaking the thermal technique a couple of years ago. But because of the Arab Spring and financial crisis, the Middle East region slowed down progress; so there is now pent-up demand in the desalination market, and membranes will be chosen over thermal.

What are some of your toughest times?

We've gone through three economic downturns. For a small company to go through an economic downturn is very tough as you do not even know how you could pay yourself much less your staff. And if you don't pay them, they leave, and you are finished. How are you going to pay the rent? How are you going to maintain the whole building? At every economic downturn, I would worry day and night about how to get that extra dollar and how to locate that small pocket of opportunity. But I always had to stay optimistic. When you are a small company, you take on the role of the sales manager, logistics manager and everything else. So instead of you calling say five customers a day, you call twenty or fifty during an economic downturn so that hopefully one of them will respond positively. These small, little things keep you going. You never give up hope. You have got to always stay positive and, of course, that is easier said than done.

There have been times when I was so down at night that I think to myself, "What's the problem? Why can't I just give up? I have a Chemistry degree and can go back to being a chemist or a teacher." It did not help that my classmates also frowned on my work and tried to persuade me to become a housing agent or broker—I would at least earn more money and not "work like a contractor". Having said that, a few of my classmates were very supportive and even gave me money for lunch when I had no money in the first few years of setting up the business. I was already 28 then, and it was so difficult to make ends meet. I was worried all the time.

Sometimes, when I wanted to have a good meal, I would have to be thick-skinned and reach out to my friends who were making more money than me back then. They were all very nice and encouraged me but they also chided me because they felt that I was making my own life difficult. I recall one dentist friend who was very dear to me. She suggested that I try to do something else, but I said no. I shared with her that my business was scalable and has room for expansion when I make it big, whereas hers was like selling *char kueh teow*—each plate had to be fried by the hawker himself or herself. She remembers this of course! But at that time, honestly, I was very down, but I still maintained an upbeat disposition. I assured her that she did not have to worry as I will persevere. Of course, it's easy to say these things, but I felt then that I was only "talking big" and had really no idea where I would go to get another sale the next day.

When was your breakthrough moment?

You just persevere, hand-to-mouth until the sudden economic upturn in 1998 and 1999. The year 1997 was a very bad year and, at that point, we were in China. But suddenly, there was an influx of multinational foreigners wanting to have a slice of China, and we serviced them. We were English-speaking and knew the local language, so we became the perfect bridge, and the companies trusted us. I built many plants in those few years, and that actually propelled us to head back to Singapore. I had by then amassed a portfolio of recycling jobs and was able to sell to the Jurong Bird Park. That really was a breakthrough, but the key is to first wait out the storm.

Has your leadership style changed?

I have to keep on learning. As shared, I like to be hands-on and knew every tool that was placed in my storehouse. But today, I cannot operate like that. I cannot micro-manage and look over people's shoulders. I told myself that I have to behave like a CEO and not a boss of the company because that means that I will not be able to expand.

I also started observing many businesses around me and saw that they are not able to secure a breakthrough because they held on to too much by themselves. They did not share and failed to bring in new talent. You must have a renewal of talent in order to expand. Can you imagine when we were listing the company, we had only 30 staff? Today, we have over 2,000. An operational manager in a company with 30 staff is different from an operational manager in a company with 2,000 staff. We must be able to recognise that and help the older staff feel comfortable with the new changes. We need to assure them that they are still relevant even when the company is getting bigger. Of course, some are unable to take the change but what is important is that you keep trying your best to keep upgrading. Either you upgrade their skills, or you have to bring in more capable people.

These scenarios and work challenges are totally different. Back then, we were only doing smaller jobs for, say, a $200,000 plant. Today, every one of our jobs is valued at hundreds of millions of dollars which requires a different skill set altogether. The level of skill is unimaginable so you have to bring in the right talent to manage your risks along the way in order to scale up the company's operation.

I am glad that I am a degree holder because I am able to gain information easily from the Internet, and I am interested in the philosophical and conceptual levels of thinking. I remember somebody telling me, when I was still quite small, that growing a company is like transforming from a cocoon into a butterfly. If the cocoon always thinks its current structure is okay, then it will never become a butterfly. If I keep thinking that I am unable to fly, then I will not be able to fly. It is important to believe in changing your structure, which is your manpower and operations. This means you must be able to bring in the right people with the right capabilities in order to bring about a big change in the structure to allow you to fly.

It is a great metaphor for me, and it suddenly dawned upon me that yes, I cannot continue in this family business type of structure—in the end, everyone pulls everyone else down. The real breakthrough is when I went into headhunting a couple of years after I listed. I realised that I am able to oversee one project, but I certainly cannot look after ten projects. I can visit one country for one meeting, but I cannot go to ten countries. I needed to bring professionals into the company and started to really open up. Of course, some of my staff could not accept this change and left, but I knew that this is part of the company's natural transition and progression, and I am happy that they found somewhere else that they could be happier in. We also started to create our own corporate culture as we got bigger.

Do you think your gender has aided or impeded you?
I never think for once just because I am a woman that I had to study fashion design or whatever. I just did what I liked and ignored the noise. When I went to China, they looked at me as if I was a school leaver and didn't think very much of me, but I ignored them and continued working.

Your industry is male-dominated, so how did you handle the pressure, and did you feel that you had to work harder?
Knowledge is power. It all depends on how you carry yourself. When I was very young, I was in Indonesia and had a meeting with a room full of men. They did not seem keen to listen to me as they must be wondering who is this little girl? Luckily, I was able to speak Malay, so I presented in Bahasa and they could understand, even though Bahasa Indonesia and Malay are a little bit different. I was only 28 years old that year. What do you expect? You stand in front of all the men and you are ignored, so you just have to focus on what you know. Once you present, you show that you know your stuff and can command a kind of respect—they'd sit up to listen to you.

I never for once thought that I needed to prove anything because I am a woman. I look squarely at the facts and am always myself. I think it's very important to be yourself. The more you try to make it sound like you are somebody else, the worse it is, and people will look at you differently.

A lot of entrepreneurs may have a great idea, good products and good suggestions but they give up easily. They don't persevere enough. As an entrepreneur, whether you are male or female, perseverance is a must-have. As I said, water is a sunrise business and is becoming more and more scarce. Population and industrial growth also mean there is more polluted water everywhere.

Do you think there are natural abilities between men and women?

Of course, in business, you have both genders at work, but I also agree that there are certain jobs that are more suitable for a man than a woman and vice versa. For example, I would not send a woman to be Head of Sales in Saudi Arabia as the region is very male chauvinistic. The woman can still advance in her career but perhaps in Southeast Asia.

If a culture is unable to accept women in the public sphere, you have to respect that. Of course, these Middle Eastern companies like to meet the boss, so I show up. When I do, I carry myself well and don't do things that irritate or annoy the other culture. Should the culture require me to wear a headscarf, I make sure that I have the headscarf on tight.

What was your biggest takeaway from all the different cultures you have worked with?

People respect you if you respect their culture. Sometimes my managers may criticise a different, foreign culture, but I always remind them to be respectful because we are going to their land and home, not vice versa. We chose to go to them so we have to be respectful of their local culture and customs, or we won't be successful.

Every venture is a lesson, and I never had it smooth sailing. You go through a lot of ups and down but at every down, we learn something as long as you hang on and persevere. We are grateful that Asia has grown very strongly so we get a lot of our revenue from Asia and we are from here so it is easier to handle and adapt. We also do see a pick up from the Middle East, as well as Africa, so it is always important to be very respectful of the differences in culture when we are there.

How was the experience being a Nominated Member of Parliament?

It was an eye-opener for me. Up till then, I only knew about the business world. The experience opened me up to a different perspective on politics, and it was very good education for me. It also built up my courage as well. The first time I entered Parliament, I had to stand in front of Mr Lee Kuan Yew and had to speak in front of him as he looked at me intently. I remember being overcome by a feeling of awe and I told myself I either make it or I'm dead!

After a while, I learned a lot of things from him, and I respect him greatly, which made me feel all the more justified that I left Malaysia for Singapore. Entering Parliament also enabled me to see that this was, and is, the right country for me, as Singapore is akin to an enterprise and is always in survival mode just like my company. There is almost no difference. For survival, you sometimes have to do things that you ought to do even if you may not like it. Putting politics aside, I was happy that I was able to be in Parliament with the late Mr Lee. I got a chance to see him, talk to him, and it was really my privilege.

How has your success changed you?

If I say I didn't change, it is a lie. At least I know that what I have done has given many opportunities to other people, especially to my childhood siblings. At least I am able to say with a clear conscience that whatever steps I've taken, there is no looking back and I want to continue to move forward and do good.

Do you have any regrets in your life?

I don't think I have any regrets not being a wife and mother. Every time I look at the smiles on all my siblings' faces—these are all the children who were adopted together with me under the same roof by *por por*—I feel that I have done right by them.

Many people have asked if I regret not knowing who my parents were. I say no regrets because I think life is such that you need to keep counting the blessings, not the misfortunes. If you keep counting your blessings, you will be a much happier person and it naturally stays with you. My grandmother has given me a happy childhood. Although we were very poor, she provided an environment where I could be happy and free. On the other hand, some families may have wealth, but their children are so repressed that they are not able to do what they like to do. The parents may be forcing their children to have top marks and are never satisfied—98% is not good enough, you need to have 100%!

Sheryl Sandberg said that women can "have it all". Do you agree? How would you define "having it all"?

I really admire Hillary Clinton despite all her critics. She had it all, in a way. I believe if a woman sets her mind to what she wants to do, she can do it. What's wrong with becoming a mother and having a successful business? What's wrong with having a family and still be able to juggle if you have an understanding spouse? I think there's nothing wrong. For me, I chose my career and have no children. I see nothing wrong with that at all too. The one thing I learned in life is that I should never look back and regret.

What would you tell a staff who is torn between family and career?

When my secretary first had a baby, I told her to hire an assistant when she returns from her maternity leave. I do not wish for her to work too late now that she has a family. She did and was very thankful that I thought of her. She's been with me for close to 18 years.

Do you think you have sacrificed anything along the way?

No. It's unimaginable even to me how far I have come and the opportunities I have been able to create, so I do not see that I have sacrificed at all. I look at the place I live in now and how I lived back then and go, "Wow."

Back then, I stayed in a place called Wah Loong in Kampar which was a notorious drug addict area. Everyday, I would be afraid that I could get stabbed or robbed or cheated. You can ask any Malaysians in Perak, they will know where Wah Loong is.

What do you do to unwind?
I give myself a little bit more time to travel now. I also like the arts in general as it is still my passion. I like to draw and love to buy paintings. I used to paint. I can't paint anymore as I have no time. I was, in fact, the best painter in class and my teacher told me not to lose my talent. Today, my artistic expression is suppressed but I do let it go from time to time. In fact, I decorated this place myself.

So you are a Renaissance woman! But would you say you are more science-oriented or arts-inclined?
I pressured myself to be good in science because I thought that was the more secure path forward. Honestly, I think I am naturally more artistic, but I trained myself to be a scientist and an engineer.

What annoys you?
Shoddy work, because I am a perfectionist. And I don't like people who just take things for granted despite having opportunities.

What makes you happy?
Even up till now, closing a big deal makes me happy.

Is there a cause you would champion or campaign for?
I am not an extremist. I always look at views from both sides, so I won't champion anything as I feel that there are two sides to every coin.

You said you like philosophy, so what has been your guiding principle?
I always tell myself that since I have achieved so much, I have to be

merciful. I should not push things too much as different people develop at different speeds and are all born with different talents and proficiency. One has to be magnanimous in whatever one does. This is my philosophy.

When I go to developing regions, say, Yunnan or anywhere, I see the children and I will sometimes take photographs with them and tell them that they must continue to do what they do well. Of course, I may also give him or her some money because it reminds me of my childhood. I recall that on a lucky day, a customer may give me five ringgits and I would be so delighted!

How best do you want to be remembered?

There are so many capable, famous people in the world. I don't need to be remembered. I am just happy that I was given this opportunity. I don't really think like that because all the great men and women die sooner or later.

What would you say when you meet God?

I will definitely meet Him, and when I do, I will thank Him for what He has given me.

Would you consider yourself a Madonna, Maverick or any other M word?

I am neither, but I am Married to My Work.

The Wunderkind Grocer

NICHOL NG

As the Managing Director of FoodXervices Inc Pte Ltd, Nichol oversees 150 employees, 3,000 customers, 4,000 line items, and an annual turnover of close to $45 million. She is responsible for sales, marketing, customer service, human resource, finance and business development. Driven by her passion for and interest in food, as well as a desire to deliver service with a heart, Nichol bought over the family business and rebranded the company in 2007. Nichol is also the Managing Director of sister companies GroXers Inc Pte Ltd, PlotX Inc Pte Ltd, LogiXtics Inc Pte Ltd, and X Properties Inc Pte Ltd.

Prior to this, Nichol graduated from the National University of Singapore with a degree in Economics and Japanese Studies. She was a marketing executive of MediaCorp Radio, where she was part of the team in charge of rebranding all the MediaCorp radio stations, including Class 95FM, Gold 905FM and Y.E.S. 93.3FM.

In 2012, Nichol established The Food Bank Singapore, which aims to be the prevailing, centralised coordinating organisation for all food donations in the country. She is also the President of ONE Singapore, a nonprofit organisation that is dedicated to raising public awareness and taking concrete actions to make poverty history.

***

With her flaming red hair, flamboyant clothing, mile-high heels and strong, take no prisoners, #girlboss demeanour, Nichol Ng is every inch the intelligent man's fantasy: strong, sophisticated and sexy. (Sorry, she's happily married, y'all.) But underneath that tough, food warrior armour is the poor, little rich girl who has gone from riches to rags to a self-made food-empire queen and who has battled an eating disorder for over 25 years.

Having known Nichol for close to two decades, I can honestly attest that she is a wunderkind. While most of us battled identity, relationship issues and focused on building our wardrobe and shoe collection in our 20s, Nichol had her head fixed squarely on her shoulders and was focused on rebuilding her family business. She set out to take on a male-dominated world while marching stridently on her platforms, dressed in brightly coloured maxi dresses. It is unsurprising nobody takes her seriously until they see her composure at work.

Her measured confidence comes from a deep wisdom far beyond her years coupled with a humility that makes her immediately approachable. There is nothing to dislike about her, which is annoying, as we are often made to believe that perfection does not exist. She seems to be the yin and yang balance of creativity and logic, artistry and analytics, boldness and level-headedness—and all this while being a full-time working mother of three, and a wife to her long-time partner, Eddy.

I was late for over an hour for our meeting as I was delayed at another interview. Nichol waited for me patiently in the car park of Scotts Square in her Porsche Cayenne and gave me no flack for having made her wait. Instead, she offered that the wait time allowed her to catch up with work emails and gave her much needed me time in the privacy of her car. I know of no other CEO who would take being made to wait for over an hour this lightly; her kindness and compassion are truly heartfelt.

Her story is one of growing pains, reversal of fortunes, a life-long love-hate battle with food and an irrepressible energy and respect for life as well as a thoroughly inspiring account of how she rebuilt her family's business after it was razed to the grounds.

Buckle up, read on, have a bag of chips or two handy, though I am not sure Nichol would approve—then again, maybe she would.

***

Share with us your background.

People usually see me as a poor, little rich girl. My dad had a food distribution business which my grandfather founded. My grandfather moved from China to Singapore in the 1930s and started a glamourised provision shop in Rochor Road. My dad was the second youngest of nine children. When he was growing up, things were not easy. Even though I have never met my grandfather, my dad would tell me stories of how he would have to retrieve small green beans that fell on the floor as every bean was precious and how he had to sleep under the accountant's table. My grandfather literally raised nine children from that little shop house. That was basically how we started.

My maternal grandma used to run a Chinese restaurant on top of a laundromat where Paragon is now. After her O Levels, my mum helped with odds and ends as a cashier in the restaurant, and that was how she met my dad. He would buy her a packet of lemon tea and asked the restaurant staff to hand it to her. They soon got married when mum turned 19. My dad was seven years older.

My mum had never really worked a day in her life, and it was evident they had very different temperaments. She was whimsical and wore super short skirts and high platforms in the 1970s, even though she was never slim. She was, however, very attractive in her own way and many men wanted to date her. She had a mind of her own and always wore her nails painted, unless there was a funeral. Dad was, by contrast, calmer and more serious; a traditional Chinese man who did not believe in romantic overtures.

Nonetheless, they got married at Neptune Restaurant with nearly 1,500 guests. I was born exactly nine months later so I was definitely a honeymoon baby. A year and a half later, my younger brother, Nicholas was born. In fact, my mother had a miscarriage before him so that's perhaps why I am so close to Nicholas. Mum raised us, as dad was busy building the business. But I have to dedicate time to talk about my dad as whatever happened to him shaped the person I am today. Most people don't know about this story so I would like to share.

People you interview would share their success stories, their hard knocks and how they rose from the fall. Life is a cycle and so things do come and go. My dad started working in the shop when he was 15 back in 1985, making $100 a month, working seven days a week. And he took over the business with my uncles when my grand-dad passed on in 1977. He expanded the trading business, dealt with alcohol and tobacco in an open market, selling Hennessy and XOs. In the 1990s, he ventured into movies. In fact, we even made Hong Kong movies, so I met Leslie Cheung and Anita Yuen when I was in secondary school. He was trading hundreds of containers of consumer products, such as shampoo brand Head & Shoulders, and shipped them to China, which was still a closed market then. He also distributed Aiwa in Taiwan and even started the first duty-free shop in Maldives.

The head office was then in Thong Teck Building in Orchard Road, which occupied two and a half floors. Back in the heydays, there was a golf putt in his office and we had a view of the American Club, which was a big deal. I also recall seeing government officials when we opened for business. We also constructed a building at Toh Tuck Road and had offices all around the world—Switzerland, Hong Kong, China, Europe and even in India. Our company turnover between 1995 and 1997 was approximately US$250 million a year. It is fair to say that my dad was a very adventurous, very bold man—even though he was media-shy.

At the pinnacle of his business empire, he even owned helicopters and a fleet of planes in India. He also built a house perched on the top of Windsor Park Hill in the Thomson area. The house was enormous and had a door that looked like something from Jurassic Park. It had a pool that would put some luxury hotels to shame and there were hardly any walls as it had floor to ceiling glass panels. The house also had an underground studio-cum-cinema where we could watch people swimming in the pool! I called it the Glass House on the Hill. But the whole irony was that we never moved in as we lost that house, but more on that later.

Suffice to say, I had a privileged upbringing, but even after my dad's trading business had taken off, we continued to live in our humble terrace house in Serangoon Gardens. Weekends as a primary school student included shopping at the luxury and designer shops, such as Club 21 at the Hilton Hotel. I wore brands like Salvatore Ferragamo, and I have memories of having my parents drop me off at the Louis Vuitton store. I recall we would get locked in as a means of security surveillance as there were just too many Japanese tourists in the store back in those boom days. So, yes, I would say I had a taste of the good life even though my mum instilled in us a sense of humility.

My dad was an excellent businessman, but he trusted the wrong people and expanded too quickly over too short a time. Like typical early successes, most never entertain the thought of failure nor anticipate falling out of favour with the banks. So, when things hit the dust, it turns very bad, fast. First, my dad and my uncles were all declared bankrupt, shortly before I entered university. Then in my third year of university, OCBC Bank came with security guards and a warrant to seize our house and everything in it. Just like a television drama, we were made to vacate the house in 30 minutes and were told to only take our identification documents with us.

My mum was in a total state of loss, and I began to feel that I had to take responsibility as the oldest child. I was always raised to think like the leader of the pack even though I was just slightly over a year older than my brother. We lost our Glass House on the Hill, the office in Orchard Road, the newly constructed building, the Mercedes, all our club memberships and privileges but what pained us most was losing our humble family home. We lost everything overnight and scrambled to rent a roof over our heads. But we stuck by each other as we were a very close-knit family.

Did you have any inkling of what was happening?

To be fair, I knew that things were not going well. There were signs of my dad's impending business failure. After my O Levels, I expressed my interest to read Hospitality in Switzerland but my dad didn't let me, saying that I should spend time with mum in Singapore. So, I headed to a local junior college and barely scraped through my A Levels. I then shared with my dad that I wanted to read Business in an overseas university, but dad dissuaded me again, so I ended up reading the Arts in National University of Singapore. My brother, on the other hand, was sent to a boarding school in Australia from the time he was 15 because he fared poorly in Chinese.

Anyhow, I made my own pocket money by teaching phonics to preschoolers while in university. Prior to that, I worked in the kitchens of Delifrance, and that was where I met my now husband. While things were bad, I was thankful the government could not seize my dad's CPF, because that was how he managed to afford my university fees. In fact, my then boyfriend, now husband, had to give me an allowance to survive. Because all my uncles were bankrupted and none of my other aunties would undertake any risks, my mum who has never worked a day in her life was made the director of Ng Chye Mong Marketing, which was the subsidiary food compnay that my dad managed to retain. It was a business she knew nothing about. That was basically the foundation of the next phase of my life.

Before I graduated, my dad once asked me what he should do with his father's business. I remember saying that although it was not very profitable, food was always viable business. It did the job of providing for my dad, uncles, covered our overheads and that it could be an opportunity for my dad to start all over again. As soon as I turned 21, I was made the director of the company. It had an annual turnover of US$7–9 million, a contrast to the US$250 million we were used to—it was a drop in the ocean—but that became our bread and butter and formed the basis of our family business.

How did your father and you react to this change from riches to rags?

I am sure many men would have committed suicide to see themselves fail so miserably, but my dad held on, though his health really suffered. His heart problems took a turn for the worse, and later he was diagnosed with stage three salivary gland cancer in July 2014. His face had to be permanently altered to remove the tumour. He spent nearly 40 days in hospital, half of which was spent in the ICU. He went through four operations over the course of a few months and had no insurance so we chalked up nearly half a million in medical bills. I was seven months pregnant during that time and reflected that what my dad went through was really due to accumulated stress over the years. Up till the day he died on 30 April 2016, he still found it hard to let go of the business.

As for me, I am eternally thankful that my parents raised me to be humble and grounded as I am sure many others in my shoes would have blamed their parents for their fall from grace but I never did. In fact, one of the reasons I feel compelled to have an all rounded life is because I witnessed that there is really no satisfaction in the singular pursuit of money. My dad certainly made his millions but no one knows his story. Which is why, I am determined for us to be known as changemakers in the industry so that we toil for a bigger purpose in life as seen in our work in The Food Bank Singapore, One Singapore and Support for Eating Disorders Singapore. I want my children to know there is really more to life than just money.

Do you think your leadership qualities were shaped by what you went through or were you always a natural born leader?

I was raised in a Catholic environment, attending St Francis Xavier kindergarten followed by a decade of education at St Nicholas Girls' School. I've always felt that I was second best in school because I was in the Express stream, while everybody else was in the Special stream. But the irony is, even from a young age, all my teachers could discern that I had leadership qualities. My principal, Mrs Hwang, told my mum that

I had keen leadership skills and would contribute to society even though I was not one to excel in academics. It was a very powerful statement for an 8-year-old to hear, and my principal gave me many opportunities to grow under her charge.

I was made a head prefect when I was in Primary Six and Secondary Four. In fact, I was the first head prefect from the Express stream and all my friends were the "renegades"—unbuttoned pinafores, long nails and floppy fringes. I had to be their discipline mistress to "catch" them in class. But I think they enjoyed the "prestige" of having a head prefect in their class, which was the top leadership position in school.

My secondary school years flew by but I recall celebrating the 55th anniversary of St Nicholas at Singapore Indoor Stadium. The performance involved 3,000 students from Primary 1 to Secondary 4, and it was a huge honour to be part of something so grand in scale. As Head Prefect, I was tasked by Mrs Hwang to feed the younger students. Even at that age, I recalled having a bigger perspective of things to come: that leadership and service was as important as academic excellence. On top of that, there were other overseas trips, student exchanges and other similar opportunities for growth and development. At Catholic Junior College, I was also made the President of the Students' Council, and I was probably one of a couple of females in a history of male presidents.

As shared, university was a turbulent time, but I was also very active on campus. In fact, I was really more a full-time union member and part-time student. I spent days sleeping in school although my mum forbade me to live in the student dormitories—she knew that she would not see me if I did! In my final year, I was made the Vice President of the Student's Union and was in charge of all the orientation activities. I was also the chairperson of the Business Committee that worked on soliciting sponsorships. It was then that I realised I enjoyed marketing—that got me thinking.

I never had strong ambitions but I knew I wanted to have my own business. Since I was 16, I kept an idea file, and I had in mind a name for the company which was Sassy Chix & Company. I envisioned that my office would be at the Grand Hyatt, where the present day Bang

& Olufsen store stands. I also wanted to own a creative and interesting fashion café and even started crafting menus! Anyway, I finally graduated from university, which was a relief to everyone at home—even though Nicholas was still studying in Canada. In many ways, Nicholas was shielded from the financial despair as he was not in Singapore and did not undergo the trauma that I experienced when we had to vacate the house. As a result, Nicholas was always a little more sheltered—though he has matured over the years.

Share with us your previous work experience before becoming the director of FoodXervices Inc.

My first job was at Mediacorp in the year 2000. The global markets were not doing well and getting a job was not easy. I must have sent out close to 90 hard copy resumes to banks and media companies—we had no email then—and I knew I needed a job.

So I started work in a marketing role even though I had no prior experience. My direct superior was Florence Lian, a vice president who was highly experienced. She gave me many opportunities and I learnt everything I could from advertising to television to radio when I was there. This job was a blessing too as it made me realise that marketing was fluid and could be applied to anything from watches, to food, to even yourself. I thoroughly enjoyed the creative process. In total, I spent two years in Mediacorp before deciding to take a six-month sabbatical because of my eating disorder.

I know the eating disorder is a huge part of your life. Share with us your struggles and how you managed to eventually overcome the condition.

Most people would never guess that I have an eating disorder because I am confident and seem to have the world under my feet. In fact, my first recollection of being conscious of my weight was when I was three or four years old.

Back then, Nespray ran a commercial of a ballerina whose mother praised her for being her "best little girl" and "my pride and joy"! That spiked my interest in ballet so my mum took me to a famous ballet school at Thomson. The ballet teacher took one look at me and told my mum that I was "too fat for ballet". My mum told her off, "Who do you think you are? My daughter wishes to learn ballet and you tell *that* to a child?" On hindsight, I was neither pudgy nor obese, but I've always had a bigger build and am taller than the average Singaporean. Somehow, that comment stuck in my head in the years to follow.

It didn't help that my uncle enjoyed teasing me as I was bigger and one and a half heads taller than my scrawny little brother who was a picky eater. So I began to dread the annual Chinese New Year reunions. I knew that I would have to bear comments like "Why are you so fat and your brother so skinny?" The relatives do not mean ill but they do not realise that it really hurt a growing child, and later a young lady.

By the time I turned seven, I knew something was wrong with me. I felt the need to be "perfect" as I believed that I was somehow "imperfect". The eating disorder manifested in my need to prove to others that I was accomplished—it probably underscored my need to excel in leadership. When I was 11, my mum had to take me to a dietitian as she knew that I was obsessed with my weight. Back then, your weight was displayed in the report books and I was in the 120 percentile range. The British dietitian I went to gave me 16 huge multivitamins to swallow per dose, and dictated that I could not have any carbohydrates at all—at 11 years old! I was also told to be selective with my vegetables and was only supposed to eat leafy greens like lettuce.

When you are at such an impressionable age, everything the professional says is regarded as the gospel truth. I dieted severely for two weeks but did not lose any weight because I had reached puberty and had started menstruating. Again, I know now that it was my hormones that were at work but I did not know that then. The dietician, whose practice has since closed down, did not clarify that fact for me either. I started to have a burning desire to lose weight as I felt that I would be more perfect and better liked.

At 13, I read the tabloids and discovered bulimia and anorexia.

Magazines in those days were not as enlightened and seemed unaware of the effect its articles had on young readers. These teenage magazines would tout phenomenal weight loss by glamorous celebrities and feature their diet and slimming habits, which included the use of laxatives and slimming pills. Of course, I was inspired by what I read and also started taking the pills. I quickly became quite obsessive by the time I turned 14 or 15.

Back in the day, you could walk in and purchase these pills with no questions asked by the pharmacist. I would "cycle" my diets and the longest track record was fasting for five whole days with no food and drinking only water. When I took my first mouthful of a Filet-O-Fish five days later, I wanted to throw up. I instinctively knew that I had a problem but I couldn't seem to escape from it. I weighed myself twice a day and remained obsessed about my weight all those years.

When I turned 16 after the O Levels, I bloated up as I hibernated at home. I ate only when I was behind closed doors. At 85kg, I was at my heaviest. Prior to starting junior college, I starved myself for two months to lose all the weight again as I wanted to look good for the boys and be at my physical best in junior college. A Levels was a stressful time and I suffered from peer pressure. Just then, one of my friends read an article in Cleo about eating disorders, and he suggested that I may have a problem as he has never seen me eat. Indeed, since I was in Secondary Two, I never ate in front of anyone.

When I was 18, I went to see a GP and told him that I suffered from gastric and "an eating issue". He asked point blank if I wanted to lose weight. I said yes and he offered to guide me. At that point, I told myself that if *even* the doctor was telling me to lose weight, then I must really have a weight problem! I tried to stop taking the laxatives, but I couldn't, and I got bloated because of water retention. It was like being on drugs, and it was a vicious cycle. I was resigned to a life of routine dieting. I did the same thing while in university—party, eat and consume a concoction of laxatives and slimming pills. I kept myself active as a coping mechanism, but the disorder got worse. Once, after starving for three days, I had a craving for wanton mee and my mum bought it for me. I could only manage two wantons and I could not eat anymore. I headed to my room and cried out of sheer helplessness.

I was utterly depressed during that time, and I was also experiencing crunch time in Mediacorp. The hours were long and irregular and it was not uncommon for me to work till 2 a.m. I relied on 3-in-1 instant coffee mix and suffered from severe mood swings. One morning, I woke up and started passing out blood while I was in the toilet. By that time, I had put my body through 11 to 12 years of abuse, and I knew that I needed help.

One of my colleagues directed me to her GP. The GP asked if I suffered from piles, but I decided to confess that I had an eating disorder. She told me that I was the first Asian who has shared that with her and quickly wrote me a referral letter to IMH (Institute of Mental Health). She diagnosed me as a bulimic with signs of anorexia. Ironically, that diagnosis made me feel as if a whole weight was lifted off my shoulder. Someone was finally acknowledging that something was wrong and even provided me with a structured programme, clear solutions as well as access to support groups. She also suggested that I learn to overcome and eventually get rid of the stigma of this disease. Up till today, I am still seeing this doctor.

But, being the person that I am, I felt that more has to be done and I wanted to work towards helping to remove the stigma about eating disorders. At that time, many parents and victims were unwilling to speak up. There were stories in the press about children eating no more than two tablespoons of rice out of the fear of getting fat. I thus decided to share my story with the media and soon, the magazines and *The New Paper* started coming to me for exclusive interviews on the issue.

An eating disorder never really "disappears". Share with us how you are today and what do you do to cope with the condition.

Twenty years on, I still visit my psychologist once a month. My pregnancies can be very trying, especially my first, as I still had a fear of eating and could only manage a meal a day. This affected the growth of my baby and my gynaecologist had to work with my psychologist to find a solution that is workable for me. Like any sufferer of an eating disorder, it will take a long time before I am completely out of the woods.

This has become a cause that I champion. I used to manage the support group emails and I had many parents writing to me. My goal is to share my story and tips on recovery to all, especially young girls out there. Women bear such a huge burden of having to look good and stay slim and yet bear the brunt of having to get pregnant and birth beautiful babies. We need to somehow "get it all together"—have a career and raise a happy family so there are many personal pressures and societal expectations. It is not easy and we certainly cannot do it alone. I want more people to know what I went through so they don't have to suffer in silence. I believe it is not just up to the media or dieticians to deal with this problem; it is a societal problem that we all need to contend with. Eating disorders are common—men, women and children are all susceptible.

It is ironic that my whole life seems to revolve around food. My psychologist says it is a normal phenomenon for most sufferers of eating disorders to be obsessed with food in all aspects of their lives.

Share with us how you turned your father's business around and started FoodXervices Inc.

After leaving Mediacorp, I went on a solo holiday for two months. I went to the United States then headed to Hong Kong and Penang with a girlfriend. I took the time to clarify my intentions and found that I was keen to start a F&B business. My husband Eddy loaned me $10,000 to become a shareholder, and with that, I started a sandwich shop at Clifford Centre. It lasted just under five months and had to shut down due to a problem with the food court.

After that, my dad approached me to help him with his business. None of my cousins wanted to help and the business climate was particularly bad after the SARS outbreak in 2002. During that period, all the F&B outlets were hit badly as people stopped dining out, staff stopped coming to work, and everything came to a standstill. In addition, everything in our company was done manually and *handwritten*, even though we are talking about just 15 years ago.

When SARS hit, we were forced to find new systems of working that did not rely exclusively on human labour. In addition, one of our biggest hotel clients, now known as the Fairmont, wanted to consolidate all their suppliers from a pool of 100 or so to only 11 and we were one of the suppliers selected. Our office only had two computers and no one knew how to use them, so my dad suggested that I help to service this account. One of the first things I did was to look into the computerisation of the purchasing system so that all information would be properly documented. That really was the start.

I have always had a keen interest to run my own business, loved food, cooking and hospitality, so it seemed like the perfect fit. When I joined the company in July 2002, I embarked on a crash course to understand the business. We had a small team with two to three staff in customer service and sales, but we had a steady flow of business. We are unlike any other food business I know because we do not function like wholesalers and are able to "break bulk". Everything we sell can be sold in piecemeal quantities so you can basically order two packets of salt, three packets of flour and five packets of rice. As long as you meet our minimum order, we will deliver.

When I took over, I was a delivery girl, the only sales person, marketing executive and customer service executive. All our invoices were handwritten in carbon copy invoice books. During Christmas, my customer service staff would write invoice after invoice till her hand blistered. Furthermore, we did not have a customer list and our inventory list ran on an old DOS system. My delivery staff would make deliveries without a shirt on and I had to ask them to wear shirts! To make matters worse, there was no clarity of brand, pricing or details, so it was utterly inefficient.

As there were no proper systems in place, I took two years and met with 10 vendors to finally create an invoicing and ERP system. After three years, we finally created a system that was user-friendly to my staff who had never touched a mouse before nor worked with computers. I wrote memos in Mandarin and spoke dialect, and I realised I had entered a man's world.

What changes did you make to scale up this otherwise traditional business?

I started to research on the business and learnt that foodservice is a mature industry in the United States and other parts of the world, but it is not as structured in Asia. I began to see this traditional business as very viable and saw that we could edge a bigger piece of the pie. I also saw that we had an advantage as pioneers as we are able to amass a bigger customer base and a wider product range.

Currently, I have over 2,500 customers and over 4,000 products, so you can imagine my warehouse is a nightmare. For example, Shangri-La may order 50 bottles of ketchup to the poolside, three packets of Tabasco to in-room dining, so it is all very miscellaneous but we are able to undertake that in a way that no other wholesaler can because we are able to break bulk.

The other service that we have always undertaken is product sourcing. Back in the day, it was as simple as a "local sourcing" so a chef or buyer may ask us for "two packets of this sauce from ABC." Our staff would then take his bicycle to purchase the product, run the delivery and collect the payment and we profit on the "mark up" as we provided a service. Sometimes, our clients may require a specific organic product in Cold Storage and we would purchase it for them. We have also received requests from SATS; their special First Class VIP flyer only drinks a brand of skimmed milk and so we would deliver three cartons of that milk to them. Sometimes, I have to pick it up myself but such is the nature of the business and I am used to it. Relationships and service are at the core of our business even till today. In fact, we'd go as far as to say that what we provide is a food concierge service.

By my third year in the business, I felt that we had a very distinctive service and I was ready to do something special—to reconceptualise, repackage it and launch us as a brand. It is best to think of us as a huge hypermarket. There were plenty of Chinese family businesses doing this so when I decided to technologise, I also wanted to look into renaming as well as curating a repertoire of products as we were always seen as a trading company.

My dad and uncles did not believe in being a sole distributor as this meant that we would be controlled by the brand. They believed in trading or parallel importing as Singapore is a free port, so there was money to be made. As the F&B industry progressed to more professional and sophisticated levels, I realised that we needed specific brands. I reckoned that since we were selling so much of a particular product, we might as well create our own so that we can control the factory, price and brand identity. This was key to me as I wanted us to be recognisable.

My uncle told me that I would "sure fail" as he believed that locals would not want our in-house brands because they were used to household brands—and he was right. We did fail at the start, but we persevered. I told myself that even if I sold only 10 packets, I would try my best. We created our own house brands that we still use today—Bello and Groxers are some of just the few that were crafted as we saw a need.

Between 2004 and 2005, I started to revamp many products and processes. When we were moving the office from Sin Ming to Bendemeer, instead of merely sending them one notice, I inserted a slip in all our invoices to alert our clients early to ensure it was at the top of their mind. What I wanted to do was to make the shift gradual. I did not want a complete overhaul overnight, so I did not change our logo at the start, but I simply made people take notice that we were moving and modernising.

People did start to take notice. My hair was already red then, and I would wear three- to four-inch heels to cart goods into the wet kitchen. The chefs must have been thinking, who is this girl! You must remember that up till today, most of the business owners are older males in their 50s and 60s. Here I was in my 20s and looking like a young punk who did not know what she was doing! After a while, I started to win them over as they learn that I knew my stuff. In addition to personal interest, research and self-development by experimenting with recipes, Googling and cooking, I even wrote to Sysco Corporation, the largest food service company in America.

Like an eager schoolgirl, I submitted a request to visit their facilities and asked them to grant me a full-day training session—and they actually agreed! I flew to their office and received a crash course in sales training. I saw how the sales staff did the calls and it was all very new to me. I realised there is a huge gap in Asia and our level of service compared to theirs was like night and day. At Sysco, their staff guides the customers on how to plan their own restaurant from day one—business plans, signages, printing of napkins and, of course, the food supplies. They are able to provide consultation on anything from the types of tables and chairs to the kinds of insurance needed. In short, they were order makers not order takers. This is what we are working on right now.

The other thing I learnt is how to chase for payment professionally, which means offering solutions instead of sending a debt collector. So a typical conversation would go, "Hi Mr Customer, we are aware you are two months behind your payment. Is there any problem? If need be, we have connections with the banks who may be able to help you with your finances." By offering solutions, you build bonds.

I learnt what I could from Sysco about professionalising the business and kept what I learnt as an inspiration for bigger things to come. It was a one-stop shop, so the customer does not need to order from multiple suppliers and can benefit from the convenience. In Asia, the mentality was different. Even if it was one packet of salt, the customer would have three suppliers just to ensure they get the best price. I told myself that the business model and culture has to change and that I had to streamline the processes. Singapore is so small and does not need so many suppliers to service just one client. There was inefficiency, high logistical cost and high carbon footprint.

So in 2005, I was inspired and decided to make the changes to our way of working from ERP to sales, branding and the threshold was logistics because that was a man's world. It was difficult for me to communicate with the logistics team, so I told my brother that I really need help. He got one of his staff at Tiger Beer to help me, but I shared that I needed him to work together to completely revamp the company. In short, I needed a revolution, a fresh look, because I was not only revamping the business operations, but its entire brand identity.

What motivated you or provided you with the gumption to undertake such a gargantuan task in your 20s?

Honestly, no one else in the family wanted the business as it because it was still laden with debt and the brand had its own baggage. My cousins were used to working in cushy jobs and drawing high salaries, while our work was tedious with long hours without a break. However, I felt that I had put in so much effort and time that I had to safeguard my own interests as well as the longevity of *ye ye*'s business. In 2006, I discussed with Nicholas that I wanted to buy over the company. I was going to take the company in a totally new direction—with new name, look, invoice, patents and new trucks. That was how FoodXervices officially started.

Nicholas and I registered the company and left Ng Chye Mong behind. Even my father didn't know. Of course, they soon heard about it and told me that I would fail because Ng Chye Mong was a trusted name. Despite the naysayers, I bit the bullet and shared with my uncles that the change was necessary and it was the only thing that would guarantee our existence for the next 20 to even 100 years. And with that, we went from a beige Ng Chye Mong to FoodXervices Inc, which is stark black with green.

Even though Nicholas and I were the only shareholders and directors at that moment, we actually spent millions to buy over the customer base and product lines. We did not want any family disputes and it was a very clean handover with proper invoicing and payments. It was a tough journey unlike what most people think. The business was not handed to me on a silver platter, it's more like an Ikea plate.

Many are surprised that even though I was only in my late 20s, I was capable of mature thought. That is because I often reflect on life and was forced to grow up overnight when my dad went bankrupt. By the time I turned 28, I knew I was ready to take over the business. I did not let any of our old staff go. In fact, they still work for me till today, which is proof that I won them over. I function more like a peer to them than a boss. I worked long hours and showed that I could work the warehouse, take calls and make deliveries. When I first took over, the staff were afraid that I would fire them. Instead, I shared with them that I wanted them to grow along with the company and promised that they would all be upskilled and retrained. All I asked was that they keep their minds open. I shared with all my team that there is no "iron rice bowl" or "forever job" these days, so all I ask is that they give their best when they are here, learn as much as they can and leave a better person. This would mean that I have added value to their life.

In 2007, the market was rife with rumours that we were bought over by an American firm and many wanted to know how much we were paid. I shared that FoodXervices Inc and Ng Chye Mong were two separate entities, and that FoodXervices Inc belonged to my brother and me. Word soon spread to the media who liked the way we transformed ourselves from a 70-year-old business to a fresh, bold identity. Our new look attracted new customers with companies that are also forward-looking. There was also a new mindset amongst the workforce—with new hires, new general managers and new business owners who started to look at business differently. It was not merely about price, but quality control and even on corporate social responsibility. It seemed like the industry woke up and became more interested in working with partners who had global visions and perspectives.

I changed our traditional trading mindsets to focus on building brands as well as opening doors to partnerships. For the past decade, we have more than 30 brands that we work directly with, ranging from Unilever to McCain. In 2008, Kimberly-Clark actually came to us, which was a huge feather in our cap. Nobody would think that a non-food company like Kimberly-Clark, the world's number one paper company, would partner a food company. We took over their lodging business, which is their largest business in Malaysia and Singapore combined. 3M came after that, followed by a suite of brands who started to see that we had the experience, know-how and professionalism. Coupled with a team that is young, energetic, willing to try and daring to experiment with new ideas in the market, brands saw that we could drive our company and their brands to the next level as well.

How else are you driving service and innovation in your business today?

We started putting our suppliers' products on our product list. More importantly, our own sales team started learning about their products so that they could sell them. That is an important motivator when working with global brands, which prioritise knowledge and professionalism. So when working with Kimberly-Clark's toilet paper, we are able to share about everything from what is recycled content, to what is virgin pulp, to the number of ply, to what is best for wiping your bottom.

Basically, we made our staff become "customer champions" because we know the customers very well but it also helps that we also become "product champions" for our brands. This is a very powerful partnership. In fact, my brands and my sales team would visit our customers together, so it is a win-win partnership for all of us. Unilever, for example, would have us go into their kitchens. They would train us every two months on their products or new offerings. Aside from the margins, it is a good learning curve for all of us. Honestly, the margins may not be great, but there are intangible rewards that come with it. More importantly, these are global brands and MNC companies, which means they see something in us.

We are also moving into solutions selling and technology. In our latest product catalogue, we created an augmented reality app to go along with the magazine that brings products, recipes and visuals to life. On top of that, we also launched our own procurement platform where F&B owners can perform tasks such as their stock management, purchasing and inventory control. This is all in line with our philosophy to see how we can digitise and move the industry forward while enhancing our own efficiencies.

How is it like working with your brother?

Nicholas joined me in 2008. By that time, he had worked at Tiger Beer for about five years and learnt from the ground up. As luck would have it, he had met one of the managers at Tiger Beer in Singapore when he was back for the university summer holidays and was offered a job right away. Nicholas joined Tiger Beer immediately after he graduated and by

Chinese New Year, he was in Chinatown selling beer. It is good that my brother went to work for another company first and gained experience before he came back to join me, so he was not a greenhorn.

My brother and I work in similar ways in that we are not afraid to get our hands dirty. We do not have a top-down approach but are instead like peers to our staff. We are, however, completely different people, I am patient, mild and never raise my voice, while he is hot-tempered. But that works for us as we balance each other with our strengths and weaknesses. We have never had a fight as siblings, and I dare say we are closer than ever, although we are now parents. The irony is that we like working with each other so much that we started a charity together—as if it was not enough to run four companies and conduct a huge revamp!

What are some of your biggest accomplishments or milestones in FoodXervices Inc?

When we bought over the company, its turnover was approximately $13 million. This year, we are talking about $45 million.

We are huge if you take into perspective that I have orders as small as one to two bottles of ketchup. You can see that I have had to make countless trips in order to make those millions! I am not like Indoguna or Culina; they specialise in fine foods. I do not have deep pockets and don't do lobsters or foie gras. So it is all the small things that make up our business. We are proud of that but most importantly, we know that we have turned Ng Chye Mong around so much so that people now see FoodXervices as an entity of its own while continuing our grandpa's spirit. Ideally, we would like to continue this business for the next 100 years, which is why we started diversifying.

In 2008, we started GroXers, a retail arm. We had never done retail but we started doing business with Cold Storage and NTUC FairPrice. The following year, we started our online home delivery as we saw that retailers charged an arm and a leg to deliver to customers. We felt that since we have our own logistics team, it made perfect sense to deliver to Shangri-La Hotel in Orange Grove and then head to a private condominium in Grange Road with no sweat off our backs. We also own 30 trucks with a logistics team of 80. We are looking forward to moving into our own building in 2019.

We also started PlotX Inc, a holding company for our businesses in China. We currently own two mountains where we grow our own tea, which we sell to the Chinese market, and a plantation of 250,000 chestnut trees, with all the chestnuts are sold to Japan. That was the older side of the business. As young business owners, Nicholas and I do feel that we have a responsibility to attract young talent who can succeed our family. We do not want our business to wind up closed due to poor succession planning.

While this is a sunset industry, we still believe it is viable. For us, it is no longer just about bottom line anymore, but thinking about what is good for the industry. We need to make changes, even at the risk of failure. We are aware that we do things that are out of the box and not in the average person's comfort zone such as B2B credit card payment. In the United States, it is common for companies to pay each other through a B2B credit card or a corporate card. I maintain that the liability should be handed over to the bank, not us, the suppliers. People here in Asia are still slow to adapt to that sorts of idea, but we pushing boundaries and hopefully, someday we will be able to make changes in that area.

What is on the horizon for you and FoodXervices Inc?

We are looking at a lot of mergers and acquisitions now as we believe that there are smaller companies in Singapore that are worth buying over. Another way that we can expand is to buy or set up our own F&B outlets because if I wanted to sell my french fries and hot fudge sauce, it is best I have my own café that sells french fries *with* hot fudge sauce.

In addition, there are many F&B players now that import their own products, but I still think that there is still a piece of the pie for us to help our F&B customers who do not import. The industry is very competitive now, so either you expand or you keep to a niche. The in-betweens with no sound branding are either going to fold or get bought up.

We took the last nine years to build as we are planning to go regional and duplicate our business in developing countries like Malaysia, Cambodia and Indonesia. We have big American brand owners who are asking us to have a presence in Cambodia and have given us verbal agreements that they will appoint us as their partners. We are certainly headed in that direction as our customers, such as Four Fingers, are going regional, so we realised that we would need to travel with our customers. In a way, this is a less risky endeavour as we would have a ready pool of customers.

We are also focusing on China and may decide to drop our agriculture business as it is no easy feat maintaining that. We may look at ways to revamp the tea and chestnut business and give it new lease of life, but we have no concrete plans as we have been focused on Singapore. Many people have suggested exporting overseas, but my theory is that it is harder to succeed in Singapore than just shipping 100 containers overseas. I believe if you can make it in Singapore, you can make it anywhere. That was the foresight we had so we were not anxious to follow the trend and expand to the Middle East and instead chose to take our time. I give myself a 30 to 40 years horizon to get to where I really want to be, so I am in no rush.

The next few years will be exciting as we look forward to expanding our product range, customer base, go regional, start F&B outlets and maybe even establish an F&B consultancy service. We are currently already doing this informally, but we may formalise it into a service business.

How do you keep yourself inspired and motivated?

Inspiration strikes on nights when I am breastfeeding my kids or have a quiet moment. I also like to watch documentaries and the news, and I like learning about other leaders. I am thankful that I have a brother and fellow management person that hardly disagrees with me and we give each other space to execute the ideas that we want. And yes, I am infinitely thankful that I do not have to report to the seniors anymore.

It has been a painful process. My husband and my brother can vouch for me that I have had so many days where I would just sit in the car crying, thinking that I should just give up. The meanest words can sometimes come from the people who are closest to you. Much as they would want you to succeed, they also want you to fail—it is their ego talking, they want you to follow their tried and tested methods. When I was a young twenty-something, with no experience and confidence, those words really do take you down. My dad, before he passed away, was my harshest critic. He did not think we were successful as we had yet to hit the $250 million mark he achieved years ago. But I know that we are like the phoenix rising from the ashes and that the next five years will be a turning point—so just watch out for us.

Share with us more about your husband, Eddy.

There are two EDs that form a big part of my life: one is eating disorder, the other is Eddy, my husband. We met when working at Delifrance. We were chalk and cheese; he was outgoing, and I was shy even though I was active. He was a wild child and I was the typical good girl, even though I look as if I have a wild streak. Our family backgrounds were completely different. I was the "rich kid" that mum would drop off to work at Delifrance where I would make $4.50 an hour. In fact, I would get my mum to drop me further away from work because I did not want to seem like a snob.

My husband, in contrast, comes from a small Malay family and has two older sisters. His parents were each other's first love and are still together. However, his dad was physically aggressive and abusive towards him when he was young. He was a good looker and was popular with the girls, but he was hot-tempered and is a straight shooter. One day, he asked me out. Eddy is two years older than me and was ready to embark on a career with Singapore Airlines as a flight steward when we met, and now we have been together for over 20 years.

Our love story is difficult not because of the religious differences but we were very different people with different upbringing and educational backgrounds. But I knew all he needed was someone to believe in him and for an opportunity to bloom. He needed his own space and time to explore as he embarked upon a career that required frequent travel. I was liberal and gave him the green light to explore the world, meet other people and date other women. He was not ready to be a husband and father, though he knew I would be a good wife and mother. It was a mutually agreed open relationship. I myself did not date as I was focused on my career, but I told him that after he has seen the world, if he still believes that I am the right person for him, then we would start making plans for the future. And he did. He came back and popped the question when I was 29 turning 30—though I took two years to eventually say "yes" to him.

Eddy has been my biggest fan and supporter and has seen me through the toughest times. He saw me transform from a chauffeur-driven girl to a young lady who lost her familial home. During my darkest days, he provided me with an allowance while I was in the university. Even though we had unhappiness in the early years, he has been my one constant pillar of strength, and he believes wholeheartedly in my capability and thinks the world of me. In life, we all need someone like that.

Were there difficulties in pursuing a bi-racial relationship? How do you overcome the challenges as a couple?

My parents initially disapproved of our relationship, so we did not make it official. When I decided that we are going to get married, I formally introduced him to my mum. I will always remember the first time they formally met at the high tea in Grand Hyatt. She gave him a very hard time over the session. Today, they are buddies and are similar in many ways.

The initial apprehension could be accorded to our religious and lifestyle differences—Eddy is a Muslim, and I am raised a Buddhist though I am exposed to Catholicism. But Islam was unknown to us then. My mum asked Eddy if he was going to practice polygamy and Eddy said that it is difficult to marry more than one wife today, and he would need the approval of the first wife before he could marry the second one. Also, there must be a valid and legitimate reason, such as her inability to conceive or her having a physical disability.

The next test was my maternal grandma as I was very close to her. I used to head down to have dinner with her after work. It was hard for me to break the news to her initially, but I was surprised that she took it in her stride and even made special arrangements and prepared an array of seafood to cater to his Muslim diet. Communication was a challenge at the start as Eddy speaks only basic Mandarin and *por por* only speaks Cantonese. Yet, after the initial meetings, they were able to connect in their own way.

I am glad my *por por* saw us marry as she passed away suddenly a year later. It was a very trying time. Even though Eddy was Muslim, he took part in all the Taoist death rites. He would offer incense, sit through the prayer sessions and was even the pallbearer at the ceremony in Mandai Crematorium. He went above the call of duty and performed tasks that even my own Christian relatives would not do. When asked why he felt compelled to partake in all the rites, he would answer that my grandma was the only grandma he knew. My relatives were touched by his gesture, and so was I.

That was also a turning point for me and I embraced Islam. I still go to the temple as we both believe that we embrace religion in our heart, and that in spite of the different religions that exist, there really is only one God. Eddy encouraged me to take my time to convert to Islam. The process was not the easiest and there were one-on-one classes to attend. Our wedding was a two-day affair as we had the Chinese tea ceremony as well as the traditional Muslim rites. The next day, we had the Chinese wedding dinner and the Malay community celebrations. I broke down during the Muslim rites as I did not know what was going on and felt utterly helpless. Eddy intuitively understood my fear and stood resolutely by me. It was a life-changing moment and I knew that from then on that we are a *real* family.

We did not marry simply because we have dated for a long time. In fact, we are happier married than when we were dating! And now that we are parents, we are enjoying ourselves even more and looking forward to attending our children's graduation, retiring together and planning for the rest of our lives ahead.

Do you identify as a Muslim woman? And how has that changed you as you clearly have not adopted the conventional dress code of a Muslim woman?

Yes, I am Muslim as that is a requirement when you marry a Muslim man. Of course, there are those who choose to emigrate and not convert, but I believe I have to respect Eddy's family as they, too, have embraced my family and all the quirks that come with it. Being Buddhist also makes it easier as we are less bound by convention. We practise forbearance, openness and compassion, so there is a lot more flexibility. Buddhism is also about inculcating in oneself the right values.

Eddy has never stifled my sense of fashion and never told me to "cover up" even when I was visiting his parents. Of course, when I do visit the mosque, I would dress appropriately. My husband has been very gentle and subtle with his religious observances, requirements and expectations of me. His take on the true meaning of Islam is refreshing and sensible to me. As long as one believes in one God, and that all the other practices, such as fasting or saying prayers five times a day, can be embraced at one's own time. What is important is doing good and being committed to charity, which is a key tenet of Islam.

He was against doing anything against one's will or out of hypocrisy. He said he did not need to have a wife who was all covered up in public but eats bacon in secret. But, in fact, I do abstain from pork as I am not a huge fan of it anyway. He also shared that in the Quran, it is stated that fasting had to be done willingly and not as a chore or a burden. Fasting is not merely about the physical act of starvation, instead, it is about getting rid of our vices, improving our temperaments and is an overall cleansing of mind, body and soul.

Eddy and you come from distinct family backgrounds. Most people who do not know you may assume that Eddy "married well". But in fact, it was Eddy who gave you your first real roof over your head after your dad's bankruptcy.

Yes. Eddy trusts me with all his income and empowers me to manage our finances. When he turned 30, he bought a two-room apartment under my name before we were even married as a proof of his love, trust and devotion to me. The property was worth over $600,000 then. For someone who came from a humble background, it was a mean feat to be able to do it by himself.

When we decided to marry, we were able to buy my family's first home using the profits that Eddy received from selling the apartment. And it was significant because it was the first house that my family lived in that we owned, and did not rent, for over a decade. I am touched by Eddy's love—not many spouses would welcome the wife's family. Eddy was raised and lived in East Coast so it was also a change in mindset for him when he agreed to purchase our family home in Serangoon Gardens that was familiar to my parents. We now live in a three-storey semi-detached house. My brother moved out after he got married, and my dad passed away last year. My mum still lives with us and my three children. My mum cherishes this house greatly as she is afraid of losing her home again. She was tired of being at the mercy of landlords and now finally feels safe in the home that Eddy and I created.

Do you think your gender has aided you in your career?

Absolutely. In fact, I honestly enjoy being a woman. People have asked if I would prefer to be born a man and I would say, "Hell No!"

I like the softness that we have, our emotional side and the steely determination that many men fail to possess. I am very thankful for my principal in St Nicholas' who set my views right early in my life. She always reminded us that we had to be "all rounders"—good daughter, wife, mother, leader and we also had to be good in the kitchen and at work! It sounds so traditional and Confucian but isn't it what society needs right now?

As women become stronger, we have also tended to forget that our original role was to look after the family and keep the family balanced. I am a very bold, avant garde, forward-thinking, modern woman, but Eddy takes the lead at home and I enjoy playing second fiddle, which is probably why the relationship lasts for more than 20 years. By the way, my hobbies are baking, cooking, knitting and sewing. Can you beat that?! (*laughter*)

How has motherhood changed you?

I've always been maternal, so that has not changed. I mother my employees, and they know that I care. But after being a mother, I also learnt to prioritise as I have always placed everyone before myself. It is part of my eating disorder, but now that I have my own children, I realise that I need to look after myself before I am able to look after my children.

I have always envisioned having six to 12 children and knew that I was going to enjoy motherhood. But the experience has been surreal, and I am actually even more productive now that I am a mother. I am very hands-on and take care of my children after work. I want my nanny to rest at night as I need her energy in the day to care for my children. So, after work, I shower my children, take them to the park and cook with them. My five-year-old started cooking at two and is able to prepare scrambled eggs and bake cookies.

I am a free-spirited mum as I believe a child needs space to develop his or her individuality. While I can be firm on certain issues, I have never laid my hands on them and my husband would vouch for this. I haven't scolded them since they were born and I talk to them every day. It has helped me keep a very positive outlook.

My experience with motherhood and childbirth have been pleasant, and my deliveries tend to be swift. This could also be in part due to my active lifestyle as I practiced pilates and used to head to the gym a lot. I have no fear of childbirth and I do it all without pain relief. It isn't about pride, and I am not boasting that there is no pain. But I chose to go without an epidural as I wanted to know what it feels like to "push" when the time comes and so that was the route that I chose.

Other than the pimples on my face during the early months of pregnancy, I enjoyed all of my pregnancies. In fact, I don't even buy new clothes and wear my jeans up till I am six to seven months pregnant.

Motherhood is one of my biggest inspirations. When I look at my children, I get ideas because they are so open and free. I think I am at my most productive or creative when I am feeding my children.

You have accomplished so much. Do you have plans or expectations of your children to follow in your footsteps?

I would say there are no plans because I want them to pursue what they enjoy. They need to have a passion for what they do and if they are not keen, they do not need to manage the company the way I do. We can establish a Board so that they can be part of the Board and be indirectly involved. I always tell Eddy that the best legacy we can leave is a bunch of happy, well-brought-up children. No one is going to remember how many millions I left behind. It's a cliché, but true.

I don't expect my children to be high flyers or scholars. I just wish for them to find contentment in life and genuinely live life to the fullest. I must have taken this from my mum as she has never curtailed my dreams nor stopped me from doing anything that I wanted to try. This allowed me to test and fail, repeat and learn, to become the mother I am today.

Now that you are a mother, what would you like to see changed in the workplace?

We should have flexible work hours, so that mothers can come into work at 8 a.m. and leave at 5 p.m., and the party animals in their 20s should be allowed to report to work at 10 a.m. and head home at 7 p.m. In fact, that is the system in our company. After being a mother, I began to have a deeper appreciation for issues such childcare. In our new building, we are hoping to have a pre-school tenant. I want to attract mothers as well as the young ones, and I want to create a family-friendly environment that supports family.

Each time I interview a female candidate, I do ask them about their views on marriage and motherhood as I want them to know that I fully support them having a family and a career. I wish to empower them and even enable them to have flexi-hours or work two to three days a week to enable them to be a working mum. I know this is still a new concept in

Singapore and the industry at large is not quite open to the idea yet, but I am. I do not believe that we judge our employees based on the hours they work and it does not mean that a staff who works from 9 to 5 is a good employee. It is sad when I see many mothers curtail their careers for their child and I wish to be able to contribute to that change.

I also hope to be able to help bring down the cost of pre-school and pre-nursery education in Singapore. Getting pregnant is free and delivery is cheap, but the cost of raising a child is high. Even if you chose to take your child to the NTUC nursery, it could still cost up to $1,000 a term. A regular office worker with two or three children earning $2,000 a month would find this a heavy financial burden. Furthermore, most childcare centres close at 7 p.m. and it does not help working mothers who have to rush frantically to beat the traffic to get to their child. It is just too stressful to live and work like this on a daily basis.

So I am thinking that pre-school childcare is another viable business that I may want to look into. Remember that I wanted to have my own café as a teen? I could extend this idea to encompass a kids' cooking school together with my café. I am all set to look into this once I am in my early 40s and am done birthing everyone. I will start looking into my own dreams then.

What is your favourite food?

I have always loved the big Fuji apples since I was a child. My mum would buy the $50 ones when I do well in the tests, so I associate Fuji apples with feeling rewarded!

Given what you know now, what would you say to a younger version of you?

Give yourself a break!

What are you most proud of?

That I am effectively bilingual and not just someone who "eats potatoes". (*laughter*) I am also proud of the fact that I may not be famous or rich but I know that I can be a catalyst for change in this lifetime.

How would you like to be remembered?

Currently, I just want to be remembered as a good mother, wife, food banker, and as someone who has contributed to society. Being a good business person ranks tenth in my life as making money isn't the key but being a change maker is. I may not be Mother Theresa, but if I can impact someone else's life, I would like to do that.

What would you say to God?

I would tell Him or Her, "Thank you very much for giving me the life that you did, because I wouldn't change a thing."

Would you say you're a Madonna, Maverick or any other M word?

I would say I am a Maternal Maverick. While independent, I have the patience to groom and nurture dreams and ideas, and sustaining an idea is even more difficult than coming up with one.

The Gentle Warrior

IVY SINGH-LIM

Ivy Singh-Lim was born in 1949 to Bachoo Singh, a direct descendant of the Rajputs, and his Chinese "common law" partner, Tan Lay Koon. She dabbled in marriage, travelled the world and took on various odd jobs before settling in at British American Tobacco (BAT) where she became a formidable marketer.

She met her now husband, Lim Ho Seng when she was 33 and the two married in 1982. At 40, Ivy took over the helm of her father's company and grew his business to new heights. She also served as the President of Netball Singapore for 14 years and worked to popularise the sport.

Her life then took an unexpected turn when she found herself the owner of a farm, Bollywood Veggies, which she has now developed into an education centre with a restaurant and a museum. She later became President of the Kranji Countryside Association, a group she founded to enable her passionate advocacy for the farming community, as well as enabling Singaporeans to commune with nature and to nourish their souls.

She was inducted into the Women's Hall of Fame in 2014 and continues her contribution to society through her farm and The Gentle Warrior's Trust for women. She stars in a weekly digital talk show called "Coffee & Whiskey with Ivy" on Happy-TV.

***

Suffice to say, there is never a dull moment speaking with Ivy. Our interview in her popular bistro, Poison Ivy, was filled with hearty interruptions from staff coming up to check in with her, customers professing their glee at the food and the farm, as well as gushy fans who see her as some sort of goddess.

Ivy grew up as the proverbial wild rose in a men's world and is elsewhere described as being the result of a union between the lion and the phoenix—her Indian father and her Chinese mother. The Rajputs were a warrior clan named after the lion so warrior blood coursed through Ivy's veins from birth. Her temperament has also been described as being akin to the five cardinal virtues of the phoenix, the Chinese mythological bird: benevolence, uprightness, wisdom, faith and respect. The last one, I argue, can be contentious given her devil-may-care attitude towards people, ideas or situations that she deems preposterous. She does not suffer fools and certainly does not mince her words, and she does have some very strong words to say towards our government. In fact, some of her strongest critiques came with so much vitriol that I found myself having to research studiously into the cases she raised as evidence. But to be fair, she is polite to a fault when it comes to the elderly. I know as I saw how she attended to my 81-year-old father with much grace and respect. It is no surprise why she has proclaimed herself the Gentle Warrior.

Unlike the 45th U.S. President who is almost always guilty of making accusations with no proof, and then scrambles to find ways to back up his untruths, Ivy speaks many truths that may seem like hot air at first because of her theatrical flamboyance, but upon research, her charges are watertight. These instances are well documented, though unpublicised because the authorities do not wish to invite media scrutiny.

Ivy is the sort that does not back down from a good fight and she would fight all the way to the end to prove her point. The ability to do so is, of course, abetted by the fact that she can afford the legal fees. One gets a sense that she fights and makes a show of herself to represent the underdogs who may be charged for speaking their minds. These regular Singaporeans may never get their fair day in court, may be held in "detention without trial", and may not have the means to wrestle it to the end with the powers that be.

One such high-profile demonstration of her seemingly unhinged antics was seen when she won a case in court. She thanked the judge and pumped her fist, saying "Majulah Singapura!" She then kissed the ground outside the Subordinate Courts and had her head shaved by her husband all in full view of the public. The uninitiated passerby may be forgiven for thinking that Ivy seems stark, raving mad. But once you scratch the surface you'll find that underneath the aggressive exterior lies a woman who genuinely cares for people and the society.

Ivy speaks loudly with animated gesticulations and much bravado, but she is a self-professed patriot and expresses her love for Singapore, even as she decries its idiosyncrasies. Hers is not an unmediated tirade on the establishment; it stems forth from her encounters with injustice that she does not shy away from sharing. In fact, writing about Ivy proffers a different sort of challenge to the Singaporean writer—the challenge of self-censorship. Her language is so, shall we say, "colourful", that it makes the convent girl in me blush. These are words that I would utter in the company of my best friends in Hokkien, but perhaps not the language I would use in the media because it may live on in posterity. Her speech, peppered with scatological references and open criticisms of the government, also run contrary to the usual guardedness of media practitioners in Singapore. It is clear Ivy knows these unspoken rules but she has no intention of abiding by these conventions.

There is no subtext or subtlety with Ivy Singh-Lim. In fact, her loving and supportive husband, ex-head honcho of NTUC Fairprice affectionately calls her "a terrorist—a snakey, quarrelsome and troublesome Indian". She says what she means, though she does not always mean what she says, as she has, in the course of our interview, threatened to wreck literal carnage on the orifices of various individuals and institutions. She may not be everyone's cup of tea, but she certainly is mine. She is a breath of fresh air and a welcome change and to an otherwise staid and conservative Singapore.

With Ivy, she gets not just the last word but the first word too—like in our interview. I had no chance to set the stage before she hijacked the conversation by voraciously sharing with me her fondness for her personal assistant, Manda, and did not back off even when I tried to get a word in. So I did the next best thing: I took a backseat, strapped on my safety belt, tucked into the delectable array of dishes—Warriors Platter of Sambal Tofu, Honey Sesame Chicken, Pineapple Fish and Warriors Chicken Curry—and surrendered to the rollercoaster ride that was about to begin. Just don't say you were not warned.

***

Manda is an interesting kid who walked into my life six years ago. She came here with a bunch of girls and I approached to tease them as I usually do, and also to find out what they were doing at Bollywood Veggies. Manda replied that she was with a group of girls from Boston University and expressed her desire to work here.

I looked at her and said, "Why on earth would I employ you? You look like a bloody gangster." I asked, "Where were you schooled?" and she said, "SCGS and Raffles Girls'." I said, "Any donkey can go there" and asked her about her university and she said, "Boston University." So I said, "Boston as in Boston, America, or Boston, Middle Road, Singapore?" and she said, "Boston, America."

She said she was studying journalism and I asked, "Why would I employ a journalism graduate and what can you do for me?" and she said, "I'm cheap, cheerful and I'll do anything as long as it's not against my principles." I then asked her "How much is cheap?" and she mentioned the price. She said the reason she wanted this job was because her dad just gave her a car, but she would like to pay for it herself. So I thought, "Very good lah!"

I employed her and she became my personal assistant and scribe. Fast forward six years, Bollywood Veggies is gaining popularity and I'm getting interviews left, right and center, so Manda ended up putting her journalism skills to practice! That's how it started. She's never left and I even sent her to Lee Kuan Yew School of Public Policy."

You said Manda "walked into your life". Did your husband do the same?

My husband is a darling but nowadays he's getting old and grumpy. He's 74 and is my second husband. I'm a very unusual person. As soon as I got my freedom at 21, I got married. I married someone absolutely poor, and after seven years, I thought, this is it. I knew I never wanted a kid so I sacked him and was single for seven years. I was drinking, smoking and doing all the other evil things in life. I even worked in a tobacco company, BAT, and one day, I went to the NTUC supermarket and met this man. He pretty much had a sign that said "buy one get one free"—he has a daughter though he was never married. To me, that was a sign of a responsible person and soon after, we got married.

My husband is my muse and my soulmate. When we first got married, my temper was worse than it is now. I would read the newspapers and I'd say "These f****** bastards!" And he'd say, "Darling, don't swear." People have told him, "Your wife is terrible." And he'd say, "I married her and I love her because of that."

You shared that your father was a wealthy landowner. Share with us how much land your family owned back then.

Our family used to own the whole of Simei, about 6.5 million square feet. I was born in 1949 and back then, we owned what was known as the "Third Mile" which ran from modern day St Andrew's School to the river and Woodsville Estate. We had so much property, but 30 years ago, the government took 6 million square feet and paid us only a dollar per square foot. They took all the sand and put it all in Marine Parade. But back then, we were still happy as we had 500,000 square feet, where my papa had over a hundred houses which was rented to the British army and the locals. In 1988, we rebuilt the estate that now stands opposite the Simei MRT station.

How did your papa make his wealth?

My papa came to Singapore when he was around 14 years old in 1920. By the time I was born, he was super rich. From what I gathered, my first mother was Cantonese and didn't have any kids of her own, but she inherited a son from her previous marriage, who was just five years younger than my mother. My brother, Andrew, is still alive and is in his 80s. According to Andrew, papa made metal trunks for ships and also sold flour and spices after the war.

When he made his money, he used it to buy land. His philosophy was to always invest in land. He believed that a fool and his money would soon part ways and figured that he might give all his cash to a woman he meets. But if he invested all his money in land, he would have to wait to liquidate it, so by then, his madness for the woman might have ended. That was his logic which served him well. So by the time I was born, he was already super rich and we lived in Moonstone Lane, which he owned.

My father's life started in Colonial Bar near the Rex Theatre building at the corner of Serangoon Road. I believe my father ran a restaurant downstairs, and also ran a gaming house. He met my mother, consort number two, who used to live in Veerasamy Road. My mother was only 16 when she met my papa. My maternal grandfather had died suddenly, otherwise, he would not allow his Chinese daughter to be number two to an Indian man.

All of us were born in the KK Hospital. When my youngest brother was born, we moved to Rose Lane in Tanjong Katong as papa had bought a property from Cathay Organisation even though his office was in Malacca Street. I remember it was a long office and always smelt of spices. So whenever I go into a spice shop, it would remind me of papa and my childhood.

You never had a day of poverty, so how did you become so streetwise and come to care so much for the masses?

As a half-Indian and half-Chinese, we were raised by servants and educated in Christian schools. In our house, the gardener is Malay-Muslim, the servants are Cantonese and Hokkien, which also explains why I am able to speak all the dialects. We were raised by servants and bodyguards who taught us to hunt and fish. We needed to learn how to be self-reliant and to defend ourselves, because kidnapping was an everyday thing back in the day, and especially because we were super rich. That is also why I am so bloody fierce, and if I can get kidnapped in Singapore, Singapore really has no hope, man. In fact, when I first moved here, the police were so anxious and were always driving up and down because it was a jungle. But I had no fear.

Anyway, my father never made us Hindus or Christians and just told us to be who we think we are. He built a Hindu and a Taoist temple, the Tua Pek Kong temple in Moonstone Lane. But he was also supportive of other religions. When there was a church event in school, my papa would just ask, "Do you need money or do you need to bring some food?" He never put down other religions.

The thing is, when you are young, you don't know whether you are rich or poor, Indian or Chinese, because we all just played and ate together. The neighbouring unit was rented out by rooms, so I played with all the poor children. Our gates are never closed. We shared with them whatever we have and vice versa. If I were to drown in a *longkang*, they'd save me. My classmates would tell me that they knew I was rich as I always had the most pocket money, nicest pencil cases, biggest house and I always paid for their food. I was always like the leader of the pack though all my teachers loved me as I was respectful and was even made a prefect.

I think this current government has made things worse. They keep harping on this Chinese, Malay, Indian distinction and this is where it has become a problem. Like me, I'm not a bloody Indian, and I'm not a bloody Chinese. I'm a Singaporean, just as Americans are Americans. Whether you are black, blue or brown, you'll say you're an American. The government wants to keep things that way to divide the bloody donkeys so that they can rule.

As far as I'm concerned, politics and religion created God and Government and it has kept women *out*. They introduced another G for Ghost to keep Man down. There you have it, the three G's. I'm the fourth G, Gentle Warrior. I'm not frightened by God, Government or Ghost.

This is how we were raised. People ask me how I can be Singaporean and so outspoken. And I say, that is because we were super rich, super intelligent and my papa told us to never worry about anything or anyone except to make sure we are not dishonest, unkind and to always be fair. And most importantly, to always help everyone in the community. That's all there is to it.

A totally honest person and a born leader would not care and not be frightened. Mostly people are fearful as they are compromised—they worry about their parents, husband, religion and they all begin to feel compromised. For me, my parents never curtailed my lifestyle though I would never dare smoke or drink in front of my papa. In school, we were not frightened of our teachers as our papa and the servants imbued in us a sense of responsibility. When I grew up, I wasn't afraid of my employer and couldn't give a damn if they sacked me. As we were wealthy, I worked to keep myself occupied.

When I got married, I didn't give a damn too. I mean, I love and respect my husband, but if he gives me grief, I will happily kill him too. I have my own opinions and am entitled to them so why should I give a shit about what you think about me. It's my life. If my husband can't take me as I am, he would have run away a long time ago, but he's a strong man.

How is your relationship with your mother?

As far as my mother is concerned, I think she would have killed my papa long ago but she was too young. You see, my papa recruited a third woman into his "stable". She was Teochew, and had a couple of kids with her shortly after my youngest brother was born. Then he had a fourth, fifth and a sixth partner. I thought, he finally ended with six so that he could rest on a Sunday.

My mum had to put up with this because she was not educated and did not have the support of her family. Besides, my papa helped all three of her brothers through school in one way or another, and even supported one of them through law school in the UK. Honestly, they would not have accepted my papa if he wasn't rich. They called my papa *lau hor* or tiger. My papa supported everyone and even paid for my mum's youngest brother, who is 85 years old now, to study Law in England.

Clearly, your father influenced your values and ethics. What were your views on marriage shaped by?

My father didn't want me to get married. On both occasions when I wanted to get married, he asked me "Why?" Now I understand. As I did not want kids, am rich and beautiful, why get married? You see, he probably knew the apple wouldn't fall far from the tree and was afraid that I would be bored with my husband since I certainly didn't need him for financial security. He was trying to tell me, "Think carefully before you get married." I didn't, and that is why my first marriage ended up in divorce.

I learnt a lot from my papa as he was always very caring and helpful to the workers and people. I saw how he would give the milkman food whenever he comes, even when the food was specially prepared for him. My papa was very frugal and not flashy. He never had a watch, never wore socks, ate at home every day and never travelled.

The other key thing was that he sent us to the right schools and we had a Christian education. I went to St Anthony's Convent Kindergarten till Secondary Two when I left for Katong Convent. That is also why I eventually became a warrior as KC made you look more holistically at life. Both schools imbued great values in me and I would have become a nun if I stayed on. In many ways, I had the best of both worlds—a convent education as well as discipline from the family. If you don't have discipline and responsibility, you'll end up becoming a rude, young, obnoxious punk with no respect for the law. But once you teach a kid discipline, responsibility and all that sort of stuff, then they are on their way towards something greater.

Given how privileged you were, could you hold down a job?

I had several jobs before I started working for BAT in 1977 and I worked for them for 12 years, which was my longest held job. It was never meant to be a career as I get bored easily. In 1989, I went back to the family business to help develop the properties in Simei because my youngest brother had retina detachment and almost went blind and my papa was very sick.

My father's company, incorporated in 1947, was called Indo-Australian Trading Company Private Limited. When I quit my job to run the family business, we were then in the midst of building 68 semi-detached and terrace houses. When we completed that, we developed Rose Lane where we had our family house. We closed the company eventually because when you are in a family business, not everyone has the same vision. Some may be happy with 10 million but another may want a billion, so there is bound to be unhappiness. In the end, we wound up the company.

To date, my youngest brother and I still privately own many properties, as our values are quite similar. When Ho Seng, my husband and I went to Perth for our honeymoon, we both wanted to retire there. I wanted to liquidate my assets to migrate because it was a great place with a wonderful lifestyle. But my then BAT boss, Kim Siang, said, "Yes, it is beautiful. But after six months, you will get bored with your husband and will definitely get divorced. I tell you what, let Ho Seng develop his career and you both go to Perth for holidays." Suffice to say, that was the best advice ever given to me. We are still married.

Was your husband already in NTUC (National Trades Union Congress) then?

He was never in NTUC. When I married him in 1982, he was the number one in SILO (Singapore Industrial Labour Organisation) and PIEU (Pioneer Industries Employees Union). He was employed after a fiasco by Phey Yew Kok[1] who was then the Secretary General of NTUC. On 1 May 1983, SILO and NTUC Welcome were merged to form NTUC Fairprice. My husband was the one who drove the merger to success.

My husband wanted to retire at 55 so that we can move to Perth,

1 Ivy segues into a side story on Phey Yew Kok, whom she declares to be smarter than Lee Kuan Yew but is a crook. He was one of the most powerful union leaders in Singapore, holding the post of NTUC Chairman and heading SILO and PIEU, and their supermarket chains. He was an elected Member of Parliament when he embezzled money from the unions, SILO, the supermarket, and went into hiding. His arrest and sentencing marked a chapter in Singapore's union and political history.

but he ended up retiring a year earlier. See, what happened was, at that time, my brother, Mohan had developed 40 apartments in Perth and I went over to help him complete it. Just then, my best friend also quit as the financial controller of Standard Chartered Bank to retire with her sweet, Christian husband in order to embark on their travel plans to commemorate their 25th wedding anniversary. But, in January he had a heart attack and died. It really made us see how short and unexpected life can be and that we should live a full life everyday.

How did you come by the idea to start Bollywood Veggies?

On a trip when I was flying back to Singapore with my husband, I read the news about a farmer in Lim Chu Kang. I said to my husband "Darling, look, there *is* land in Singapore! The bloody PAP is talking c*ck!" So, once we touched down, I got our driver to take us there and I learnt from one of the the owners of Green Circle that there's a tender in September. We saw it as yet another sign and did the math to see if we could afford to live in the Kranji countryside for the next 20 years.

So okay la, we are rich people and we need about $20,000 to $30,000 a month to live. Why? First of all, I drink, so I cannot drive. My husband doesn't drive because he's spoilt, and my mother is also spoilt. So between the three of us, we need at least two drivers. I need a secretary because I'm just lazy and I also need a bookkeeper to keep track of my money and a housekeeper. I also have a Caucasian driver and a housekeeper in my home in Perth. We fly and live first class both in Singapore and in Perth.

Which is why this discovery of land here in Singapore is just so ideal. I said, "This is it. This is my calling." And so we came back. I think the universe decided that I should come back because shortly after our return, Mohan decided to return too. He then agreed to take a legal case defending a taxi driver who was scammed by the cash-back scheme which originated in Hong Kong. All our leaders in HDB and the banks knew about this scam, which was promoted by many housing agencies. Because he was a whistle-blower, he was crucified by the government, and it took us seven years to fight the case before the judges in the Court of Appeal found him innocent and said that the case should never have come to court in the first place.

Share with us about the court case you personally had to deal with. The BCA (Building and Construction Authority) tried to take me to court and I fought the case. Again, it's very simple. They said they sent me a note to do an inspection of my building and I said didn't receive it. When I finally received it, I wrote, "Dear Donkey, don't waste my time."

There was a recession in 2009, and I told the authorities to come and inspect my properties. I have both TOP (Temporary Occupation Permit) and CSC (Certificate of Statutory Completion). There is no sewer line in this part of Singapore. Building a septic tank costs a lot of money and I'm one of the rich and responsible farmers who can afford it, so I told them to come and inspect instead of making me pay extra money for an inspection as I am already investing a lot to develop the area. For example, there were no buses and we are already providing chartered buses to come into the area. Finally, they inspected and they passed my house, but then insisted on inspecting the rest of the property. So I wrote to the commissioner and to the minister, but they all came back with the same responses. I said, "Don't be a goose. Stop regurgitating the law. Fly here and have a look." The goose didn't fly here but sent me summons instead! So I decided to defend myself in court.

When we went to the pre-trial conference, even the judge agreed with my course of action but advised me that in order to challenge the existing laws, I had to take it to Parliament, so I told him I had written to the minister. Anyway, to make the long story short, I complied with what was required, but one month later, I was told that I had to plead guilty to one charge. What on earth for? The judge said "Miss Singh, you should ask your brother for advice." So I said to the judge, "Your Honour, thank you very much for your kind heart." I went out and told those bastards, "Do you know why my surname is Singh? I am not a Sikh. I am a Rajput warrior. Do you know what we do when we catch an enemy? I f*** you in your backside, so make sure your arse is clean." So, I got a super-lawyer, Engelin

Teh, and of course, we won the case. But it cost me $700,000. What on earth for? I want to know now, how much did it cost the state to bring me to court and for what?[2] I plan to sue BCA for malicious prosecution soon.

And you wish to do so to make a statement?
Yes. This is the thing, all these bastards in power think that at the end of their life, they will have a pot of gold waiting. But hello, it's the guy with the horns that's waiting for you. This is the trouble, the dishonesty is disgusting, but we have impressed upon the world how wonderful we are. People compromise their principles and that's why the world is what it is today.

Do you think it is also because the government has made our lives here so comfortable that we are lulled into a false sense of contentment and have lost our principles?
It's not just Singaporeans. The average human being is a bozo who just cares about feeding themselves, having the latest technology gadgets, and they don't give a damn about anybody else. That's basically it—simple. I tell you something: it's going to blow up. It's a matter of time.

I'm sure the universe brought me back here so all this could happen. I started this Kranji countryside idea and look, this thing is beautiful. You can't cement the whole of this country. The trouble is our leaders all come from poverty-stricken backgrounds and when they see land, they don't see life. All they see are opportunities to build more shopping centres and condominiums and to line their own pockets with their exorbitant salaries. They say we have 50 years of great governance, but there are so many Singaporeans, not foreigners, who earn less than $2,000 a month. How do they live? And these bastards have the audacity to say we have a meritocratic society? Come on, give me a break, man!

2 Ivy was brought to court by the BCA after failing to comply with the inspection orders despite five deadline extensions. She faced two charges: failing to have her farm inspected and not engaging a professional engineer to carry out the check. Ivy retaliated by disputing the claim. The defence by Engelin Teh challenged the validity of the notice and charges, and presented evidence that there had been occasions when Bollywood Veggies did not receive mail sent to its address. Bollywood Veggies was acquitted of the criminal charges.

If you have a car bumper sticker, what will it say?
Simple. "Get rid of evil men and stupid women." Look at the bastard men running the world and all the women who are supporting them. The stupid women, instead of running to look for the culprits who are throwing babies in the river, they run to collect and cover the corpses of all the babies. Look at Modi, he wants to defend our sea lanes. What has India got to do with the South China Sea? Why doesn't he defend his own country and people, especially when his women and children are being raped and he can't do anything about it?

Did you not once say you would like to form an all-women party?
If I was younger, yes, maybe. You see, the universe has been protecting me. My classmate, Teo Soh Lung was one of those arrested by Lee Kuan Yew.[3] Soh Lung was arrested at 40. At age 40, I was going to stop working and go into politics. I wanted to make a difference to my community because I'm rich, powerful and I didn't want children, so what else could I do with my life but make the community stronger? But just when I was considering politics, my youngest brother had retinal detachment, my father died, and I had to go back to run the family business.

If I had known Soh Lung was arrested, I would have gone to the Whitley Detention Camp to kick the door down and Lee Kuan Yew would have arrested me as well. And in my 50s, I didn't want to get myself locked up. Why would you want to go down that path and get arrested? You can't do anything from there and once you get locked up, half the people will think you're wrong and you can't make a difference, so what's the point? I'm a warrior, not a fool. A warrior fights battles slowly to win the war.

And plus, we really wanted to go to Perth to retire but before I knew it, we found this beautiful land and started this. I thought, if I do this well, I can also make a difference without going into politics. Besides, I

3 In 1987, Teo Soh Lung, a lawyer, was detained under the Internal Security Act (ISA) of Singapore together with other persons for purported involvement in a conspiracy to overthrow the government by force and replace it with a Marxist state.

am already giving them a firing every day on the phone or speaking to ministers about what is ailing the system whether they like or not. If they are not happy, they can arrest me and put me in jail. They have tried to do all sorts of things but they failed because I have God, Allah, Buddha, Jesus and Prophet Muhammad on my side. I'm confident of it.

And now that I am past my 60s, I'm old with less energy and limited time. And honestly, where can I find nine other people with exactly the same values as me to form a party?[4] Impossible.

Why do you think you haven't been censured like the bloggers Roy Ngerng or Amos Yee? What is your strategy?

I think I make responsible statements. I have black and white proof of everything I've told you. When I say they are corrupt, I have black and white proof of it. If I call the prime minister stupid, that's up to me, it's my opinion. How can they arrest me for calling somebody stupid? I do think he is stupid and that is why so many people are having to suffer and earning so little money—because he doesn't know what the hell is going on here.

It is an opinion and not an accusation that they stole money or something. I don't think they are corrupted in the sense that they steal money officially, but look at how much they have been enriched in one lifetime? That is something that everybody knows and nobody dares to say. Somebody should ask them to declare their wealth since the day they started in politics. Ask them to declare how much they are worth then? Thailand does it, so why doesn't Singapore insist on it?

With Roy and Amos, I think the authorities got carried away. They are trying to scare the younger generation because they know the younger ones can make a difference. And the young people don't worship money as a god. That's the most frightening thing for them. You see Manda, my scribe—she's rich, intelligent, effective, fearless. And there are more and more honest and fearless people these days. And the point is, when you have all these fearless people, do you want to change your system of government and have them on your side, or have them join ISIS and shoot you? Which would you prefer?

4 At least 10 Singaporeans are needed to form a political party in Singapore.

I am not harmful. I love my country. I am a builder, not a destroyer. But sometimes, you have to destroy to build something better. The people who are out there poor and helpless have no one to help them and they live in total frustration and disappointment. All they need to do is get hold of a gun and they will shoot because they just don't care anymore.

What is your net worth and how much have you spent on Bollywood Veggies?

Well, I think I am worth \$20 to \$40 million according to the property market, but Bollywood Veggies is not an investment. For us, we just see it as a lifestyle and a purpose. We live here and we don't care if we make money or not. We employ May, who sells her book *Scaling Walls* and she makes her money from that. We employ all sorts of psychedelic people with lots of attitude. There's Donna who is a lawyer who studied in Australia and runs my events department.

You see, when I went to America close to 50 years ago with my cousin, I remember a white boy carrying my bag to my room and he made breakfast for us the next morning. I asked him if he was the owner and he said he's the manager and is paid by his boss to look after his business. I asked him how much he was paid and he said \$10 an hour and that he was a graduate of University of Berkeley. So I told him that I would double his salary if he could take three days off to drive my cousin and I around California. The deal was that he would teach me all about America and I will share with him about Asia.

The first thing we did was to go to his house—it was then that I realised that he was well-to-do and that the rich may share a house to go to the university. But most times, when people share a house in Singapore, they tend to be poor. When we got to Lake Tahoe, we all swam in our underwear to show him that despite the colour of our skin, we're all the same. It was also then that I realised how super efficient the Americans are and I learnt from that experience as well! That's also why I have never turned on a computer in my life because anything a monkey or a machine can do, I don't do. I do things that cannot be done by a computer like thinking and creating and farming. Because if you can be replaced by a machine or a monkey, what's your worth? Think about it.

I noticed you seem to have a very inclusive taskforce. Tell us more about that.

Actually, I didn't plan for that nor am I one to advertise. All I do is that I always believe and pray to the universe and people just come. When we wanted to make this a tourist attraction, I went to STB (Singapore Tourism Board) and the stupid woman there told me farms in Singapore are not unique! So when I was invited to the Uniquely Singapore launch, I said, "You honkey donkey, yellow monkey, don't come to my farm anymore, or I'll put you in the compost! And you white monkeys too!"

I then went to see Vivian Balakrishnan who was then the Minister of State for National Development. I said, "Minister, you know my name is Ivy Singh, we've never met before." He said, "Ivy, I know everything about you, and I said you will go far." I said, "Minister, this is my card, I have a story to tell you. When you have time, please let us know." And he was good. He followed up and emailed us and soon, after that, our young farmers created a map and a blueprint for the Kranji countryside, and that's how this all started! That's how it all morphed! He got those idiots in SLA (Singapore Land Authority), AVA (Agri-Food and Veterinary Authority) and URA (Urban Redevelopment Authority), etc. to change the guidelines and that's what has happened. People think that I am so clever to have done this and I said, "No lah, I just look at the white man. Whatever the white man does, we will do. When the Chinese get rich, they drive a white man's car and drink a white man's wine. So let's face it, why won't they emulate a white man's lifestyle?"

But this country thinks that you're going to sit in your office all day and technology will do everything. Ask the prime minister to come out here and help me technologise my farm. Unfortunately, it's not that I dislike him or the government, but I dislike the fact that they are hypocrites. If they are unhappy with me, they should have the guts to come and talk to me about it. I'm not trying to run my country down. What I'm saying is do something about our beautiful country just as my father did when he first came here as a poor, uneducated, 14-year-old Indian. And look, he did so much for our country and even produced a genius like me.

Your father truly believed that Singapore was the land of opportunity and in many ways, so do you.

Of course! All countries are like that, but most Asian countries always end up having a bloody dictator who will screw it up somehow or other and leave a legacy of having so many left behind! And don't tell me this country is not screwed up, because when we get into a big recession, we're all going to eat sh*t.

Do you see that we seem to defer to authority as part of our Asian psyche, whereas the West focuses on the rights of the individual?

Yes, but don't forget, while the Americans did have a headstart, they still managed to take care of the community. Look at Bill Gates, Warren Buffet—they both give their money back to the community. Yes, there are always going to be people left behind, but you must still try your best and hardest to lift your finger. That's why I say, get rid of evil men and stupid women and bring the world back to paradise.

I get it—Bollywood Veggies is your way of giving back to society. You created an alternative Garden of Eden. So tell us more about the other projects you have in store, such as the museum and the culinary school.

The culinary school was an accident. See, they allowed the farmers to create a museum in this area. So, since I love to build, I decided to create a museum on my 60th birthday instead of buying a Bentley. It is also because this area here tends to get very packed so I needed more space to house the visitors in case it rained. And so, that was how the museum started. It will also have a cooking school which can empower women. If the women can cook and sew, they can make a living. As for the artworks in the museum, it wasn't planned. One day, in walks this blonde lady who asked me what I was going to showcase in my museum and I shared that it would be a Food Museum and she ended up painting 24 beautiful paintings for us!

I also say my prayers. Most people think I don't pray. In fact, I pray deeply and strongly and I pray for good things. But I also pray for those who should go, to go. I believe I'm also like God because I can create, destroy and nurture. People always think God is merciful and kind. Please lah, God doesn't give a shit. If He is so wonderful, why does He send all the misery to the poor countries? Why would there be tsunamis, earthquakes and typhoons? Because it is nature—that is what the Ice Age and Noah's Ark is about. It's the movement of the planets. So what we should do as an endangered species is to try and help our own species.

For me, I don't care as my mother, my husband and all my puppies would have died when I die. I have nothing left behind that I worry about, but it is the people who have children and grandchildren that should make a concerted effort and do something about it. It is the governments that are creating more problems by spending so much money on guns and bombs to shoot at each other and at the neighbours, which is really not helping the people.

Is what you are doing here sustainable?

It can be, provided you work hard. We should have more people, like us, who are rich and like to help. When I grow old, I'll move out of my bungalow and build a small retirement unit here. The younger generation can take over to support a circle of life. If only we could all create a circle of life around us instead of a circle of destruction, that would be brilliant! I think the British left us too soon, and Lee Kuan Yew and Mahathir set us back many years. Just look at how long it takes to cross the Causeway.

Having spoken to you for an extended period of time, I realise that while you use profanities, speak of destruction and paint doomsday scenarios, your philosophies and beliefs are quite the contrary. You seem to truly want to create and foster an environment of love.

Jesus made a mistake when he spoke too gently. I won't make the same mistake. Of course I love my land and I love my charmed, fortunate life. I have never turned on a computer or cooked in my entire life so I am useless, yet I live such a charmed life. Which other country would have given me this opportunity? I love this country so much that I think no one here should have to suffer.

My father gave so much to this country and yet 95% our land has been taken away. And even then, I don't mind. But what have they done with all that land now? They take away our land for a dollar per square foot and build HDB (Housing Development Board) flats, and they say they don't make money from selling the flats? They are dishonest bastards. Where do you think all the reserves in Singapore came from? From land acquisition, their biggest money churner! Ask them to look at it and stop being dishonest. That's all I need them to do and start to help the people who really need help. Recently, there was a report that 26% of those receiving assistance from Comcare[5] are employed and the response from the government was that they had to "find out why they need more money when they are working." It is simple, you donkey, they are not earning enough!

You're saying, "Why spend the money on research when you can spend money to fix the problem?"

Exactly! They spent $7 million to work with a French company on research, to make them richer than they already are, to find out who are the drunkards are. They probably come back with the report that the Malays are drug addicts, the Indians are drunkards, the Chinese are gamblers and the Eurasians are a bit of all of the above. That's what pisses me off. The government once asked, "How can we move from good to

5 Community Care Endowment Fund is set up by the government to address the socio-economic needs of low-income Singaporeans and their families.

great?" The answer is simple—be honest. We don't need intelligent people in the government. We just need honest people. And the argument is if you have to pay the ministers a high salary for them to be honest, then you should just get rid of them!

What other daring exploits have you done that we have not heard of—aside from you kissing the ground or shaving your head bald?
Basically, "no" is never an option for me. When I was 17, my girlfriend and I stole a chicken. We were in a bungalow which had everything for a barbeque except meat, so we hunted our neighbour's chicken, killed, barbequed and ate it. When I was younger and more wicked, if I am in the car with my driver and I spot a plant I don't have in my garden, I will jump out, cut a part of it and bring it home. It is not because I am a destructive person, but I like a good challenge and it is always for a good cause and for the betterment of the people. My husband was very convinced I will be the first woman to be caned. And yes, up till today, I still carry a knife wherever I go.

Share with us your appointment in SPCA (Society for the Prevention of Cruelty to Animals).
So, recently they made a new rule for pet licensing, so I wrote in to share that they should make an exception for farmers. I suggested that we should have a bulk license as we actually help to take care of the dogs so that they do not wander on the streets and end up at your gate. And do you know what was the response I got from AVA? Close the gate! Can you imagine how stupid the AVA is?

I spoke to K. Shanmugam about the ridiculous story and he referred my case to Desmond Lee who said he could not make an exception, to which I said, "Tell Desmond Lee, I know his parents, Mr and Mrs Lee Yock Suan. I will place nine of my dogs in my Jaguar, ten of my dogs in my Pajero and we will drive to the Istana and release my dogs at Orchard Road." I told Shanmugam that I was not being rude, but I need an option, so he suggested that I work with an NGO.

Just then, I learnt that SPCA is moving to the Kranji countryside so I decided to reach out to them and help them as well. At that time, they needed $1 million to complete their new facility and I decided I will go in there as Fund Raising Vice Chair and try to change the rules and regulations so that we will not have so many strays.[6]

I love dogs, but we don't want rabies. It is already in Penang and Bali so it is a matter of time before it gets to Singapore. The recent tuberculosis and hepatitis C outbreaks prove that our ministers don't understand what the real threats are. The real dangers are not dissidents, but diseases, especially in a global hub. Every day, thousands come to our airport, how do we screen them all? So the biggest concern should be disease and our lack of food production as we currently produce only 8% of the fish and vegetables we consume! Over 90% of the food we consume in the country is imported! So it is about time for a revolution.

What is your management style?

My management style is simple. I like to be happy, so make me happy. Don't think you are smarter than me because if you are, then you cannot be working for me. I'm a caring but strict boss and I don't take nonsense. If you are tired, rest. If you're hungry, eat. If you are sick, see the doctor. Don't work here for $700 and spend your money on cigarettes. Why would you want to smoke for? Stop smoking, stop drinking, except once a year on New Year's Eve, you're going to drink with me. The rest of the time, you work and you rest. That's all.

Tell us what is the toughest thing you faced.

The only time I was really sad was when my dad died. After the cremation, I came back to the house and I cried. I had my father till I was 40 years

6 The SPCA's new facility costs $7 million which includes a shelter, adoption centre, education centre and clinic. Ivy invited friends and fellow farmers to the fundraiser and also offered to hold SPCA talks at her farm while the building was under way. Minister and animal lover K. Shanmugam attended the event and even shared that he wouldn't mind working here as "it's a nice place full of living things that don't talk back to you." The MP for Chua Chu Kang GRC, Mr Yee Chia Hsing, also made an appearance, much to the pleasure of Ivy.

old. My father was like the godfather and my mum was uneducated. Suddenly, I felt like I was the last one standing. I was very broken-hearted and I went back to run the business. Of course, all my brothers started fighting with each other. At one stage, I even contemplated shooting them all to run the business with my sisters-in-law and my mum. The other time I was really sad was when my Great Dane died. I was very broken-hearted as he was the love of my life.

What would you say to a younger version of yourself?

Darling, look in the mirror. You are beautiful, young, intelligent and powerful for a reason. Why did the universe make you special? And when you are special, you will be different. Like Manda, she is a young person with very strong views and that is why she can work for us. I trust her with my life and my money.

Many people think they must have their own flesh and blood. To me, relatives are related by marriage and marriage is disposable. And blood? Blood is cheap and you can get it at the blood bank. Real family is the people who love you—my dogs, my drivers, my staff, my maids and my friends. Not all my relatives love me.

Favourite swear word?

F*** Off—because the first word has to do with sex and the second has to do with travel.

How do you best want to be remembered?

For what I am, a pain in the ass.

What will your epitaph say?

Here lies a woman who did whatever she wanted and said "F*** Off" to the world.

If you met God, what would you say?

You're a f***ing idiot aren't you, because you are a man like Adam who did not know what Eve was really after. Why create Paradise only to allow evil men and stupid women to destroy it?

What would you define yourself as? A Madonna, a Maverick or any other M word?

No M word—I'm the Gentle Warrior. No other word fits me.

The Music Maestro

SIOW LEE CHIN

Praised by the American Record Guide as "a distinguished cultural asset of international stature", and The Strad as a "trailblazing role model for string players," Siow Lee-Chin's Gold Medal victory at the 1994 Henryk Szeryng International Violin Competition launched her career as one of Singapore's first soloists on the classical stage, wowing audiences in more than 20 countries across five continents from Carnegie Hall to Osaka Symphony Hall. Her performances have been viewed by millions on BBC World News, China Central TV, America's CBS, National Public Radio, and Singapore's Mediacorp.

As a soloist, she has collaborated with renowned conductors and orchestras from the Royal Philharmonic and Danielle Gatti to the Houston Symphony and Andreas Delfs; and performed in the presence of celebrities and dignitaries from Elton John to former U.S. Secretary of State Henry Kissinger. In June 2015, she took centre stage performing at the Southeast Asian Games Opening Ceremony for an audience of more than 40,000 and reaching many more through web broadcasts.

She started her violin studies with her late father Siow Hee Shun, and traces her musical lineage to Henryk Wieniawski and Eugène Ysaÿe, the King of the Violin, through his disciples who were her teachers at Curtis, Oberlin and Mannes: Aaron Rosand, Jascha Brodsky, Felix Galimir, Almita and Roland Vamos. Today, she continues their pedagogical tradition in her work with young people all over the world from Beijing's Central Conservatory of

Music, Chicago Institute of Music, Singapore National Youth Orchestra and she is also Professor of Violin at the College of Charleston.

Lee-Chin confidently bridges the East and West, personalising familiar favourites with Asian motifs and introducing Asian composers to the West. In 2015, she performed the world premiere of Air, a piece specially written for her by acclaimed composer Yao Chen, to open Singapore's Golden Jubilee celebrations in the City of London Festival. That same year, Straits Times Press published her memoirs "From Clementi to Carnegie: The Journey of Singaporean Violinist Siow Lee Chin". In 2017, she premiered Air and Singaporean composer Kam Kee Yong's Chinese Rhapsody at Carnegie Hall.

***

In the beginning, our correspondence was undertaken by Lee-Chin's manager who had the unenviable task of trying to coordinate our distinct schedules across oceans. I did not know what to expect, except that I knew musicians were an erratic bunch—passionate and truly sensitive. After all, it is that nuanced sensibility that they take to their craft.

I am not one to be easily intimidated, but I am no classical music aficionado and can barely pronounce some of these European names. I figured I would refrain from speaking too much about classical music as that was not my strongest suit and besides, I contended that she had given far too many interviews on that subject. What should we speak about then? After all, she is a writer, too, having written her own memoir.

But all my fears and questions were unfounded the minute we started chatting. It was a conversation between two artists working with the East and West—we are both children of the diaspora, we are teachers who love learning and mentoring and, above all, we are daughters of amazing fathers. But it was the last one that sealed our mutual understanding.

Beyond making music, cultivating the arts, fulfilling our dreams of leading a better life and creating a better world, what bound us together is that shared sense of love and affection towards our fathers. We are both grown women in charge of our own destinies, but we yearn every day to have our fathers with us so that we could be at home, safe and comforted in the knowledge that we can always be daddy's little girls.

But do not mistake Lee-Chin for a sappy lass. Her discipline, steely willpower and determination have led her to leave Singapore as a young teen, only to later take on the classical music world by storm to become the highly respected artist that she is today. In recent years, her optimism and strength have enabled her to overcome her brush with cancer as well as a devastating accident that threatened to end her ability to play her beloved violin. This Clementi girl is living proof that Henri Matisse was right when he said that "Creativity takes courage."

Lee-Chin's story is not one of instant success or overnight sensation, but that of a stalwart artist who crossed oceans to break barriers while fighting against fear, self-doubt and numerous slammed doors, to emerge as a resplendent phoenix in the gilded concert halls of Carnegie.

***

Lee-Chin, thank you for talking to me. We are doing this with the help of technology through Skype.

First of all, I am thrilled to be included in this very diverse compendium of incredibly interesting women that you have carefully curated and selected! I am deeply honoured. I have to admit: I would love to do what you are doing. In fact, there is nothing more I would love than to have a role-reversal and interview you and all these accomplished women! What a great way to learn from such inspiring role models! (*laughter on both sides*)

You are too humble, Lee-Chin. So let's start the interview formally using the title of your book, *From Clementi to Carnegie* as a launchpad. Clearly, you have no pretensions about your

humble beginnings, which makes a great conversation starter. So please enlighten and share with us about your early struggles.
In order to tell my story, I need to tell my dad's story first. His background is absolutely amazing. The fact that he became a violinist was in itself is a miracle and the fact that he was alive to play the violin was another miracle.

See, when he was nine years old, he was grievously injured by the Japanese during the Occupation. Despite being bayonetted, he cheated death and survived. Luckily for him, a kind Malay lady who witnessed the incident applied medicinal herbs on my dad's wounds. He started to get better and the rest is history. Isn't that already amazing?

My dad had a tough life and lost both his parents as well as five of his siblings. So, you can only imagine the kind of trauma he endured as a young man. Growing up, I never knew this. It was not until a couple of years prior to my departure for the U.S. that Dad decided to share with me the cause of the visible scars on his body. I was shocked beyond belief.

The other miraculous thing was that no one else in Dad's family was into music. His Hakka family members were all businessmen and nobody was in the arts. So my dad was a real black sheep. And of all things, he fell in love with, specifically, the violin.

Dad did not have a lot of money so he saved up money for a year in order to buy himself a violin and eventually saved more to finance about one year's worth of violin lessons. He was determined to master the instrument. Just by doing that, my dad will always be my role model. In fact, he got so good at it, he was given an opportunity to pursue his violin study in England. However, as luck would have it, he met my mother just then. So he gave up his love for the violin for the love of my mother. Mum was soon pregnant with me and I think, in many ways, my dad transferred his love, desire and passion for the violin onto me.

I was scarcely three months old when he wanted me to play the violin. But he was never a stage parent. He was just extremely enthusiastic and very, very supportive. All he wanted to do was to share his love for music with his children. And somehow with me, the violin really resonated.

Even at a young age, before I could really understand anything that was going on, Dad already got me to listen to classical music. I did not have the vocabulary but I remember being taken by the sheer elegance of the phrase. I would be enthralled by its arch and its beauty though I had no idea what all that meant. What I could sense, though, was the intense passion and that was very intoxicating. And so I would listen, enthralled, and I would look up from time to time and see my dad and mum standing over me, sharing with me their passion and their love for music. I would learn later that the strife for something is in itself something great.

But like any child, we grow into rebellious teenagers and somehow, in the years before I went abroad, I suddenly developed a love-hate relationship with the violin. I loved performing and wanted to do my dad proud but it is tough for any teenager to come to terms with the endless hours of practice needed to become a successful violinist! As a teacher today, I find myself in my dad's shoes, reminding my students to practice, but I was in their shoes not so long ago! I know how hard it is to keep pushing on and to accept delayed gratification. But thanks to Dad's patience and encouragement, I found my own passion for music and my ticket to see the world.

When I was about 15, the famous American violinist Aaron Rosand was in Singapore to perform with the Singapore Symphony Orchestra. Dad always encouraged me to perform for visiting artists, so I took the opportunity to play for Mr Rosand, not knowing that he was recruiting for the Curtis Institute of Music, one of the top American music conservatories! I was a little nervous, so I asked Aaron Rosand if I could warm up first. "Sure, go for it," he said.

Instead of warming up with a scale as most would, I was so flustered that I launched into the *Cadenza* of Paganini's *Concerto No. 1*, which was the piece I was learning then. Amused, Mr Rosand said, "If you're going to warm up with that, what are you going to play next?"

The next thing he said changed my life. "Would you like to study with me at Curtis?" Right there on the spot, he offered me a place, on full scholarship, at one of America's most prestigious music schools.

It was a huge decision for my parents to let me go abroad on my own at such a young age. But Dad had no hesitation. He had such immense passion and belief in me and made me believe that I could do anything I wanted if I worked hard at it. He was very much a no-nonsense Chinese man and lived by the mantra, "Do not worry about the harvest. Keep sowing and the rest will take care of itself."

Honestly, I was just too young to fathom how scary going abroad all by myself could be. If you asked me if I would do it now with the benefit of hindsight, I would say "No way!" (*laughter*) Looking back, it was all one big adventure and I was fortunate that my father had such a passion for music. The popular choice of study then was Medicine, Law or Engineering. So what I chose was not popular at all. But my dad not only encouraged me, he was full of conviction that it was the right way forward for me.

Is it a stereotype that most of the children who study classical music came from money? In the U.S., did you ever feel a disparity between those who "have it" and those less privileged?

I am generally a positive person, and I must say while I was in the U.S., I did not feel that I lacked anything. Besides, everyone at Curtis was on scholarship. In addition, there was no minimum age. For most colleges, you have to be at least 18. But at Curtis, you could be 12, 13 or eight years old, and you could get in if you could play well. It was a very meritocratic environment and that was the yardstick.

I think I was very, very fortunate because I didn't get the sense of what it meant to "have it" or "not have it". I truly believe that the most important thing you can give to a child is love, confidence and time. And, they will look at the world in a very different way. That was what I felt. My family was rich—not financially but psychologically. So for that, I know I am very blessed and I was never envious of any of my well-to-do classmates who went on holidays to faraway places and came back with stories of exotic foods or sights they had visited. Oh, but when I went to Philadelphia, I fell in love with the strawberry cheesecake the very first time I saw it. I had to have one almost every other day and gained like 20 pounds! (*laughter*)

Who were your mentors or role models when you were in Philadelphia?

My other key support, besides my family, was Lady McNeice, wife of Sir Percy McNeice, the first President of Singapore's City Council. She was like the grandmother I never had and was my patron. My education in the U.S. was also sponsored by her foundation, the Loke Cheng Kim Foundation. She was an incredible philanthropist who championed arts education and the environment long before such causes became fashionable. Her gifts came not just in financial form but also in the generous amount of time she spent with the scholars she sponsored.

Lady McNeice made me feel special and would invite me to tea at her home every time I returned to Singapore. She would share with me her love for botany, photography and all kinds of things. When I asked her how I could ever repay her, she encouraged me to "pay it forward and to do something for somebody else."

I must say that her words have stuck with me and became one of my driving forces. When I was writing my own book, I researched on my teachers and their teachers, and realised there is this debt of gratitude running through an amazing lineage of great musicians, composers and teachers. So, I felt that I had a deep sense of duty and an overwhelming feeling that I had to pay it forward because I had been given an amazing opportunity in my lifetime.

Share with us what it was like back then when you started doing tours and performances. Did you feel that you bear the responsibility of having to excel as an Asian and a woman artist?

Yes, indeed. Breaking new ground is never easy. When I embarked on this career, I had no notion how to do it. There were no road maps or guidebooks. There were few local role models or contacts I could call upon, except my teachers, so I had to learn to be creative and resourceful. I think that the American proactive mentality really helped and taught me to not wait for something to happen but to get out there and make things happen. I learnt quickly that I had to carve my own path.

In my profession, being a woman also has its challenges. We are expected to be glamorous, be good at what we do, and make it all seem effortless! The challenges that Sheryl Sandberg wrote about in *Lean In* resonate deeply with me. In the book, Sheryl said that women were built to be nurturers, not breadwinners, so in order for us women to take care of the family and be on top of our career, we have to be very strong. And yet, strong-willed women are viewed differently from men! Strong-willed men are not frowned upon as it is seen as their nature as providers and hard negotiators. It is not easy when women have to stand up for themselves!

Ah, I have a cute story to share. I was in my 20s and I had a manager—in fact, at one point, I had three managers. Anyway, one of my managers from Europe would get me these amazing solo engagements with orchestras. But, he was always late in payment. In a worst case scenario, I didn't get paid at all. He gave excuse after excuse, until I had enough. I decided to stand my ground. I had no choice, it was my bread and butter. He had scheduled me to play at a concert in Germany. Before I went on stage, I summoned all my courage to tell him that unless he paid me there and then, I was not going to go on stage!

To be honest, I was terrified that that would be the end of our relationship, but at that juncture, he pulled out a wad of cash and handed it to me. I had nowhere to place the money, so I stuffed it in my bra and headed out on stage! My heart was pounding but the opening bars of Bruch's Scottish Fantasy calls for a calm and meditative melody. I had to switch my emotions within a split second in order to get into the mood of the piece. Being an artist may seem glamorous, but there's so much more to it than meets the eye!

So that night, you were spectacularly, shall we say, well-endowed?
Yes! I think these are the things you do not get to learn in school. Schools teach you the foundation and fundamentals, but they don't necessarily teach you to survive and thrive in the real world. I have so many life lessons like that—moments where you just have to figure things out on your own.

When I first began my career, I thought "Wow, I am the only Singaporean soloist out here." There were very few Asians and even if you did know of each other, there was no opportunity to sit down, have a meal and bond. Recently, when I was invited to give a talk at a book festival, I was mesmerised by the fraternity, openness and willingness to share their experiences, craft and technique. There is nothing more I love than being in an environment where musicians and artists can talk, network and share our resources to make our work better.

Similarly, I think Singaporean artists and creative arts practitioners should network, share and really try to understand one another. I think there is an innate sense of competition as we are a small country so there is a feeling that "if you succeed, it means I lose". In actuality, I feel that by being open and generous, one receives more.

Do you think the Asian concept of "face" impedes growth? How do you reconcile and resolve this?

Yes, it is a dilemma and I had to be very creative. I would also ask myself, what are my resources? What is special about me? I had to sit down and really look deep into myself and be completely honest. What are my strengths, my weaknesses? Invariably, my identity as a Singaporean is a double-edged sword. We do not have a huge population so we do not have a lot of bureaucracy, but this also means we don't have critical mass.

Once when I was about 20, I won a competition and was given a chance to give a recital at Carnegie Recital Hall. But that week, Yo-Yo Ma was playing in New York, and I remember thinking, who is going to come and listen to me? I was a budding artist with few connections. Then, I recalled a story my father once told me about the famous Polish-Mexican violinist, Henryk Szeryng, who had embassies from both countries sending limousines to ferry him when he played in town. In my naive mind, I thought, "I have to call my embassy!" So I paid a courtesy visit to Ambassador Chan Heng Chee, who was also Singapore's Permanent Representative to the United Nations in New York.

To my surprise, Ambassador Chan was kind enough to listen to me.

I shared my predicament and presented my observation that whenever I attended a concert by a Japanese artist, I would see many Japanese in the audience. Could Singaporeans do the same? I asked Ambassador Chan, "Can we encourage Singaporeans who are living abroad to support their own artists?" I think what I said must have resonated with her.

If my memory serves me right, Ambassador Chan made a call and introduced me to the Singapore Airlines office in New York. Then, I had to go talk to them and present my case. My story has a happy ending: SIA invited their special guests to my recital and threw a beautiful reception at the famed Russian Tea Room. The turnout at my Carnegie debut was beyond my wildest dreams. It was sold out!

The thing is, when you show others the value in helping you, chances are, people will be willing to lend their support. But of course, I needed to put in the hard work to become an accomplished violinist. So, I advise young people not to be afraid to ask, but ask graciously and reasonably. And if you are turned down, do not be discouraged or take it personally. You simply try again and again and again. That is what I had to do. For every Yes I get, I get hundreds of No's. But people only see the Yeses and go "Oh my gosh! Why is she given so much?!"

Yes, I firmly believe the harder you work, the luckier you get.

I agree with you. There is definitely an element of luck, but you have to work at it. Many people only see the "luck" but they don't realise the time, energy and tenacity required, because let me tell you, rejection is no fun, especially for sensitive souls. Every time you pluck up the courage to ask for something, you are putting yourself on the line and setting yourself up for rejection and it doesn't feel good.

There is another incident I recall. For the longest time, the Singapore Arts Festival would always invite an international orchestra to perform, but there was never a Singaporean soloist involved. It is very expensive to engage a visiting orchestra and it is certainly a big break for any local artist to be able to collaborate with them. When I first learnt that the Dallas Symphony was going to perform at the Festival, I remember thinking to myself "Wouldn't it be nice to have a Singaporean artist perform as soloist?" So I decided to ask if I could be given a chance. I had no idea just how hard it would be. I knocked on door after door until my knuckles bled, before realising that this honour was not going to be handed to me on a silver platter.

But as luck would have it, a well-known ambassador from Mexico who happened to love the violin, came to one of my concerts and we chatted. He shared that he knew the conductor of the Dallas Symphony and told me, "While I can't promise you anything, I will deliver your case to him." I thought I would not hear anything of it, but a short while later, I received a call and the conductor from Dallas asked for me to be the soloist with the orchestra in the Singapore Arts Festival! And so, for the second time in my life, an ambassador had been instrumental in stepping forward to help a young artist! I became the first Singaporean musician to play with a visiting international orchestra. Honestly, I am surprised today that I had such pluck and tenacity then!

Fast forward to the nation's 50th birthday bash two years ago, everything was very rah-rah Singapore. Singaporean artists have certainly come a long way. I can see how things have progressed. It seems easier to be a young artist in Singapore today, though I would say being an artist anywhere is never easy.

Do you think us Singaporean artists need to make a name for ourselves overseas before we are recognised back home? What is your advice to them? And just how do you think we can try to change that mindset and attitude towards local artists?

We make a change by having a conversation, by making our experiences known through a piece of theatre or music or even a book. That is powerful. That is one of the reasons why I wrote my book. I wanted people to know that life is not a slam-dunk. So, starting a conversation is a very important step.

I think it is typically true that no prophet is accepted in his own homeland—you have to make it elsewhere before you come back.

Unfortunately, most people have a herd instinct and with something as intangible as the arts, most do not know what to make of it and gravitate towards mass consensus. That is why having more dialogues is important.

My advice to all aspiring musicians: Don't wait for things to happen. I learnt to create opportunities for myself and some of my biggest gigs came from my own efforts. Everyone's circumstance is different and unique. Fundamentally, one must love what one does. Pursuing the creative arts must be a calling, as there is no guarantee of success. You must love it so much that life becomes unbearable without it… you must want to pursue it wholeheartedly and not look back! With passion, patience and perseverance, the sky's the limit.

Let's look at it from a performer's perspective now. As a director, I can put on the same show, but I can tell you there is a stark difference between performing for a local crowd and a foreign audience. What are your sentiments?

Yes, playing for a home crowd is the toughest for me. But, it's also the most fulfilling as I get the most support and the warmest applause the minute I step on stage! Of course, there will also be naysayers who diss you but I revel in that challenge. It makes me want to work harder and get better in what I do. The striving keeps me humble and allows me to grow.

Clearly, you must have had your fair share of harsh criticisms? What are some of the worst things that were said about you?

I don't know, nor do I remember. But I do remember someone wise once said, "You're not as fantastic as the great reviews, nor are you as terrible as the bad ones." When I receive positive feedback, I remind myself that I am fortunate, and use that to propel myself to move forward. Life is always a balance. I don't think I can win over everybody. That is just not realistic. I believe that you win some and you lose some. I have come to terms with that. Not everybody is going to love you but not everybody is going to hate you either. As an artist, one must have faith in yourself, remain positive and work hard. The truth will reveal itself in time to come.

I can imagine it's a hard reality to face. As artists, we are sensitive because we do pour our souls into our art, right? We want to pretend that it's not personal, but it is personal at many levels.

Exactly. It is indeed very personal which goes back to my point about having conversations. When I met a very successful woman not too long ago, she was complaining how difficult and unfair the world has been for her and my jaws just dropped. I'm like, "You too, really?" When we experience negativity, we may tend to think that we are the only ones at that point in time, but we learn to let go and see that it really is not personal. I tell myself, forget individuals who have been unkind and move on to other people who love and adore you. But yes, it is easier said than done as we are sensitive and it takes us a while to lick our wounds.

Recently, I read that one of the younger Hollywood actresses, Jennifer Lawrence, caused a controversy as she said she was too shy to demand an equal paycheck as her male co-stars. She did not speak up in order to not be perceived as a prima donna. This is pervasive. As women, we face that struggle.

You have made some radical decisions. You were in New York and headed to the Midwest. Then, from being a star performer, you decide to become a teacher in Charleston. Tell us about your unconventional choices.

In classical music, it is not uncommon for artists to combine a performing career with concurrent teaching appointments at universities and conservatories. I consider myself fortunate to be enjoying the best of both worlds! Everyone's path is different. We have to find our own way rather than follow the herd.

When I left New York, people thought that I was crazy because the Big Apple is seen as the epicentre of the universe. But at that time, I was so busy making ends meet that I lost the joy and meaning of making music. It was all about survival and putting bread on the table. On reflection, I felt that I needed to grow as a musician and wanted to invest in myself.

It so happened that my friends had told me about this amazing couple, Almita and Roland Vamos, well-known violin pedagogues and faculty members at the Oberlin Conservatory of Music who have taught prominent musicians and produced many competition prize-winners. I went to meet the Vamoses. To my delight, they accepted me as their student and, joy of joys, Oberlin offered me a full scholarship for the Artist Certificate program!

Oberlin is a little university town in the Midwest where the cost of living is much cheaper than New York. Freed from the worry of having to make ends meet, I focused on polishing my craft and learning from the Vamoses. They were great teachers and knew how to get the best out of each student. Practically every week, at least one of their students would return with a win from a competition! It was truly inspiring.

So I stepped up my game, and in 1994, won the Gold Medal at the Henryk Szeryng International Violin Competition, which launched my concert career as a soloist. Before long, I was living my dream, travelling the world and performing concert tours. I do believe that it is important to follow your inner voice. Don't go with the crowd. Having the right mentors also makes a huge difference.

Thanks to the Vamoses, I also discovered my love for teaching. One day, I was in Chicago catching up with Mrs Vamos when she casually mentioned that she was going on sabbatical and needed a replacement to take over her class at Oberlin Conservatory. The next minute, she looked at me, as I turned slowly to look at her: eureka! A flash of inspiration connected us! So I interviewed for and got the job. You could say I was handed a Rolls-Royce for my first job. The Vamoses were known as "the Pied Pipers of Oberlin". Talented students from all over the world came to study with them.

These days, a teaching position is much sought after. Many artists are teachers and academics in addition to being performers. Personally, I love it—it is a harmony of yin and yang. When you perform, you take in the audience' gratitude and appreciation for your craft, and in teaching, you give back.

I taught there for a while before I got the position in Charleston, which I also fell in love with because it is a beautiful city—it was voted the USA's No. 1 city for five consecutive years by *Condé Nast Traveller*! It's been home now for 15 years. The longest time I have spent in one place other than Singapore. I have been on the move as I am unable to keep still. It's my personality. I like variety, challenges, diversity and change.

Share with us some of your toughest times.

2012 was a particularly difficult year for me. My father and Lady McNeice passed away. I also had a car accident and was diagnosed with cancer. It was just bang, bang, bang. I mean, what was going on?!

This really forced me to assess what was important in my life. But yes, my dad's passing was obviously the single hardest experience for me. We were very, very close and I felt like the prodigal daughter because he wanted me to be closer to home but I always thought I would have more time. I would come home every summer but I did not realise that the end was so near. When I saw him in the hospital, I was shocked—he couldn't even recognise me. The nurses said he had been unresponsive for weeks. I was heartbroken.

Instinctively, I reached for my violin, and started to play his favourite piece, *Jeanie With The Light Brown Hair* by legendary violinist Jascha Heifetz. Then something miraculous happened. Within minutes of hearing the music, tears began rolling down his cheeks. He started to slowly come out of his shell. It was truly unbelievable. Bit by bit, he became more lucid and started to recognise me. Slowly, his blood pressure went back to normal and he could even sit up!

I continued to play but I had just gotten off from the plane and was tired and emotional so I fumbled. I mumbled under my breath that I should practice, and to my surprise, my dad echoed my sentiments and said in Mandarin, "Ah, you need to practice!" I didn't know if I should laugh or cry at that moment, but it was wonderful. It still remains one of my favourite stories to share as it exemplifies the power of music.

So after your dad's passing, you left for China. What made you do that?

It was quite out of the blue. After Dad's passing, plus the trauma of my accident and the bout with cancer, I needed a change of environment to recharge. Around that time, somebody asked me for an opinion about a new school in Suzhou and asked if I knew anything about the Suzhou Industrial Park (SIP). I said that as Singapore was involved in SIP, she could be assured that the area would have great infrastructure and a conducive living environment. I basically gave her the thumbs up. The next thing I knew, I was invited to consider a professorship at the music academy!

I guess I saw it as a sign after Dad's passing that I had to return to Asia and help pay it forward by helping to start a school. The opportunity to be part of a founding team to help shape a curriculum was very enticing. In addition, it was to be the first music conservatory in China to teach in English, in partnership with New York's Bard Conservatory, a very established, prestigious liberal arts school. So I thought, "Why not?" In hindsight, I learnt a lot while I was in China, met many Singaporeans and made many new friends.

How did that Chinese experience change you?

I never felt more Singaporean than when I was in China! I realised that the Singaporeans in Suzhou are really proud of Singapore. When I attended a big National Day celebration there, I met so many Singaporeans and even did the *yam seng*. It was quite a thrill to be the first professional musician from Singapore to be based in the Suzhou Industrial Park. Of course, Suzhou is steeped in history and it was inspiring to be immersed in the artistry and heritage of this ancient city. So I am sure your next question would be why did I return to Charleston?

(*Laughter*) **Yes, of course, how long were you there and why did you return to Charleston?**

I was in Suzhou for two years and I still continue to have many projects with the Chinese. I do wish to continue developing my presence there, but

I must say that after I have experienced cancer, health is very important to me and is my priority. I am familiar with the healthcare system in America—the doctors, medicine. Above all, the real issue that I grappled with in China was the pollution.

That is tough and it was a real struggle. I felt as if I was torn between two lovers and Suzhou was asking, "Are you going to marry me?" and Charleston was saying, "When are you coming home?"

Ah, you are a lucky woman. This is a happy problem.
So, yes. I picked Charleston, where my partner is. Plus I had tenure waiting. But I have been going back to China and also performed at Suzhou's International Arts Festival. Honestly, my life is so much more enriched after the China stint.

I recall a colleague of mine encouraging me to take the unknown route. He shared that every time he was at a crossroad, he would take the unknown path to challenge himself. I am that way too. I am thankful to have seen more of the world and have richer experiences to share.

That is absolutely true. So what do you think are your biggest takeaways from your experiences in Singapore, China and the U.S.?
I don't know if I am the most qualified person to make sweeping observations, but drawing from my own personal experience, I feel that each country has its strengths.

The Chinese are so hardworking and have admirable work ethics simply because competition is so stiff and everyone craves that one, big break. They are hungry for knowledge and are always on the lookout for opportunities. For example, I had a Chinese student living in Wuhan who would make a 10-hour trip every week to Suzhou just to have an hour's violin lesson with me. He made this trip every week, for two years. That is the most admirable thing. His father comes with him, too. So you see, it is not just about having the money. They have the dedication, time and hunger to learn. I was so touched by their efforts and was truly honoured. In return, I imparted as much as I could to this young boy.

Across the board, I really think the Chinese students are very hardworking and have great respect for their teachers and the education system. As a professor, you feel gratified because they appreciate your wisdom and teaching. That's very rewarding for an educator.

The downside is that China is "chaotic"—for a newcomer, there is definitely culture shock. What you think is impossible is possible and vice versa. In that sense, I did spend quite a lot of time trying to figure out how things work, so that was tough for me as I was more accustomed to the structure and systems in America.

And speaking of America, I can say I most admire their sense of entrepreneurship, invention and creation. I am grateful for the collaborative culture and openness that has allowed me to thrive and grow as an artist. For example, after arriving in Charleston, I co-founded the Charleston Music Fest, which involved growing a new chamber music series from the ground up, securing sponsorships, building relationships with fans and programming concerts. As a musician, one can take on many different roles—a performing artist, entrepreneur, fundraiser, festival director and educator. It's been an exciting and fulfilling ride!

Singapore, on the other hand, is very small and nimble. There is an easy accessibility and it is less formal than the U.S. I mean, can you imagine going to the White House to have tea with the President? I have met several of our Singapore presidents, movers and shakers, and that is a very gratifying experience—to know that your craft and your work is appreciated at a national level. The upside is obvious: we can be seen and heard. Through just one article in *The Straits Times*, you could potentially reach out to practically everybody in Singapore. That is certainly not the case in the U.S. or China. These countries are far too big so national engagement is a huge challenge. The downside in Singapore is that there is not enough diversity among the decision-makers. But in general, I'll say Singapore is in a sweet spot. It has the best of both the U.S. and China, but it is on a much smaller scale—that is both our strength and our weakness.

Speaking of connection, is there a fraternity among Singapore violinists? Do you keep in touch?

Certainly I feel that we could do a better job of making an effort to stay in touch and get to know each other better as a collective. Besides this, I feel it is also important to recognise our pioneer artists. Without them, Singapore's arts scene would not be what it is today. When I gave my recital at Carnegie Hall recently, I was thrilled to champion the work of Singapore's pioneer composer, Kam Kee Yong. As a Singaporean artist, it was very meaningful for me to premiere a Singaporean work to a global audience in New York.

Whenever I'm home, I also try to schedule masterclasses to work with young violinists. In recent years, I've given masterclasses for the Singapore National Youth Orchestra and schools like the Nanyang Academy of Fine Arts. I've also been getting to know the violin teachers in Singapore and must give them credit for doing a great job! It's been a joy to work with their students. I am proud that Singaporean violin students are doing well internationally—coming up tops in music competitions, being accepted to world-class music festivals, like Aspen Music Festival, and in conservatories like Juilliard and Curtis.

The world is a big place, there is always room for collaborations and I would love to do more, especially to nurture younger violinists.

So tell me, what prompted *From Clementi to Carnegie*?

Many reasons. One of it was that I wanted to debunk myths and misconceptions that my journey to where I am today is one of "luck". But more importantly, I felt that I needed to share the story about my accident.

Just a paper cut on the fingers can affect violin playing, so can you imagine how hard it was for me to get through my accident with my left arm broken and not knowing if I could ever play again? The physical pain and loss is one thing but it was the emotional trauma that was most trying. Playing the violin is not just my career, it is my life and passion, and I was nearly deprived of it!

In the beginning, even performing simple actions such as washing my hands or taking a shower was tough because I couldn't raise my arm and it hurts just to move my shoulder. I could not tie my shoelaces or a pony tail—all the little things that I took for granted became exceedingly difficult. When I first picked up my violin, even playing a scale, something a beginner can do, was hard. Every note was shaky. Psychologically, it was a huge setback. My violin is my voice and the thought of not being able to express myself was terrifying. I had to rebuild from scratch and it was the words of my father that really uplifted me and kept me going.

When I was little and didn't want to practice scales, he had gently chided me, "There is beauty in the mundane. Think of these scales like little pearls. When you do it nicely, everything is round and white and pure." I clung to those words as I picked myself up. Note by note, scale by scale, I worked on putting my life back together again.

I was so glad to be back on track 100% that I wanted to turn my experiences into a source of positive inspiration. Over the years, I have kept little diaries of things that have affected me emotionally. Interestingly, it was the late President Wee Kim Wee who suggested that I do so. He was a newsman and said that I might forget my stories as the years rolled by. I am glad I did. By the time I wrote my book, I felt as if I had all these stories that were screaming, "Write me, write me!" I also wanted the book to honour all my teachers, mentors like Lady McNeice, and above all, my dad.

Knowing what you know now about yourself, what would you have done differently?

I don't like to second-guess myself as it's pointless, but I would have taken better care of myself physically by exercising more.

What are your greatest strengths and weaknesses?

My can-do spirit and my fear of taking financial risks.

What irks you?
Dishonesty.

Which composition best represents you?
Tchaikovsky Violin Concerto, fiendishly difficult but utterly satisfying.

What would you be if you didn't play the violin?
An interior designer—to spend other people's money indulging on beautiful things. Seems like a great profession!

How do you want to be remembered?
A fearless and passionate artist, who chased after her dreams despite many obstacles.

When you meet God, what would you say?
I gave it my all. Hope you approve!

Would you define yourself as a Madonna, Maverick or any other M word?
Musical Maverick! I am a fan of thinking outside the box, taking the road less travelled and relishing the uncommon harmonies.

The Sweetest Sensation

JANICE WONG

Chef Janice Wong's never-ending passion for culinary art has propelled her forward to test the limits of dessert making. The native Singaporean has learned from some of the world's best chefs, including U.S. luminaries Thomas Keller and Grant Achatz, virtuoso Spanish chocolatier Oriol Balaguer, and prodigious French pastry chef Pierre Hermé.

An undisputed favourite amongst sweet-toothed Singaporeans, her dessert restaurant 2am:dessertbar has redefined the dessert experience, pushing the boundaries between sweet and savoury, with carefully researched progressive dishes. In 2014, she also launched her eponymous sweets concept, JANICE WONG. Chef Janice has received worldwide recognition for her cutting-edge creations and is a regular on the global pop-up circuit—proof that 2am:dessertbar is more than just a sugar rush. She has twice been named Asia's Best Pastry Chef by the prestigious San Pellegrino Asia's 50 Best, in 2013 and 2014.

***

As her staff led me through a seemingly endless maze of chocolate bonbons, edible artworks and pineapple tarts, I felt as if I was Alice in Wonderland, falling happily down the rabbit hole. All I remember wishing was that an "Eat Me" invitation would magically present itself somewhere in that pristine kitchen so that I could partake in some of that yummy, tantalising, sweet goodness that has taken much of Singapore, and now Tokyo, by storm.

Then as if by magic, she appeared, dressed every inch the chef. Her diminutive frame took me by surprise as I realised that her reputation precedes her, and I was expecting a towering Amazonian woman to appear and say, "I am Janice. Hear me roar!" But Chef Janice is quite the opposite. She looks and feels like your precocious little teenage sister, on the cusp of junior college-hood, who may suddenly get infatuated with boys having been raised in an all-girl convent—until she speaks.

When she did, I could instantly see why the self-styled visionary, artist, author, culinary stylist and photographer, continues to inspire and fascinate the media with her creative concoctions and penchant for edible art. She is the perfect embodiment of yin and yang, science and art, and she speaks in a deliberate, almost careful manner while describing some of her most amazing edible art installations.

In fact, in 2011, she fashioned seven pieces that completely transformed the studio space. That feat launched her as a credible food artist and she has since then been commissioned by galleries, restaurants and clients both local and overseas to craft what she calls "interactive art". Her website states that Janice is taken by "a pursuit for perfection in imperfection", and an "appreciation of imperfection in perfection". The Japanese have a term for this, *wabi-sabi*. While no literal English translation for this term exists, suffice to say that *wabi-sabi* understands that tender, raw beauty of a grey December sky, which acts as a backdrop to the aching elegance of an abandoned old shed. It celebrates the cracks and crevices, rot and rubble that time, weather and, increasingly, Man have left behind. To discover *wabi-sabi* is to see the singular beauty in transience and what can be more transient than food? Now, imagine encapsulating all that beauty in a singular chocolate bonbon. Ah, now you begin to understand why Japan and now the world at large has, too, begun a love affair with Janice.

But, Janice's early successes can be attributed to two major unhappy episodes: a head concussion and a failed romance. The former led to a sudden change of heart and, literally, mind as the impact of the accident seemed to awaken her right brain, resulting in the birth of fiery passion and creative energy. The searing pain from the latter led her to find other channels of artistic expression in food, which led to her book writing, her subsequent edible art creations, events catering, and now her foray into food manufacturing. She has built a veritable food empire that bears her name JANICE WONG in bold letters—a daring departure from the Eurocentric, male-dominated names in the food world.

From a little-known national squash player to a burgeoning food entrepreneur to a media-celebrated edible art artist to today's emerging luxury brand owner, Janice has journeyed far. Some may say revenge is a dish best served cold; but for Janice, letting go, getting peace of mind and securing personal success in an increasingly global arena definitely tastes much, much sweeter.

***

Share with us your background and your influences growing up.
Very simply—the diversity of the coaches I was exposed to really shaped who I am today. I am continuously pushing myself to do better, to think and be different. That's how we move. There has not been one "normal" day here in the past 11 years and there never will be.

But to take it back to the start, I grew up in Singapore. I was born here and I lived in Chinatown until I was three. Hong Lim Park is very memorable, that was where I would play and hang out with grandma. Hong Lim Hawker Centre still remains, with many of the same vendors even though I have seen two generations come and go. The Hong Lim hawkers have seen me grow up and I recognise a few of them as they know my parents well. I grew up living with my grandma as my parents were always working. My dad got posted to Japan when I was like one or two. I later joined him between the years of three to seven though he was away for seven to nine years. I came back to Singapore for school and my dad was then posted to Hong Kong.

I read that your father was a businessman and an investor.

He does bond trading. When he was posted to Hong Kong, I went with him as there was a good school there—the Singapore International School.

I was there for the two to three years that he worked there and met many Singaporean kids living in Hong Kong. Most of them have the same story. I guess you could say I was exposed to a great deal of diversity from a young age—different cultures and food. I also had to adapt as a young child to fit into the school system. Unlike the average Singaporean, I had four primary schools, two secondary schools and was always moving around. I said many hellos and goodbyes. I also had to learn to be very independent. I took the public transport in Hong Kong to go play squash at the age of 10 or 11.

My parents were always looking out for me but I was given a lot of freedom. I guess I had a headstart as Hong Kong was very competitive. There were only two classes offered at the primary level in the Singapore International School so you can imagine the competition. Even at that level, I remember having to do my homework and Ten Year Series till midnight. After that, I came back to Singapore to begin my secondary education, and it was just as competitive, if not more. You can say my constant moving around as a kid and having to find my place in new cultures really shaped me.

So all your early influences were largely Asian: Singapore, Hong Kong and Japan.

Correct. I was at the American International School for three years in Japan, and Singapore International School for two years in Hong Kong. I started playing squash at the age of 9, and that also instilled a kind of discipline in me.

In many ways, you were like a military baby but you are an expatriate kid.

Yes, so that was my past. Aside from schools, I was also very competitive in sports that exacted discipline and 100% focus. We used to practice hitting the ball at least a hundred times. Squash also required me to wake up early in the morning. I would have my training, then breakfast, and head to the class.

When I was back in Singapore, I went to Methodist Girls' School but I was training for squash intensely—at least once a day. Between junior college and the start of my university, I trained twice a day for the Nationals; we had like 14 competitions a year. I competed in squash until I went to University but I decided to quit after the Asian Championships. I was already in the line-up but I dropped out two months before the competition and they had to do another trial to find my replacement.

Why did you do that?

Because I thought I had enough. By then, I played the sport for a decade and felt that I was going nowhere with that. I remember when I was in my first year in Anglo-Chinese Junior College, I trained twice a day for the Singapore Junior Championships in Chennai. It was very tough juggling my studies and squash.

I had to sacrifice a lot of my time and there was very little government support. We would go out and compete but we had to sponsor our trips and tournaments ourselves. It just didn't make sense. You would do your country proud but you had to pay for all your own expenses? Many of us dropped out of squash back then, about 17 years ago, as the government was only keen on investing in football, swimming and table tennis. In contrast, I saw all these amazing athletes around the world being celebrated and supported. They had a well-defined structure and they could make a great career out of sports but Singapore only emphasised academic studies, which is not a bad thing. But as a result, many of us dropped out and went into our second career choices.

But, I didn't stop challenging myself and played nine or 10 different sports while in university. In fact, I also played squash for the varsity championships that required almost no commitment compared to what I was used to doing. I also started to play tennis simply because I wanted a challenge and because I loved it. I also played touch rugby, soccer, badminton, basketball, javelin and tennis.

So how did your passion for the culinary arts even start?

After I quit squash, I suddenly had all this time on my hands to explore. I was 20 years old and decided to take the time to travel to Australia while I was a student in NUS (National University of Singapore) and even started learning different languages. I had already taken French in school and even tried studying French and Japanese at the same time. I failed, of course—I had to choose one so I focused on French. That also gave me an insight that there was a learning curve to most new ventures.

Anyway, I was on a six-month programme in Melbourne, Australia. While I was there, I discovered my love for the farms, the culture, fresh produce and ingredients. That was where and when my interest in food all began. I had to feed myself and bought my own groceries. It was also a welcome change from my strict athlete's diet. I started to discover fresh produce and would experiment with cooking.

And then I went to Tasmania to explore the farms, but I met with a car accident the moment I touched down. I smashed my head on the windscreen and there is a scar right here to prove it. I received about 20 stitches and had a skin graft. There were another 30 stitches down my foot. I had many stitches everywhere and that was…

Life changing.

Correct. After that, I started to lose my memory. I never recovered, or rather, there are things I can't remember, but it was then that this whole art thing came into my life. I have never been art-trained or art-schooled but for some reason, my brain just switched and I started cooking.

Do you suffer from short-term memory loss now?

I will probably not remember your name or the way you look after a year. I tell people I have a bad memory but I'm still praying for its restoration. I am a Christian and my grandfather is a pastor. And I also find it very hard to learn any new languages or anything new for that matter. In the meantime, my life is changing and I wouldn't give this up for anything. I am a very organic person and accept whatever comes or goes. I also became very zen and calm after the accident. My parents initially thought that I had become a totally different person as my temperament changed. I also started painting in 2007, three to four years after the car accident, and started cooking a year after that and decided to open a restaurant.

Did you quit NUS?

I wanted to but decided to respect my parents' wishes. Anyway, the other interesting thing about the accident was that I was bestowed the gift of the gab and could do public speaking after I made a full recovery. I used to always get nervous, but now, I am able to give speeches like a train. I could talk and talk and captivate the crowd, and even started doing TED talks and food shows.

You shared that you started cooking and decided to open a restaurant but there must have been a process. Share with us that story.

It all started with a strawberry. After I was well, I went back to Melbourne in 2006 to visit a strawberry farm. When I had my first taste of strawberries from the ground, what I tasted was not only sweet and sour, I also savoured the different dimensions of flavours, such as earthiness. I knew I had to recreate these amazing food experiences from Australia back home in Singapore. When I returned, I decided I wanted to open a dessert bar and so I did in 2007.

After NUS, I left for Cordon Bleu in Paris and did a basic course for three months. Instead of continuing with a longer six- or nine-month course, I decided to pursue an internship in a proper kitchen. I knew that studies were important but I wanted real action, and the best way was to get in the kitchen and start learning from the best chefs. I remember meeting with Justin Quek and asking him how I could get an internship with Les Amis, and Chef Gunther took me in for six months.

In 2006, I also took part in a cooking reality series called Star Chef on Channel 8 and ended up getting placed second in the TV show. It was a three-month process where I had to cook a dish based on a different theme every Sunday. I remember that my brain was so fried, literally. I had to create my recipes, perform my trials over Wednesday, Thursday, Friday; film on Saturday and compete on Sunday. It required a lot of stamina, but that was where my sports experience helped greatly.

Gunther was helping me, loaned me his kitchen and gave me advice. The journey was amazing as I got to push myself to the limit. It was like being on MasterChef and even in that short span of time, I became so much better. I learnt that I had to be mentally prepared, stable, sharp and have no margin for error. There is no space for any failure in my career.

Share with us what you did after the TV stint.

I wanted to work as I needed to get respect from the industry. I figured that I was young, female and I would need to lead a team of at least ten. I didn't have the expectation that my team has to be younger than me and be all women. I knew I had to earn respect and create and showcase my unique philosophy. I could not simply burst onto the scene announcing that I want to cook good food. I knew I had to find my philosophy and story.

So after Les Amis, I went back to Melbourne and interned at Fenix, a molecular gastronomy restaurant that has since closed down. Raymond Capaldi was the chef, and when I there, I actually saw plates and pots go flying in the air, and he would swear a lot. There was a lot of fear in the kitchen, so I lasted only one week. After that, I worked for a fortnight in The Botanical.

I was in New York for 90 days till my visa expired, and on the last month, I actually performed two jobs. From 4 p.m. to 1 a.m., I was at a dessert bar, and by morning, I was in Aquavit, Chef Marcus Samuelsson's place in New York. It's a great restaurant with Swedish influence, and I wanted to learn as much as I could. I had all this curiosity and hunger that I used to have for my sports. I came back to Singapore and headed to Chicago and Spain where I did many different stints. When I returned to Singapore, I opened 2am:dessertbar.

How did you finance all your travels? Do you think you could have gotten ahead so far so quickly if you had been from a lower-income family?

From working part-time as a squash coach. I had some savings from my sports grant and was doing a lot of odd jobs that supplemented the travels. It helped, of course, that Dad paid for tuition and also gave me €10,000 for Cordon Bleu and my time in Paris. I relied on my savings to feed myself though I knew Dad would always give if I asked but I never dared ask for more.

So 2am launched you.

2am began when I was 24. I wanted to find an edge in pastry making and wanted to think differently. I saw that there was no plated dessert degustation menu in Singapore at that time. It was hard to find a high-level sweets restaurant. I knew I wanted my first restaurant to feature beautiful, plated desserts that you could admire and appreciate. The challenge was that it would be an after-dinner option so it would appeal to a late crowd. We didn't have much of a high tea culture in Singapore back then so I would not have had the tea-time crowd. So it was, of course, very challenging in the beginning.

But Singapore loves fads, so any new place is always successful. It may be misleading at the beginning as you may be up, running and pumping as everybody wants to go to this new place to "check it out" but things may not be so rosy after six months. I am glad the road was always quite smooth for me as we consistently created new dishes and had new ideas. It helps that I am fidgety and did not want to be content with just one menu. Only having one menu is not sustainable in Singapore.

You became a girl boss by the end of 2007. Share with us more on that journey.

I had all this ambition and I did it myself. I hired my interior designer to control the construction. It was a nightmare dealing with contractors and screaming matches ensued. I recall our electricity went out on the first day of our soft launch. We had 40 people for a post-wedding celebration on a Sunday, and I was like "Oh my God!"

Partly because my memory does not serve me well, and because my schedule was jam-packed, the years flew by. There is something new every day. After the electricity outage, we shut for a month and reopened in mid-August. All this time, I was paying my lease that was about $20,000. I was trying to speed up the process and went to PUB (Public Utilities Board) but long story short, I had to wait another month, so our grand opening was not till 10 October, or 1010.

I even handled my own marketing and PR even though I studied Economics and am not trained in that area at all. My first interview was with *8 Days* where I had a two-page spread, and they featured my time in New York. I remember saying that I want to build a brand though I had no real idea what that meant. Today, when interviewers ask me what my vision is in five or ten years, I am able to share in greater detail.

But what I did know was that in business, sustainability is very important. Everybody talks about sustainability but, in Singapore, you can't be fully sustainable as we do not have all the systems in place to recycle. It is way too costly to do all that. So if my focus was business sustainability, then I knew what I needed and had to build a brand.

Today, I have two brands, 2am:dessertbar and JANICE WONG, even though when I started I had no idea what that meant at all. I knew the media loved us as the new kid on the block, so I decided to focus on building PR. Social media was not as crazy as it is today but I decided to start blogs as well as a Facebook page. We had some difficulty telling our story in the beginning but it has certainly changed over time.

Now that you have successfully created your brands, how do you define branding?

Building a brand is all about time. You can't build a brand in half a year. It doesn't work that way. I don't have 200 million dollars to open shops all over the world. So as a small eatery, I started from scratch. Yes, my father helped but it was not as if I could splurge on two, three restaurants all at once. So the key for me was to start very humbly. I also realised that it was all about telling a good story.

How did your edible art installations begin?

I have to share with you a longer journey before we get there. By 2007, I had a menu of desserts with alcohol but you see, in 2008 and 2009, business declined, so I knew we had to keep changing and rethinking. I tried to introduce vegetables, beetroot, yoghurt and fresh produce in my desserts but it didn't work. So I started experimenting with creating savoury desserts. At one point, I had a miso dessert that captured the five different tastes in one dish. That worked out so well.

So every year, I would have a new idea and new inspiration. We rode on trends as well, and invested in a coffee machine and brewed our own coffee. Back then, not many F&B places would roast their own coffee. I thought it was very important to pair my coffee and my plated desserts. In fact, in 2014, we even extended into teas. Now, we have eight types of JANICE WONG teas that you cannot find anywhere else, such as popcorn tea.

Anyway, to back up, we kept improving ourselves, and soon, we were not just a dessert bar but had everything from cocktails, to wine, coffee, tea to high tea degustation. That made a great impact on the business as it allowed for people to have a full experience. So that takes me to 2011. It was a great year and I was by then already in an 18-month long relationship. I was dating an Italian chef. We were engaged but I caught him cheating and my world came crashing down. I remember that day very clearly. I couldn't work. I was crushed and I realised that I was so fragile. I thought I was a strong woman and a leader of a full team, but I was crushed, so I went on a break to Amsterdam for three days.

Just three days? I would be there for three months.

Yeah. (*laughter*) No, no. I did not want to cry over spilt milk and started thinking, "How do I fix this?" I knew I needed to get this out of my system as I was hurting so bad. Amsterdam cleared my head. I went there with a good friend and he really helped me to heal. When I returned to Singapore, I decided to churn all that bad energy into a beautiful book. So, by 2011, I came out with my own book, *Perfection in Imperfection.*

Out of all that hurt came a beautiful story, just like a phoenix rising from the ashes.

Yes, and it became more and more beautiful. The book took two to three months to create. I like to work fast and I self-published. Even though I enjoyed photography, I engaged Kelvin Koh to take the photos for me. But I take my edible art photos myself which leads me to your question on edible art.

I had to do a book launch for my 400 guests. I started to think, "How can I get them to taste the book? By then, I had already ventured into catering services, but I was bored of servers going around with spoons. I wanted to feed them and yet give them a unique experience. That was how I started the edible art installations. I ended up creating seven installations to allow my guests to "taste the book". This was the first of its kind in the world, and I was only 28.

The media and the art world loved it and ate it all up, literally.

Yes, that's when I started to travel for art. In fact, in 2015, we did 48 exhibitions. It is a lot of work, and I am really blessed to have a huge kitchen and a real good team now. But in the beginning, I managed with one or two chefs. Each piece can take several weeks.

Back then, I had to work at 2am:dessertbar which led me to eventually open the 2,000 square feet 2am:lab in 2012. It was in Fusionopolis and is supported by the Singapore Tourism Board. I wanted it to be a nonprofit space to experiment with recipes and share them on the online platform. That was very important to me. We had an open kitchen and a lot of videos on the wall that I called a flavour wall. It was very beautiful and we also hosted many private dinners there. I decided to move the lab to Tokyo three years later, and that worked out even better as we get to create a lot of good recipes with good produce.

By 2012, I have started to work on even more art even as I was working on private dinners and numerous events. I have now made these into my stable of services. I travel to Japan eight times a year. We have a team running the lab and we develop and work on commissioned projects. There are about three to four of them in the team. They take on projects for us and we get hired to develop recipes for manufacturers who will, in turn, produce and distribute in bulk. One creation can be multiplied in the hundreds of thousands. I love doing that—create something and then blasting it out.

Share with us your thought process. How did you go from chef, to artist, to caterer, to manufacturer?

It really stems from my inability to stay still. Once 2am:dessertbar was stable after three years, I knew I wanted to expand as I could only serve a maximum of 120 people per night. For art, it was a little bigger, say, 1,000 people could eat my art. So the next venture was to go into dinners and food catering. Once I was there, the next logical step to scale up to is to venture into food manufacturing.

By 2014, I wanted to do go into manufacturing and develop new sweets—healthy pastilles from bamboo shoots, and that was a resounding success when I first launched it at the Sweets and Snacks Expo in Chicago. But I didn't have the resources to continue on that scale of production even though a hospital was keen to order. I decided I had to think big. I needed resources to support all my different channels while micro-managing my art.

But that same year, I met my business partner, Manoj Murjani of TWG Tea Company, at a Tom Ford event who shared that he wanted to invest in my brand. We shared the same vision, and I was looking for a partner who could help me grow the business, so it was a definite "yes" for me.

What were some of the changes that happened with the partnership?

When Manoj came onboard, we renovated the dessert bar and gave it a new look. We also found and invested in a factory since I needed all this space for the amount of art I am doing. In fact, previously I had to throw away many edible art pieces because I could not store it. He also enabled me to create and build my eponymous JANICE WONG brand.

By the end of 2014, we had done a lot of research and we were ready to launch JANICE WONG in 2015. It is a very bold move as pastry or sweet brands are usually fronted by a European name and they all tend to be male. I have an Asian surname and I am a woman so we broke so many new grounds. Having a pastry shop frontage in Japan with my name is definitely ground-breaking. I wondered if we could really pull this off but we stuck with it as there is just no other better name as I am, after all, the creator.

What other names did you tinker with?

There was Sweet Shop, Janice Sweets, Shop JW. We had so many variations and created copious designs that all had great depth and meaning. Mark de Winne created our font, called Imagination Sans especially for me, because I am 50/50—50 percent play, 50 percent consistency. That is how the logo came about and it was in line with my philosophy. For example, an éclair is an éclair but I will place art on the top of it. I have photos of all the fashionable cakes and sculptures that I have done.

Edible art is a game changer and now, there are events around the world that provide edible art as a means of consumer engagement. So we were pioneers in generating a whole new food culture and classification all on its medium and terms.

What is the key difference between your two brands as they are both sweet?

JANICE WONG and 2am:dessertbar is my partnership with Manoj. I partnered with Japanese airlines ANA for my dessert bar in Tokyo. Lumine had approached me prior to opening a new mall, NEWoMan at Shinjuku

Station. And I was like, "This is fantastic!" Ours is a joint partnership and the idea is to get a managing partner for it. JANICE WONG Dessert Bar in Tokyo opened on 15 April 2016 just over a year ago.

What do you have in store for Japan in the near future? What will you do to entice their palate?

It is not just Japan but Hong Kong too. I don't even know how to pinpoint exactly when my love affair with Japan and Hong Kong began, and it could be my time spent in both places as a child. But since I set my heart and mind on them, it has been non-stop planning and changes. There is no fear and I am really loving the process.

I am also partnering with New World Development to open a restaurant in Hong Kong. They had approached me to do a franchise for 2am:dessertbar and it will be called COBO HOUSE by 2am:dessertbar—there will be a lot of art in it. As Hong Kong's first dessert bar that espouses a farm-to-table philosophy, the restaurant demonstrates its sincerity about food with its own rooftop garden, with sand from Okinawa, where the menu's organic herbs and edible plants will be grown. I will create sweet and savoury dishes with the fresh produce and the dishes will be experimental as I will see what is available in the Hong Kong market. The style of cooking will be as simple as possible as I will focus on the fresh ingredients and the plating details.

I also decided to retain my brand 2am:dessertbar, but when you say 2am, it sounds like a place for the late night, so I decided to modify it with its location as a prefix. COBO HOUSE is an 80-seater, 3,000 square feet restaurant. As it is a big place, we have 35 to 40 staff in Hong Kong. In Japan, we have 15 staff.

Now, for some trivia. Which chef has influenced you most?

Grant Achatz, the chef and founder of Alinea, in Chicago. I worked with him for just one week a decade ago but he impacted me greatly. He was always looking at things differently as he creates a consumer experience that is wholly unique.

Who has been your greatest mentor?
My father is my greatest living mentor, and Coco Chanel is my perennial inspiration.

What are three things you can't do without?
I'll say four. My mobile phone and my laptop are connected. I also need chocolate and empty notebooks to jot down my ideas.

What do you do for leisure?
Yoga clears my mind and works my body. I also enjoy diving as you don't have to speak to anyone and can just be one with nature.

What dessert best describes you?
Cassis plum. It looks and feels feminine, but there is a surprise element to it.

What's your ultimate comfort food?
Tiramisu.

What would you say when you meet God?
Thank you for letting me do what I love. It has been a great run.

Who do you identify yourself with—a Madonna, Maverick or any other M word?
Madonna is good.

The TV Darling

XIANG YUN

Xiang Yun is a veteran actress with over 30 years of on-screen experience, endearingly referred to as Mediacorp's "Ah Jie". As a television actress, Xiang Yun has starred in leading and supporting roles in popular Mandarin drama series such as "The Awakening" and "The Price of Peace", as well as English series "Sweet Dreams & Turtle Soup". Her work has garnered her a loyal following and widespread local recognition. She was awarded the Best Supporting Actress at Mediacorp's annual Star Awards in 1998, 2000 and 2001.

She has since forayed into hosting, and her easy-going, affable style has met with highly favourable reviews. Xiang Yun has also ventured into the theatre, starring in Mandarin productions such as "December Rain", "Butterflies are Free" and "Peranakan Ball". Her silver screen debut, "I Not Stupid", remains one of the highest-grossing Singaporean films of all time. Xiang Yun is a household name and is married to the ex-Mediacorp celebrity, Edmund Chen, who is also this author's eldest brother.

***

Before I become sister-in-law and family, I was a groupie. Okay, not a groupie but I certainly was a fan. Back in the 1980s, between copious rewinds and replays of Wang Chung's *Let's Go Baby* and Air Supply's sappy love ballads, there really was not much else in entertainment. So, I dare say that most of us grew up watching *The Awakening*, singing the lyrics of its theme song.

Later, as a gawky 12-year-old, I, like every schoolgirl had an autograph book, except mine was cooler than the rest. My book was a prized possession filled with photos and signatures of Caldecott Hill's hottest and biggest stars because my brother, Edmund Chen, was a full-time artiste at Singapore Broadcasting Corporation. It meant only one thing: that he was useful in securing for his baby sister autographs from the nation's top stars.

Amongst all the coveted items, Xiang Yun's was the prize. She was Singapore's biggest star and she, above all other celebrities in my book, gave me the most street cred. I felt like the Greek goddess Athena presiding over everyone in my school. Take that you school bully! But my life was to get even sweeter one evening when my brother, unannounced, brought Xiang Yun to our humble abode and shared with us, in the confines of the kitchen, behind her back, that she was going to be his wife! Gasp! Xiang Yun? My sister-in-law! That was out of this world, and I scrambled to get my Mandarin in order. Honestly, my ability to even hold a conversation in a Chinese dim sum restaurant is all thanks to Xiang Yun. I was so enamoured with her that I took my Mandarin classes seriously thereafter.

Twenty eight years on, I am so proud to say Xiang Yun is still my *da sao*, as I call her affectionately. The entertainment business is harsh, and a marriage under the spotlight surrounded by prying journalists can easily take its toll on anyone. I have watched my brother and sister-in-law weather through the harshest storms and know that what they have today is hard fought and well deserved. Through it all, Xiang Yun has managed to age (this is a bad word in TV land) gracefully under the media glare and has remained television's evergreen darling. Her kindness, humility and well-loved candour is real—Xiang Yun is a Singapore's sweetheart, a small town girl who made good.

Her hawker background is well known to all, and she has taken that humility with her all through the years. To all the haters, there is unfortunately no other "mask" beyond what you see. With Xiang Yun, what you see is really what you get, a tough concept for most cynical urbanites to contend with. Yes, I have seen her down and out. Yes, I have seen her scream at her husband and be stressed out over her children. Yes, I have seen her weep off camera as we trade stories on love, family and relationships. But isn't that real life?

To me, *da sao* has always had that grace, wisdom and fortitude that transcends time and space. It is a fundamental kindness and worldliness that comes with years of living, playing the real-life roles of daughter, wife and mother, coupled with decades of walking in someone else's shoes as the script dictates. A career in the media and acting is not for everyone—the pressure of the cameras, the incessant public scrutiny (and cruelty) as well as the need to take on different roles can take its toll on a lesser individual, but *da sao* has carved a niche for herself. Her acting craft is the stuff that younger starlets hanker after, her perennial grace is something that all Singaporeans can attest to, as they see her on their screens night after night for close to 40 years.

***

Obviously, I know you far too well since you are family. But can you share with our readers more about your background, your family and your influences? Basically, who were you before you were Xiang Yun?

I was born into a poor family. What I can recall from my earliest memory was that my father did not hold a stable, regular job. He ran a business when I was growing up, but was cheated by his business partner and lost his money. My father also befriended some gambling addicts. So you can say our family was rather unstable. My mother had four girls and a boy. Because of our financial situation, she took on many jobs—school bus attendant, egg-seller and a helper at a hawker stall. She basically did everything she could to keep the family going. Being the eldest child, I went everywhere with her and got a chance to experience many different types of odd jobs.

We never had excess food and always had to eat sparingly. A simple dish of rice and two scrambled eggs would be devoured by the whole family. If there were prawns, which was rare, we could only afford to eat one each. We simply did not have the luxury to have more than one portion because there were seven of us in the household. I certainly did not expect that there would come a day when we would have more food than we could eat.

I was closer to my dad growing up. He had no temper and loved me very dearly. My mother, on the other hand, is Cantonese, and whenever my parents had a tiff, she would yell. My father was soft-spoken, and I think that was precisely what irked my mother. He was also very handsome and many women were attracted to him. My mother was always jealous, so much so that I used to say "Even a gust of wind brushing up against my dad would cause her to be jealous." (*laughter*) Up till the week of his death, my parents still argued. When he passed on, my mother said wistfully, "We will not have a chance to quarrel anymore." I knew then that fighting was their way of bonding and she misses him every day.

You were one of the first artistes in the then Singapore Broadcasting Corporation (SBC), now Mediacorp. What made you even start acting? Back in the day, acting was certainly not seen as glamorous and was, in fact, frowned upon.

Before SBC, I joined an acting class at the then Radio Television Singapore (RTS). It was still a black-and-white TV era and we formed a pool of RTS's part-time actors and actresses. Back then, the money we got was so little. We were paid about $7 per day as an extra, and we even had to provide our own costumes for the shoots. I remember that my first major role in a TV drama came even before I was contracted as a full-time actor and I didn't have any proper paperwork done. I was to play a university student and then a career woman, and I had to borrow all my costumes from my colleagues. I was only a teenager and didn't have sophisticated clothing required for the part! You know, looking back, you could say I pursued acting because I did not know any better. It was a simpler world then and I was very young and naive. All I thought was that if I liked acting, I should pursue it. That's it. It was not about fame or fortune.

My foundation in acting was firmly set when I was part of a theatre group from Rediffusion, the cable radio pioneer in Singapore. In fact, you could say that most of the actors who ended up signing contracts with SBC were largely from the theatre groups emanating from Rediffusion. Back in that day, we were very giving in spirit, time and energy. We knew that we could not make money from the arts but still, we persevered. We would be so excited and passionate about acting that we would stay overnight even after filming has wrapped as we had so much to share and talk about. Even the ones who were married with families did the same. It was a very different time and no one was tainted by money, just sheer dedication to the craft.

When SBC did ask me later to sign on as an actress, my father, who was a traditional man, was dead set against it. He was under the impression that the media industry was a "dirty" one and did not see it as reputable. He felt that actresses had to sacrifice their souls and, more pertinently, their bodies as part of the business. We took over half a year to debate and consider this as a family, but eventually, I insisted on signing the contract. This was largely due to Li Ming Fen whom I still regard today as my benefactor. She was my producer and has become a pastor in recent years. She gave me many opportunities while I was acting part-time and instilled in me a great sense of confidence.

What made you realise you could act?

Actually, I had no knowledge of acting at all, but I had a very good command of Beijing-accented Mandarin. At Rediffusion, all broadcasters were required to have excellent fluency, but I had kept a low profile. My sole involvement then was to provide canned laughter and clap my hands at the appropriate juncture as an extra. But my command of the Chinese language did not go unnoticed in the acting classes. Honestly, I don't think I was cast because I could act, I was cast because my Mandarin was good! Besides, the standard in the acting classes was neither high nor professional.

You became a household name in *The Awakening* as the lead actress, Ah Mei. Share with us what that experience was like, and take us through the acting climate back then.

The telecast during the black-and-white TV era was once a week or even once a month. There were not many productions and thus also fewer opportunities to learn. Today, the new actors get so much more exposure and opportunities than we did. For us, we had a very steep learning curve with limited exposure and learning platforms.

The Awakening was a real departure and an awakening for us as actors because the series was created by a team of Hong Kong professionals. They ushered in a whole era of change and they raised the standard of television with their presence. In particular, I will always be grateful to Director Jiang Long. He was my first professional director and he poured his heart and soul into every scene. I learnt so much about the craft just by working with him.

In one instance, the Ah Mei character I played had to be seen sobbing and running into a house in a rubber plantation. I could not cry on cue but Jiang Long sat with me and coaxed me into my character's emotions. He taught me how to manipulate my state of mind and mood, and waited for four hours for me to get into my character. He was my first and greatest teacher. I went from knowing nothing about acting to understanding what it took and meant to be an actor. In my amateur days, we thought acting merely meant reading from the script.

Actress Zhu Xiu Fong made a very firm impression on me. On my first day at the studio, Xiu Fong was playing the part of a dying mother giving her final instructions to her children, and she wept real tears! I was so moved by her acting that I started to cry fairly loudly and had to be asked to step aside as I was disturbing her and the filming process.

At that moment, I thought, "Wow, how does one weep?"

During the process, I learnt about acting technique. I may not have had the life experience to know what the character went through in my early days, but I began to understand the importance of research, preparing for a character, and understanding the character's objectives and motives.

Even though I became a household name at a young age, I was still seen as the girl from the hawker centre. My more established and experienced colleagues who came from better backgrounds would tease me and call me "the hawker centre girl". I was young and naive then and was affected by these comments. I also felt handicapped when I had to play the part of a rich girl. I had never come into contact with wealthy individuals and did not know how to act or feel. So I researched by going to the movies and reading books that feature the lifestyles of upper middle class characters. So yes, at the start, I had to rely on imagination and imitation.

Gradually, as I matured through marriage, motherhood and the diverse encounters with people from all walks of life, I began to understand people better and began to really enjoy acting. All these life experiences really shape you, and the craft grew on me. In fact, acting became a source of stress relief for me at one point in my life. All the sadness and stress I felt in my daily life were channelled to my on-screen character and I just bawled when the script called for me to! Similarly, when I play a happy character, I become energised and excited.

So when I started, acting as a career didn't cross my mind. I saw it initially as a means to get a small but stable income. My pay at Rediffusion then was $350, but SBC offered $800 which was a lot of money to a 19-year-old. I was terrified about signing a three-year contract, but I wanted the financial independence. Today, 30 years on, I have signed countless contracts.

You have achieved so much and have so many career highlights. But, what to you are your personal milestones in the past 40 years?
Definitely *The Awakening* because it established my acting career in Singapore.

But, the next milestone is after the birth of my son. I was certain that my career would go downhill. I had very limited acting opportunities then and felt that I had been quietly forgotten by viewers. A new batch of actresses like Zoe Tay had come to the fore and was steadily rising in stardom. I tried changing career paths and became an insurance agent, thinking that given my tough background, I would survive. But I was very unhappy. Many prospects and clients entertained my calls purely because I was an actress and they wanted my company. I recall one incident keenly. A prospect requested to meet at 12 a.m. and I knew he was not interested in purchasing a policy, all he wanted to do was to drink and talk. I made up my mind then to stop and went back to focus on my acting.

Upon return, I relished and treasured every opportunity, even though they were scarce. This period also gave me a deeper appreciation of every role I was given, not just the sassy leading lady. I began to have a better understanding on how to nuance my characters and how to immerse myself fully in the role. I was then given a very precious opportunity in 珍珠街坊 (*Around People's Park*) where I had a "character makeover" and took on a role outside of my standard repertoire. I played the part of a mentally-ill tissue paper seller.

In one scene, I had to sell tissue paper at Orchard Road. It was a pitiable role and I certainly looked the part. As the cameras were hidden, no one could tell it was me and I actually sold about 20 to 30 dollars' worth of tissue paper! This experience really boosted my confidence as an actor. I recall once I was shopping for Lunar New Year decorations in my acting costume, and I heard an uncle saying to his son, "Walk quickly." He really thought I was mentally unsound. All of a sudden, I felt both very sorry for people living with mental illness and for myself. The struggle became real for me. That was a breakthrough role for me and I realised the beauty of creating "reality". I found myself really growing as an actor, especially as a character actor. I began to invest a lot into creating a strong backstory for every character I play—that to me is half the battle won.

For that role, I received the Best Supporting Actress award at the annual Star Awards. Ironically, this came just when I thought my days on screen were numbered. I was really beginning to understand acting as more than a job or a passion, but as a real craft that had to be continually honed. I was also very fortunate to have been cast in more long-form dramas after the birth of my daughter.

The other career highlight is *The Little Nonya*. It was a great script and, in my opinion, one of the best creations in recent years. My screen character was a lonely, downcast and sad person who works in the kitchen. Honestly, we were making up a lot of the characters as we went along because we did not have the full script for the series. But the director really propelled us to give our all. This pressure was a great boost and pushed us all as an ensemble collectively forward. I began to practice inhabiting my role the minute I started to put on my costume.

In one scene, I had to scold Jeanette Aw's character firmly and reminded her that we had to have dignity even in poverty. I did not know what happened, but it seemed as if my character took possession of me. I recited the lines effortlessly as if they were my own words. Every emotion, nuance and cadence was so vivid for me. I remember it was a dark set-up because it was an intimate, sombre scene, but I only needed only two takes. I won an acting award for the role too—it was a great experience and a career highlight.

You seem to really get method acting and immerse yourself in the role. Meryl Streep and even Marilyn Monroe have been quoted saying that they take some of the character's drama into their own lives. Have you had encounters like that?

Yes, there is a tendency. But now that I am more experienced, I know how to get back to reality quicker. Back when I was younger, I would carry some of the personalities of the character even after completing the shoot. For example, I played the part of a quarrelsome lady in *Happy Fish* and all my scenes required me to find fault and quarrel with everyone. After the filming have wrapped, I realised I had inherited my character's bad temper. Previously, I would often weep as most of my characters were pitiable, long-suffering types; but that role made me bolder and I started learning how to pick a fight, quarrel and argue!

I think this is an unspoken reality of all working actors. I guess you can say I am very fortunate to require a shorter decompression time, quite simply because I have a family that keeps me busy. I honestly cannot afford to be locked up in my character's world for too long after the shoot. I do see it happening to new actors and share with them that they must take the time to renew and recuperate after a long two-, three- or even six-month shoot. The longer they carry around unhealthy energy, the worse it is for their bodies.

So how do you keep the momentum going, watch your sanity and your health over these long shoots?

I would go jogging and eat healthily. I take good care of myself and ensure that I do not to fall ill during the shoot. I just completed a 170-episode long-form drama that took about ten months to complete. Personally, I know that age is catching up and I am not physically as fit as I was before. Previously, I could go on without much sleep for seven to eight days. I even mastered the art of sleeping while standing up. All I needed to unwind was a good meal to pamper myself and I could get back into the fray. Nowadays, I cannot go without sleep for even a day. I would not be able to eat normally if I do not have ample rest, and it will affect me a lot. So I am very mindful of my own health and even started taking supplements.

How do you think the scene has changed since you have been in the business?

I feel so very fortunate to be working as an actor and bearing witness to Singapore's media scene, watching the industry progress and be part of its history. (*laughter*) For many decades before the advent of the Internet and social media, television was the trendsetter for most of our viewers. Our industry was at the forefront of cultural shifts and changes.

Let me give you an example. Back in the 1970s, cosmetic products were dense and often made of wax. The make up look was thick, heavy and unnatural. Colours like blue and purple were in fashion, and we used it even though it was not made for the Asian skin. When I started acting, this style was not suited for my age and skin tone, but viewers who saw this look wanted to emulate it. Later, the cosmetic industry and the aesthetics started to evolve. By the 1990s when Zoe Tay came onto the scene, the style was sexier and cheekier, a departure from our goody-two-shoes persona in the 1980s. Permed "bedroom" hair was in and even though I was always more conservative, I had to evolve with the times. I have seen how our make-up, style, fashion and our entire aesthetics change. We went from black-and-white TV to colour TV, to the media dominated landscape we live in today. As artistes, we are the champions of change and have to find our own way even with all the constantly evolving trends.

The other key difference is our short attention span. Nowadays, audiences demand pacier dramas, so we need to tell our stories in faster speed and shorter time. But what is certain is, the entertainment industry will always play a significant part in everyday life, quite simply because it helps to provide an escape and ease some pressure off the daily toil.

It's great that you mentioned the evolution of entertainment. What are your thoughts on reality TV show celebrities and overnight sensations such as bloggers?

To be very honest, I was not entirely happy about their entry, even though I accept their existence—but this is what society subscribes to and demands today. I suppose every generation will see things from a different point of view. For instance, in the 1970s, concert halls and live theatres were very popular and were the main sources of entertainment for the masses. Back then, when people watched a series, they would talk about it for days!

Now, bloggers and vloggers call the shots and they are the stars of today. What I do marvel at is their independence and their amazing ability to market. You have to acknowledge that their advertising and marketing techniques are outstanding. They have high energy, move fast and they do have a lot of talent, but they need to learn to be patient.

Today, our audience demands continuous engagement and stimulation, and instant gratification. They lead such fast-paced lives, they talk about you today and they forget you the next. It is difficult to capture their attention and you may not have the loyalty of your fans they way you had them in the past.

As a veteran actor, what do you think we can do to improve the standard of acting and productions?

I think we need a lot programme exchanges with overseas professionals. Even though the locals complain about our programmes, they still support it and, in fact, we actually attract a lot of foreign viewers. We receive many letters from overseas and our social media feeds are awash with fans from abroad. Singapore has a huge migrant Chinese community and they, too, have taken to watching our Mediacorp dramas. It does show that we still are relevant and have a wide viewership.

We also need to stay vigilant on the viewing patterns of our viewers. They were taken with Hong Kong dramas, then Taiwan and now Korea. But I also recommend that we stay ahead of the competition and watch what is being made overseas. Some of my friends would prefer to complain and I would advise the against naysaying but instead put our brains together to create improvements and change.

My friends from Hawaii have watched *Little Nonya* and loved it. Do you think Singaporean audiences are too critical?

I have a friend who is in the media business and he actually says that Singapore dramas are comparable with Hong Kong but somehow Singaporeans tend to think the grass is greener on the other side. So I think we have to take all criticism with a pinch of salt. We must not always slam our local productions. Instead, we just need to keep growing, improving and doing our best.

There is no fairness in this industry, especially when you are a public figure. I liken us to being on display at a shop—I see myself as a commercial product. The customer has the power to buy, walk away from or even diss the product. But as an actor, what I can strive to do is to establish good rapport and relationships with my audience. I appreciate all the support I receive but not everyone has to support me, I do not expect it.

After all these years, I still publicly acknowledge and appreciate my fans. I am still amazed that I get recognised even on my day off. I still feel bad if I turn down a fan request for a photograph with me when I am not appropriately attired, for instance, when I am at the petrol kiosk. The reason I decline is that I may not be looking too presentable and I know some of these photos may live on in Facebook and the Internet. But these days, I must say I am now more aware and make an attempt to dress up even on a day off so that I can entertain these requests from fans—I do not like disappointing them. I think it is very important to never be proud or self-centered.

So, what do you think is the secret to your success, having been in the limelight for so long?

I, too, am not sure how I braced myself through the trials and tribulations, but I do believe we must do everything wholeheartedly. I am a firm believer in Buddhist philosophy and have spent a lot of time reading up about this. I used to have the erroneous impression that as long as I was a faithful believer, I would have happiness and perfection. It was not till later that I learnt that there is no way to attain perfection in life. Eventually, the only things you can pursue are reality, charity and beauty. You come to terms with who you really are, you create good work and do good for others, and from there, natural beauty will emanate and that is what will last.

How is it like ageing in front of the camera and the public?

I was fearful of ageing. I was used to playing the role of a leading lady or the spunky lass. But after the delivery of my two children, I was immediately relegated to playing the role of an "auntie". I cried the first time someone addressed me as Auntie. But something happened when I turned 40. My outlook on life suddenly changed. I realised that even though I could not control the physical changes over time, I did not have to dread ageing—in fact, I started to rejoice! I began to see the beauty and confidence of a lady in her 40s, a lady who is enriched in every aspect of her life, physically and emotionally. I also began to appreciate how her life experiences will enable her to understand herself and others better.

I now get to play older women in their 50s and 60s, and these roles are richly fleshed out characters written for me, so I do feel very fortunate. Although occasionally my characters are the "recycled" maternal roles—a naggy, mentally-ill or dull mother. So what I do is that I try to infuse every role with something different. Even if I do get similar lines, I use a different method to bring out the character's essence. The goal in all my creations is to be able to touch the hearts and minds of the viewers.

I hope to have more opportunities to be involved in films. Film production is much more rigorous and more defined than television drama production. I gain a deep sense of satisfaction from it because it is a very exacting art form.

This industry is known to be bitchy and cut-throat. How did you survive and have you ever fallen prey to it?

I am happy to say that I have never been bothered by it at all. Perhaps, ignorance is bliss. I was initiated into the industry at a young age and in a simpler time so somehow I just always understood it as a game and grew alongside it. But the spoken word has the power to destroy. I recall in the 1950s, a Hong Kong actor committed suicide because of gossip and rumours. His final note said, "You cannot control one's tongue." It really illustrated how devastated he was. The death of this particular actor was etched in my mind and served as a cautionary reminder for me to not be affected by the remarks of others. I do not take comments to heart, nor do I bother with what others say about me.

To me, everyone is entitled to their own point of view, but I do not like to gossip and stay clear of such situations. When journalists approach me for a comment on another actor, I would abstain from giving an opinion. I grew up in a large family and bore witness to constant quarrels and arguments, and saw how damaging words could be. These served as a cautionary reminder to me, and I tell myself all the time to not be involved in other people's squabbles.

How do you feel when you see your co-actors, such as Huang Wen Yong, passing on?

Wen Yong has been my acting partner pretty much all my life. We made our debut as an on-screen couple in *The Awakening*. During the 40th anniversary of MediaCorp, we re-enacted the roles of Ah Shui and Ah Mei. We laughed for such a long time as we couldn't fit into our costumes anymore. He was still healthy then, and I recall him saying, "Xiang Yun, we must always remember the blessing that *The Awakening* has brought us." I agreed. We had forged such a long career and starred in numerous dramas together. Audiences would always remember us as television's golden couple.

When he passed on, I was truly saddened. Not simply because I lost a partner, but also because we have gone through so much together. When I was at my lowest point, he was still active in dramas, even though he was no longer the leading man. Later, when I got out of my casting rut and started gaining my second wind as a character actor, he was sidelined. I saw his dejection and how he was consumed by this despair. In many ways, his anxieties got the better of him and I saw him age with some element of grief, regret and depression. His wife is my old friend, and I am close to his children. I was very sad at his passing and can only hope that his family will go on to lead better lives.

Indeed it is. Let's talk about your marriage to my brother. You both dated at a time when romance with co-stars was frowned upon. How did you handle it?

Yes, we had to date secretly. I was such a typical Singaporean girl and I wanted to get engaged to acquire a HDB flat. In our traditional worldview, once you are engaged, you were considered married. We were thinking to get a house first and hold the customary wedding later. But somehow, word of our engagement got around, and soon, it was in the news. We wanted to do the right thing so within a short time and before I knew it, I had entered into another phase of life. Edmund was raised more liberal and more westernised than I was and he gave me a lot of confidence. We marched boldly forward because Edmund rolled with the punches. That aspect I learnt from your brother—to take life by its horns and live daringly.

What is it like being married in the public eye?

I think it was very tough for both of us as we were the first celebrity couple in Singapore and this attracted a lot of attention. We did find it difficult in the early years of our marriage because of the differences in our upbringing. I came from a very traditional Chinese background, where my mother literally told me to manage my marriage wisely. I was not to return home after fighting with my husband. I had to resolve and figure everything out on my own. Times have changed and social mores are different. As people attain more independence, divorce and remarriage have become options but I do not see them as options at all.

To me, a family that fights, laughs and celebrates together—stays together. No matter how Edmund and I fight or squabble, we know we want a complete family and that means we will work out our own differences. Honestly, my parents always fought when I was growing up and I lived in fear that my own marriage would end up in a divorce. But because I was so terrified, I have great conviction that I want to provide a harmonious family for my children.

Is it hard being in the same industry as your spouse?

I feel it is really not easy especially in terms of family and time management. When Edmund and I both had shoots, we would have to leave the children at home with the caregivers and my parents. Even though my parents were happy to care for the grandchildren, it was still tough as there was a generational barrier.

When Edmund first decided to make the decision to sacrifice his career and leave Mediacorp to care for the children, I grappled with whether I could accept my husband working from home. I was so used to the traditionalist idea that men are breadwinners and women are homemakers. There were even rumours that Edmund merely wanted to idle at home and live off his wife. These were so unkind and untrue. My husband showed that he could work diligently from home, channel his energy towards our family, raise the kids and yet still manage to have a successful career, even breaking a Guinness Book record amongst other things. Today, there are more families like that, but I must say, back then, we broke with convention.

What happened in 2003 precipitated this. My daughter was three and learning to walk and she hit her face on a hot iron. We rushed her to the hospital but the accident left a scar on her face. Thankfully, you cannot see it today. To add to that, my son had a serious eye infection and needed a cornea transplant. That was a huge wake up call to us as parents. It was a very trying time for us and Edmund slipped into depression. When I saw him so broken, I pleaded with him to be strong for us and the family. I wanted him to still go out to work as that was what I thought was expected of a husband and a father. But finally, I relented as I saw that he was truly saddened by his children's various accidents and wanted to be the primary caregiver. I took about two to three years to finally come to terms with the sacrifice he made for our family.

I have learnt that much as I wanted to be the final decision maker because I am a mother, I also needed to learn how to respect my husband as a wife. I realised that I needed to give him the responsibility, credit, confidence and peace of mind to raise our children and care for our family. I no longer see a need to fight over authority as this only affects the morale of the family.

How is it like dealing with the loss of privacy and what sacrifices have you had to make along the way?

My whole family and I are used to it, and they too know that they are also part of the media equation. When I was at my peak, the reporters even took an interest in my parents and would head to my parents' vegetarian hawker stall in MacPherson market to try to get some snippets of news. One time, my mother was hit on the head by a brick that fell in the toilet and that also made the headlines! There was no social media then and the newspapers were circulated nationally so everyone would know everything!

The entry of social media gave rise to new situations and circumstances. My children have both parents in the limelight and grew up with the media. When we used to go on outings as a family, Edmund and I would negotiate with the children and ask them to behave well. I do think that this can be rather unfair on them as children—sometimes they may just need to misbehave. As parents, Edmund and I have also learnt to let go and we see that we must allow our children to be who they are.

Ironically, now that they are older, they are more aware of their status as children of celebrities and understand that they will somehow always be under public scrutiny. They have grown up well-adjusted and handle media attention well. In fact, we had a gathering at home with my siblings a few months ago and something silly took place. I used my cellphone to capture the moments and it was my children who asked me not to post the photos online. They were more conscious of the power of social media and the notion of privacy than even I was! (*laughter*) But even your side of the family is savvy with the media, and have handled that with much grace and sense of humour. It is the norm for us, isn't it?

Would you encourage your children to go into media?

They have the freedom to choose their own path, as long as they are able to be upstanding members of society and contribute to it. All I wish for is for them to be happy. This is of the utmost importance to me.

How do you best want to be remembered?

There is no need to remember me. I feel that life is but a gust of wind we are all passersby. If I leave this world, then just let bygones be bygones. I just want to make sure I have lived my life to the fullest.

If you met God, what would you tell him?

Why did you bring sadness, disease, suffering and war to us? Why can't this world be a more beautiful place? But it is fair to say that many may have great blessings but do not know how to experience joy as well. You know, it may be fair to assume God doesn't have the answers either.

Would you consider yourself a Madonna, Maverick or any other M word?

I will say that I am a Madonna as I am very simple and steadfast at heart, but my work demands that I become a Maverick and I have embraced that over the years. I will also say Mother as I regard that as my most challenging, yet fulfilling, role!

Acknowledgements

My deepest appreciation and respect to all the women who have generously given me their time, bared their souls and allowed me access into their highly functioning minds. To Cynthia, Fanny, Halimah, Heng Chee, Ivy, Janice Koh, Janice Wong, Jennie, Lee-Chin, Min, Nichol, Odile, Olivia, Sylvia, Theresa, Tjin and Xiang Yun—you are all Madonnas and Mavericks in my book and eyes. I hope you continue to inspire the world with all that you do and touch.

To Lee Lee and Aunty Phyllis, thank you for helping me with the transcripts. These women speak fast and furious and I know it isn't always easy trying to decipher our private conversations in public spaces, but I am so grateful to you for coming with me on this journey.

To the team at Marshall Cavendish, especially to Sophia, my editor for all your ideas and inputs; my publishing manager, Melvin and my publisher, Mei Lin for believing in me for the third time. Thank you for the patience and I am already looking forward to the fourth!

To my family, my constant pillar of support, it is hard to be away from all of you and I miss you all the time.

To my husband Lee, for always loving me. Writing is a lonely activity and I have been so unwell. You have cared for me tirelessly even as I am unable to hike the mountains with you now and for a long time to come. We shall scale metaphorical mountains together. As they say, when God gives lemons, make lemonade and we can make them super tangy, tart and yummy.

As always, to Mummy and Daddy, for I am nothing without your selfless love and dedication. I love you very much and hope to always make you proud.

About the Author

Firebrand Dr Loretta Chen is a multi-hyphenate and a tour-de-force: leading creative director, marketing powerhouse, leadership trainer and bestselling author of *Woman on Top: The Art of Smashing Stereotypes and Breaking All the Rules* and *The Elim Chew Story: Driven by Purpose, Destined for Change*.

Chen was the Creative Director of The Activation Group, a turn-key creative agency with offices around Asia. During her 16-year career, she helmed campaigns for luxury and international brands and directed theatrical productions in Asia, the U.S., Canada and the Edinburgh Theatre Festival. She was also the International Consultant to Druk Holdings and Investments (DHI), the government investment arm of the Kingdom of Bhutan.

She holds a Doctorate in Philosophy and a Certificate in Leadership from Harvard University. She is a Visiting Professor and Guest Speaker in numerous institutions including Stanford University, University of Hawaii, University of Southern Maine and the Colegio de San Juan de Letran in the Philippines. She is also Adjunct Professor at Argosy University and Leeward Community College.

Other career highlights include having her eponymous radio show on Lush 99.5FM, instituting a Young Designer's Scholarship at Raffles Design Institute and being voted one of Asia's Most Inspiring Women. Her entrepreneurial ventures include design agency The Barefoot Group, the world's first TCM wearable device by Kang Healthcare and Our Green Tara, a leadership and coaching outfit. Chen also worked with innovative automobile and clean energy company, Tesla.

Chen believes in compassion, karma and loves the mountains, oceans and taking on unknown adventures. She is living her dream and now resides in Hawaii with her husband and three cats.

Madonnas and Mavericks marks her third book with Marshall Cavendish.

For enquiries and collaborations, log on to www.drlorettachen.com.